CALLED UNTO HOLINESS

The Story of the Nazarenes:
The Formative Years

Church History Commission
Mendell L. Taylor   S. T. Ludwig
J. Glenn Gould   Westlake T. Purkiser

CALLED UNTO HOLINESS

THE STORY OF THE NAZARENES:
THE FORMATIVE YEARS

Timothy L. Smith, Ph.D.

Nazarene Publishing House
Kansas City, Missouri

Copyright 1962 by Nazarene Publishing House

ISBN 978-0-834-10282-8

LIBRARY OF CONGRESS NUMBER 62-11409

PREFACE

"The perfect historian," wrote Lord Macaulay, "is he in whose work the character and spirit of an age are exhibited in miniature." While no historical endeavor can possess the qualities of absolute perfection, it is evident that both the Commission on History and the author have endeavored to present fully and accurately "the character and spirit" of the Church of the Nazarene during the formative years of its development. The quality and scope of this volume compliment both supervision and authorship, and the gratitude of the church is hereby expressed.

While the orderly presentation of historical facts has its value, the full purpose of this publication is much more broad and significant. History has underscored consistently the fact that, while later generations may improve the facilities and techniques of a spiritual movement, rarely do they improve on the spirit of the founding generation. Furthermore, it takes but one generation, ignoring or distorting the spirit and basic issues, to change for all the future the course of any spiritual enterprise.

The driving force in the lives of early Nazarenes was a sense of mission, to the accomplishment of which they were utterly dedicated. This sense of mission was rooted in a vital experience of scriptural holiness and the implications of such an experience in life. Thus a fundamental purpose of this volume is that "the character and spirit" of our Zion may be made clear and the essentials emphasized in such a way that Nazarenes everywhere may experience a new appreciation for the church and a renewed sense of mission.

This historical record, then, goes forth dedicated to a clearer and more intelligent understanding of the Church of the Nazarene by both members and nonmembers. May the blessing of God, by the Holy Spirit, attend this project, making it an effective and worthy witness to the saving and sanctifying grace of our Lord Jesus Christ, and bringing glory to His worthy name.

BOARD OF GENERAL SUPERINTENDENTS
Church of the Nazarene

TABLE OF CONTENTS

CHAPTER I. THE HOLINESS REVIVAL, 1858-88   11
The Modern World Challenges the Old Faith. The Holiness Revival in the Methodist Churches, 1865-85. Interdenominational and International Aspects of the Movement.

CHAPTER II. THE CHURCH QUESTION, 1880-1900   27
The First "Come-outers." The Pursuit of Unity and Loyalty. The Loyalists Face a Mounting Crisis. Holiness Social Work.

CHAPTER III. NAZARENE BEGINNINGS IN THE EAST   54
The People's Churches: Holiness and Congregationalism. The Methodist Preachers Delay Decision. A Middle Way: The Evangelical Association and New England Methodism. William Howard Hoople and the "Pentecostal" Churches in Brooklyn.

CHAPTER IV. THE ASSOCIATION OF PENTECOSTAL CHURCHES, 1897-1907   74
The Growth of Denominational Fellowship. H. F. Reynolds and the Search for a Superintendency. The Pentecostal Collegiate Institute. The Establishment of Foreign Missions in India and the Cape Verde Islands. Retrospect: Radical Experience and Conservative Churchmanship.

CHAPTER V. PHINEAS BRESEE AND THE CHURCH OF THE NAZARENE   91
The Making of the Man. The Holiness Revival in Southern California. The Founding of the Church of the Nazarene. Characteristics of the Early Nazarenes.

CHAPTER VI. THE NAZARENES BECOME A NATIONAL CHURCH   122
The Dawn of the Idea of a National Holiness Church. The Growth of the Church in California. Nazarenes in the Northwest. How Bresee's Church Came to the Mississippi Valley.

CHAPTER VII. FROM THE CUMBERLAND TO THE RIO GRANDE: THE HERITAGE OF HOLINESS IN THE OLD SOUTHWEST   151
Robert Lee Harris and the New Testament Church of Christ. The Beginnings of Denominational Organization. The Holiness Movement in Eastern Texas. The Holiness Association of Texas: Peniel. The Independent Holiness Church: Pilot Point. The Rising Star Union of 1904. The Holiness Church of Christ, 1905-8.

CHAPTER VIII. THE PENTECOSTAL MISSION IN TENNESSEE, 1898-1915   180
The Holiness Movement Comes to Middle Tennessee. An

Undenominational Path, 1901-7. The Postponement of Union with the Nazarenes. The Last Years of the Pentecostal Mission. The Progressive Movement in American Religion.

CHAPTER IX. UNION AND LIBERTY—ONE AND INSEPARABLE 205
First Steps Toward the Union of East and West, 1906-7. Forging the Links of National Fellowship. Erasing the Mason-Dixon Line. The Meaning of Pilot Point.

CHAPTER X. SOME UNHERALDED ACCESSIONS, 1908-15 224
The First Fruits of Union. Success and Failure in Other Merger Efforts, 1908-15. The Midwest Becomes the Nazarene Heartland. The Pentecostal Church of Scotland.

CHAPTER XI. ACHIEVING THE INNER REALITY OF UNION 243
Unfinished Business. The Early History of the General Superintendency. The organization of Foreign Missions. The Harmonizing of Educational Activities. The Establishment of a Central Publishing House. A Churchly Way of Life.

CHAPTER XII. THE TRANSITION TO A NEW GENERATION 272
A Crisis of Leadership. Liberty Versus Unity. The Rees Dissension. H. Orton Wiley and Northwest Nazarene College. The Fear of Spiritual Decline in the Second Generation.

CHAPTER XIII. THE LAYMEN'S HOLINESS ASSOCIATION ON THE NORTHERN PLAINS 298
The Origin of the Laymen's Movement. A Methodist Association. Wesleyan Fundamentalism. Uniting with the Nazarenes. The Nazarene Response to Fundamentalism.

CHAPTER XIV. THE RENEWAL OF LEADERSHIP AND THE RESURGENCE OF EVANGELISM, 1921-33 322
The Enlarged Role of Education in Denominational Strategy. The Inner Life of the College Communities. Christian Education in Local Congregations. The Committee System of General Church Administration. R. T. Williams and the Forming of the General Board. Evangelism at Home and Abroad.

A FORWARD GLANCE 349
NOTES 353
INDEX 403

INTRODUCTION

As we approached the Fiftieth Anniversary of the Church of the Nazarene, it became evident that the founding fathers were rapidly passing away. Important information that had a bearing on the early history of the church was passing with them. Also, many significant documents scattered in all parts of the nation, Canada, and the British Isles needed to be collected and filed in a central depository.

If all this vital information was going to be saved and incorporated in the history of the denomination, something had to be done to garner it. To make sure this early history was preserved, the Board of General Superintendents appointed a Church History Commission in 1955. The commission was charged with the responsibility of collecting historical data, capturing the spirit of the formative years, and planning for the writing of an official history of the Church of the Nazarene.

In May of 1955 the commission held its first meeting. At that time Dr. Timothy L. Smith was appointed the author for the history. The following pages are the product of a united effort to give the church an authoritative, documented, and dramatic account of our heritage. The manuscript has been carefully reviewed for accuracy and clarity in numerous conferences between the commission and the author.

The Church of the Nazarene is a Wesleyan denomination whose organization on a national basis took place at Pilot Point, Texas, in 1908. Its membership at that time was drawn from associations of churches which had appeared within the previous two decades in cities and towns of the northeastern and far western states, as well as in the South and the Middle West. None of these parent bodies had originated simply as secessions from the Methodist church, however. They were, rather, products of a spiritual awakening which during the previous half-century had cultivated among many denominations the doctrine and experience of Christian perfection, or entire sanctification. The history of the Church of the Nazarene, therefore, properly begins with the story of what was called the "holiness movement" of the nineteenth century.

John Wesley, the founder of Methodism, taught his early preachers that the central aim of Christianity was to restore sinful men to holiness of heart and life. To be sure, Wesley shared the orthodox conviction that fallen man could do nothing to save himself apart from the grace of God. But he declared that the atonement of Christ had secured for all the power to repent and believe the gospel, and so to be freed from the bondage of sinning.

There remained within the heart of converted Christians, however, an inner bent toward evil which was the bitter fruit of Adam's fall. He called it "sin in believers." To Wesley and his followers, this individual inheritance of "original sin" was neither guilt for Adam's first transgression nor simply the frailty of mortal flesh but a diseased condition of the soul. He was less concerned with the diagnosis of the affliction, however, than with proclaiming the divine remedy: an experience of entire sanctification, which, by comparison with one's conversion, was "a second blessing, properly so-called." Beyond forgiveness lay inward healing; after justification, a purifying of the heart.

Through this scholarly work Dr. Smith has made an invaluable contribution to the literature of the denomination, and the church world has a historical study that gives a new perspective on the way the Wesleyan tradition is being perpetuated in the twentieth century through the Church of the Nazarene.

We commend this volume to the reader. Dr. Smith has combined the skill of the historian with a warm personal interest in the church until the reader feels a part of the moving drama taking place. As you peruse these pages we trust you will receive both inspiration and instruction from the reading.

CHURCH HISTORY COMMISSION

CHAPTER I

The Holiness Revival, 1858-88

The Modern World Challenges the Old Faith

On the eve of the American Civil War the stream of holiness preaching in the United States approached flood stage. A great revival swept the nation in 1858. Hundreds of mammoth daily prayer meetings broke out almost spontaneously in New York, Philadelphia, Chicago, and nearly every city and town in the northern states. Ministers and laymen of all denominations took part. Churches everywhere scheduled special services. A half million persons were converted. The deepening of moral conviction hardened resistance against the sin of slavery, soon to be done away in the Civil War, and rejuvenated as well the crusades against intemperance, Sabbath desecration, and neglect of the poor. It also inspired hundreds of Christians to seek holiness of heart and life.

Just before and during the revival, pastors in Buffalo, Boston, and New York invited Charles G. Finney to conduct union services in those cities. Finney had had few such calls to the East since 1839, when he and Asa Mahan, together with other professors at Oberlin, a Congregationalist college in Ohio, had professed and begun to proclaim the grace of entire sanctification. Though never as clear or consistent in their teaching as Methodist theologians wanted them to be, Finney and Mahan thereafter preached holiness all over the country.

One of their admirers, William E. Boardman, published also in 1858 his book *The Higher Christian Life*. It soon made the author famous in both the United States and England; various publishers sold nearly 200,000 copies. Boardman sought to make the experience more appealing to all denominations by describing it in terms which neither Methodist nor Oberlin preachers had used before. In New England, the same year, A. B. Earle professed sanctification; he was for the next decade the most influential Baptist evangelist. First at Fall River and New Bedford, Massachusetts, then at Tremont Temple, Boston, Earle launched the career of "interdenominational" soul winning in which he made the "rest of faith," as he called it, his most prominent doctrine.

Meanwhile, among the Methodists, the long campaign to restore the Wesleyan experience to its central place in that denomination proceeded with new earnestness. Phoebe Palmer, wife of a New York City physician, had for twenty years conducted in her home the "Tuesday Meeting for the Promotion of Holiness." Hundreds of Methodist preachers, including at least two bishops and three who were later to hold that office, were sanctified under Mrs. Palmer's influence. The *Guide to Holiness,* printed in Boston, publicized her work and served as well to unite and inspire the clergymen great and small who shared her concern. True, conflicts were brewing in some local sections of the church; that in western New York produced the Free Methodist secession in 1859. But the Palmers and other holiness evangelists were never in such demand at camp meetings and revivals as in the years just prior to the Civil War.[1]

Many believed, in 1858, that the gospel of Christian perfection was the key to a century of spiritual progress. Fifty years later, when the followers of Phineas F. Bresee, H. F. Reynolds, and C. B. Jernigan met in the tiny Texas town called Pilot Point to unite the fragments of the holiness movement, that doctrine had become an embattled creed. Graying divines cherished still the dream of an interdenominational crusade for a national Pentecost. Bresee and Reynolds professed similar optimism, declaring that consolidation of the perfectionist forces would achieve that goal sooner. But sober men knew that the strongest argument for "organized holiness" was the aggressive nature of its opposition. For a half-century thereafter the experience of sanctification thrived chiefly in the small Wesleyan denominations. Only by the mid-twentieth century, when these groups numbered perhaps a million adherents and a new atmosphere of spiritual hunger prevailed in the church world, could hopes arise for the restoration of the quest for perfect love to an important place in Protestant religion.

What happened so to frustrate the dreams of 1858? The early chapters of this book will suggest a number of possible answers to that question. One of them, however, we can note at the outset: the one hundred years between 1858 and 1958 were a century of social upheaval and spiritual confusion.

The American Civil War, lasting from 1860 to 1865, ushered in a new era in our nation's history. An urban and industrial society rapidly replaced the simple agricultural environment in which Thomas Jefferson and the author of the McGuffey readers had lived out their days. Commerce and manufacturing lured hundreds of thousands of young people from the farms of the Old World and the New. In the cities and towns, these newcomers often lived in miserable, disease-ridden hovels. They endured periodic unemployment and faced multiplied temptations to drunkenness and vice. Roman Catholic immigration entirely changed the complexion of cities like Boston, Lowell, Pittsburgh, Cleveland, and Chicago. Barriers of language and religion only complicated the bloody strife which soon broke out between wage earners and employers.

Farming, meanwhile, became a speculative enterprise. The new machines which Cyrus McCormick turned out encouraged immigrants and native-born Americans alike to go west to seek their fortune. Millions of acres beyond the Mississippi were laid to the plow. Overproduction and chronic depression resulted, heightening rural suspicions of the wealthy and creating a new sectional discord, West and South against the urban East. Feelings reached white heat in the middle 1890's, when William Jennings Bryan, the "Boy Orator" from Nebraska, first ran for the presidency.

As the twentieth century came on, the effects of the industrial revolution appeared more sweeping still. The farm-to-city movement became a torrent. Though federal law tended to restrict Catholic immigration from southern and eastern Europe, Dixieland Negroes now moved in large numbers upon Detroit, Chicago, Indianapolis, New York, and Philadelphia, creating grievous tensions. Meanwhile, mass education and the allurements of city life quickened the pace by which young people threw off parental restraints and discarded old values. The daily newspaper, the popular magazine, the moving picture theater, and the automobile, radio, airplane, and television each in turn increased the passion for movement and distraction. They spread novel ideas and made tragedy and scandal the chief topics of thought and conversation. On another level, the new university graduate schools at Harvard, Yale, Johns Hopkins, and Chicago popularized theories about man's origin and nature, his social relations, morals, and religion which challenged the older Christian outlook. Their departments of physics and chemistry turned out white-robed scientists and technicians who soon replaced the black-garbed clergy as the recognized experts on the good life.

That the churches were all this while falling under the spell of wealth and power did not make the task of holiness preachers any easier. Denominational executives imitated the methods of business tycoons in building up the strength and income of their organizations. Local congregations neglected spiritual matters to pander to the social wants of their people. In the seminaries, to be sure, earnest men grappled with the new learning and the ethical issues which urban poverty and industrial strife had raised. The new faith of modernism which they brought forth was deadly serious about righting social wrongs. But it rejected the ancient doctrines and the old-fashioned revivals which hitherto had made the war on sin effective. The masses of churchgoers either misunderstood or suspected it. To most laymen, the "social gospel" seemed nothing more than a sanction to church festivals and Sunday school dances. The shallow faith prevailed that education, democracy, and liberal Christianity were soon to usher in earth's most glorious age.

Two world wars, a paralyzing depression, and widespread fear of atomic warfare shattered the dream. A time of heart searching, conducive to a revival of earnest Christianity, seemed in order. In some cases, however, the pendulum swung too far. Two forms of Christian pessimism echoed the cynical mood which enveloped society at large. The plain man's fundamentalist movement despaired of the world's conversion. The theologian's "New Orthodoxy," learned, Calvinist, and crusading, made conversion itself an experience of despair. Both recognized the terrible reality of man's sin but neither proclaimed a Saviour who was able to cleanse it away.

In the last days, God had promised to pour out His Spirit on all flesh. Sons and daughters would prophesy and young men see visions. It was not enough simply to cry that the stars were falling.

Popular psychology, sometimes masquerading as Christianity, prescribed confident thinking as the antidote to anxiety. By this an individual was supposed to be able to redeem himself from defeat and despair. But Nazarenes at mid-century were convinced that the means to both personal and social health was the love of God shed abroad in men's hearts by the Holy Ghost. Thus the sixth decade of their history as a church found them intent upon discovering more effective ways to point the world to Christ and holiness.

The Holiness Revival in the Methodist Churches, 1865-85

The Civil War left in its wake a moral and spiritual crisis which prominent Methodist pastors believed could be met only by a return to the faith of their founders. John C. McClintock, chairman of the committee in charge of the celebration of the denomination's one hundredth anniversary in 1866, declared that Christian perfection was the central theme of the Bible and the chief goal of Wesleyan piety. "It may be called fanaticism," he said, "but that, dear friends, is our mission. . . . If we keep to that the next century is ours." McClintock the following year became the first president of Drew Theological Seminary, near New York City. He chose Randolph S. Foster, author of *Christian Purity, the Heritage of Faith*, to be professor of systematic theology.[2]

During the centennial year, weekday holiness meetings multiplied in many cities. Dr. and Mrs. Palmer enjoyed a highly successful tour of conference camp meetings in New York state, Michigan, and Illinois. They conducted revivals at several Methodist colleges, including one which lasted three weeks at Garrett Biblical Institute, near Chicago. There Frances Willard, future president of the Woman's Christian Temperance Union, professed sanctification. In New York, meanwhile, John S. Inskip, chairman of the Methodist preachers' meeting, led a series of discussions which gave rise to the first "national camp meeting for the promotion of holiness."[3]

This gathering, held at Vineland, New Jersey, in 1867, bound together a rising group of young men who made a specialty of the "second blessing." John Allen Wood, pastor at Wilkes-Barre, Pennsylvania, and William B. Osborn, a presiding elder in southern New Jersey, seem to have suggested the national camp. Other sponsors were Alfred Cookman, a distinguished Philadelphia minister; George Hughes, pastor at Trenton; Lewis R. Dunn, of Central Church, Newark; and Bishop Matthew Simpson, the denomination's most illustrious preacher. So extensive were the fruits of the Vineland assembly that these men formed the "National Camp Meeting Association for the Promotion of Holiness" and planned a similar gathering each year.[4]

Their meeting for 1868 was held at Mannheim, Pennsylvania. Bishop Simpson preached the opening sermon from the text in Rom. 8:14, "For as many as are led by the Spirit of God, they are the sons of God." Inskip followed in the afternoon. When, that night, Alfred Cookman gave his spiritual autobiography, a newspaper correspondent wrote that "men fell under the mighty power of God in all parts of the ground" in a scene equaled only by "the wonderful Pentecostal season" the following evening. Large congregations from New York, Brooklyn, and Philadelphia maintained prayer-meeting tents in the grove. Scores of ministers sought holiness. German-speaking leaders of the Evangelical denomination professed the experience in such numbers as to stamp that church with perfectionism for fifty years to come.[5]

Thus by 1869, when the association went to Round Lake, New York, on the Troy Conference grounds, the national camp meeting had become a major attraction to Methodists. Twenty thousand persons were present the first Sunday, despite an agreement forbidding railroad travel to Round Lake on the Lord's day. Bishop Simpson conducted a mammoth Communion service that afternoon, at the end of which he exhorted the clergymen present to consecrate fully their all to Jesus. "You need, and may have, a fresh anointing just now," Simpson cried. Only men who possessed "apostolic power" could channel toward godliness the tide of heathenism which was rolling in upon America. "O Lord," he prayed in closing, "clothe us with salvation! Help us to preach Christ as we never preached before . . . His blood cleanseth, cleanseth, CLEANSETH . . . The blood of Jesus cleanseth from all sin!"

A week later four hundred persons, many of them ministers, professed to have received during this meeting "the consciousness of sanctifying grace." Invitations for the next year's camp poured in from conference officials all over the East and Midwest. Three were selected, each near an urban center of the church: Asbury Grove, a few miles north of Boston; Oakington, Maryland, on the railroad between Wilmington and Baltimore; and Des Plaines, Illinois, site of the Chicago District camp meeting.[6]

Likewise, 1871 was a banner year. At the urgent invitation of Asbury Lowery, an Ohio presiding elder, and the aged Bishop Thomas A. Morris, the national camp convened first at Urbana, Ohio. A correspondent to the *Methodist* wrote that "doctors of divinity, professors in literary institutions, officers of the General Conference" and "men of wealth, position and power" flocked to the altar seeking holiness. Forty preachers of the Cincinnati conference, hitherto divided on the subject, "unanimously resolved to bury all differences, and go home to preach a full and present salvation." At its close, Alfred Cookman led most of the association's workers back to Round Lake. The second engagement there proved as momentous as that two years before.

Inskip took another party to the West Coast for meetings at Sacramento, Santa Clara, and San Francisco. An eyewitness reported that he saw many prominent leaders of the California conference "stricken to the ground by the power of God" and lying for hours "filled with glory." Two presiding elders, the editor of the *California Christian Advocate,* the president of the University of the Pacific, and nine pastors signed a testimonial honoring these heralds of holiness for awakening "godless California" to its need.[7]

In the five years following, twenty-four "national" camp meetings took place: two of them at Knoxville, Tennessee; three at Old Orchard Beach, Maine; four under a great tent in Baltimore and Washington; and others as far west as Iowa and Nebraska. Daily "experience meetings" for clergymen and special hours for young people, children, ministers' wives, and businessmen were features of each gathering. The mass Communion service was more than a novelty. It symbolized the churchly bonds of the leaders and exalted at the same time the atonement of Christ, through faith in which seekers might expect the promised cleansing. The association itself remained a tightly knit circle of Methodist ministers. They allowed only those in full agreement with their doctrine and experience to preach, in order, as they explained it, to maintain a spirit of "harmony, love and union" on the grounds.[8]

Between national camp meeting engagements, members of the association promoted the holiness revival in many other ways as well. As early as 1869 they launched in Philadelphia a weekly paper, the *Christian Standard and Home Journal.* John

Inskip was the first editor. The next year William McDonald founded in Boston a monthly magazine, the *Advocate of Holiness*. In 1873 an affiliate publishing company took over the *Standard,* under the presidency of Washington C. DePauw, Indiana glass manufacturer. Both presses issued a stream of books and pamphlets, swelling that which still poured from the office of the *Guide to Holiness.* Dr. Palmer had purchased the latter in 1863, moved it to New York City, and made his wife editor in chief.[9]

The leaders of the movement also served as evangelists in hundreds of camp and revival meetings. "Camp Meeting John Allen," sanctified at Vineland, became a revered figure in Maine. William B. Osborn devoted several years to developing the Ocean Grove, New Jersey, campground, soon the largest in the nation. Dr. and Mrs. Palmer led the daily holiness meetings there for many years. Alfred Cookman continued the annual round of Methodist camps in the middle Atlantic states, as had been his custom since 1857. He led scores of ministers into the grace of perfect love. Shortly before his sudden death in the fall of 1871, Cookman preached before President U. S. Grant at Ocean Grove, and before Massachusetts notables at Martha's Vineyard. Bishop Simpson spoke at Cookman's funeral and R. S. Foster, who had succeeded John McClintock as president of Drew Seminary, declared, "The most sacred man I have known is enshrined in that casket."[10]

John Inskip, meanwhile, resigned his Baltimore pastorate in the spring of 1871 in order to give all of his time to evangelistic labor. Bishop Edward R. Ames invited Inskip to accompany him that summer as preacher to the St. Louis, Kansas, Missouri, and Nebraska annual conferences—an auspicious beginning to a brilliant ten years' work. When, in 1881, William McDonald joined Inskip in a round-the-world mission, their annual conferences, the New York East and the New England, enthusiastically commended them to overseas Methodists, as did the presiding bishops, Thomas Bowman and Matthew Simpson. At Lucknow, India, they found their old friend William B. Osborn serving as presiding elder on the South India Conference, recently organized out of William Taylor's free-lance missionary work. Bishop Stephen M. Merrill participated in their meetings at both Bombay and Lucknow, preaching earnest sermons on the baptism of the Holy Ghost.

Other champions of holiness invested their time in educational, administrative, or literary work. Daniel Steele was elected the first president of Syracuse University in 1871, shortly after he professed sanctification. From there he went to Boston University as professor of New Testament Greek. From 1886 to 1891 he held the chair of systematic theology as well. He wrote many influential books on perfect love. Lewis R. Dunn published numerous articles in the church journals, in addition to several books. Asbury Lowery edited the *Christian Standard* after Inskip gave it up, and served thereafter as pastor and presiding elder. He contributed to the organization of the Epworth League in 1887. William Nast, the founder of German Methodism and an active member of the National Association, encouraged the drive to make holiness the dominant theme of the German-speaking churches and camp meetings.[11]

The support of the bishops was from the outset a key factor in the spread of the revival. Edmund S. Janes, senior to Simpson and Ames, was a close friend and admirer of Mrs. Palmer. He wrote a glowing preface to the book of testimonies which she published in 1867. Four of the eight new bishops elected at the General Conference of 1872 were pronounced friends of holiness: Randolph S. Foster, Stephen M. Merrill, Jesse T. Peck, and Gilbert Haven. The first two we have noticed earlier. Peck, author of *The Central Idea of Christianity*, which the Methodist publishing house reissued in 1875, had contributed often to the *Guide to Holiness*. He urged the conference which elected him to revise the doctrinal statement on sanctification so as to commit the church wholly to the "second blessing" view. Haven had defended the work of the National Association while editor of *Zion's Herald* in Boston, and wrote the introduction to George Hughes's history of the national camps.[12]

The bishops of the southern church in 1870 publicly mourned the neglect of the experience of perfect love "as a distinct and practicable attainment." "This was a paramount theme in the discourses of our fathers," they declared. "If we would be like them in power and usefulness, we must resemble them in holy consecration. Nothing is so needed at the present time throughout all these lands as a genuine and powerful revival of Scriptural holiness."[13]

Two incidents which took place after 1880 illustrated the hold which the revival gained upon the minds of Methodists.

At the first world conference of Wesleyan denominations, held in London, in 1881, John P. Newman, soon to be a bishop in the M.E. Church, North, delivered an important address on "Scriptural Holiness, and the Special Fitness of Methodist Means of Grace to Promote It." In the discussion which followed, Bishops Simpson and Peck as well as prominent southern and English divines supported Newman's conclusion that the "second blessing" was an integral part of the "common belief and the experience of the church." Washington C. DePauw, head of the National Publishing Association for the Promotion of Holiness, was one of the three lay delegates present from America. He had recently made a large gift to the Indiana college which thereafter bore his name. In the meeting which the conference set aside for testimonies to sanctification, DePauw cried,

> We must come back [to the "old landmarks"] by consecrating ourselves and our homes, our lives, our pocketbooks, our business, everything we have to Christ. . . . Brethren, I think we have fallen away in this. And now I want to say I have long ceased to measure arms with God. . . . He can fully cleanse any man. . . . Glory be to Jesus! the blood hath cleansed.[14]

The other event was the celebration in New York on February 9, 1886, of the fiftieth anniversary of Mrs. Palmer's "Tuesday Meeting." Though its founder had passed away ten years before, two bishops, Edward G. Andrews and W. L. Harris, and scores of prominent clergymen gathered at St. Paul's Church to do honor to her memory. John P. Newman, who was then pastor of the Metropolitan Church, Washington, D.C., reported the meeting for the *Christian Advocate*. He described Phoebe Palmer as "the Priscilla who had taught many an Apollos the way of God more perfectly." Willard F. Mallalieu, elected to the episcopal chair at the preceding General Conference, wrote that, more than at any time in the history of Methodism, God's people were seeking the blessing. J. R. Jacques, president of Alfred University, lauded the Palmers for their loyalty to the church and opposition to divisive or fanatical tendencies. They had been, he noted, catholic in spirit and strong in their protest against the growing love of luxury and wealth. Two hundred and thirty-eight weekday holiness meetings were by then operating in every major town in America and a dozen foreign cities. Scores of publications emulated the *Guide to Holiness*.

These facts were evidence, Jacques said, that Dr. and Mrs. Palmer had created "a system of evangelism of no mean event in our current church history."[15]

Many such occurrences demonstrate how fully the leaders of the holiness revival had overcome early fears that they might incite secessions from the church. The strength of their propaganda, in fact, lay in their constant appeals to the memory of Wesley, Fletcher, and the first American bishop, Francis Asbury. So successful were they in identifying sanctification with Methodist orthodoxy that opponents were hard pressed to find ground upon which to stand without laying themselves open to the charge of heresy. Later on, in the early 1890's, those who first published extensive criticisms of the doctrine had to acknowledge their divergence from Wesley's views. Only then, as we shall see, when the bright hope faded of sweeping the whole church into the pursuit of perfect love, did responsible champions of holiness drift toward secession.[16]

Interdenominational and International Aspects of the Movement

What makes the story of the holiness revival among men outside the Methodist church important is that they so often took the initial steps toward organizing new denominations. Among the Nazarene "founding fathers," for example, William Howard Hoople was a Baptist, Edward F. Walker a Presbyterian, J. O. McClurkan a Cumberland Presbyterian, and A. M. Hills and George Sharpe, of Scotland, Congregationalists. Edgar P. Ellyson and Seth C. Rees were Friends, and John W. Goodwin an Advent Christian. Most of these men had previously been active in interdenominational associations which paid scant heed to the desires of Methodist officialdom. They were all heirs in some measure of either the Oberlin or Keswick movements, both of which had leaned toward congregational and independent church government.

After the Civil War, William E. Boardman and A. B. Earle found Presbyterians and Baptists everywhere willing to listen to the promise of the "higher life." Earle conducted a long union revival campaign in Park Street Church, Boston, in 1866. He then went to California for two years, at the invitation of the San Francisco ministerial association. In the 1870's, A. P. Graves, one of Mrs. Palmer's converts, carried forward this Baptist phase of the work. In Boston, Charles C. Cullis, an evangelical Episcopal layman, opened a mission, a training school, a publishing business, and a rest home for sufferers from tuberculosis, all dedicated to propagating the higher life.

Meanwhile Boardman, Henry Belden, and Asa Mahan preached in camp meetings and revivals all over the East. Mahan expressed gratitude that the American Board of Commissioners for Foreign Missions had abandoned their former prejudice against candidates who espoused the "second blessing." In 1873, when a national conference of Congregational churches met at Oberlin, its members asked the aged Finney to preach on the baptism of the Holy Spirit. The same year Dwight L. Moody, who had for many months past enjoyed the higher life, opened the meetings in London, England, which made his name a household word on two continents.[17]

The national camps inspired many Quakers also to seek what they considered to be a Methodist version of their historic experience of the "Inner Light." David B. Updegraff, son and grandson of Friends ministers of Virginia, experienced sanctification in his Ohio home in 1871, after hearing the testimony of an acquaintance who had been at Round Lake. He immediately began work as an evangelist. Before the year was out Updegraff had won over Dougan Clark, professor of Bible at Earlham College, Richmond, Indiana.

These two led the holiness awakening among midwestern Friends. Clark wrote several thoughtful books and Updegraff edited the *Friends Expositor*. Both received support from Calvin W. Pritchard, editor of the influential *Christian Worker*, published at Chicago. The international Friends assembly which met at Earlham College in 1887 adopted a thoroughly Wesleyan article on entire sanctification. By that time Ohio and Indiana yearly meetings had become strongholds of perfectionism. Both sent out scores of young ministers who placed the same stamp upon the trans-Mississippi sections of the society. Clark was ousted from Earlham in 1892, however, and Rufus Jones replaced Pritchard as editor of the *Christian Worker*. In the twentieth century, Cleveland Bible Institute (now Malone College) served as the holiness educational center for midwestern Friends.[18]

How natural, then, that Lewis R. Dunn should have boasted in the *Methodist Quarterly Review* in 1873 that Episcopalians, Quakers, Presbyterians, and Baptists were forsaking sectarian controversy to proclaim with their Methodist brethren the purifying grace! Dunn and other members of the National Association in fact regarded themselves as pioneers of Protestant unity. Where Christlikeness is prominent, George Hughes wrote, minor distinctions of doctrine and government melt away. The Palmers insisted to the last that their labors were "unsectarian." All hands rejoiced at the interdenominational flavor of the weekday meetings and national camps. By 1880 the "Western Union Holiness Convention," held first at Jacksonville, Illinois, drew representatives from fifteen denominations. When, a few years later, Deacon George Morse and Dr. E. M. Levy, the Baptist founders of Douglas Camp Meeting, Massachusetts, announced a service for Baptists and Congregationalists only, a capacity audience thronged the large tabernacle and three hundred persons testified to entire sanctification.[19]

A religious movement which exerted such influence upon the chief American revivalists inevitably spilled over into England. The writings of Charles G. Finney, Phoebe Palmer, T. C. Upham, and William E. Boardman had circulated widely there by the time of our Civil War, and Finney had made two memorable visits. After the Awakening of 1858 spread overseas, Mrs. Palmer and her husband sailed on a four years' tour which created a minor sensation in English Methodism.

The Palmers preached for weeks to packed houses at Leeds, Sheffield, Manchester, Birmingham, and dozens of other places. On their return, James Caughey, who had twice before conducted long campaigns in England, departed to carry on the crusade. Caughey stayed three and one-half years and reported over 10,000 converts. Thereafter, British Methodists championed sanctification more unanimously than their American cousins. When John Inskip and William McDonald arrived in 1881, both the "General Committee" of the Primitive Methodist church and prominent Wesleyan pastors welcomed their work. At Leeds, they saw scores of ministers profess the experience. Thirteen hundred persons were converted in one service.[20]

Meanwhile, Dougan Clark and Asa Mahan carried the good news to English Friends and Congregationalists, and William E. Boardman helped inspire the large summer conferences which bore permanent fruit in the famous Keswick Convention. Boardman and R. Pearsall Smith, a brilliant but erratic young Presbyterian minister, were thrown together in London during

Dwight L. Moody's campaign of 1873. They joined in a small meeting for holiness at the London Y.M.C.A., in which Smith's wife, Hannah Whitall, daughter of a Philadelphia Quaker family, took a leading part. The following July, a wealthy squire invited to a convention on his estate these two and about a hundred others, mostly clergymen and students from nearby Cambridge University. A similar conference, held the same summer during vacation time at the sister university, blossomed into the "Oxford Union Meeting for the Promotion of Scriptural Holiness." Huge crowds flocked to the town. Asa Mahan was present and preached the first sermon. Though Boardman and the Smiths were not in charge, their personal influence was very great. At both meetings, influential preachers from Germany, France, and the Lowlands experienced sanctification.

The next July a mammoth encampment at Brighton drew 8,000 persons. Here Pearsall Smith witnessed the climax and the collapse of his career. During the preceding winter he had returned briefly to America, then answered an urgent invitation to go to Germany. In Berlin, the emperor's court preacher arranged a large church for his use. Immense crowds attended Smith's services in Berlin, Cologne, and other cities. In succeeding years a company of wise and respected ministers, aided by Methodist missionaries from William Nast's following in America, made the "higher life" movement a significant factor in the religion of Germany. Back in Brighton, Smith cried, "All Europe is at my feet!" But his runaway enthusiasm provoked British preachers to banish him to America. He never recovered from the emotional shock of this event. Hannah Whitall Smith devoted the next few years to caring for her ailing husband and writing *The Christian's Secret of a Happy Life*.[21]

At the Brighton convention, however, Canon Harford-Battersby, vicar of Keswick, one of the loveliest rural settings in all England, had arranged for an open-air conference in his parish. The meeting was made an annual affair. In ten years Keswick became the chief center of holiness teaching in England. It was in some ways a British equivalent of the national camp meeting movement. There, however, Calvinist and Church of England clergymen provided the chief inspiration and support. The shirt-sleeve exuberance of the American camp meeting gave way to a more thoughtful atmosphere. And individual experience turned more often toward social need, despite the encouragement which Anglican participants gave to the mystical element in holiness teaching.

Partly on account of these reasons, the tendency grew rapidly at Keswick to explain the baptism of the Spirit as an enduement of power rather than a cleansing from sin. Boardman, who made London his permanent residence after 1875 and appeared regularly at the conference, became interested in faith healing, following the example of Dr. Charles Cullis, in Boston. The premillennial interpretation of the prophecies of Christ's second coming also became a cardinal point in Keswick doctrine. These teachings—the denial of the eradication of inward sin and the emphasis upon premillennialism, faith healing, and the "gifts of the Spirit"—opened a wide breach in the holiness ranks. The conflict spread to America when Dwight L. Moody, R. A. Torrey, first president of Moody Bible Institute, Chicago, Adoniram J. Gordon, father of Gordon College, Boston, A. B. Simpson, founder of the Christian and Missionary Alliance, and the evangelist J. Wilbur Chapman began to propagate in this country the Keswick version of the second blessing. As we shall see, this controversy vitally affected each phase of the founding of the Church of the Nazarene.[22]

One other transatlantic holiness movement, the Salvation Army, came from England to America in the 1880's. It wedded Christian perfection to urban social work. William Booth, a Methodist New Connexion preacher sanctified under James Caughey's influence, withdrew from his conference to become an evangelist in 1861. He began four years later to hold tent and street meetings in the poorer sections of London, under the auspices of a nonsectarian mission. This group reorganized in 1878 as the Salvation Army, with General Booth as commander in chief. The movement grew so rapidly in the United States that when Booth and his wife, Catherine, first visited this country in 1886, he found 238 corps organized under 569 officers. Eight thousand persons heard him at one service in New York. Mrs. Booth's two books on sanctification, *Godliness* and *Aggressive Christianity*, had already circulated widely in America, with the blessing of Daniel Steele and the holiness press.

Samuel Logan Brengle, a brilliant young divinity student at Boston University, fell under the spell of the Army about the time he received the baptism of the Spirit in 1885. Brengle went to England and accepted appointment among the lowliest of Booth's followers. In a few years he had become the organization's principal spiritual leader. His campaigns in the United States and Canada, as well as in Scandinavia and Australia, inspired thousands both in and outside the Salvation Army to the quest of perfect love.[23]

Thus from Vineland Camp to Keswick and the London world conference of Methodism and back again to Boston, New York, and Chicago did the fires of the holiness revival burn. Finney, Boardman, and Phoebe Palmer had kindled the hopes of an idealistic age. The doctrine of entire sanctification, like the crusades against slavery, drunkenness, and pauperism, appealed to a widespread confidence that all the world's evil could be done away.[24]

The holiness movement was born of great revivals. It prospered from the newly employed energies of laymen and women preachers. And it was in large measure centered in the cities. Urban pastors and evangelists who ranged freely over two continents, rather than rude frontiersmen, gave the awakening its original impetus and direction. The rural surroundings in which camp meetings and summer conferences took place could not hide the fact that most of the leaders and participants were city dwellers. The tented grove provided a welcome refuge from the city's anxiety and tumult.

Nevertheless, as we shall see in a moment, the rapid pace of social change soon created conditions in urban Christianity which led to a conflict over holiness. The increase of wealth and social pretension in city congregations of humble origin did not fit the pattern of perfectionist piety. Nor did the new goals by which church administrators planned their work. The outcome, after a brief struggle, was the organization of a dozen new Wesleyan denominations, of which the Church of the Nazarene was to become perhaps the most significant.

CHAPTER II

The Church Question, 1880-1900

Why did the holiness revival lead to the organization of independent churches, despite the frequent pledges of loyalty which its leaders made to the older denominations? The answer to this question is by no means simple, but it is fascinating.

By 1885, the sweep of the awakening into the Midwest and South was producing two more or less distinct groups. One, largely rural, was more emotionally demonstrative, emphasized rigid standards of dress and behavior, and often scorned ecclesiastical discipline. The other was urban, intellectual, and somewhat less zealous about outward standards of holiness. Its leaders were eager for alignment with all in the older churches who would share their central aims.

Those who earliest left the church came from the first group. Members of the more conservative party withdrew only under great provocation. Many of them lived and died in the church of their fathers. This was true of the Boston leaders especially —Daniel Steele, William McDonald, Charles J. Fowler, and Bishop Willard F. Mallalieu—as well as of Henry Clay Morrison of Kentucky and J. O. McClurkan, of Nashville, Tennessee.

Four factors entered into their decision to stay or leave: (1) the persistent opposition of ecclesiastical officials to independent holiness associations and publishing agencies; (2) the recurrent outbursts of fanaticism among persons who were members of the associations but not of the churches; (3) the outbreak in the 1890's of strenuous attacks upon the doctrine of sanctification itself; and (4) the increasing activity of urban holiness preachers in city mission and social work.

In all cases, however, as we shall see in a moment, the exodus was intermittent and disorganized. Independent bands and congregations arose in response to local situations. They usually included persons who formerly belonged to several different communions. And they coalesced slowly and rather haphazardly into organized denominations.

Neither the origin nor the subsequent history of the Church of the Nazarene can be understood without a knowledge of the two holiness traditions, urban and rural. The founders came from both. Both had great gifts to offer the young denomination —the one a determined stand against worldliness and a healthy suspicion of ecclesiastical machinery, the other a national vision and a solid respect for learning and the Wesleyan tradition. To balance them one against the other has been the task of Nazarene churchmanship ever since the union at Pilot Point in 1908.

The First "Come-outers"

A series of premature secessions which extremists provoked in the Middle and Far West around 1880 seriously complicated the relations of the holiness movement to the churches. It put the more responsible leaders on the defensive, forcing them to profess full loyalty to the older denominations during the very years when official but covert resistance to their doctrines was reaching the danger point.

The careers of four men illustrate this story well. Daniel S. Warner founded the Church of God (Anderson, Indiana) in 1880. Hardin Wallace paved the way in Texas and California for the Holiness church. John P. Brooks, editor for the Church of God (Holiness), formulated the theory of "come-outism." The fourth, S. B. Shaw, of Lansing, Michigan, tried but failed to bring about a national holiness union which he hoped would bypass the church question entirely.

D. S. Warner's Church of God carried the nonsectarian traditions of the holiness revival to such extremes that he rejected entirely the idea of an organized denomination. Local congregations kept no membership records and were bound to others only by the fellowship of the Spirit. The founder believed that he was commissioned to unite all Christians on the basis of Jesus' prayer recorded in the Gospel of John, chapter seventeen, "Sanctify them . . . that they all may be one."

Warner's wife was the earliest to fall by the wayside. She announced in 1884 that she was "thoroughly convinced that this effort to unite God's people by calling them out of the churches is not God's plan of unity." It simply "cuts off a few by themselves, who get the idea that none are clearly sanctified unless they see as 'we' do." Although Mrs. Warner professed her love for all who were associated with the movement and especially for her husband, she deplored their surrender to "the same self-righteous pharisaical spirit" which "Christ rebuked and denounced when he was here on earth." Absurd fanaticisms, she noted, were already cropping out here and there.

Nevertheless, Warner's concept of the church appealed to a widespread suspicion of ecclesiastical machinery. The Church of God has persisted into the twentieth century to become one of the stronger of the small holiness denominations. It maintains a college and publishing house at Anderson and carries on an extensive missionary enterprise.[1]

John P. Brooks and Hardin Wallace were Methodist preachers who were sanctified in an awakening which swept rural Illinois around 1870. Like dozens of other preachers of many persuasions, they joined first in the work of the Western Holiness Association and, later, the Illinois Holiness Association. Several Methodist presiding elders heartily supported them. Brooks edited for many years the *Banner of Holiness,* published at Bloomington. His address at a conference held under National Association auspices in Cincinnati in 1877 typified the group's prejudices. It denounced the "easy, indulgent, accommodating, mammonized" kind of Wesleyan preaching which tolerated church parties, festivals, and dramatic presentations and "erected gorgeous and costly temples, to gratify its pride." Ten years later Brooks had abandoned entirely his earlier loyalties and was writing *The Divine Church,* a volume which became from that day onward the textbook of "come-outism." He was by then editor of the *Good Way,* a magazine published by the struggling group in Missouri and Kansas which eventually became known as the Church of God (Holiness).[2]

This movement had grown out of the Southwestern Holiness Association, organized among Kansas and Missouri ministers, chiefly Methodists, in 1876. Six of its 182 members decided to withdraw from their denominations in 1882, on the grounds that insistence upon church loyalty was subjecting converts to pastors who were enemies of the second blessing. They won the right to continue in the Southwestern Association, however, and prevailed upon that body to sanction the organization, when necessary, of independent holiness "bands." At this point many prominent ministers withdrew, shattering whatever influence the association had exerted upon the older communions.

Within three years the "One New Testament Church" idea had prevailed among the leaders who remained. Their concept was that Christ was the Head and the Holy Spirit the sole Executive of the true Church. Its congregations were to be gathered from the world and "set in order" according to what was thought to be the New Testament pattern. Dissension continually wracked the bands, however, first over opposition to the sacraments and church discipline, then over the question whether elders or congregations were supreme in the New Testament order.

All of this was a scandal to the Methodists, whose passion for holiness was never as strong as their devotion to discipline. "Come-outism" became a favorite whipping boy of all who opposed the second blessing and many who did not. T. J. Wheat, a Missouri presiding elder, wrote the denominational newspaper in New York in 1888 that the leaders in the holiness movement were "all or nearly so, zealous advocates of come-outism." For the last ten years, he charged, the holiness associations had been "a standing menace to the spirit of the Gospel of Christ. . . . They have been, and are today, religious anarchists."[3]

Interestingly enough, Isaiah Reid, J. B. Creighton, and J. A. Kring, all of whom later became Nazarenes, were at different times associated with congregations of the Church of God (Holiness). Such staunch exemplars of the district and general superintendency as our present leaders, G. B. Williamson, D. I. Vanderpool, A. E. Sanner, and the late R. J. Plumb, were in their youth nurtured among them.

Long before Brooks moved to Missouri, Hardin Wallace had begun the holiness revival in Texas. Wallace's first meeting was at Calvert, in 1877. He then proceeded to Ennis, Denton, Bremond, and Corsicana, preaching sometimes in Southern Methodist and at others in Cumberland Presbyterian churches. Key Methodist ministers at first supported his work and numbers of them professed "the blessing." Within the next year W. B. Colt, M. L. Haney, and other Illinois evangelists appeared in Texas to help the movement on. Soon, however, as a contemporary account put it, the requirements of the doctrine as presented placed so many restrictions upon worldliness, and called for so much cross-bearing and self-denial on the part of church members that strong opposition sprang up against it, and as this opposition was especially strong on the part of the wealthier members of the churches, the presiding elder and numbers of the preachers soon arrayed themselves against the doctrine.[4]

The embattled leaders organized the Texas Holiness Association at a camp meeting near Corsicana in October, 1878. Methodist and Cumberland Presbyterian laymen were in charge. The association held ten annual camp meetings in different localities, each of which generated revivals in the churches nearby. From the beginning, Wallace had organized his converts into independent "bands." These grew in number as the awakening spread. The bands were interdenominational and without any stated discipline. They sometimes accepted the ministry of preachers whom neither God nor man, seemingly, had ordained. Under such circumstances, outbursts of fanaticism and extreme claims to "Spirit-guidance" inevitably occurred, strengthening the hand of the opponents of the revival.

Responsible Methodist clergymen thereupon organized in November, 1883, the Northwest Texas Holiness Association. They made their constitution the Bible and Wesley's *Plain Account of Christian Perfection* and agreed to receive none who were not members in good standing of the M.E. church. They also promised to conduct no meetings on any charge save at the invitation of the pastor and the official board. "We thus shielded the movement from fanatics and 'come-outers' on the one hand," wrote B. F. Gassaway, the president and Hardin Wallace's first Texas convert, "and on the other [we] sought to convince our brethren in the conference that we proposed no movement that was not sane and conservative." The association was remarkably successful. It founded a half dozen permanent camp meetings, including famous ones at Waco and Scottsville in Texas.[5]

Wallace, however, had already moved on to southern California. He held meetings early in 1880 at the First M.E. Church (North) in Los Angeles, organizing a holiness group there and at several other places. These bands he united in the Southern California and Arizona Holiness Association. When Wallace returned to Los Angeles the next spring, however, he found most of the churches closed to him. He launched a weekly gathering on the courthouse steps and held tent meetings at many points between San Diego and Santa Barbara. Despite the fact that numerous clergymen in the Baptist, Congregational, and Northern and Southern Methodist denominations professed sanctification, bitter opposition to the band meetings prevailed.

"It soon was known as a painful fact," so a picturesque chronicle runs, "that much of the past work had been destroyed through the constant opposition to clear testimony. . . . Many felt convicted to throw off the yoke of bondage." Chief of these latter was James F. Washburn, of Artesia, who encouraged a number of bands to organize as independent holiness churches. At the annual camp meeting of the Southern California and Arizona Holiness Association in 1883, Washburn and two Presbyterian ministers carried that organization with them, despite protests from the Methodists. They secured the adoption of rules forbidding members of the association "to wear or sell gold as an ornament," to use or sell tobacco, or to belong to a secret order. They recommended that the "Holy People" organize bands, erect tabernacles, shun musical instruments in worship, and "dress in plain raiment."

Thus was born the Holiness church, over which Mrs. James F. Washburn eventually assumed chief leadership. Intense persecution together with the puritan plainness of their rules combined to retard their growth and keep them confined to very small towns. Only twelve congregations existed in 1888, none of them in Los Angeles. Two young converts, Dennis Rogers and George M. Teel, both almost totally without formal education, returned to their native Texas and planted first bands and then Holiness church organizations along the agricultural frontier in the northern part of that state. Most of these eventually died out, and Rogers later joined J. B. Chapman and C. B. Jernigan in organizing the Independent Holiness church, another of the parent bodies of the Church of the Nazarene.

In California, however, the leaders managed to weld together the congregations of the Holiness church into a genuine denominational order, destroying in the process, of course, much of the freedom in which they had come into existence. "We must beware of unholy desires for personal independence," one wrote in 1892, "which allies liberty with license and makes it akin to come-outism, which, if left to run its course, will end in anarchy and ruin."⁶

The Pursuit of Unity and Loyalty

Meanwhile, back in rural Michigan, where both Oberlin and Methodist perfectionism had cast deep roots, S. B. Shaw dreamed more of uniting the holiness advocates upon the radical platform than of starting another denomination. He held revivals and camp meetings continuously under Methodist, Free and Wesleyan Methodist, and United Brethren auspices. But when the National Camp Meeting Association came to Lansing for one of its campaigns, its leaders drew Shaw's fire both for their firm allegiance to the Methodist Episcopal church and for the liberality which some of them displayed on matters of dress, membership in secret orders, divorce, and so on.

Shaw was in theory as sharply opposed to come-outism as to sectarianism, despite the fact that by 1884 the Michigan State Association, of which he was president, had adopted a statement of doctrines and rules for its members and set up a plan for the formation of holiness bands. Actually Shaw tried to mediate between all groups. Originally a Methodist, he joined first the Wesleyan Methodist and then the Free Methodist church in search of a sympathetic fellowship. He forsook each in turn because of opposition to his work with the "undenominational" association. "Come Methodists, come Baptists, come Presbyterians, and Mennonites, and U. B.'s, and Salvation Armyists," Shaw wrote, in announcing the "Michigan State Campmeeting" for 1887,

> come come-outers, come everybody, . . . and let us all get melted down before God, so we will not have any feelings toward each other in opposition to perfect love. May God save us from narrow-minded selfishness and bigotry, save us from sin of all kinds.⁷

Interestingly enough, Shaw and other radical leaders were chiefly responsible for the Chicago Holiness Assembly of 1885, which brought together representatives of all the groups organized in the United States to promote sanctification. Among these were over a dozen state associations and four larger regional ones, the Western, Southwestern, Pacific Coast, and Union—all of which were interdenominational—and a half dozen denominational societies, of which the Methodist "National" was by far the most important. Shaw first suggested such a meeting in his

Michigan Holiness Record in 1884. He hoped it would bring about a "National Interdenominational Association" strong enough to unite and discipline the work and yet elastic enough to leave separate units "free to carry out independent plans and measures." John P. Brooks seconded the idea in the *Banner of Holiness*. Brooks proposed a planning committee chiefly made up of midwestern firebrands. The project quickly gathered wide support.

When, however, the assembly convened at Chicago the following May, conservative leaders were on hand in such force as to secure the election as permanent chairman of George Hughes of New York City, secretary and historian of the National Campmeeting Association and Dr. Palmer's successor as editor of the *Guide to Holiness*. Hughes forthwith proposed that the delegates transact "as little business as possible" and seek instead a "gigantic" baptism of the Holy Spirit. The chairman later refused even to permit the gathering to hear a letter from James F. Washburn on the subject of organizing independent churches. The assembly adopted instead a "Declaration of Principles" which enjoined church membership on every converted person (Washburn's California group allowed this privilege only to those who professed sanctification). It declared holiness to be "not a disintegrating but a conserving force" and rejected any really new departure in national organization.

The Chicago Assembly was the first of several successive crises in the church question. It demonstrated that those whose chief interest was to convert the older denominations, particularly the representatives of the National Campmeeting Association, were still in effective control of the movement. Shaw's *Michigan Holiness Record* could take comfort only in the fact that some "radical work" was done amidst the gathering's tumultuous prayer meetings. Many, he reported, pledged to take a "narrower way." "Gold watch chains, gold cuff buttons and even bows on a hat went for Jesus' sake," and ministers of many denominations were "slain under the power of the Spirit."

By 1890, Shaw had followed the example of Warner, Brooks, and Wallace and organized his followers into the Primitive Holiness Mission. The editor of the Oakland, California, *Holiness Evangelist* reported this event with "deep and inexpressible sadness." The latter could not understand, he said, why "holy men who have been put in the stocks of . . . sectarian church government, and beaten from pillar to post by the sect principle and spirit" should "go to work and organize another sect, and thus perpetuate the very evil which has met them at every turn in all the sects."[8]

From the middle 1880's onward, therefore, a lengthy argument raged between those who believed that separate holiness denominations were necessary and those who relied upon associations to carry on the work. The argument was complicated at every stage by the easily revived memory of the excesses of the "come-outers" and by the fact that radical leaders were usually in the vanguard for secession.

No large group ever pulled out at one time. The great majority professing sanctification clung to the older churches and, hence, to the association idea. Their successors to this day maintain scores of annual camp meetings and provide the chief support for such colleges as Malone and George Fox (Friends), Asbury and Taylor (Methodist), and Vennard College, God's Bible School, and Cascade College (all undenominational).

As the crisis in church relations deepened after 1890, however, ecclesiastical pressures forced the associations to become interdenominational. The inroads of fanaticism meanwhile required them to tighten their rules. Thus by 1897 the National Holiness Association, hitherto Northern Methodist, had shifted the center of its attention from the East to the Midwest and was striving to become the sort of inclusive body S. B. Shaw had advocated at Chicago in 1885. It proclaimed a doctrinal code and banned those who made healing, premillennialism, or Keswick views their "hobby." At the Chicago Holiness Assembly of 1901, Shaw found himself in accord with prominent clergymen of many denominations. The gathering signaled the triumph of his unsectarian position, but produced no really effective organization. Three years later Henry Clay Morrison and other southern leaders formed the Holiness Union, which sought to unite the whole movement below the Mason and Dixon line.

More limited in scope but similarly undenominational were J. O. McClurkan's Pentecostal Alliance, which drew together missions and churches scattered over central Tennessee, New England's Central Evangelical Holiness Association, and the Holiness Association of Texas, organized in 1899. All of these played important roles in the origins of the Church of the Nazarene. Both the Iowa and the Northern Indiana holiness associations, the two strongest in the Midwest, welcomed members of all churches. Presbyterian A. B. Simpson's Christian and Missionary Alliance, which championed missions and divine healing as well as holiness, meanwhile evolved slowly into a separate but "interdenominational" communion. Organized in New York City in 1887, the Alliance soon spread to all the major cities of the nation.[9]

On the other hand, passing years witnessed the retreat of the original "come-outers" from congregational sovereignty toward a limited superintendency. A dozen denominations thereafter set sail in the narrows between "anarchy" and ecclesiasticism. Many of these flourished in cities under conditions quite different, as we shall see, from those which Brooks and Wallace had faced. Such were Phineas Bresee's Church of the Nazarene in Los Angeles, the Association of Pentecostal Churches of America in Brooklyn, and the Pentecostal Mission in Nashville, all parent bodies to the present Church of the Nazarene, as well as the Metropolitan Church Association, an emotionalist offspring of the movement centered in Chicago.

Other sects emerged in a rural and radical setting. The Tennessee-Texas area produced the New Testament Church of Christ and the Independent Holiness church. These two merged in 1904 and then joined the Church of the Nazarene in 1908. The Holiness Baptist church, a tiny group in Arkansas, stood apart. Far away to the East, seven ministers expelled from the New Brunswick Baptist Association organized the Reformed Baptist church in the Maritime Provinces of Canada. By 1895, seven years after its founding, the denomination reported thirty-three congregations, of which twenty-seven had constructed their own meetinghouses. In the Midwest, meanwhile, the smaller Methodist communions flourished alongside such organizations as the Ohio Yearly Meeting of Friends, a separate communion in all but name, and the Mennonite Brethren in Christ. Here also came into being in 1903 the Apostolic Holiness church, under Seth C. Rees and Mrs. M. W. Knapp, widow of the founder of God's Bible School, Cincinnati. The group gathered strength in rural Kansas and Texas and eventually became a part of the Pilgrim Holiness church.[10]

An interesting question is, Why did not those who seceded from the old denominations join one of the young Wesleyan churches already in existence? True, some did unite with the

Free Methodists, who had been uncompromisingly perfectionist since their origin in 1859. This denomination spread slowly through the West and South in the wake of the rural revival. The Methodist Protestant church, dating from 1832, adopted a specifically "second blessing" creed in 1877, and became a haven for a few sanctified Methodists in Texas, Louisiana, and Mississippi. The Wesleyan Methodist Connection, which had originated in the antislavery agitation of the 1840's, took the same step in 1887 and filled a similar role in sections of New York, Ohio, Indiana, and southern Michigan. In Pennsylvania, the Evangelical Association keynoted sanctification among the German-speaking population.[11]

But most holiness people stood aloof from these. One reason may have been that a tide of nonsectarian feeling bore along the first wave of secessions, whereas the Wesleyan bodies had developed rigid patterns of faith and order. Distance and isolation, moreover, made it difficult for regional groups, as for example the holiness Baptists in Canada and Arkansas, to establish fellowship with others. A third factor may have been simply personal: the withdrawing leaders were often restless individualists, unable to accept much real discipline save their own. Probably most important, however, was the fact that Baptists, Congregationalists, Friends, and Presbyterians—even sanctified ones—found it difficult to become Methodists, "Free," "Wesleyan," or otherwise.

In any event, whenever a new denomination emerged, the old arguments over "come-outism" cropped up again. The secessionists insisted that they had actually been crushed out. The loyalists maintained that perfect love and sectarian schisms were incompatible. Both were, no doubt, partially right. Certainly, responsible leaders left the old churches with great reluctance. And they always disavowed both come-outism and sectarianism when announcing their departure.

In retrospect, the embarrassment which the earliest secessions brought to the more conservative leaders of the holiness revival gives them a significance all out of proportion to their size. They illustrate also the growing urban-rural cleavage of the movement. From our vantage point seventy years later, the rural leaders seem to have differed only in the *degree* of their adherence to puritan standards. And they spelled out the reasons for their attitude with surprising good sense. All holiness preachers made a strong issue of worldliness in dress and behavior in the nineteenth century. In this they were out of harmony neither with evangelical tradition nor with its objectives current at the time. Leaders in both the Northern and Southern Methodist churches, for example, strenuously opposed the growing indulgence in theatergoing, fancy dress, and other frivolities and scorned raising money through festivals and suppers.[12]

The growth of wealth, the rise of cities, and the decline of the ideals of industry and abstinence were a challenge to the old faith. The new sects, however radical, did not create new doctrines or standards, as some of our sociologists have recently said. They simply re-emphasized the old ones when the drift of society was in the opposite direction.

The Loyalists Face a Mounting Crisis

While the debate over "come-outism" raged, two serious developments compelled leaders of the conservative wing of the holiness revival to re-examine their professed loyalty to the older denominations. Ecclesiastical officials, particularly Methodists, laid increasing pressures upon the independent agencies which supported the movement. And a series of major assaults on the doctrine of sanctification appeared in public print.

Late in the year 1881, a company of the most eminent Methodist champions of the second blessing requested the northern bishops to arrange under their own chairmanship a great national convention for the promotion of holiness. Daniel Steele, Asbury Lowery, John Miley, professor of theology at Drew Theological Seminary, and Milton S. Terry, professor at Garrett Seminary, were in the group who signed the appeal. Their chief argument was that the work of sanctification, which had spread so widely in the previous decade, could "never become universal in the church if left to independent organizations and unrecognized agencies."

The bishops replied in a letter which professed the "entire allegiance" of their number to Wesley's doctrine but which bluntly rejected the proposal. "It is our solemn conviction," they declared, "that the whole subject of personal experience . . . can be best maintained and enforced in connection with the established usages of the church." And they agreed that it was all too true that the holiness associations segregated a part of the church from the whole, thus tending to produce alienation.[13]

This declaration was in line with the policy which the board of bishops had followed since 1856. But the incident gave opponents of holiness an officially acceptable line of attack and, at the same time, drove a wedge between its champions and the great body of moderate men in the church. For, the argument now ran, if the bishops and theologians of the denomination had acknowledged entire sanctification to be fundamental in Methodist religion and thrown their weight in its support, independent publishing and camp meeting associations were no longer a necessity but a nuisance.

J. E. Searles framed the reply of the National Association to this argument in 1887. That organization was still greatly needed, he said, both to continue the work already begun and to shield the state and local associations, many of which were loosely organized interdenominational bodies, from unsound or fanatical tendencies. Even though the doctrine of holiness "is clearly and fully taught in our schools," Searles declared, "it seldom finds its way into the pulpits and prayer-meetings of the churches." Too many ministers knew of sanctification only from theory, not practice—and this when the rapid growth of urban wealth and refinement was mounting a fearful challenge to personal consecration. "Nothing but the earnest preaching of this doctrine and experience," Searles warned, "can save our great Methodist church from religious formalism, and the spirit of the world. Our danger increases with our increase of numbers, and popularity, and wealth."[14]

In any event, the leaders of the movement showed no intention of abandoning the agencies which had brought the interest in Christian perfection to such a high pitch. John Inskip died in the midst of preparations for a mammoth convention held in connection with the General Conference at Philadelphia, in 1884. The national unit encouraged the organization of dozens of state and local associations. By 1888, 206 holiness evangelists were giving all their time to the work, most of them without regular assignment from ecclesiastical superiors. The *Christian Witness,* published in Boston, the *Christian Standard,* organ of the National Association, and the *Guide to Holiness,* now edited by George Hughes, were only the most prominent among a score of periodicals whose distribution inevitably competed with that of the official conference journals. The great camp meetings which the associations established, many of them interdenominational and all of them out from under the control of presiding elders, were a constant source of friction. Only slightly less trouble arose when the national group arranged to use conference campgrounds for their own highly publicized gatherings, inevitably draining away support from the stated sessions.[15]

The rollicking story of the elevation in 1884 of the freelance missionary evangelist, William Taylor, to the bishop's chair illustrates both the solid respect which holiness leaders had won among the rank and file and the dismay which their vast array of extra-constitutional activities brought to the hierarchy. Taylor was one of Phoebe Palmer's trophies of grace. He had spent the years following the Civil War establishing "self-supporting" missionary ventures in South America, Australia, and India. An incorrigible individualist, he ignored the Methodist Board of Foreign Missions while raising large sums and recruiting helpers at holiness camp meetings from Maine to Oregon.

All hands agree that Taylor's work was substantial. The South India Conference was formed from his labors in 1880. Two years later, however, the General Missionary Committee denied the right of Taylor or any person other than its regular appointees to organize Methodist Episcopal churches outside the United States. His South American congregations were declared "out of order" and their pastors commanded to return home.

Taylor at this point accepted the status of a local preacher and appeared at the General Conference of 1884 as a lay delegate from South India. Toward the end of that conference Daniel Curry, editor of the *Methodist Quarterly Review,* rose to propose the election of a missionary bishop for Liberia. Curry had long desired to see a Negro clergyman in the episcopal office. After the motion carried, however, an obscure delegate nominated William Taylor. The idea took the conference by storm and Taylor won on the first ballot, 250 to 44, despite the frenzied maneuvers which Curry and the members of the Missionary Committee made to stop it.[16]

The new bishop immediately launched an aggressive program. He spurned the $3,000 annual salary which the Missionary Committee set aside for his use after the Book Committee, regularly responsible for episcopal salaries, had refused to pay him. He knew he could raise greater amounts by his usual methods. Douglas Camp Meeting alone gave him $2,000 in two years.

Taylor took with him to Liberia Mrs. Amanda Smith, a colored evangelist. She helped him turn the Methodist mission there into a holiness crusade.[17]

The General Conference of 1888 only partially sustained Taylor's position, amidst keen embarrassment all around. The long address of the church fathers to that assembly laid bare the problems which independent agencies posed to a denomination accustomed to tight discipline. The address contained, to be sure, a ringing affirmation of the bishops' devotion to the doctrine and experience of Christian perfection. Methodism was "rooted and grounded in this faith," they said, and all of its means of grace were designed to promote holiness. But other paragraphs defended their recent policy of refusing to appoint regular ministers to the office of evangelist and urged upon the conference "some official supervision or limitation" of the work of "voluntary alliances, leagues, unions and associations."[18] Clearly, peace could be had only on condition that the leaders of the second-blessing movement turn over the work entirely to the bishops, and trust these chosen leaders to further Wesley's doctrine in the church.

A similar impasse developed in Southern Methodism as soon as holiness associations became numerous there. Spokesmen for the latter insisted that they were the most devoted of churchmen. Far from being responsible for the "fanatical extremes" of "come-outism" which had "brought the cause of holiness into such disrepute in California, Missouri, and in parts of Texas," they claimed to represent the only organized bodies seeking to channel the universal yearning for perfection into paths of loyalty to the church. Leonidas Rosser, a Virginia presiding elder, pointed out that Methodism itself began as "a great holiness association . . . organized in the Church of England." The address of the Southern bishops for 1894 brought this argument to a bitter climax. They denounced the "party" which had sprung up "with holiness as a watchword" and which maintained

> holiness associations, holiness meetings, holiness preachers, holiness evangelists, and holiness property. . . . We do not question the sincerity and zeal of these brethren; we desire the church to profit by their earnest preaching and godly example; but we deplore their teaching and methods insofar as they claim a monopoly of the experience, practice, and advocacy of holiness, and separate themselves from the body of ministers and disciples.[19]

The same year the Northwest Texas Conference adopted resolutions which, in the name of peace, practically outlawed the second-blessing doctrine. The conference affirmed its devotion to entire sanctification and the duty of its members to preach it, in return for which the Northwest Texas Holiness Association agreed to disband. The latter action left the Waco camp meeting an orphan, and gave opponents of the movement freedom to invoke church law against unauthorized evangelists. When, despite the protest of the pastor and presiding elder, Henry Clay Morrison conducted a meeting at Dublin, Texas, in 1896, he was tried and expelled from the church. His appeal to the Kentucky Annual Conference finally carried on a technicality. Morrison agreed to conform to the law and friends patched up the quarrel. Afterwards he withdrew from the church, only to return again. But the General Conference of 1898 made the prohibitions against unauthorized evangelists stronger than ever. Robert Lee Harris, Bud Robinson, W. C. Wilson, and many others who later became Nazarene leaders broke with Southern Methodism over this issue.[20]

The second development which disrupted the loyalties which bound Methodist conservatives to their church was the outbreak of a doctrinal controversy in which the teachings of Wesley himself came under public attack. In earlier decades, critics of the "second blessing" had professed great respect for the founder. They contented themselves with publishing fragments of his writings which seemed to prove that Wesley questioned the idea of an *instantaneous* second experience, or that he discouraged testimony to it and left undefined the precise nature of the "sin in believers" which it eradicated. The holiness specialists managed by the 1880's pretty well to demolish these arguments and to make the veneration of Wesley their most powerful weapon. This fact in part explains the unanimity with which Methodist officialdom professed loyalty to the doctrine while opposing measures designed to promote it.[21]

In 1888, however, J. M. Boland, a preacher in the Southern church, published a volume called *The Problem of Methodism,* which declared that Wesley got his notion of "sin in believers" from the Calvinists and that he erased it from the Articles of Religion in 1784. Furthermore, Boland maintained that, regardless of the founder's views, the Bible taught that the experience of conversion encompassed both the forgiveness and entire sanctification of the soul. A brief article in the Southern *Quarterly Review* praised Boland's book and called for the elimination from Methodist doctrine of "all that recognizes a 'second change.' "

Forceful rejoinders appeared at once, and the debate was on. Leonidas Rosser, who later became a bishop, wrote a full-length reply. A half dozen essays appeared in the *Review*. One by S. H. Wainwright, missionary to Japan, demonstrated that Wesley's omission of part of the Ninth Article of Religion from the Methodist creed was for other reasons than its statement on "sin in believers." George H. Hayes added fuel to the fire in 1891 with *The Problem Solved,* a book which shared Boland's rejection of the second blessing, but for opposite reasons. Hayes argued for the Calvinist idea that depravity is inseparable from the mortal state. This prompted an even more formidable defense of Christian perfection, spearheaded by John J. Tigert, who became editor of the *Review* in 1894. Tigert promptly closed the columns of that journal to all material which contradicted traditional Methodist theology. He acknowledged that he did not profess entire sanctification, but he believed in it and thought its champions were on the front lines of the church's crucial conflict with worldliness. In May, 1895, Tigert published an article by O. E. Brown, professor of church history at Vanderbilt University, which maintained that all the standard theologians of Methodism, including the more recently accepted ones, agreed upon the instantaneous availability of entire sanctification, though not all believed this was the only way to attain it.[22]

Boland continued to insist, however, that his theory was based upon both sound psychology and the Bible. He had, he said, relegated the "residue theory" of "sin in believers" to the scrap heap, and Methodists might as well accept the fact. But he could scarcely be expected to rest his case on rational arguments alone when another kind was so ready at hand. Hence, with heavy sarcasm, Boland denounced in 1893 the holiness preachers for thinking themselves "heaven-appointed custodians of this sacred ark of Methodism." They had established independent associations and periodicals, erected holiness schools and colleges, and flooded the countryside with harebrained young evangelists, some of whom dared even to impugn the integrity of bishops of the church.

It was a telling blow. That the church fathers echoed the same language in their address of 1894, quoted above, cast a shadow on their professions of loyalty to Christian perfection, despite the efforts of John J. Tigert, and the bishops themselves, to prove they were sincere.[23]

The career of B. F. Haynes, a prominent Nashville Methodist who was one day to become the first editor of the Nazarene *Herald of Holiness*, illustrates the confusion which reigned over the question at the headquarters of Southern Methodism between 1894 and 1900. Haynes was a former presiding elder, whom Bishop Hargrove removed to a hard-scrabble circuit in 1891, as a part of a wholesale effort to discipline the conference for its devotion to the Prohibition party. The conference established a journal, the *Tennessee Methodist*, to defend its course and made Haynes editor. The scrappy publicist soon became convinced, however, that efforts to reform the church were less important than a restoration of "individual unworldliness—personal, whole-hearted, uncompromising consecration of heart and life to God and humanity."

At this juncture a holiness evangelist arrived in Nashville. Haynes found the blessing and committed the *Tennessee Methodist* to the cause, this at the very moment when the *Nashville Advocate*, newspaper for the whole denomination, was taking the opposite stand. Although the Tennessee conference voted in 1895 to continue Haynes's paper as its organ, its resolution specified that the endorsement "should not commit the conference one way or the other in regard to the question of the second blessing theory of sanctification." Haynes thereafter engaged E. M. Bounds, for many years an editor of the *St. Louis Advocate* and more recently of the *Nashville Advocate*, to deepen the perfectionist content of his paper. But by the time of the conference of 1896 his cause was lost. That body disowned the *Tennessee Methodist*, despite Haynes's plea which underlined the "phenomenal inconsistency of a Methodist conference repudiating its conference organ, because it teaches a Methodist doctrine."

Haynes continued to publish the journal as a private venture for four more years, under the name *American Outlook*. He sold it at last to J. O. McClurkan, who changed the name to *Living Water* and made it the organ of the Pentecostal Mission. Bishop Joseph S. Key, a staunch friend of the holiness leaders, appointed Haynes pastor of a large congregation at Lebanon, Tennessee, in 1898. A sweeping revival followed. The next year Bishop Galloway removed him to a miserable charge with the remark, "You have ruined our church at Lebanon." Haynes accepted the presidency first of a tiny Methodist school at Pulaski, Tennessee, and, thereafter, of Asbury College, a struggling institution which Henry Clay Morrison and the second-blessing preachers of the Kentucky conference were supporting. In 1909 he moved on to the holiness college at Peniel, Texas, and joined the Church of the Nazarene. "My life has been simply one of protest," Haynes wrote later in his autobiography; "my voice and pen have been kept busy in dissent." Such was the fruit which these years of controversy bore.[24]

In 1895 a similar public debate broke out in Northern Methodism, sparked by James Mudge's volume *Growth in Holiness Toward Perfection, or Progressive Sanctification*. Mudge was much less revolutionary than Boland had been. He did not deny the traditional doctrine that believers were sanctified after they were justified. He did, however, acknowledge his divergence from Wesley's view of an instantaneous experience and denounced as well the sectarian and divisive tendencies of the second-blessing movement. Here was middle ground clearly acceptable to many of the bishops; segments of the official Methodist press issued favorable reviews at once.

Daniel Steele and Lewis R. Dunn, the chief literary lights of the holiness party, published book-length replies to Mudge's volume. Every holiness periodical—by then there were dozens—pitched into the fray. Dunn attacked especially Mudge's libel that those who professed sanctification believed they had attained all excellence and spent the rest of their lives in mutual congratulation. On the contrary, Dunn pointed out, none preached, wrote, and labored so much for growth in grace as the advocates of perfect love. Asbury Lowery, a former presiding elder and evangelist, denounced Mudge in the *Methodist Review* for superseding faith with works in the quest of holiness and for brashly belittling John Wesley's scholarship.[25]

The noise of this battle had not diminished when D. W. C. Huntington, chancellor of Nebraska Wesleyan University, published *Sin and Holiness*, an elaborate reworking of J. M. Boland's thesis. In the South, meanwhile, Wilbur F. Tillett, dean of the theological faculty at Vanderbilt University, picked up Mudge's ideas and carried them even further. The holiness leaders quickly realized that the Methodist colleges and universities would no longer shelter their defenders.

How far matters had gone is evident from the fact that in 1904 Bishop Willard F. Mallalieu, a close friend of Daniel Steele, wrote the introduction to George W. Wilson's attack on the young intellectuals called *Methodist Theology vs. Methodist Theologians*. Wilson traced the decline of vital piety and the increase of worldliness in Wesley's church to the new heresies of Borden Parker Bowne and James Mudge, whom he quite uncritically lumped together. "New England Methodism, where much of this new theology is born," Wilson wrote, "is slowly dying. Revivals are scarce. An increasing proportion of our members dance, play cards, attend theaters, and absent themselves from revivals." Actually, the sequence of events had been the reverse. Worldliness had begotten spiritual compromise, making the atmosphere favorable to theologies which explained away the call to Christian perfection.

Whatever the cause, the doctrinal controversy brought deep gloom to those who preached the second blessing. "Spiritual matters with us are not specially hopeful," William McDonald, Inskip's successor as head of the National Association, wrote Phineas Bresee from Boston in 1895. "Fairs, church theatricals, and higher criticisms seem to take the lead, and those who inquire the way to Zion are only here and there a traveler." The same year Isaiah Reid, western editor for the *Christian Witness*, seconded Beverly Carradine's suggestion that the time had come to establish holiness colleges and to separate entirely the movement's publishing ventures from church control.

But Reid urged his readers not to withdraw from their denominations until absolutely compelled to do so. He had experienced his fill of "come-outism" years before, in the Church of God (Holiness). Nor would fleeing from Southern to Northern Methodism, he warned his brethren in Texas and Kentucky, be anything more than moving "out of one frying pan into another." The world had "no quarter for a real holiness man." The "war to extermination" which seemed to have begun in Southern Methodism was not a matter of longitude or latitude.

In the next ten years Asbury, Texas Holiness University, and Meridian College emerged in the South and God's Bible School, Taylor University, Chicago Evangelistic Institute, Cleveland Bible Institute, and Central Holiness University appeared in the Midwest. All these were either Methodist or interdenominational. Literally scores of smaller schools, serving one or the other of the holiness sects, came into existence about the same time. These schools, like the camp meetings and periodicals which supported them, all became instruments for the creation of separate holiness organizations.[26]

Holiness Social Work

The decisive factor which alienated many urban holiness leaders from the older churches was their participation in nondenominational mission and social work. Some of the movement's finest souls turned away from sterile controversy to evangelize the poor. Their labors produced a class of converts who could scarcely be made to feel at home in the stylish churches "uptown." The inevitable result was the organization of independent congregations.

From the days when Charles G. Finney helped inspire the antislavery crusade and Phoebe Palmer instigated the first settlement house in New York City slums, the experience of perfect love had driven men and women to the relief of human suffering. From 1860 onward, holiness people established scores of missions and rescue homes for the victims of the white slave traffic. They founded hospitals and orphanages to care for unwed mothers and their children, provided for impoverished immigrants, and returned thousands whom they found on Skid Row to their native countryside.

The spread of the Salvation Army to the larger towns of America after 1880 greatly quickened all this activity and linked it even more positively to the perfectionist crusade. Some mocked at the idea of preaching holiness in the red-light districts. But General Booth, that tender tyrant of perfect love, thought the lowest class would not trust any religion which failed to magnify the power of God's grace. He also knew that his volunteers could be neither recruited nor kept from sin unless they were fully consecrated, wholly sanctified men and women.

The vast company who thus engaged in holiness social work in the last fifteen years of the century learned new reasons for rejecting the smug Christianity prevalent in the churches. The record of their labors appears in marvelous detail in every periodical promoting sanctification. In rural Texas, for example, numerous rescue homes and orphanages flourished, one of which, at Pilot Point, entered significantly into the origins of the Church of the Nazarene. Many of the evangelists there spent their summers holding free-lance tent meetings in the countryside but moved to some promising town when winter set in, and opened a holiness mission. In the East, A. B. Simpson's Christian Alliance Bible School trained young people for the foreign field by sending them out in bands to New York City's missions, hospitals, and jails. "Nearly all the students are from humble stations in life," one of Phineas Bresee's converts wrote back home in 1895, "and many have had very little educational advantages, but they are ones whom God has found He can trust."

Elsewhere, C. W. Sherman operated the Vanguard Mission in St. Louis, specializing in rescue work. He published a fine paper to which Mrs. R. B. Mitchum, a leading woman preacher in the New Testament Church of Christ, often contributed. H. D. Brown, pioneer district superintendent in the Northwest, passed from a Methodist pastorate in Seattle into the Nazarene fold by way of the Washington State Children's Home Society. This organization, which Brown headed for many years after 1903, won national recognition for its plan of orphan care. The holiness evangelist Charles N. Crittenton spent the latter part of his life erecting a chain of rescue homes which bore his name from Maine to California. Nazarenes actively supported his work in places like Lynn, Massachusetts, Little Rock, Arkansas, and Los Angeles, California.[27]

Much of what was done for alcoholics, "fallen" women, and orphans had little to do with the church question, of course. What is most significant for this chapter is the holiness mission work which sought to provide a church home for *families* who had crowded into the poorer sections of the cities after 1880.

The bishops of the M.E. Church, North, had for decades warned their followers against neglect of the urban poor. They at first encouraged the establishment of mission churches. They became more cautious, however, when parishioners who professed sanctification led the way in such projects and occasionally converted the missions into independent holiness congregations. Many Nazarene churches originated this way, including the oldest one, at Providence, Rhode Island, as well as those at Washington, D.C.; Calgary, Alberta; Little Rock, Arkansas; East Liverpool, Ohio; Lynn, Massachusetts; Omaha, Nebraska; Minneapolis, Minnesota; Spokane, Washington; and Colorado Springs, Colorado. Isaiah Reid wrote in 1895 that the First Church Mission, sponsored by the principal Methodist church in St. Louis,

Missouri, had become "the natural rallying center for the holiness movement in the city." Later, in an extended article on the subject, Reid declared significantly: "In many of the city churches the holiness evangelist has no standing room. In the mission he has."

By 1897, great cities like Chicago and Brooklyn and Cincinnati were filled with such ventures. At Evansville, Indiana, C. W. Ruth found that the Union Gospel Mission was a thriving institution managed by "holiness people from the various churches." A thousand people attended his revival there night after night. In Spokane, Washington, Dr. D. N. McInturff, formerly pastor of the First Methodist Church, established the People's United Church. It was completely Methodist in both doctrine and polity, save for a strong stand on woman's rights. Within twelve months McInturff had gathered seven hundred members, instituted a Bible school, and made plans to organize groups in the surrounding towns. Rev. Fillmore Tanner, later a Nazarene charter member there, was secretary of his missionary board. At the time of the founding of our church in Spokane seven years afterward, missions flourished under the auspices of the Salvation Army, the Door of Hope, the Volunteers of America, and the Nazarenes—holiness advocates all.[28]

Even had there been no secessions from the churches, however, the interdenominational character of much of this mission work would have been enough to provoke ecclesiastical suspicions. This fact is well illustrated in the story of Phineas Bresee's endeavors at Peniel Hall, Los Angeles, in 1894-95.

Rev. and Mrs. T. P. Ferguson had conducted the Los Angeles Mission, ancestor to Peniel, since 1886. Early in 1894 an Englishman named G. B. Studd, brother of C. T. Studd, gave them money sufficient to construct a fine building. The Fergusons recruited Phineas Bresee, one of the most prominent Methodist ministers in southern California, to join them in the work. Bresee had occupied all the important Methodist pulpits in the area and was reluctant to leave Los Angeles, where his large family was happily situated, in quest of another suitable charge. Apparently he had no thought of breaking with the friends who only two years before had elected him their delegate to the General Conference. He preached frequently at the district camp meetings and served on most of the important conference boards and committees.

Either the presiding bishop or persons influential in the Southern California conference, however, blocked Bresee's request to go to Peniel Hall under a "supernumerary relation," the legal term for the status of a regular minister placed on special assignment. But the new mission hall was nearing completion, and he had given his word to the Fergusons. After three days of prayer, Bresee asked for a "location," that is, an honorable release from his duties to the Methodist conference. The call of the poor had joined with his concern for an unfettered holiness crusade to pull him out of the church. One would like to know just how this man of God prayed, and what his brethren thought, when, that afternoon, he gave the invocation for his last session in a Methodist conference.

Peniel Hall, "large enough to seat 900 persons, light and comfortable," as the *Los Angeles Times* reported, was dedicated on Sunday, October 21, 1894. Dr. J. P. Widney, a wealthy Methodist layman, president of the University of Southern California, and Bresee's close friend, led the praise service at nine-thirty. Dr. Bresee preached at eleven from the text, "And Jacob called the name of the place Peniel: for I have seen God face to face, and my life is preserved." John A. Wood, author of the famous book *Perfect Love* and an evangelist from Massachusetts long active in National Association work, preached at night. Bresee announced that Joseph H. Smith, another eastern evangelist prominent in National Association affairs, would begin revival meetings soon. Dr. Widney urged the young people to enroll in his Training Institute, in which Bible and practical nursing were to be the principal studies.

In the initial issue of their monthly paper, the *Peniel Herald*, Dr. Bresee declared:

> Our first work is to try to reach the unchurched. The people from the homes and the street where the light from the churches does not reach, or penetrates but little. Especially to gather the poor to the cross, by bringing to bear upon them Christian sympathy and helpfulness....
> It is also our work to preach and teach the gospel of full salvation; to show forth the blessed privilege of believers in Jesus Christ, to be made holy and thus perfect in love.

Here were holiness and humanitarianism working hand in hand, as in the days of Wesley. And sectarian feeling was rejected: "Peniel Mission is thoroughly evangelical but entirely undenominational," the *Herald* declared. Its superintendents would welcome help from all "earnest souls . . . who have any time over and above the work in their churches that they desire to give."[29]

Bresee knew, however, that he could not accept some volunteers at face value. Holiness missions all over the country had suffered from the cranks and the hobbyists on the Second Coming or divine healing who had tried to take over the work. Amanda Smith, a woman of much sound sense, wrote the *Christian Witness* in 1897 that some of the missions which flourished in Denver, Colorado, spread "the wildest teaching in fanaticism" that she had ever met with anywhere. "Lots of people," she commented, "seem to like to be fooled." Of this Los Angeles had already had its share.

Hence Bresee wrote in December, 1894, that he had "stated as publicly as practicable, from the beginning of the planning for our work, that . . . an organization of the workers" was necessary. Moreover, he noted, the organization must take into account "those that are being gathered in, who have no church affiliation, who need care and fellowship, and a place to find a home and work." On behalf of the four superintendents, therefore—himself, Mr. and Mrs. Ferguson, and G. B. Studd—Dr. Bresee printed the statement of belief to be required of all who wished to associate themselves with Peniel Hall. It was a broad one, "embracing in simplest statement . . . a few of those essential things which are the common inheritance of the children of God." But it was enough to fend off the firebrands. The statement, containing only seventy-four words, was the archetype of the earliest Nazarene creed:

> The Peniel Mission is an organization for Christian service and fellowship. It will be required that those who seek to become members of the Peniel Mission be sound in the faith on all the main points of Christian doctrine, which may be particularized as follows:
>
> 1. The Divine inspiration of the Scriptures, the Old and New Testaments.
> 2. The Trinity of the Godhead, Father, Son and Holy Ghost.
> 3. The Fall of man, and his consequent need of Regeneration.
> 4. The Atonement of the Lord Jesus Christ for all men.
> 5. Justification by Faith in Him.
> 6. Sanctification by Faith in the cleansing blood of Jesus Christ, and the Baptism of the Holy Ghost.
> 7. The Resurrection of the dead.
> 8. The eternity of Reward and Punishment.

What Bresee intended, apparently, was a combination of the interdenominational mission idea with that of an independent church, the former for the workers and sponsors who had no thought of forsaking their old allegiances, the latter for the converts and others who had no church home. In this and many other respects, as we shall see, Peniel resembled very closely the Pentecostal Mission, which J. O. McClurkan founded in Nashville between 1899 and 1901. Neither was quite a church, neither simply a mission.

Interestingly, Seth C. Rees, a Friends holiness evangelist who later played a striking part in Nazarene history, launched a similar but quite unsuccessful venture in Chicago around 1900. And at God's Bible School, Cincinnati, Mrs. M. W. Knapp led her deceased husband's movement in and out of another effort along the same line. In all these cases, the leaders had to provide an organization strong enough to restrain fanaticism but loose enough to attract support from persons still loyal to their own churches.[30]

Regardless of forms, Bresee's main object in Los Angeles was to build a great "center of holy fire" which would stir the whole city. Staunch Methodists like William McDonald, J. A. Wood, Joseph Smith, H. C. Morrison, and Beverly Carradine applauded him. McDonald, war horse of the New England movement for the previous thirty-five years, seriously considered coming to southern California to end his days at Peniel Hall. Joseph Smith wrote home to the *Christian Standard* after his revival at Peniel in December, 1894, that it had been "the most easily managed meeting" he ever conducted.

> No fanaticism to restrain. No indifference to impede us. All love: no censoriousness; no controversy; no criticism heard; no fear either of any fairs or festivals, or Christmas shows to come afterward, and eat up the fruit of the revival. It was a modern Pentecost.

Beverly Carradine led a twenty-day meeting the next May, during which the hall was filled every night. At its end A. C. Bane, pastor of the M.E. Church, South, in Los Angeles, wrote in a Methodist paper that sanctification was "sweeping everything before it. The spirit of John Wesley must rejoice."[31]

John Wesley's successors, we may be sure, did not rejoice. For the previous twenty years the Methodist bishops had faced a growing cleavage in their communion. Its gravest aspect was the estrangement of the church fathers from Methodism's most earnest and sacrificial souls.

The bishops in both North and South were mostly spiritual men. They were sane, conservative, and anxious to keep their denominations evangelical and strong. On the one hand, wealthy city congregations and their cultivated pastors had rebelled against the class meeting, the revival, and, especially, the old "standards" by which holy living had been evidenced. More recently, this part of the church had seemed an easy prey to the young university and seminary men who were rapidly forsaking traditional theology. The bishops needed the holiness revival, if for nothing else, to help stave off this attack from the liberal left. But the second-blessing preachers had been generally critical of episcopal authority. Some of their number had fellowshiped radicals who had joined the earliest secessions. Now, in the 1890's, all of them seemed bent on missionary and evangelistic activities which were independent of Methodist polity.

From 1895 to 1905 many Northern and Southern bishops sponsored a serious campaign to bring the great body of their preachers back to the quest of perfect love. Samuel Ashton Keen, an Ohio pastor and presiding elder, held "Pentecostal Services" at scores of annual conferences, by appointment of the presiding officers. In Ohio, Indiana, Iowa, Nebraska, and Washington state especially, as well as in southern or "border" conferences where Northern Methodism was a minor denomination, this strange campaign was remarkably successful. But the long-run result was simply to produce a second crop of prospects for a distinctively holiness church and to keep alive the camp meetings where suspicion of the hierarchy flourished steadily, year after year.[32]

Meanwhile new outbursts of fanaticism, this time centered in the cities, sickened the average churchman and at the same time forced the holiness leaders on toward stronger independent organizations. The seeds of holiness sectarianism germinated everywhere. How some of them bore fruit in the parent bodies of the Church of the Nazarene is the subject of the next few chapters of this book.

CHAPTER III

Nazarene Beginnings in the East

Boston had been a major center for the holiness movement from the days in 1839 when Timothy Merritt founded the *Guide to Holiness* there. It remained so right down until 1910, long after the Methodist conference had turned its back upon the "second blessing" and Boston University had substituted personalism for Pentecost. William McDonald, Inskip's successor as head of the National Holiness Association, was a lifelong resident of the Puritan City. The *Christian Witness,* which McDonald and Joshua Gill published there, was the most influential periodical in the movement. When McDonald retired in 1897, he asked his brethren to elect as president of the association Charles J. Fowler, Methodist pastor at nearby Haverhill, Massachusetts. They agreed to do so despite the fact that the real center of the holiness movement had shifted west to Chicago. Meanwhile, Daniel Steele continued to write a weekly column for *Zion's Herald,* the New England conference paper. And Bishop Willard F. Mallalieu, from Abingdon, another suburb to the south, labored long into the twentieth century to restore the doctrine of entire sanctification to a central place in Methodism.

It is not surprising, therefore, that the oldest of the congregations which united in 1907 and 1908 to form the Pentecostal Church of the Nazarene originated around the shores of Massachusetts Bay. Religious developments in the East were a generation in advance of those in the West. Its universities welcomed the new liberal learning earlier. And the growth of its cities, with all the resulting social and religious conflicts, preceded similar developments in the West. Hence the crisis among conservative, loyalist champions of holiness came to a head sooner in New England than in Illinois, Tennessee, Texas, or California.

The People's Churches: Holiness and Congregationalism

The history of the Nazarenes in New England properly begins with the story of the organization on July 21, 1887, of the People's Evangelical Church in South Providence, Rhode Island.

In the early 1880's, T. J. Everett, pastor of St. Paul's M.E. Church, Providence, led his congregation in seeking the blessing of entire sanctification. He secured Miss Lizzie Boyd, a woman evangelist, to assist him in revival services. A powerful awakening gripped the church, climaxing in scenes of great emotional fervor at the Methodist campground in Willimantic, Connecticut.

The two pastors who succeeded Everett, however, failed to carry on the work. A socially ambitious group of laymen, whose wives were active in the Ladies Aid, employed a professional chorister and engineered an extensive remodeling of the church building, on the promise that no part of the structure would be used for money-raising suppers or entertainments. The paint was scarcely dry, however, before the pastor attempted to push through a resolution authorizing these activities. This was early in 1886. When the official board firmly resisted him, the pastor took steps to compel their consent. He meanwhile refused to allow the installation of Fred A. Hillery as Sunday school superintendent and canceled the "holiness meeting" which was hitherto a regular part of the church's program. At this juncture a new pastor, E. D. Hall, was appointed. Hall recklessly continued the policy of his predecessor, denounced the majority of the membership in public and in private, and defied the Sunday school board.

As the tension approached a breaking point, George E. Perry, a local preacher, announced a cottage prayer meeting at his home. The result was the organization on May 12, 1886, of the South Providence Holiness Association, with Fred Hillery as president. Sixty members of the church soon joined. They began meeting regularly on Friday evenings, carefully choosing a time which would not interfere with other church activities. By August, a rented hall was necessary to accommodate the crowds. It was then an easy next step to secure holiness evangelists to conduct special services. G. N. Ballantine, a Baptist pastor in Groton, Connecticut; E. M. Levy, Baptist pastor in Philadelphia; and H. N. Brown, a Methodist from Connecticut, appeared during the fall. The group recovered a long-lost sense of brotherly fellowship by prohibiting mention at their meetings of the troubles in the church. And they also carefully continued their support and faithful attendance at all the services of St. Paul's.

Pastor Hall, however, refused any compromise. He removed Hillery, Perry, and G. H. Spear from their positions as class leaders. Spear had long been a pillar of saintliness in the church. Hall then warned Hillery that any such movement as the association, whatever its name, was "in the disciplinary sense an act of insubordination." Hillery's answer appealed significantly from the Methodist *Book of Discipline* to the Word of God:

> When I am forced by ecclesiastical authority, without regard for the Bible, to comply with those requirements which are to prove disastrous to my spiritual life, and also that of my brothers and sisters, I am constrained to regard self-preservation as my first duty and accordingly so act. . . . When the Discipline is used to crush and annihilate that which is spiritual and godly in the church and which it was originally designed to *protect,* I say it has been *perverted* and *abused.* . . . We are Methodists, and as such, desire to "worship God in the beauty of Holiness." If we have taken a position contrary to the Discipline it is because we have been driven to it by the continued pressure of ecclesiastical power executed by three different ministers.[1]

A full year was to pass before the association organized as a church. Meanwhile the members endured a steady stream of public and private abuse, hoping for redress. The pastor dissolved the three classes formerly led by Hillery, Perry, and Spear. In October he publicly assigned these "disorderly" members to a class which was to meet under his direction on Friday nights—the same time as the weekly services at the hall. Only one appeared at the appointed hour. Thirty-eight others sent their regrets, but declared their willingness to attend on any other evening.

Matters came to a sad climax on Sunday, December 5, when the church caught fire while the noontime "holiness meeting" was in progress at the hall some blocks away. The building was totally destroyed. This tragedy, which under more thoughtful leadership might have provided an occasion to unite the opposing parties, resulted only in dividing them further. Early in January, 1887, the pastor removed from office all Sunday school teachers who belonged to the holiness association. Hillery's group at once notified their presiding elder that they must now institute at the hall a Sunday school and other services which directly conflicted with those at the church. These would continue, they said, "until these wrongs which we have suffered are rightly adjusted." The only consequence was that Hillery was tried and expelled from the Methodist church. A month later his appeal to the quarterly conference was rejected. When the annual conference which met in April granted no relief either, forty-eight persons notified the hapless pastor that they were withdrawing from the church and forming an independent congregation.[2]

The People's Evangelical Church became almost at once a nucleus around which other congregations and holiness bands united. An independent group which had been organized in 1882 at Rock, Massachusetts, out on Cape Cod, was the first to establish fellowship. By September, 1888, when Hillery began publishing a little monthly called *Beulah Items*, another congregation had been organized at Attleboro, Massachusetts, fifteen miles north, and holiness meetings were in progress at nearby Pawtucket. Four months later C. Howard Davis, a young Baptist evangelist, organized the Mission Church in Lynn, an industrial city just north of Boston, fifty miles away. Representatives of these and a few other bands and associations met frequently that winter in "all-day holiness meetings," where the freedom and joy of the Spirit erased for a while the bitterness which had surrounded their birth.[3]

The annual New England Union Holiness Convention, composed of the outstanding "loyalist" leaders, could scarcely give its blessing to such a movement. Its session at the Bromfield Street Methodist Church, Boston, late in March, 1889, adopted a resolution which said: "We favor no come-out-ism from the churches because of opposition or indifference therein to this doctrine, but we approve rather of remaining in our providential places and there witnessing both to small and great . . . and doing as best we can to aid all the legitimate work of the church." The convention did, however, sanction the formation of local bands and associations and approved such extra meetings for the promotion of holiness as did not conflict with the regular services of the church. The delegates also declared their hearty sympathy and fellowship toward "those who have been excluded from the visible church for their adherence to this doctrine and experience."[4]

Throughout the next year the work of the independent groups expanded. Bands formed missions, and missions grew into churches. In Keene, New Hampshire, F. L. Sprague, a Methodist layman, inaugurated the Bethany Mission, and purchased and remodeled an abandoned church for its use. Local holiness associations at Quincy, Stoneham, Chelsea, and Somerville, all suburbs of Boston, sent delegates to the all-day meetings. In the fall of 1889 a Mr. McFarlane, from the Stoneham group, initiated regular services at Malden. The meetings continued through the winter there at the Young Women's Club Rooms. Mrs. S. A. Hanscome was principally in charge. Many were saved and sanctified. "Some found church homes, for we had no thought of organizing our work," Mrs. Hanscome wrote later. But other "neglected ones" came in, "persons who had not a home feeling in the churches, and began to ask for church privileges." On August 15, 1890, C. Howard Davis came from Lynn to organize the Malden Mission Church, under a covenant which declared it to be independent of any "denominational creed." Davis accepted responsibility for the pastorate of the new flock, along with that of his Lynn group, but placed Mrs. Hanscome in actual charge.[5]

Earlier, on March 13 and 14, 1890, representatives of most of these groups had met at Rock to organize the Central Evangelical Holiness Association. They declared their object to be "to promote scriptural holiness by united council and action, and to give strength and encouragement to all those who from loyalty to this divinely inspired truth are without the privileges of real Christian fellowship." Membership was confined to representatives of "holiness churches, associations or bands" and such ministers or evangelists as should make application and secure the approval of the executive committee. Laymen who were not members of any society might become associate members only. W. C. Ryder, pastor at Rock, was elected president; Fred A. Hillery, vice-president; C. Howard Davis, secretary; and Benjamin Luscomb, soon to be pastor at North Attleboro, treasurer. Other members of the executive committee were Aaron Hartt, perennial song leader at Douglas camp and now in charge of the meetings at Pawtucket; and F. W. Plummer, a Baptist evangelist who had recently organized a congregation at Harwich, on Cape Cod. F. L. Sprague's mission in Keene joined the next year.

As might be expected, these preachers were all firm believers in the congregational system of church government. Good Baptists like Dr. Levy had comforted and aided the Methodists among them during their earliest tribulations, and had encouraged congregations to ordain as pastors laymen like Sprague and Hillery. Most of the other ministers had been ordained previously in Baptist or Congregationalist churches. Union councils of ordination thus became the source of apostolic authority. "Recognition councils" met in good Baptist fashion to receive new societies into the fold. Independency, congregationalism, and perfectionism were thus linked by hallowed bonds. "We believe in Christian Holiness," C. Howard Davis wrote of the Lynn group in 1889, "and perhaps that is the reason we are an independent church."[6]

The Methodist Preachers Delay Decision

The Central Evangelical Holiness Association did not, however, continue to grow at a rapid rate. The chief explanation for this fact is that "loyalist" clergymen took steps to divert the drift toward independency into other channels. William McDonald and Joshua Gill began to promote in 1891 an organization called the General Holiness League. This association enrolled *individuals* as members, thus providing brotherly ties for those who felt themselves excluded from their churches, but its leaders firmly opposed the founding of independent congregations. Instead, they instituted local interdenominational "leagues" in many New England towns. The only prominent leader to support this movement outside New England was Evangelist Martin Wells Knapp, who was thus to straddle the issues in the church question until his death. Knapp left a local unit at nearly every place he labored in Michigan and Ohio.

Remarkably enough, the League actually helped to draw the loyalists out of the church instead of keeping the drifters in. For the organization could not exist without sanctioning the independent holiness meetings so objectionable to ecclesiastical officials. This issue came immediately to a head. In April, 1892, the New England Methodist Conference met at Haverhill, in the church of which C. J. Fowler was pastor. It adopted resolutions which warned that all meetings of any character which were not under the control of pastors were "in conflict with the order and discipline of the church" and justified punitive action against their sponsors. Interestingly, Fowler had earlier secured permission of the committee on public worship to have Joseph H. Smith, holiness evangelist from the Philadelphia conference, conduct afternoon "Pentecostal meetings" during the Haverhill sessions. And Daniel Steele, a member of the committee which brought in the resolution, presented a significant minority report. Though expressing regret for the friction and disharmony which holiness meetings had caused in various places, Steele proposed that pastors be directed either to take personal charge of any which were held in their parishes or else to appoint and supervise another leader to do so. The *Christian Witness* noted with regret that Steele's report was "applauded but not adopted." At the end of the conference J. N. Short, one of the most aggressive holiness pastors, was transferred from the Central Methodist Church in Lowell to a struggling charge in Beverly.

At the annual meeting of the General Holiness League that fall, both independents and loyalists were fully represented. McDonald's opening sermon threw down the gauntlet to the church. The League had become necessary, he said, because "the churches will not allow the professors of holiness to peacefully remain and enjoy their liberty." There were no "come-outers" in the organization, he said, but some were there who had been put out, or who had to go out to maintain fellowship with their holiness brethren. J. N. Short, H. N. Brown, and H. F. Reynolds, all one day to become Nazarenes, served as a committee on revision of the constitution. The delegates elected McDonald, Fowler, Deacon George Morse, and Reynolds as president and vice-presidents in that order. Gill was made secretary-treasurer, Hillery recording secretary, and H. N. Brown field agent. Short, F. L. Sprague, Aaron Hartt, Dr. Levy, and M. W. Knapp were named "managers." Clearly, matters were approaching a crisis. But still most of the preachers delayed a decision.[7]

They were moved to patience in part by the news of what was happening in the Green Mountain State of Vermont. Hiram F. Reynolds, a promising young minister in the conference there, had persuaded his brother, E. E. Reynolds, to join with O. J. Copeland, a layman from Montpelier, and several others in organizing the Vermont Holiness Association. Copeland deserves much of the credit for this movement. His wife had been sanctified at Douglas in 1887 and immediately thereafter founded a holiness meeting in her home, in the Phoebe Palmer tradition. Students at the Vermont Methodist Seminary, located in Montpelier, attended often, among them the Reynolds brothers. Interest grew also from the appearance in 1886 and again in 1888 of the National Holiness Association leaders at the conference campgrounds at Morrisville. A. B. Riggs, a minister in the conference who was later to become the founder of the

Nazarene church at Lowell and a pillar on the New England District, had led Hiram Reynolds into the experience of sanctification.

The plan of the Vermont Holiness Association was to purchase tents and conduct conventions and revivals throughout the conference, but to do all in full loyalty to Methodism. They decided to place H. F. Reynolds in the field as a full-time evangelist, and he requested the Methodist conference held in April, 1892, to grant him leave to accept this assignment. A lengthy debate broke out on the floor. Several protested that the existence of the association implied "that the rest of us do not do this, and that all our meetings are not holiness meetings." Others, however, testified to the good work which was being done, and the request was granted. Within a few hours Bishop E. G. Andrews sent word through A. B. Truax, Reynolds' close friend and presiding elder, that a presiding eldership was open to the young evangelist if he would accept it. Reynolds rejected the offer, however, and launched into a round of revivals and conventions for the association. He and others in the group also began attending various meetings in Boston and joined the Holiness League. In this way they developed a working fellowship with F. L. Sprague, C. J. Fowler, and especially H. N. Brown, a Connecticut evangelist who had been presiding for several years at Silver Lake Camp Meeting in south-central Vermont.[8]

The holiness revival thus came much later to isolated rural Vermont than to the rest of New England. And with it came no wildfire of fanaticism. The leaders were substantial men whose work seemed for several years a vindication of the loyalist policy. Soon, however, they were caught up in the same crisis which had led others to leave the church. And in their case the issue was intensified by their reaction against the cultivated, worldly Methodism which they now saw at close range or. their frequent visits to Boston and New York.

A Middle Way: The Evangelical Association and New England Methodism

Back in the Puritan City, the loyalist ranks were already beginning to break under ecclesiastical pressure. Joshua Gill and John Short began reluctantly to lead a substantial party of Methodists into the Evangelical Association, a German-speaking Wesleyan denomination centered chiefly in Pennsylvania. Early in 1892, the *Christian Witness* had carried news of extensive holiness revivals among the Evangelical people, first at district and then at conference camp meetings in eastern Pennsylvania. Gill and others soon realized that here was an answer to the church question which did not involve the perils of independency and which would enable them to continue as members of the Methodist family. The young editor organized the First Evangelical Church of Boston in the late fall of 1892 and secured the ancient Jesse Lee Chapel for a house of worship. The next year Short gave up his attempt to remain in the Methodist conference and came to Cambridge, across the Charles River from Boston, to organize an Evangelical church there. In a little over a year Short's congregation numbered 100 members. Several ministers hitherto active in the Central Evangelical Holiness Association threw in their lot with the denomination also, notably Aaron Hartt in Pawtucket, and George N. Buell at Central Falls, Rhode Island. Gill, who was soon made presiding elder for all New England, publicized the work steadily through the *Christian Witness*. But he never at any time subjected that paper to his own ends nor in any way closed its columns to news of other groups.

In March, 1895, Bishop Thomas Bowman paid a first visit to New England. "He found the work of the Evangelical Association progressing satisfactorily," the *Witness* wrote, "and predicts a bright future for the church here." Events of the next few years bore out his prediction. New churches were organized in 1895 at Lynn, Salem, New Bedford, Everett, and Chelsea, Massachusetts, as well as at Woodsville, New Hampshire, and Ringfield, Maine. The group at Lynn set to work in a hall located across town from that where C. Howard Davis' congregation worshiped. The following March, Bishop Bowman returned to organize 14 preachers into an annual conference which claimed 620 members and reported $11,000 raised the previous year. A remarkable spiritual tide swept the conference session; "people wept and shouted" as if "Pentecost was repeated." Bowman appointed Gill presiding elder of the Boston District, which included all of southeastern New England, and placed Short over the churches north and west of the Charles River.

During 1896 and 1897 new congregations of the Evangelical Association appeared in Stoneham, Quincy, East Boston, and Somerville, all near Boston, as well as at Providence, Rhode

Island, and New Haven, West Haven, and Bridgeport, Connecticut. Apparently the respectable standing of the denomination made it much easier for local holiness bodies at these places to organize themselves as churches than had been the case when the only alternative was an association of independent congregations.

Most of these flourished from the start. Many constructed substantial chapels. Each instituted a churchly program of youth, missionary, Sunday school, and social work, to supplement the program of revivals. The form of government was, of course, strictly episcopal. The conference was composed exclusively of ministers, ordination took place at the hands of the bishops, and Gill and Short appeared regularly at each place to conduct "quarterly meetings." A holiness camp meeting established at Allentown, Pennsylvania, in 1897, served for a brief period as a meeting ground between New England and Pennsylvania representatives of the church. Bishop Bowman preached at its first session.

A conference made up of men who had been so recently manhandled by ecclesiastical officers, however, could scarcely be expected to develop overnight the inner unity and subjection to discipline which the Evangelical bishops desired. Short, Hartt, and Buell were strong-willed men who realized that the denomination was the heir rather than the agent of the holiness revival in New England. They were reluctant to surrender the control of congregations which they had gathered from the highways and hedges to German-speaking bishops who lived five hundred miles away. Short especially refused any longer to accept the fate of removal from one pastorate to another each few years.

All these factors lay back of the division which, shortly after 1900, rent in pieces the New England Conference of the Evangelical Association. Hardly a congregation escaped without a split. Part of the Cambridge membership followed Short into an independent organization. They built a new house of worship two blocks away from the old church. To this congregation, eventually the Cambridge Church of the Nazarene, Short was to preach for the next thirty years. The Everett group withdrew in a body in 1899, under Aaron Hartt's leadership, and managed to take their property with them. Practically all the seceders joined William H. Hoople, F. A. Hillery, and H. F. Reynolds in the Association of Pentecostal Churches of America and, eventually, the Church of the Nazarene. The estrangement which existed for many years between the Nazarenes and the Evangelicals in New England—the only two holiness denominations which made much headway there—stemmed directly from this period of dissension.[9]

But the division of feeling was not characteristic of the earlier years. Throughout the decade of the 1890's a remarkable spirit of unity prevailed among all the holiness people in New England, regardless of how they were solving the church question. Short and Gill preached at all-day meetings at Hillery's church in Providence and conducted conventions for C. Howard Davis in Lynn and W. C. Ryder at Rock. Representatives of all groups appeared prominently on the program of the Boston Holiness League after 1895. Although most of the congregations in the Central Evangelical Holiness Association united with Hoople's group in 1897, the *Christian Witness* continued to report regularly the annual meetings of the former body, and men from all parties appeared on its platform. Even as late as 1905 it was not unusual to find Hillery, Daniel Steele (still a much-loved Methodist), Joshua Gill, H. F. Reynolds, and Baptist Deacon George Morse on the same program at the famous Monday holiness meeting held at the Bromfield Street Methodist Church.[10]

Looking backward, we can see that the interdenominational holiness camp meetings were an important unifying influence. At Douglas and Rock in southeastern Massachusetts; at Portsmouth, Rhode Island, where Seth C. Rees was cultivating a perfectionist awakening among the Quakers; at Silver Lake, Vermont; and at Staten Island, New York, "independents," "Pentecostals," "Evangelicals," and "loyalists" joined hearts and hands with Congregationalists, Baptists, and Friends to lead believers into sanctifying grace. In 1895, for example, the executive board at Douglas included three Baptists, two Methodists, two Congregationalists, one independent, and two who had recently joined the Evangelical Association. All but two of the preachers at the first four days of the camp that year eventually became Nazarenes: H. F. Reynolds, H. N. Brown, William H. Hoople, A. B. Riggs, John N. Short, John Norberry, F. A. Hillery, and F. L. Sprague. The other two were Joshua Gill and Dr. Levy.

In New England, therefore, the "church question," though earnestly debated, never really disrupted the fellowship of the holiness preachers, save when the Evangelical Association's conference divided over episcopacy and other matters. C. J. Fowler, president of the National Holiness Association, actually encouraged the growth of the independent movements, particularly the Association of Pentecostal Churches, about which we shall learn more in a moment. Fowler attended many of the annual meetings of Hoople's group and endeared himself to the hearts of Nazarene pioneers. The administration building at Eastern Nazarene College was later named for him. Throughout the twenty years from 1887 to 1907 the *Christian Witness* carried as detailed accounts of the work of independent, Evangelical, and Pentecostal congregations as of those still loyal to Methodist discipline. Long after men like Hillery and Reynolds had made their break with Methodism, presiding elders in rural districts of Vermont, New Hampshire, Maine, and upstate New York employed them as speakers and workers at district and conference camp meetings.[11]

All hands rejoiced in 1896 when the National Association was invited to hold a convention at the First M.E. Church, Syracuse, N.Y., under the auspices of the Methodist preachers' meeting in that city. The local presiding elder served as chairman and H. N. Brown, a member of both the National and the Central Evangelical holiness associations, was one of the principal speakers. The following spring Syracuse University conferred the D.D. degree upon J. B. Foote, who had served as secretary to this convention and who was to be the evangelist at the Rock camp meeting that summer![12]

The fact is that in rural New England and upper New York state the openness of the Methodist churches to the old-time religion was usually great enough to make secessions unnecessary. In the cities, however, a wealthy and worldly atmosphere prevailed. The new learning of the universities and the new "respectability" of Methodist worship created a religious climate which profoundly disturbed the pious folk moving in from the countryside. Churches in Boston, Providence, and Brooklyn, as well as in lesser towns like Lynn, Haverhill, Lowell, Portland, Somerville, and Fitchburg, failed to assimilate the newcomers. Especially during the depression of 1893-97 did these cities fill up with displaced residents of the farms and small towns of New England. Such persons were prepared to find the city a modern Sodom; but they were shocked indeed to find the church in careless compromise with the world.

Among this group the longing for the religion of village church and hearthside found fulfillment in the simple preaching of ex-Vermonters H. F. Reynolds, E. E. Angell, and A. B. Riggs and "down-Easters" like Aaron Hartt, H. N. Brown, C. Howard Davis, and Nathan Washburn. Although the most important Nazarene congregations in New England originated in the cities, their pulpits and their membership rolls were filled principally by men and women who had recently come from the green valleys and white-spired meetinghouses of Vermont and New Hampshire and the isolated harbors along the coast of Maine.

The newcomers had at first directed their efforts toward reviving the old ways in churches rapidly growing both rich and proud. Conflict and confusion resulted, often as not over the newfangled fairs and festivals, the Gothic architecture, and the robed choirs so dear to socially ambitious city dwellers. The spirit of both Puritanism and perfectionism thus lay back of their heart-rending decision to form an independent church. Such a venture required great courage, and it usually produced a sense of isolation from the community. But in the summertime old and young alike could go to camp meeting and find themselves no longer alone. These gatherings thus became for the displaced descendants of the farm an annual return to both the setting and the certainties of their childhood faith. Here in the tented grove were forged the unity, the interdependence, and the common front against "worldliness" out of which a new denomination was born.

The moral metal of their souls, heated white in persecution and tempered in their tears, became the inner strength of a movement in which holiness and congregational freedom—two ancient New England standards—were twin passions.

William Howard Hoople and the "Pentecostal" Churches in Brooklyn

Nazarene congregations in Brooklyn, N.Y., originated under humble circumstances and without much relation to the inner problems of Methodism. William Howard Hoople, the son of a millionaire leather merchant, had been converted in a Congregational Sunday school and joined that church. In the early 1890's he began attending the noonday prayer meeting at the John Street M.E. Church, on lower Manhattan. There he met Charles BeVier, a zealous witness to holiness and choir leader at the largest Methodist church in Brooklyn. Hoople thought BeVier's "fanaticism" a pity, and set out to argue his new friend into rejecting sanctification. Instead, Hoople wound up finding the blessing himself. From that day forward, these two young men were the David and Jonathan of the holiness movement in Brooklyn.

True to the impulse of perfect love, they began searching for a place from which to evangelize the poor. On January 4, 1894, they began a mission in an old saloon at 123 Schenectady Avenue. This soon developed into a church called the Utica Avenue Tabernacle. Here was organized shortly before Christmas, 1894, the New York State Holiness Association, with BeVier as president, Alexander McLean and Hoople as vice-presidents, and John Norberry "Field General." The association was undenominational, the *Christian Witness* reported; its board of managers included representatives from several churches. When a second independent congregation came into existence on Bedford Avenue the following spring, a reporter (likely Hoople himself) declared:

> We are an Independent, dependent body, and are not comeouters but as none of the evangelical bodies seemed to desire to push holiness as a second work of grace, and where they had tried this it took a good deal of coaxing and teaching and then after it was about accomplished some one came along and upset the whole thing, because they had control of the temporal power and were opposed to holiness; and as our time here is short and we didn't amount to much, we thought the most sensible thing for us to do was to walk alone with the Triune God. Perhaps this may sound strange to some of my Methodist brethren, but after all you can't expect very much from one who was a Congregationalist and embraced Methodist doctrine. Holiness is apt to make us appear to the world a little peculiar.[13]

Throughout 1895 the work in Brooklyn continued along undenominational lines. Many Methodist pastors permitted the leaders to conduct conventions in their meetinghouses. The Bedford Avenue group secured possession of a former Unitarian church. They rejoiced that they were able to renovate the building completely without putting on any "church sociables" or "Martha Washington tea parties." Dr. E. M. Levy, whom the younger men jestingly called "our Bishop," came up frequently from Philadelphia to assist in dedication and ordination services, just as he had earlier done in Providence. BeVier and Hoople emerged as enthusiastic leaders, the latter professing to see in every old, disused building "an excellent place to plant a holiness church."[14]

Meanwhile, O. J. Copeland had moved from Montpelier, Vermont, to open a granite business in Brooklyn. He soon joined Hoople's group. To this small event can be traced a good deal of Nazarene history in the East. For from this point on, substantial laymen and preachers from Vermont brought a new element of strength to the Brooklyn movement. Such persons as Copeland, H. F. Reynolds, A. B. Riggs, E. E. Angell, Susan N. Fitkin, and H. N. Brown played key roles in the subsequent union with the Boston and Providence congregations in the Central Evangelical Holiness Association. They also encouraged the development of a regular denominational order designed to shelter beleaguered champions of holiness in the East.

H. F. Reynolds was the first to follow in the footsteps of his old friend, Copeland. The young evangelist decided to leave the Methodist ministry at the close of the camp meeting season of 1895. Although he had never had so many and such promising calls to Methodist churches as then, Reynolds saw that year by year his converts suffered increasing opposition from holiness-fighting pastors. He expressed the hope, however, that his decision would not cause good Methodists to shun the blessing out of fear that to seek it would mean that they must, like him, forsake their church. In October, 1895, Reynolds appeared in Brooklyn and became the first regularly ordained minister to join Hoople's association. All the other preachers had been ordained in the Baptist manner by their new flocks.[15]

Likely it was Reynolds' flair for organization which crystallized sentiment for the incorporation of the Association of Pentecostal Churches of America at the annual meeting held March 31, 1896. He it was who reported the event to the *Christian Witness*, in any case. Reynolds declared that by this act the association had taken its place as "one of the many evangelical churches in the world."

The parent New York State Holiness Association continued to serve as the instrument through which these men carried on the "interdenominational" phase of the work. It sponsored the annual camp meeting on Staten Island as well as numerous holiness conventions. C. J. Fowler, the chief worker at Staten Island camp in 1896, wrote on his return a long and significant report of the progress of holiness in New York, without, however, mentioning the existence of the new denomination. Fowler said he found the leaders from Brooklyn were able and intelligent. "There were no fads . . . There was a time to be quiet and a time for holy demonstration. People lost their strength and lay as dead for hours and lost their sin at the same time." But Fowler concluded the article with a cryptic warning which seemed in part to minimize the need of a separate denomination. "Friends of holiness," he advised, *"keep out from under the juniper tree.* Never, since the historic apostasy, have so many holiness people lived and have there been so many holiness appliances [*sic*] in the field." He pointed to the growth of camp meetings all over the country. "See what is going on in the South-land. See Godbey, Morrison, Dodge, Pickett, Carradine and a host of others, victorious from the Ohio to the Gulf." He urged his readers to "pray, but don't faint. . . . Live on this side of Pentecost."[16]

Already, however, Reynolds and Hoople had begun a series of negotiations proposing union with the churches in the Central Evangelical Holiness Association. Chief among these were Hillery's congregation in Providence, Rhode Island; Sprague's in Keene, New Hampshire; and C. Howard Davis' two churches in Lynn and Malden, Massachusetts, the latter now served by J. C. Bearse. As early as October 2, 1896, the Lynn church board wrote Hillery approving the proposed union. On November 11, Sprague, Hillery, Davis, and W. C. Ryder went to New York for a meeting in Hoople's home. Present as representatives of the Association of Pentecostal Churches were BeVier, Reynolds, H. B. Hosley, and F. W. Sloat. These men readily agreed to use the constitution of Hoople's group as a basis for discussion —proof that they recognized the superior vigor and promise of the newer movement. At the end of two days they voted to recommend union of the two bodies. During the winter, however, Ryder made plain his determination to remain independent and the Malden congregation delayed decision.

What actually happened, therefore, was that the New England congregations simply joined the Association of Pentecostal

Churches individually, usually dropping the word "mission" from their names and styling themselves "Pentecostal Societies." Lynn, Providence, North Attleboro, and Keene united in April, 1897, bringing with them three new congregations organized during the winter—Bristol and North Scituate, Rhode Island, and Cliftondale, Massachusetts. Malden came in the next year. The society at Cliftondale, hard by Lynn, was composed chiefly of Baptist folk whom a laywoman, Mrs. Mary Webber, had encouraged to start meetings in a hall. C. Howard Davis had provided ministerial leadership. More important than the coming of any single congregation, however, was the accession of Hillery's paper, now known as the *Beulah Christian*, which so long had served the limited interests of the smaller group. It now became an organ of unity and propaganda, a decisive factor in welding the Association of Pentecostal Churches into a genuine denominational fellowship.[17]

Most of the fifteen congregations which joined the association at the "union" annual meeting of 1897 were the fruit of a remarkable surge of home missionary activity around New York City. Charles BeVier organized the John Wesley Church, Brooklyn, late in 1896. Its thirty-three members were converts won in the mission he had conducted for some time on Bushwick Avenue. Susan Norris, a young evangelist brought from Vermont by the New York Yearly Meeting of Friends, was responsible for another. She experienced the second blessing at a convention sponsored by the association and joined Abram E. Fitkin in a brief series of revivals among Quakers. These two were married in the summer of 1896 and cast their lot with Hoople's company. In November, at the close of a remarkable revival held in a blacksmith shop, they organized a Pentecostal church at the Hudson Valley town of Hopewell Junction. There were sixty charter members.

Meanwhile, at Ellenburg Depot in northern New York state, E. E. Angell, a young Congregationalist, carried on for six months a revival begun under H. F. Reynolds' ministry. Several Nazarene churches owe their origins to this awakening. Hoople began that year also to make frequent trips to holiness conventions outside New York. Of his preaching at Seth C. Rees's New Year's Day Convention in Providence one wrote, "The 'old man' was nonplused and routed by the sturdy blows of this fire-baptized six-footer. The altar quickly filled with weeping seekers as soon as the call was made."[18]

The news of the union and subsequent growth of the association stirred deep interest among all the holiness leaders in the East. It crystallized sentiment for a distinctively "second blessing" denomination among some Methodist loyalists who had until then held back. Chief of these were H. N. Brown and A. B. Riggs. Brown accepted the pastorate of the Bedford Avenue Tabernacle in May, 1897. He and Reynolds set out at once to bring every independent group they knew into the fellowship of the association. Riggs joined them in the fall. He resigned his pastorate at Elmore, Vermont, to take charge first of the work in Cliftondale and then of the promising organization in Lowell. To the Staten Island camp that summer these men invited Deacon Morse of Douglas camp, and N. H. Washburn, founder of a church at Cundy's Harbor, Maine. Fowler and Beverly Carradine were the special workers. By April, 1898, eight additional churches were ready to join the association, including Malden, Cundy's Harbor, South Manchester, Connecticut, and five others in New York and New Jersey.[19] The Association of Pentecostal Churches of America was clearly a going concern.

Before we turn to the story of the subsequent growth of the association and its progress toward closer denominational fellowship, two observations are in order. The first is that in the New England movement no individual leader overshadowed the other preachers, as was true in most other parts of the country among the parent bodies of the Church of the Nazarene. Instead, a remarkable company of individualists, each at the head of an important congregation, had united under what they believed to be God's direction to found a new organization. Charles BeVier and William Howard Hoople in Brooklyn, Hillery in Providence, C. Howard Davis on Boston's North Shore, F. L. Sprague in Keene, and N. H. Washburn in Maine each enjoyed the solid loyalty and support of his congregation, a sure base of autonomy and influence. The Methodist preachers in the group—Reynolds, Brown, and Riggs—owed their positions to the prior work of the lay preachers. Though they were eventually to lead the long search for a stronger system of church government, each had for the present had his fill of episcopacy.

The Evangelical Association had already drawn off those who were most concerned to preserve Wesleyan polity and traditions. The Methodists who joined Hoople's movement were ready, for the moment, to agree with the dominant Baptist and Congregationalist element that episcopacy was inevitably a foe to holiness. They must have had some difficulty, however, with this striking statement of congregational order which was a part of the association's Articles of Faith:

> We believe each church to be complete in itself; that Christ is the Head of each and the Head of all; that the Scriptures are its sole statute book; that in the choice of its officers, in the admission and dismission of the members, and in the administration of all its affairs, each church is independent of the authority of other churches.

A final sentence relented so far as to say only "that the independence of each church is not incompatible with the association of churches for mutual fellowship, information and counsel."[20]

Here, in the need for fellowship and mutual support, and in the burning call to launch both home and foreign missions, lay the basis of the future church order. The frame of government which men like Reynolds and Brown at last devised was not imposed from the top, nor brought forward blindly out of some ancient tradition. It grew from the very nature of the Christian task, out of the practical experience of men both strong in mind and tender in heart.

The second important observation is that congregational sovereignty did not restrict the powers of individual pastors. Rather, it enhanced them. In the absence of a strong superintendency or a binding discipline, the pastor who could keep the spiritual loyalties of his flock was in the driver's seat. In Lynn and Lowell, for example, the major change in local polity which followed the alignment of these two churches with the association was that the pastor gained the power to nominate the members of the church board. As the Articles of Faith put it, "The Bishop or the Pastor—the two names being synonymous—is entrusted with the charge of the flock, the stated preaching of the word, the administration of the ordinances, and the enforcement of discipline."[21]

It was not laymen, therefore, but pastors of incurable independence like H. B. Hosley and John Norris who resisted the growth of a superintendency at every turn. Their objectives were the opposite of the "laymen's movements" which have occasionally sprung up in modern denominations. The latter seek to secure to lay leaders a large share of the administrative authority which is exercised over a united church. The aim of the former was to keep the congregations independent of all external control, so as to preserve the pre-eminence of the pastor and thus to prevent the sort of ecclesiastical domination which had originally led to the formation of the independent bodies.

The New England movement was not yet a "church," however, even in name. It was rather an *association* of churches. Most of the pastors believed that the true and visible Church of Christ on earth could be nothing other than a Bible-disciplined congregation, empowered to call and ordain its own pastor, and receive thereafter both sacraments and gospel through the Spirit-anointed ministry of this shepherd of the flock.

CHAPTER IV

The Association of Pentecostal Churches, 1897-1907

The Growth of Denominational Fellowship

Under its banner of Christian liberty the association made rapid strides in the six years following the union of 1897. The number and stability of its congregations increased along with the quality of its preachers. An ambitious missionary program in both foreign and home fields caught the vision of the laity. And a Bible institute, begun amidst great tribulations at Saratoga Springs, New York, finally got its roots down at North Scituate, Rhode Island.

Particularly important was the accession of six additional congregations in urban centers near Boston. John Short's Cambridge church, like those in Everett and West Somerville, was an inheritance from the troubles of the Evangelical Association. Those in industrial Fitchburg, Haverhill, and Lowell, Massachusetts, grew out of undenominational holiness missions. The story of the last two deserves a separate word.

When C. J. Fowler resigned the pastorate of the Grace Methodist Church in Haverhill to become president of the National Holiness Association, the bishop appointed E. E. Reynolds, brother to Hiram Reynolds, in his place. Both men thereafter supported the work at the undenominational Pentecostal Mission Hall in Haverhill, and they encouraged the church which grew out of it in 1899. Meanwhile, at Lowell, a few miles up the Merrimac River, John Norberry led a group of converts into the Wesley Pentecostal Church, organized in May, 1898. The congregation maintained close ties with the Lowell Holiness Mission, an undenominational venture out of which many of its members had come. A. B. Riggs became pastor of the new flock soon after its organization.

In 1903 a deep division split the Wesley church. Riggs led a seceding group of eighty members into the First Pentecostal Church of Lowell. By 1905 the Wesley church was making gestures at a restoration of fellowship, but to little avail. Riggs's congregation flourished from the start. Forty-six members were received the first year, thirty-two of them by "confession of faith." The fellowship of the group was marked by peaceableness and love—a spirit beautifully exemplified in one of its young men, Tom M. Brown, who down to his old age was an apostle of gentleness among the New England preachers.[1]

Elsewhere in New England the association also gained new beachheads. Nathan Washburn came from Cundy's Harbor to South Portland, Maine, in 1898, at the invitation of seven young men who had been ousted from the Methodist church for professing holiness. These seven with their wives became charter members of a new congregation. A strong body of believers soon gathered around them, many of whom had recently come from Cundy's Harbor and other towns along the coast. Across the years, Washburn's name became a synonym for piety in the seaport city.

Meanwhile, over in Vermont, the departure in turn from the Methodist fold of Reynolds, Brown, and A. B. Riggs had produced serious discussions of the "church question" among the holiness people. Two small congregations first appeared in southern Vermont, near Silver Lake Camp. Northward, at Elmore, the pastor appointed to succeed Riggs sharply opposed the second blessing. A group of laymen thereupon organized a holiness band and elected a young woman, Edith Carey, president. Soon this group found themselves forbidden to meet in the church or to testify to sanctification in public services. Similar troubles in the Methodist church at nearby Johnson, Vermont, impelled laymen from both towns to unite in a new Pentecostal congregation at Johnson. A second church was later organized at Morrisville, twenty miles away. Only the one in Johnson, however, managed to survive the bitter opposition which broke out against it.

The chief role of the Vermont churches was to raise up hardy leaders for other branches of the work. Seven of the foreign missionaries who went out in the early years were Vermonters. From the time of Reynolds and Riggs until this day, men of the Green Mountain State have been significant leaders among New England Nazarenes.[2]

Organized work in the Maritime Provinces of Canada made some progress too in the early days, although in the long run its trials were to be as great as those faced in Vermont. The holiness movement had much deeper roots "down East," to be sure. And the mass immigration of Canadians to New England factory towns created strong social and religious bonds between the two sections. A remarkable number of the association's leaders in the States were natives of Nova Scotia or New Brunswick—among them H. N. Brown, Aaron Hartt, L. S. Tracy, Isaac W. Hanson, and C. Howard Davis. Such men won converts most readily from among the half million natives of Canada and Newfoundland who were residing in the North Atlantic states in 1890. Nor did the stream of immigration abate in the next thirty years. Practically every Church of the Nazarene in New England contains to this day numerous families of Canadian origin.

This circumstance operated in the reverse direction too. Reynolds, Brown, Hartt, and Riggs always found a ready welcome for their evangelistic work in the Maritimes. In 1901 and 1902, Reynolds returned to what was by then familiar territory and organized churches at Oxford and Springhill, Nova Scotia. Later on, congregations appeared in Yarmouth, Nova Scotia, and St. John, New Brunswick. But in most other places, the Reformed Baptist church became the haven for the holiness people of eastern Canada.[3]

Far to the south, in the nation's capital, another undenominational holiness mission became the seedbed of a strong congregation. Two sisters, Phoebe and Sarah Hall, members of the Society of Friends, began a gospel work among the poor in Washington, D.C., in 1888. By 1900 many of their converts desired to establish a church home in which their children could be nourished in the faith. William H. Hoople held two revival campaigns at the Hall mission that year. Soon afterward, 32 members withdrew and asked to be organized into a Pentecostal church. Hoople persuaded C. Howard Davis to leave Lynn and go as pastor of the new flock. Davis spent two years establishing the work, at the end of which time H. B. Hosley came from Cliftondale, Massachusetts, to take charge. By 1910 his congregation boasted 261 members.[4]

Only in eastern Pennsylvania did the association fail to develop any strength. The only significant accession came in 1899, when T. L. Weiand brought the Allentown camp meeting over from the Evangelical Association. Thereafter a Pentecostal church made slow progress in the town nearby.

In the Pennsylvania Dutch country the Holiness Christian group carried on the work of organizing separate churches. The "Heavenly Recruits," as they were sometimes called, had grown out of mission and evangelical endeavors which a few independent preachers had conducted around Philadelphia after 1882. Horace G. Trumbauer and others organized a conference in 1893. The next year they took the name Holiness Christian Association, changing it to "Church" in 1897. The spread of the movement to Indiana resulted in the formation of a second conference there in 1896. C. W. Ruth, who later joined Dr. Bresee's church in California, and John Thomas Maybury, father of two generations of Nazarene preachers, were prominent leaders. Ruth, as we shall see, was more than any other single person responsible for the union of 1907. Partly through his influence, Trumbauer led the Pennsylvania conference of the Holiness Christian church into the Pentecostal Church of the Nazarene in 1908.

The Association of Pentecostal Churches did, however, gain a line of substantial outposts in western Pennsylvania. John H. Norris brought in his very strong congregation at Pittsburgh in 1899. Thereafter, starts were made in three neighboring towns and a foundation was laid for the later development of the Pittsburgh District. Farther west, two small societies at Findlay, Ohio, and Hazelton, Iowa, served only as isolated symbols of what was hoped to be.[5]

At each successive annual meeting, the reports of the expansion of the work inevitably nurtured the dream of a national holiness church. The powerful appeal of this dream explains in large measure how these erstwhile champions of independency and congregationalism could bring themselves by 1906 to propose a union with Phineas Bresee's episcopally governed Church of the Nazarene. But such a merger would never have become possible had not the easterners already developed, out of practical necessity, an effective superintendency of their own. The fascinating but elusive story of this development is interwoven with the history of the association's missionary and educational work, to which we now turn.

H. F. Reynolds and the Search for a Superintendency

Four factors contributed heavily to the decline of congregationalism among the New England churches: (1) the necessity of assigning home missionary tasks and providing care and discipline for the newer congregations; (2) the emergence of the ex-Methodist pastors to positions of relatively greater strength than that which preachers of Baptist or lay backgrounds enjoyed; (3) the breakup of the first attempt to found a Bible school, under circumstances which demonstrated the very real dangers of independency; and (4) the multiplying problems of the foreign missionary work which the association carried on in India and the Cape Verde Islands.

The "union" meeting of 1897 created a standing missionary committee, whose primary aim was to launch a strong overseas missionary program. Since this committee was the association's only general planning body, however, and included in its membership all of the chief leaders, the task of assigning and supervising the work in the home field consumed from the very first a major share of its time. An elementary superintendency thus appeared quite naturally. Its form bears an interesting resemblance to the present General Board and Board of General Superintendents of the Church of the Nazarene.

The full missionary committee, composed of a dozen or so members, nearly all of whom were ministers, met but once or twice a year. A smaller executive group carried on the work the rest of the time, meeting frequently and corresponding regularly. In 1897 the members of the latter were Hillery and Davis, representing New England, BeVier and Hosley for Brooklyn, and the chairman and secretary, Hoople and Reynolds. The executive committee passed upon the applications of preachers or congregations to organize churches, kept a tent busy on the evangelistic circuit, examined property, raised funds, and dealt with disciplinary problems. They attempted, without success, to engage first John Norberry and then A. B. Riggs as full-time workers. There were no "yes men" in the group. Thus Reynolds wrote at the close of a meeting in September, 1897, "This has been a very precious session. Good open discussions and I believe all voted in the fear of God."

Quite typical of the work of the executive committee were the actions taken at their meetings during August and September, 1898. They appointed F. L. Sprague, then in the Midwest, to seek out in that section independent holiness groups who might desire to join the association. They considered the prospects of a venture at White Plains, New York. They heard the report of the committee which had been placed in charge at Emmanuel Church, Brooklyn, during the troubles there. And they recommended the rule that whenever "a few persons" wished to organize a Pentecostal church, they must first unite in a "Pentecostal mission" and demonstrate both that their work would flourish and that they possessed the "qualifications essential to church government." By February, 1899, the executive committee had so far forsaken independency as to begin passing upon the men whom congregations had called as pastors. Two months later C. Howard Davis and H. N. Brown, one for New England and the other for the more westerly portions of the work, were appointed a committee on ministerial supply.[6]

Meanwhile H. F. Reynolds had come rapidly to the fore. He was the most able and aggressive home missionary evangelist as well as the most effective fund raiser in the group. In April, 1898, Reynolds was appointed to labor full time for the committee at a salary of nine hundred dollars a year. This relation he sustained more or less regularly down to the union of 1907. Almost from the beginning, however, and throughout the nine years following, Reynolds found that influential members of the committee balked at every step which remotely suggested a trend toward stronger organization. As early as August 11, 1898, H. B. Hosley moved that Reynolds be placed in charge of some church which would be responsible for a portion of his salary; that he discontinue camp meeting evangelism and devote more time to visiting the churches and raising missionary pledges; and that he cease direct correspondence with subscribers, leaving the pastors to handle collections, receipts, overdue notices, and so on.

What made Reynolds so useful in the task of forging the association into a united denomination was his willingness to yield to such pressures for a time without giving up his long-term goals. On two separate occasions he did accept a pastoral assignment, in order both to release more funds for missionary work and to pacify the opponents of superintendency. In 1899 he undertook the care of an independent congregation which Byron J. Rees had established at Westport Factory, Massachusetts. The following spring the missionary committee authorized him to divide the association into three sections, roughly comparable to the present New England, New York, and Pittsburgh districts, and to appoint an assistant missionary secretary over each. The plan did not work well and was soon abandoned. Reynolds now had to assume, along with pressing family and pastoral obligations, the whole load of directing the general interests of the association. Inevitably, one day he penned an abrupt postscript to a list of subscribers sent to the pastor at Pittsburgh. "Dear Brother Norris," it ran, "please can you explain why so few have paid?" Norris immediately sent thirty-two dollars in cash along with the formal notice that his church would not thereafter help with the missionary cause. Reynolds, characteristically, ate humble pie. The month of May found him beseeching C. Howard Davis to ask the Pittsburgh pastor to allow a missionary convention there in the summer, or anything else that would help him "to come into contact with Brother Norris."[7]

By the time of the annual meeting of 1902, this aggressive young ex-Methodist had learned how to work with men of independent mind so well that his successive re-election as missionary secretary became almost automatic. Part of the reason for this was his ability in raising funds. At this meeting the committee placed Reynolds exclusively in charge of the foreign task and made his good friend, C. Howard Davis, home missionary secretary. They gave the latter authority "to adopt such methods as he thinks best and to fix his own compensation." Davis' success was so encouraging that in April, 1903, the committee offered both Reynolds and Davis full-time positions at a salary of nine hundred dollars a year each, plus expenses. Reynolds, however, volunteered to support himself in evangelistic work and raise funds without pay, only stipulating that others should care for collections and correspondence. The chief reason for this was, as we shall see in a moment, the illness of one of the missionaries to India which made necessary a large expenditure for her return home. The offer was accepted. During the next year Hoople and Davis pressed the campaign for home missions and Reynolds stood aside from administrative tasks. That two such staunch independents should unite to promote and direct evangelism at home was proof that most of the leaders felt the need for some kind of superintendency.[8]

At this critical juncture, three other ex-Methodist preachers emerged to positions of great personal strength. They were thus enabled to stand by Hiram Reynolds in his quest for a stronger denominational order. John N. Short brought his Cambridge congregation into the fold in 1903. Though he had for several years been a member of the auxiliary Pentecostal Preachers' Association, Short had hesitated to unite his congregation with the association itself. That he did so in 1903 was a witness to his confidence in the stability and promise of the movement. Short was a native of Massachusetts and one of the early graduates of the school of theology which later became Boston University. He had been sanctified in 1867, under the preaching of Alfred Cookman, and had been a stalwart champion of holiness in the New England conference ever since. Beginning about 1885 he served as one of the select group who were members of the National Association for the Promotion of Holiness. Solid and scholarly in his work, humble—almost shy—of person, Short's participation was a benediction to the association in this and the following years. He was an inveterate and effective foe of fanaticism.

Meanwhile, as we have seen, A. B. Riggs was leading his Lowell congregation through deep waters and out onto a firm foundation for the building of a thriving church. Riggs was a tall, austere man. One who had never seen him exhorting sinners to repentance, his voice ringing like a buzz saw and his face lit with heavenly emotion, might indeed have thought him a typical Vermonter. The third man in this important triumvirate was H. N. Brown, who, like Short, had been an influential member of the National Association for the Promotion of Holiness. Brown's long tenure as pastor of the Bedford Avenue Church had by 1903 secured him a large place in the affections of Brooklyn laymen. He was no longer dependent on Hoople and BeVier, but stood in his own right at the head of his church. These three, Short, Riggs, and Brown, were one day soon to go to Los Angeles —the "three wise men from the East"—and initiate the union with Dr. Bresee's Nazarenes.[9] Riggs and Brown joined Reynolds and Hillery in relocating the Pentecostal Collegiate Institute at North Scituate, Rhode Island, in 1902. Their decisive action was proof that the forces of solidarity were prepared to assert their strength against those who championed independence and made way for division.

The Pentecostal Collegiate Institute

The history of the early days of what is now Eastern Nazarene College is, like that of the beginnings of the mission in

India, as much a chapter of heartbreak as of holy accomplishment. Rev. Lyman C. Pettit, pastor of the Congregational Methodist Church, a holiness body in Saratoga Springs, New York, led his people into the Association of Pentecostal Churches in 1898. He promptly began agitating for the establishment of a "Pentecostal School." A standing committee on education was appointed at the annual meeting a year later, with Pettit as chairman and Reynolds, characteristically, financial secretary. By the summer of 1900, Pettit had recruited a faculty and the *Beulah Christian* announced that the Pentecostal Collegiate Institute would begin operation in September.

Temporary quarters were arranged in an old hotel building at Saratoga. Pettit was placed in charge as president. W. F. Albrecht, a minister in the New York Conference of the M.E. church, joined the association to become principal of the school. Other staff members were Una P. Mann, from Waterville, Vermont; Lois E. Lanpher; Henrietta Moke; and Albrecht's wife, son, and daughter. "All instructors are in the experience of entire sanctification," the announcement ran. "We mean to demonstrate that heart and head culture can walk side by side. No novel reading or higher criticism. The Bible is to be 'The Great Text Book.'"

The college preparatory course followed the rigid standards of the New York State Board of Regents. The Biblical seminary curriculum was solid, but open to persons with little advanced education. "On general principles, we do not believe in the 'get ready quick' idea of preparation for the Christian ministry," the first catalogue declared. "But age and circumstances sometimes enter into the question, and so we gladly arrange special courses for those who desire to take them." Among the students who enrolled at P.C.I. the first fall were children of H. F. Reynolds, John Norris, and other preachers in the association. Some, like L. S. Tracy, were youngsters who had been inspired to come as a result of Pettit's numerous appearances that summer at camp meetings from Pennsylvania to Canada.

In the school, discipline was not harsh, at least in letter. But Tracy's correspondence with his mother and others reveals that tremendous pressure was applied throughout the year to bring every student into a profession of saving and sanctifying grace. Scenes of rather unrestrained emotional fervor were characteristic. The second year, Ernest Perry and his sister Gertrude joined the staff, and a primary school was added. Thirty-three enrolled in the college preparatory course, nineteen in the Biblical seminary, and twenty-six in other departments.[10]

But Pettit's zeal outran the limits of financial wisdom, and his personal life fell far short of the heights which he proclaimed in his sermon oratory. A new building, purchased in the summer of 1901 for $16,500, remained heavily in debt. Bills for improvements and operating expenses were secured by a second mortgage of dubious legality. The property turned out at last to have been deeded entirely to Pettit. These facts did not become clear, however, until May of 1902, when H. N. Brown visited Saratoga to investigate rumors of fanaticism and questionable moral conduct on the part of the leaders of the school. Brown found the rumors amply confirmed.[11]

But the resultant despair did not last long. With amazing speed Brown, Reynolds, and Hillery summoned a meeting of the education committee, dismissed Pettit, and disowned the Saratoga school. Albrecht and Hillery went to North Scituate, Rhode Island, in June and, on the impulse of their prayers, secured an option on a vacant academy building of grand but dilapidated construction. By August, the educational committee had organized a corporation, separate from but dependent upon the association, and secured mortgage and stock subscriptions sufficient to finance the new property. Albrecht, Ernest Perry, and some of the students went immediately to North Scituate to clean the rubbish out of the buildings and make ready for the opening of school that fall.

Meanwhile the Saratoga church called Ernest E. Angell, Congregationalist minister in East Barre, Vermont, to be their pastor. Angell joined the association the following October, and spent several years trying to restore the church at Saratoga to a useful existence. The effort was seemingly doomed from the start. He eventually moved on to be pastor of the John Wesley Church in Brooklyn. Shortly before the union of 1907, Angell became principal of the school in North Scituate. He dedicated most of the remaining thirty years of his life to Eastern Nazarene College, as administrator, teacher, and campus pastor.[12]

The significance of these developments was not lost upon men like Hoople and Hosley. The association was no longer a loose federation of sovereign congregations, but a movement of preachers and people whose unity went far deeper than the constitution adopted in 1897 would imply. Hoople was sufficiently loving in spirit and simple in heart to accept the new and stronger bonds without much protest. At the annual meetings in 1904 the missionary committee elected him "field evangelist and superintendent of home missions," at a salary of twelve hundred dollars a year. Hoople himself then moved that Reynolds be made "missionary secretary and superintendent of foreign missions," at the same salary. Hosley, however, turned sharply toward independence from this point on. But the tide was flowing in the opposite direction. In July, Hosley's brethren sternly rejected his complaints that "the sending of missionary reminders" was an "interference with the individual churches." And they persuaded Hoople to give up for the moment his plans to combine the work of home missionary superintendent with labors for Hosley's new Pentecostal League.

Hoople resigned as superintendent of home missions before the year was out, partly over dissatisfaction with the association's refusal to assume responsibility for certain of the debts at Saratoga. The movement at this point threatened to pass its founder by. In January, 1905, the education committee authorized Reynolds to act as general agent for P.C.I. Two months later, at the annual meetings in Malden, the missionary committee, by a vote of nine to one, placed Reynolds in charge of both home and foreign missionary work at a salary of one thousand dollars a year. Hoople meanwhile had taken up work with Hosley's Pentecostal League. But for the crisis which came about in the foreign missionary program just then these two might have drifted completely away.[13]

The Establishment of Foreign Missions in India and the Cape Verde Islands

More decisive than any other of the factors which motivated the drive toward a stronger superintendency was the difficulty which the association experienced in administering its missions to India and the Cape Verdes. Here again H. F. Reynolds filled a crucial role. Shortly after the union with the Central Evangelical Holiness Association in 1897, the missionary committee had appointed five persons to go to India. Rev. and Mrs. M. D. Wood, who had previously served in that country under another board, were made superintendents. The others were Carrie E. Taylor, Lillian M. Sprague, and Fred P. Wiley. The group sailed early in 1898. Reynolds, as secretary of the committee, was chiefly responsible for raising money for their passage, equipment, and first year's maintenance. In this way he first became acquainted with the laymen of all the churches.

He and the other preachers meanwhile spent endless hours devising rules by which the missionaries were to be governed and carry on their work. But distance, the problems posed by the Indian famine of 1899, and Wood's dominant personality all conspired to frustrate and obscure the plans they made. As early as February 1, 1899, H. B. Hosley had to write Wood on behalf of the association to rebuke him for his independent airs. Two months later Wiley and Miss Taylor resigned, professing great disagreement with the superintendent's policies. They were married shortly afterward, and took work under other auspices. Miss Nina E. Shroyers, who was sent out to replace them that summer, fell immediately into conflict with Wood also. The committee soon terminated her contract.

As months passed, doubts grew at home regarding Wood's loyalty to the aims of the association. Reynolds wrote a strong letter entitled "Keeping Holiness to the Front," admonishing him to preach more on this sacred theme. In April, 1901, the missionary committee turned down the superintendent's request to ordain a national preacher who did not seem to be clearly in the experience of holiness. Meanwhile Wood had opposed or disregarded the limitations which the committee had placed upon the number of orphans he might take in. Reynolds had taken great joy in persuading donors to assume the support of an orphan. He wrote dozens of letters simply to help sponsors select a Christian name for their wards. But he refused to allow the mission to be swamped with homeless children. Despite these disagreements, however, when Mrs. Wood fell seriously ill in January, 1903, the committee acted with commendable faithfulness to raise the money for the couple to return to the States. This was the year in which Reynolds volunteered to conduct the foreign mission solicitation without pay.[14]

In 1904 and 1905 eight new missionaries joined the Woods on their return to India. Chief among these were L. S. Tracy, his future wife, Gertrude Perry, her mother, Mrs. Ella Perry, and Julia R. Gibson. The three young people had all studied at the Pentecostal Collegiate Institute, and Mrs. Perry had been dean of women there. Tracy was to be a tower of strength in the mission in the days just ahead, as well as through many years thereafter. He had come from his native New Brunswick to work in the mills at Haverhill early in 1900. He was sanctified at the Haverhill Pentecostal Church and went to P.C.I. that fall on money donated by interested friends.[15]

In August, 1905, Mr. and Mrs. J. M. Davidson, who had gone out to India to be business managers, returned to New York bearing charges of maladministration against Mr. and Mrs. Wood and Miss Sprague, who now styled themselves "senior" missionaries. Out of regard for Wood's expressions of penitence, the committee kept him in service, but set up a joint superintendency composed of Tracy, Wood, and Miss Sprague. The arrangement lasted scarcely a month. The Woods and Miss Sprague resigned, carrying with them into another mission most of the native workers and orphan children. Tracy and his company set to work in quiet and noble fashion at the long task of rebuilding the venture from the ground up.

On the advice of H. F. Reynolds, Fred Hillery published a full account of the troubles in India in the February, 1906, issue of the *Beulah Christian.* At the association's annual meeting in April, Reynolds laid further details of the story before the delegates, in a manner reminiscent of a New England town meeting. These steps were necessary to salvage as much as possible of the confidence of the people who must, despite all these disappointments, continue to support the work. But in the process Reynolds found occasion to rebuke sharply the spirit of independence which had caused so much difficulty at home and abroad. "The question of organization, of authority, and of obedience," he said, "has had much to do in producing the state of affairs as they exist today." He then quoted Wood's recent letter, declaring that "if in order to gain your prayers and support we must be ruled and regulated by you, then we must, in order to obey our consciences, bid you farewell, and seek perfect freedom in other fields." The conclusion to Reynolds' report was pointed. "Perhaps," he said, "a chance to try their theories of independence will be a quick and forcible way of demonstrating their folly, as it proved to be with certain persons, leaders in schoolwork, who a few years ago wanted to be free from all control of the Educational Committee."[16]

This plain and public reference to the recent troubles at Pentecostal Collegiate Institute was a necessary part of the reconciliation which this annual meeting was seeking to make with those two stalwarts, Hoople and Hosley. As from the beginning, the willingness of brethren to suffer with one another in the spirit of holiness was the key to the unity of this strong-minded company. Hoople and Hosley were invited to describe publicly the aims of the Pentecostal League, after which the assembly voted to recognize its work as "in harmony and sympathy with this Association." Although this action was completely in accord with the association's historic policy of keeping channels of communication open to all independent holiness groups, it would scarcely have been possible without a settlement of the differences over P.C.I. The unity of spirit which resulted was essential to the much larger movement which during the following twelve months brought together East and West in the formation of the Pentecostal Church of the Nazarene.[17]

Retrospect: Radical Experience and Conservative Churchmanship

Looking back across twenty years, the champions of "organized holiness" in the East could scarcely fail to rejoice at the success of the efforts they had initiated. There were now 45 churches in the Association of Pentecostal Churches, and a total of 2,256 members. A score of strong and consecrated pastors had been raised up to lead them. Although many of the organizations were in out-of-the-way places, the greatest concentration of strength was in the urban centers. Particularly important were the attractive and well-located houses of worship which so many of the societies had erected. Their total value in 1906 was $146,000 —an increase of $26,000 over the previous year. Anyone who doubts the churchly nature of the program which the founders of this so-called "small sect" carried on needs only to visit the substantial neo-Gothic chapels which to this day have served the churches in Fitchburg, Cliftondale, Malden, Cambridge, Everett, and many other places.

As a matter of fact it is impossible to read the records of the early days without being made aware that here were men and women who sought to preserve much that was best in the tradition of American church life. They were not sectarian rebels, bent on destroying all that belonged to their memories of the old days. Nearly every congregation organized a Sunday school, a young people's society, and a circulating library of religious books within the very first months of its existence. The Methodist tradition of the class meeting was revived among them, though not without some hesitation where Baptist elements were dominant, as in Lynn. Many societies used the Methodist hymnal in worship. As early as 1899, the annual meeting of the association authorized the formation of the "Ladies' Foreign Missionary Auxiliary." Mrs. H. F. Reynolds and Susan N. Fitkin were both enthusiastic sponsors of this venture, the parent to the women's missionary organization so prominent in the later history of the Church of the Nazarene.[18]

The Pentecostal Preachers' Association, mentioned earlier, was a determined gesture at nonsectarian fellowship. It welcomed holiness advocates who had elected either to remain within the established churches or to follow an independent course. Reynolds, Brown, and Hoople beat back several attempts to confine its membership to preachers who were willing to cast their lot exclusively with the new denomination. "We must remember," their spokesman observed in 1898, "that in order for God to prosper us we must keep broad in our work, and low at Jesus' feet." The same spirit was displayed in the catalogue which P.C.I. published in 1904. "While the school is under the direction of the Association of Pentecostal Churches," the statement ran, "the plan of organization is practically interdenominational. Various denominations are represented among both faculty and students. Our desire is to spread the knowledge and living experience of Scriptural holiness rather than to attain any narrower end."

A footnote appended to that one of their articles of faith which declared the association's belief in "one God, maker and ruler of heaven and earth," reveals another facet of the character of these men. The note ran:

> We attempt not to define the essence of the Divine nature or the mode of the existence of the One True Living God. We shrink from such presumption. "Canst thou by searching find out God? Canst thou find out the Almighty to perfection? It is high as heaven—what canst thou do? Deeper than hell—what canst thou know?" What indeed, can we do but receive as little children such truth as is revealed to us, and, if our faith soar above our reason, wait the day that shall solve our perplexities?[19]

The first annual report which A. B. Riggs made to the newly organized church in Lowell in 1904 perhaps best illustrates the manner of life and spirit of joy with which these pioneers undertook their work. Riggs explained happily that the congregation had grown in both numbers and spirit. "The secret of the whole matter is perfect love," he said. "We do not see every minor thing alike in respect to all church doctrines, etc., but because of perfect love shed abroad in our hearts there has been no friction." He prophesied that if the group would continue in this way, "considerate of each other's feelings and rights," their future would indeed be bright. He rejoiced that the Sunday school had been manned by "holy men and women." The class leaders were persons whose "loyal hearts" had been "burdened with the great sense of responsibility of their classes." Their meetings had been "real Bethels, places of salvation and victory." The pastor cited as proofs of the genuineness of their piety such things as the attendance at the Sabbath morning prayer service, the presence of forty persons at Douglas Camp, the increasing interest in the weekday prayer meetings, and the devotion of the people to rescue work and relief for the poor. "Our hope in the future," he concluded, "is for all to work in humiliation and constantly seek wisdom from on high."[20]

Thus all along the eastern seaboard stouthearted men were discovering that the holiness people could achieve unity only by determining to exercise charity in incidentals. This Phineas F. Bresee had already made a cardinal point of his work in the West. Without it the union of the two movements would have been impossible.

Nonetheless, on the burning issue of entire sanctification as a second definite work of grace, wrought by the baptism of the Holy Spirit, there was no compromise. This was their central theme. Fred Hillery and C. Howard Davis wrote words and music for a song called "Be Definite," which put the matter bluntly thus:

> *When speaking of the work of God,*
> *The sanctifying grace;*
> *Give no uncertain sound to me;*
> *Give terms their proper place.*
>
> *The worldly wise men of today,*
> *Hate testimonies straight;*
> *The Dragon and his angels too,*
> *The same abominate.*

You say, Bless God, he saves me now!
You care not who denies;
But why not say, if just as true,
Bless God, he sanctifies.[21]

CHAPTER V

Phineas Bresee and the Church of the Nazarene

The Making of the Man

Dr. Bresee often said that the Church of the Nazarene was born in a holiness revival. The particular revival he meant was the one which William McDonald and George D. Watson conducted while Bresee was pastor of the First Methodist Church, Los Angeles, in 1884. But the new denomination bore so much the stamp of its founder's personality that we could rather say that it was born during the scores of revivals which shaped the character of this young Methodist preacher of the Iowa Conference in the years between 1860 and 1880.

Phineas F. Bresee was born in a log cabin in Franklin, Delaware County, western New York, on New Year's Eve, 1838. He was the second of three children. His parents, Phineas P. and Susan Brown Bresee, were both earnest Christians from their youth. As Phineas grew to manhood, his father moved first to a better farm, and then purchased a general store at the nearby town of West Davenport. The boy's advantages were few, but he improved them well. Several years at elementary school and parts of two years at an academy at Oneonta, New York, were the extent of his formal education. He was converted in a Methodist "protracted meeting" in February, 1856. Soon after he accepted an "exhorter's license," a first step toward the ministry. The next year his father visited Iowa, and decided to settle on a prairie homestead near Millersburg in that new state.

Young Bresee soon learned that Iowa was a country where preachers were scarce and traditions free. A mere boy might be admitted to the annual conference "on trial" and be assigned to assist an older man on a Methodist circuit. He joined A. C. Barnhart on the Marengo charge late in 1857. A great revival, one of the hundreds which swept the nation, broke out in various parts of this pastorate during the following year. Bresee then was appointed to his own circuit in the Dutch settlement of Pella. He was admitted to "full connection" as a Methodist minister in 1859 and ordained an elder in 1861. Meanwhile he returned to his native New York and brought back as his bride Maria Hibbard, sister to his boyhood chum and daughter of a well-known Methodist family.

Bresee requested a transfer from Pella in 1861 because he found that his antislavery convictions were an offense to certain people of southern blood. The heritage of abolitionism from the "burned-over district" of western New York always lay close to his heart. Concern for men's social needs was to remain a primary passion through his life. When the presiding elder sent Bresee to the hard-scrabble circuit at Galesburg, however, the assignment at first embittered, then powerfully challenged the young preacher. An awful impulse gripped him, he said, that the work must go forward. "It should go; live or die, it should go. I thought that the Lord would help me, but if He did not help me, it should go anyway. . . . I was in desperation." He fanned the flames of revival from one end of his charge to the other. In a single year he received 140 people into the membership of the church, bought a comfortable parsonage, and, to his great but somewhat worldly delight, purchased a fine team of horses and a new buggy for the trip to conference in the fall.

Bresee had, indeed, won his spurs as a Methodist pastor. Though only twenty-three years of age, he was appointed to a fine church in Des Moines, the capital city. Years later he told his biographer that the Galesburg charge had done him more good than any he ever had. "It broke me up, and broke through the chrysalis that was about me, and in some way taught me and impressed me that desperation, earnestness, intensity would win, God helping, in doing God's work."[1]

Thereafter Bresee's abilities were recognized and his work was uniformly successful. He rescued the Des Moines church from near financial ruin, then served two years as presiding elder of the Winterset district, covering western Iowa. He went thereafter as pastor to congregations at Chariton, Des Moines (for a second term), and Council Bluffs; then, in turn, to Red Oak, Clarinda, and Creston.

Through these years Bresee became a trusted leader in the Iowa Conference, active especially in the missionary and temperance causes. While at Council Bluffs he served for a time as editor of the *Inland Christian Advocate,* semiofficial newspaper for the conference. He was elected a delegate to the General Conference which met in New York in 1872. Though one of the youngest men present, he played an important part in securing the election of the former abolitionist Gilbert Haven to the bishop's chair.

At Red Oak, Bresee erected one of the finest church buildings in Iowa. He began his work there with his first "Home Camp Meeting." A revival broke out which lasted all winter. Hundreds of people in all walks of life were converted. During this meeting the young pastor began his lifelong custom of using popular choruses in the song services, and of training his people to do personal work during altar calls without prompting from the preacher. Here at Red Oak, also, Bresee's conviction matured that a large and commodious building was necessary to any successful gospel work. He pressed this view so earnestly that the editor of the local paper alleged that a new creed had come into being at the Methodist church. Its first article was, "Do you believe in Bresee?" and the second, "Do you believe in the early completion of the new Methodist church?" Evidently the town believed in both.

And so it was at other places where he preached. A contemporary account of Bresee's ministry at Clarinda stressed especially "the sledge hammer blows" which "saints and sinners and sin received," the pastor's "telling talks in favor of temperance," and his "rich and racy delineations of character." The writer noted also that the largest revival this church ever enjoyed occurred the first year of Bresee's pastorate and that the largest missionary collection ever taken was during his term.[2]

More important for subsequent Nazarene history than any of these events, however, was that in the winter of 1866-67 Bresee experienced for the first time the grace of entire sanctification. While presiding elder of the Winterset district, he had passed through an agonizing period of temptation to doubt. "I had a big load of carnality on hand always," he said years later, but it had appeared chiefly in impulses to anger, pride, and worldly ambition. Now, however, it took the form of doubt.

> It seemed as though I doubted everything. I thought it was intellectual, and undertook to answer it. I thought that probably I had gone into the ministry so early in life, that I had never an-

swered the great questions of being, and of God, and of destiny and sin and the Atonement, and I undertook to answer these great questions. I studied hard to so answer them as to settle the problems which filled my mind with doubt. Over and over again, I suppose a thousand times, I built and rebuilt the system of Faith, and laid the foundations of Revelation, the Atonement, the New Birth, Destiny, and all that, and tried to assure myself of their truth. I would build a pyramid, and walk about it and say: "It is so. I know it is so. It is in accord with Revelation. It is in accord with my intuitions. It is in accord with history and human experience. It is so and I do not question it." And I would not get through the assertions of my certainty, before the Devil or something else would say, "Suppose it isn't so, after all?" and my doubts would not be any nearer settled than they were before.[3]

One snowy prayer-meeting night while he was pastor at Chariton, Bresee fell across the altar of his own church and prayed and cried to the Lord for an experience of Christ which would meet his need. At the time he was ignorant of his real condition and of the gospel of holiness as well. "But, in my ignorance," he said years later, "the Lord helped me, and gave me, as I believe, the baptism with the Holy Ghost, though I did not know either what I needed or what I prayed for." He remembered that the experience took away his tendencies to "worldliness, anger and pride," and removed the doubt as well. "For the first time, I apprehended that the conditions of doubt were moral instead of intellectual, and that doubt was a part of the carnality that could only be removed as the other works of the flesh are removed."[4]

Dr. Bresee never claimed that from the time of this experience onward he was a faithful preacher of the doctrine of entire sanctification. Quite the contrary, he said later that he did not then clearly understand what had happened to him. The few who professed to be sanctified under his ministry thereafter at Des Moines, Council Bluffs, and other places owed little, he thought, to his instruction. Not for many years did he learn how to expound the doctrine in such a way as to lead others readily into the experience. In fact, by the time he moved to California in 1883, Bresee acknowledged that he was "not in the clear enjoyment of the blessing."[5]

Possibly a chief reason for his dissatisfaction with his spiritual life was the same one which impelled him to move to California—his involvement in an ill-fated gold-mining venture in Mexico. Rev. Joseph Knotts, whom Bresee had come to know first in Des Moines and then in Council Bluffs, had retired from the Methodist ministry in middle life and launched a number of business speculations. Knotts secured appointment as U.S. consul at Chihuahua, Mexico, in 1875. While there he took up options on a number of once fabulous mining properties. On his return to the States he persuaded Jay Cooke, Judge Helfenstein, and other capitalists of national reputation to join him in exploiting the holdings. Knotts made his friend Bresee his chief assistant and a director of several corporations.

In the autumn of 1879, Bresee asked for appointment to a rather insignificant church at Creston, Iowa, apparently with the purpose of devoting a great deal of his time to these enterprises. Two years later he returned to the Broadway Church, Council Bluffs, where Knotts was a prominent member. Soon after Bresee took charge of an effort to found a new congregation in a wealthy residential section of the city. Early in 1883, however, the Missouri River overflowed its banks and wiped out so much of that portion of the city as to make the new church venture futile. At about the same time Knotts received word that native laborers at the old Prieta mine at Parral, Mexico, had set off a blast which caused an underground stream to pour into the diggings. Tools and machinery in which so much capital had been invested were completely destroyed. The mine was a total loss.

Bresee was now in financial ruin. He decided to move to California, chiefly, he said, from embarrassment at the thought of "remaining in a country where I was supposed to be wealthy, when, in fact, I was very poor." He also determined never again to attempt to make money but to give the remainder of his life "to the direct preaching of the Word of God." Although his friend Knotts was nearly bankrupt too, he arranged a gift of one thousand dollars to finance Bresee's move to Los Angeles. In August, 1883, the family of seven children and two grandparents left Council Bluffs in an "emigrant car," that is, a railroad freight car fitted out for camp-style living. They arrived in southern California a week before the annual Methodist conference opened there.

Bresee was invited to preach at the First Methodist Church, Los Angeles, the following Sunday. Little did he realize that he would be installed as pastor of this fine church within two weeks. His sense of defeat at having been compelled to leave Iowa under such circumstances would also have been less painful if he could have foreseen the resolution which the Iowa Conference was shortly to spread upon its records. It ran as follows:

> Whereas, the demands of our connectional work have called for the transfer of Rev. P. F. Bresee to the Southern California Conference,
>
> *Resolved*, 1. that we deeply regret the departure of such an esteemed and valuable member of our conference, one whose work in Iowa for twenty-five years has endeared him to many hearts and who has contributed so much to the growth of Iowa Methodism;
>
> *Resolved*, 2. that we heartily recommend him to the esteem of our California brethren, and trust that he may have the largest measure of success among them;
>
> *Resolved*, 3. that should he hereafter desire to return to this conference he will meet with a most cordial greeting.[6]

The Holiness Revival in Southern California

In the congregation of the First Methodist Church, Los Angeles, Bresee came in contact for the first time with a strong company of laymen who professed sanctification. Their leader was Leslie F. Gay, in whose home a weekly meeting for the promotion of holiness was conducted. Gay had come to Los Angeles in failing health in 1874 and after his recovery became a pillar in the Methodist church. He operated for a while the first vegetable market in the city and eventually became manager of a large fruit ranch. He later entered the real estate and insurance business.

The group surrounding Gay were by 1883 witnessing the initial success of their efforts to swing the Southern California Conference into line with the national holiness awakening. When their new pastor was appointed, therefore, they began immediately to pray for him. "I instinctively in spirit allied myself with them," Bresee said later, "and, while . . . I was not in the clear enjoyment of the blessing, they seemed to appreciate whatever efforts I could and did make in assisting them in the work of holiness." As early as December, 1883, the Los Angeles Methodist "District Convention," which included both lay and ministerial representatives, made Gay, Bresee, the presiding elder, R. W. C. Farnsworth, and two other pastors "a committee to correspond with the National Holiness Association with a view to the establishment of a branch Association and the securing of competent help to carry on the work." The result was an invitation to William McDonald, newly elected head of the national organization, to come to the West Coast with George D. Watson for a series of revivals.

McDonald and Watson conducted services at Bresee's church for a period of three weeks late in 1884. The pastor said that he passed through this meeting "in general accord with both the teaching and spirit of these brethren" but he did not come to any special realization of his own spiritual lack. Afterward, however, he was awakened to pray earnestly, as he put it, for "something that would meet my needs," though he did not clearly realize "what they were nor how they could be met."[7] What happened at length must be stated in the words which Bresee himself used in describing to his close friends the experience of which he rarely spoke publicly.

> I sat alone in the parsonage, in the cool of evening, in the front parlor near the door. The door being opened, I looked up into the azure in earnest prayer, while the shades of evening gathered about. As I waited and waited, and continued in prayer, looking up, it seemed to me as if from the azure there came a meteor, an indescribable ball of condensed light, descending rapidly toward me. As I gazed upon it, it was soon within a few score feet, when I seemed distinctly to hear a voice saying, as my face was upturned towards it: "Swallow it; swallow it," and in an instant it fell upon my lips and face. I attempted to obey the injunction. It seemed to me, however, that I swallowed only a little of it, although it felt like fire on my lips, and the burning sensation did not leave them for several days. While all of this of itself would be nothing, there came with it into my heart and being, a transformed condition of life and blessing and unction and glory, which I had never known before. I felt that my need was supplied. I was always very reticent in reference to my own personal experience. I have never gotten over it, and I have said very little relative to this; but there came into my ministry a new element of spiritual life and power. People began to come into the blessing of full salvation; there were more persons converted; and the last year of my ministry in that church was more consecutively successful, being crowned by an almost constant revival. When the third year came to a close, the church had been nearly doubled in membership, and in every way built up.[8]

From this point onward, Dr. Bresee was indeed a wholehearted advocate of the second blessing. He did not, however, change his method of presentation so radically as to incur much opposition. Not until around 1890, when the holiness revival reached a considerable crisis in southern California, did he come to make that doctrine the supreme issue of all his preaching. He later regretted the indecisiveness of his earlier efforts.

"If I had known more when I came to this coast, and had had experience and sense," he declared, "I could have swept the whole of Methodism into holiness. It was not set against it enough to prevent me from putting my hands on everything in Methodism in Southern California and drawing it into holiness; but I did not know enough. I neither had the experience* nor the general ministerial wisdom to do it. I am very sorry."[9]

One justification for Bresee's moderate course was that by 1885 California Methodism seemed to be on the verge of complete acceptance of the doctrine of entire sanctification. A direct attack upon the problem might only have produced division. In May, 1884, for example, before the McDonald and Watson revival, the Los Angeles district preachers' meeting spent an afternoon discussing how to obtain and preach holiness. They then voted to reaffirm their belief in "the doctrine of Christian perfection as taught by Mr. Wesley" and to preach it to their people. Two months later, Presiding Elder R. W. C. Farnsworth published his praise of the "Los Angeles Praying Band," which met Tuesday evenings at Leslie Gay's home. It was "a holiness meeting," he said, "in vital union and harmony with our church." Farnsworth had himself served as its president, *ex officio*, in obedience to the action of the district convention the previous fall. At the district camp meeting that year, he noted, many had entered into the experience of "a clean heart."[10]

The *Southern California Methodist Quarterly*, which Farnsworth edited on behalf of the conference for several years, seems to have been entirely friendly to the preaching of sanctification. Its columns reported holiness revivals regularly, printed frequent Bible readings by Leslie F. Gay, and carried numerous articles and excerpts of sermons by Bresee, T. E. Robinson, and other leaders. The issue for March, 1885, for example, was devoted almost exclusively to the growing interest in sanctification. Arabella E. Widney, one day to become a charter member of the Church of the Nazarene, wrote against "church entertainments" which were not clearly to the glory of God. Gay contributed a biographical sketch of the evangelists McDonald and Watson. T. E. Robinson described their three weeks' revival at Bresee's church, stressing that "with true holiness comes loyalty." And William McDonald presented in this issue a lengthy argument

---

*Dr. H. Orton Wiley explained that the word "experience" here referred to mature judgment rather than to personal religious experience.—*Editor*

against the view that sanctification simply enabled the Christian to continue in the "same perfect fullness of divine approbation" which he had received at conversion.

The revival tide did not recede, despite two extended visits to southern California that summer by Bishop C. H. Fowler, an inveterate foe of what he later called "cranktification." The first conference camp meeting at the new location at Long Beach proved to be a miniature Pentecost, as the *Quarterly* reported with joy. Bresee, T. E. Robinson, and M. M. Bovard, president of the University of Southern California, all preached on the theme of holiness. Gay and other influential laymen were prominent leaders. Thirty-nine of the seventy-two who testified at the final Sunday morning love feast declared that they enjoyed the experience of entire sanctification, and many others expressed a desire to obtain it. At the last service Bresee preached from Eph. 5:25, equating the baptism of divine love with cleansing from all sin. Although this doctrine was basic to Methodism, he said, the preachers had "not always been as clear and definite in preaching it" as they ought to have been. At the close of the sermon he invited to the altar all who had "received a clean heart during these camp meetings." The congregation joined in farewell testimonies and songs, and in a display of holy enthusiasm like that for which Dr. Bresee later became famous.[11]

Those who were in the vanguard of this holiness movement were at the same time significant leaders in all the activities of southern California Methodism. J. P. Widney, a wealthy member of Los Angeles First Church and Bresee's lifelong friend, endowed a new medical college at the University of Southern California in 1885, and became its first dean. The Widneys and the Gays were the mainstays of the "District Aid Committee," an organization devoted to securing better support for underpaid pastors. T. E. Robinson and Bresee spearheaded the new emphasis on Christian education then prominent in the conference. Both urged the importance of rearing children in the nurture of the Lord. Bresee also initiated the organization of a district home missionary society, promoted the permanent establishment of the camp meeting at Long Beach, and led the Methodists in the crusade for prohibition.[12]

By the close of his term in the Los Angeles pastorate, Bresee's congregation numbered 650 members, four times that of any other in the conference. His salary was nearly twice as large as that of any other preacher of that group.

In August, 1886, he accepted appointment to Pasadena, then just a growing village at the foot of the Sierra Madre Mountains fifteen miles away. The church building was in the process of construction and the congregation contained only about one hundred thirty members. "Bresee, what are you going to do at Pasadena?" one of his friends asked. "By the grace of God," he replied, "I am going to make a fire that will reach Heaven." Almost at once he began an evangelistic campaign, preceding the services each evening with a street meeting designed to appeal to the hundreds of men employed in building new homes in the town. By the end of the year the membership of the congregation had more than doubled, making this the second largest church in the conference.

From August to January of Bresee's second year at Pasadena, 250 members joined the Methodist church. The *Southern California Christian Advocate* reported that the community was "in the full blaze of revival glory." Holiness Evangelist A. J. Bell and the team of William McDonald and J. A. Wood assisted in special services. Since it seemed impossible to enlarge the house of worship rapidly enough to care for the newcomers, the people constructed at its side a huge tabernacle, seating 2,000 persons. At the end of his second year, Bresee reported that his church numbered 700 members. His salary was $4,350, larger even than that paid at Los Angeles First Church.[13]

Meanwhile many others in the conference besides Bresee were promoting holiness successfully. Throughout 1888 and 1889, McDonald and Wood conducted revivals in churches large and small. Leslie Gay became a member of the National Holiness Association in 1887. He was one of only seven laymen from the whole country so chosen and the only representative from the West Coast until Bresee himself was invited to join in 1891. Gay also received the highest honor possible to a Methodist layman when he won election to the General Conference of 1888. Meanwhile he continued to lead the "holiness meetings" at Los Angeles First Church. The pastor there reported in February, 1888, that scarcely a Sabbath passed without persons seeking sanctification at his altars.

The editor of the *Southern California Christian Advocate* rejoiced that at the camp meeting at Long Beach in 1889 not a single altar invitation passed in which "a large number did not go forward seeking holiness of heart and life." When eastern leaders of the National Holiness Association came to Beulah Park, Sacramento, for the first "national" camp held in California in many years, the *Advocate* reported that event, too, with great enthusiasm. "The work done was in the church and for the church," the editor wrote. "All prejudices melted away before the clear presentation of the most glorious doctrine" of Methodism.[14]

Bresee himself won as much public notice for his efforts to apply Christianity to social problems during his years at Pasadena as he did for his holiness preaching. He was the first to propose that the conference establish missions to the Orientals, and founded a thriving one in his own city. He also participated in the successful campaign to make Pasadena southern California's first "dry" town. One of his temperance discourses became somewhat famous as "Dr. Bresee's hyena sermon." It so angered the liquor dealers that when the dry forces won out a mob stormed the Methodist parsonage, threatening the pastor's life.[15]

As Bresee closed his term at Pasadena in 1890, however, the holiness revival in California was reaching a new and critical phase. The increasing activity of independent holiness bands throughout the state greatly annoyed Methodist officials. Meanwhile the outbreak of the nationwide controversy described in an earlier chapter laid the second-blessing preachers under the necessity of demonstrating again and again their loyalty to the church.

Thus William McDonald wrote in the *California Christian Advocate* on New Year's Day, 1890, that the Methodist communion was the true home of "every lover and professor of entire holiness" and the most fruitful field for his labors. This was true despite the fact, as McDonald put it, that "many of her ministers, unhappily, seem to have little interest in the subject of personal holiness, and are far from being all they should be spiritually." While the last phrase provoked an immediate though anonymous rejoinder, the discussion in succeeding issues revealed strong support for Evangelists McDonald and Wood. An article on revivals, appearing in December, 1891, concluded that, although Wesley never magnified one experience to the exclusion of another, he saw clearly that "experimental and practical holiness and church aggressiveness were identical."[16]

The appearance of Bishop Willard F. Mallalieu at the Southern California Conference in the fall of 1891 increased the initial advantage which the holiness leaders held. Mallalieu appointed Bresee presiding elder of the Los Angeles district and heartily approved his plan to organize a series of holiness revivals in his territory during the coming year. By December, McDonald and Wood were back in California ready to set the project in motion. From Meridian, Mississippi, Mallalieu wrote McDonald that his heart was "wonderfully burdened for California." He had been praying that there would be "three thousand souls saved on Dr. Bresee's district this year."

The series of campaigns began at Asbury Church, Los Angeles, where Bresee had been pastor in 1890-91. The evangelists then moved on to North Pasadena. Here the pastor sought and professed the experience of holiness, and scores of conversions resulted. Thereafter, pastors of churches large and small returned to the enjoyment and preaching of full salvation. Although the response was lukewarm in congregations like that at the University Church, heretofore not noted for a "high state of spirituality," as William McDonald put it, little public opposition appeared. The new editor of the *Southern California Christian Advocate* was sanctified just in time to cancel a blast he had planned to publish against the meetings. The discussions of holiness at the preachers' gatherings in April fairly swamped those who argued that the initial experience of conversion brought all the cleansing God had provided for the soul.

The largest victory came in the last campaign, held at the First Methodist Church, Los Angeles. Bishop Mallalieu had appointed S. W. Campbell, recently from Cleveland, Ohio, as pastor of this congregation, in response to the request of certain laymen for a man who was "not radical on the subject of holiness." But the result was the same as when Bresee came there nine years before. Leslie Gay and his friends received Campbell with great tenderness, and began at once to pray for his sanctification. On the first Friday morning of the McDonald and Wood meetings there, Dr. Bresee conducted a service of testimony. At its close Campbell himself led the way to the altar. "The people cried and prayed and shouted," an eyewitness wrote, "while their dear pastor was begging for a clean heart."

Only the Simpson Church in Los Angeles refused to cooperate with Bresee's crusade. This congregation had come into existence in 1889 as a kind of symbol of Methodist aspirations for social eminence in southern California. Numerous wealthy citizens had shared in the construction of a magnificent building which seated twenty-five hundred people and boasted finer appointments than any theater or opera house in the state. Here was dramatic proof, if any were needed, that the first massive resistance to the doctrine of holiness came not so much from Methodist institutions of learning as from wealthy and worldly-minded laymen who dominated the great city churches.[17]

For the moment, however, Bresee was master of the situation. He led the delegation from southern California to Omaha, Nebraska, for the General Conference of 1892. The *Daily Christian Advocate,* organ of that conference, introduced him as a man of strong personality whose district had witnessed a general revival of great power. Among holiness circles, at least, there was talk of his being made a bishop.

That fall, however, when Bishop John H. Vincent, a determined enemy of the doctrine of entire sanctification, appeared as presiding officer at the Southern California Conference, he made short work of the revival which Bresee had begun. The evangelistic sessions planned for the evening hours of the conference were omitted. Vincent directed that the presiding elders should present reports in writing, rather than make public statements. He removed Bresee from his office without ceremony, and appointed him with thinly veiled disdain to the pastorate of Simpson Church, where the opponents of holiness were in full control. Others whom Vincent called "holiness cranks" received equally summary treatment.

Bresee's report for the year as presiding elder was, therefore, brief and pointed; it stressed especially the gracious revivals which most of the churches had experienced. "The sanctification of believers, the reclamation of backsliders and the conversion of sinners has been the chief work of most of the pastors," he declared.

> The work has been pressed in many ways regular and irregular. A good degree of help was given through the agency of our Evangelistic Committee composed of some of the chief laymen of the district, under whose advice and with whose co-operation a three

months' campaign was held of Pentecostal meetings, led by the Presiding Elder. . . .

The report also emphasized the organization of Epworth Leagues. These youth groups, Bresee said, were "leading the young people both into the richer experiences of the Christian life and out into the various fields of service" as well as "bringing many culturing influences to bear upon them."[18]

Although Dr. Bresee was happy at being relieved from administrative work, which he always disliked, the task at Simpson was almost impossible. A heavy debt crushed the church. The congregation had dwindled steadily. Very few of them were willing to accept the gospel of holiness. After a few months Bresee quietly notified the members that he would not remain longer than one year. He advised them either to unite their congregation with First Church or move out farther into a residential portion of the city, selling the property to pay the debt. The next year he was appointed to the Boyle Heights Church, Los Angeles, a substantial but much smaller congregation.

Though his demotion was apparent to all, Bresee remained high in the esteem of his brethren in the conference and was a key leader of both their evangelistic and their educational work. He was president of the conference board of trustees and the board of church extension and chairman of the committee on education. He encouraged the evangelization of Orientals and prodded the conference to favor legislation in their behalf. The presiding elders of both the Santa Barbara and Fresno districts employed him as preacher at their district camp meetings and noted happily in their annual reports that large numbers of their people had received the experience of perfect love.[19]

Bresee's relationship to the University of Southern California during these years is especially significant. He had been vice-president of the board of directors of the university since 1884, and was active in most of the new ventures which that group undertook. In 1892, Bresee and J. P. Widney set out to rescue the institution from the near ruin which unsound financing had brought upon it—Widney with his money and Bresee with his piety. Widney, who was the founder of the Los Angeles County Medical Association and the most distinguished physician in the city, had made a fortune in real estate development. He had attracted a strong faculty to the Medical School, which he headed, and had kept that arm of the university solvent by the

BRESEE AND THE CHURCH OF THE NAZARENE

simple expedient of paying the bills himself. In the spring of 1892 the directors asked him to become president of the entire university. The College of Liberal Arts was then eighteen thousand dollars in debt. Widney's first step was to set up a separate governing board for the College of Liberal Arts, both as a means of refinancing the debt and of tying that branch of the institution more closely to the spiritual leaders of California Methodism. Dr. Bresee was made chairman of this new board.[20]

At an early meeting, Bresee and two associates brought in a report concerning the philosophy of education proper to such an institution as the Methodist conference intended the university to become. The implications of Bresee's report are so far-reaching that it must be quoted in full:

> *Resolved:* That it is the sense of this board that a high standard of spiritual attainment is to be desired in our faculty, as well as high standards of scholarly ability;
>
> *That:* as a business proposition our chief reliance to offset the advantages of secular institutions must be our high moral and religious standard;
>
> *That:* to this end we enquire closely into the purity of private life and character, and soundness of Christian faith and practice, as well as nobility of spiritual life, of each person proposed as a member of the faculty. That no one be elected or retained who is not only a professed Christian but sound in doctrine, consistent in personal life, and an aggressive worker;
>
> *That:* special prominence be given to the devotional exercises of the school, that they be held before the lessons of the day, and of such a nature as will make them attractive and helpful to the students;
>
> *That:* a knowledge of God and our relations to Him as revealed to us in the Scriptures and by the Holy Spirit in the heart, is vastly more important for our students in their preparation for the work of life than mere intellectual attainment. That acquiring such knowledge requires earnest, faithful study, as well as waiting upon God, and that a systematic study of the Scriptures be made a distinct feature of the school instruction in some form and as a part of the studies of each student for each term, as soon as practicable.[21]

Little wonder that the succeeding conference enthusiastically adopted Widney's new financial program for the institution. Two of the church's most distinguished and trusted leaders were at the helm. By the time of the annual conference of 1894, the university had passed through its financial crisis, and Widney's principal work was done. Perhaps for this reason he was ready to take up a new project—association with Phineas Bresee at Peniel Mission.

Dr. and Mrs. Widney and their daughter, Arabella, had long been active in the evangelistic endeavors which Methodists carried on among the poor and unfortunate. The two women pioneered the organization of deaconess work in southern California in 1889. Bresee and Widney were members of the first executive board. Widney, like Bresee, had also been greatly interested in the progress of prohibition. He served as head of the city's nonpartisan anti-saloon league, and ran for mayor on the Prohibition ticket in 1894. He served several years as a member and president of the Los Angeles Board of Education. The only question Methodists ever raised against Widney came in 1892, when he employed a critical approach to the Scriptures in a series of articles aimed to rebuke an extreme doctrine of divine healing.

All records agree that Widney was an honored citizen of both the city and the church he loved. But, like Bresee, his abiding passion in recent years had been the evangelization of the poor and the extension of the ministry of scriptural holiness to classes which the church might otherwise miss. Few were surprised, therefore, when he joined the group which was sponsoring Peniel Hall. As we shall see in a moment, this work soon became more important in Widney's eyes than the presidency of the infant university which he had so recently and so nobly served.[22]

The Founding of the Church of the Nazarene

Although much of the story of Bresee's labors at Peniel Hall appears in an earlier chapter, we must clarify further the relation of that venture both to Methodism and to the origins of the Church of the Nazarene.

From the time of Bresee's removal from the presiding eldership in 1892, he sought appointment as a Methodist city missionary in Los Angeles. When, therefore, the proprietors of Peniel Mission invited him and Widney to join in a significant enlargement of their activities, Bresee thought his chance had come to fulfill his desire to spend the rest of his days in such work.

The reasons why Bishop John N. Fitzgerald, who presided at the annual conference of 1894, refused to grant Bresee a regular appointment to Peniel are not clear. In any case, Bresee appealed directly to his conference for a "supernumerary relation." The request was tabled, following a rather embarrassing debate. Undoubtedly theological issues played a part, but this fact does not appear in any of the Methodist records. It never seems to have been pointed out in print until a year later, when the *Los Angeles Times* reported that "those in a position to know" said that "the doctor's attitude on various doctrinal questions, notably the doctrine of sinless perfection," had been a chief reason for his leaving the Methodist ministry.

The conference records show rather that scriptural holiness was a dominant theme at the annual session of 1894. Samuel A. Keen conducted each day "Pentecostal meetings," which were fully reported in the Methodist and public presses. Bresee presided over the educational service at which Widney, as president of the university, gave the principal address. Bresee's presiding elder fully supported his request for a supernumerary relation. In his annual report, another district leader praised Bresee's work as a church and camp meeting evangelist. Despite whatever controversy was going on behind the scenes, the conference reelected Bresee a director of the university and a trustee of the Long Beach camp.

When, therefore, a few weeks later, the *California Christian Advocate* reported the first services in the new mission building at Peniel, it cast not the slightest aspersion upon Bresee, Widney, or their associates. Faculty and administrative officers of the university appeared frequently on the program at the hall. Several served as instructors in Widney's "missionary institute." Substantial Methodist laymen like the Leslie Gays were deeply involved in the undertaking. Apparently none of these persons, including Dr. Bresee, had any thought of withdrawing from the Methodist church.[23]

The first signs of an impending break came in December, after Bresee had published the "Declaration of Principles" for Peniel, discussed in a previous chapter. The declaration called for an organization of the workers which would permit persons who were not members of any church to make the mission their Christian home. The editor of the *California Christian Advocate* jumped immediately to the conclusion that Bresee was preparing to set up an independent Methodist church. He urged rather that the mission should follow an unsectarian path, accepting only persons who were members of other evangelical churches, as the Young Men's Christian Association had done.

Bresee knew that the actual result of such a policy would be to deprive a great mass of poor men of the privileges of church membership. The other leaders at Peniel agreed with him, at least for the moment. Inevitably, however, this plan called for the addition to the program of many activities more characteristic of a church than a mission. Along with the regular Tuesday holiness meeting and the noonday prayer meeting, both of which were descended from traditions by then old among holiness people, the leaders instituted a Sunday school and a Friday night young people's meeting. The latter was especially dear to Dr. Bresee's heart. Its services were soon crowded with young people recently won out of lives of sin.

One of the chief issues which separated Bresee from the Methodists, therefore, was his program for evangelizing the poor. By early June, 1895, the Methodist pastors in Los Angeles had organized an apparently competitive "City Evangelization Union." They laid ambitious plans for mission work at various neglected locations in the city. Meanwhile the *California Christian Advocate* commented that "from reports and comments in the air, it may be inferred that Peniel Hall has not the fullest endorsement of the city's Methodist pastors, and that its influence is not in the highest degree favorable to the work of the churches." The cleavage was primarily ecclesiastical, however, not theological.

The doctrine of sanctification in fact won renewed emphasis among California Methodists during the year Bresee spent at Peniel. In April, 1895, the *California Christian Advocate* printed an article by W. F. Warren, first president of Boston University, entitled "Shall I Profess Sanctification?" Warren began the answer to this question with these words: "Of course not, unless you have it; but if you are living in that blessed experience, why not tell it?" The remainder of the article was as clear and definite a defense of the second blessing as any holiness expositor had ever written. Many members of the church, Warren declared, were not aware of the privilege and duty of entire sanctification. It was up to those who knew its joys to tell others so that they might find them too. A month later two articles by C. O. McCulloch underlined in equally clear fashion the distinctions between regeneration and the experience of perfect love. McCulloch specifically denied the theory that Christians may simply grow into a sanctified relationship with the Lord. Holiness was the fruit of a second crisis in Christian experience.[24]

The immediate cause for the organization of the Church of the Nazarene, therefore, is not so much to be found in Bresee's differences with the Methodists as in those which developed between him and the proprietors of Peniel Hall. Certainly J. P. Widney must have been disillusioned when A. B. Simpson, leader of the Christian and Missionary Alliance and reportedly an extremist on divine healing, appeared as a special worker at the mission in May. Bresee on his part disagreed with Mr. and Mrs. Ferguson's insistence upon the use of young women in rescue work, and their growing interest in foreign missionary schemes.

In the spring of 1895, Widney decided to resign his position as president of the university and spend a year studying in the East. The board finally accepted the resignation, after their benefactor had turned aside repeated requests that he reconsider. Bresee, meanwhile, made plans to spend the latter portion of that summer at a series of National Holiness Association camp meetings in the Midwest. All the available evidence indicates that neither Bresee nor Widney was contemplating any change in his relationship with Peniel Mission or with the Methodist church. Bishop Cyrus D. Foss was Bresee's traveling companion as far as Colorado, and Bishop Mallalieu joined other friends in extending him a hearty welcome to the Des Plaines camp meeting, near Chicago. Between meetings, Bresee studied the work of various missions in Chicago, held a three days' revival in the First Methodist Church in Springfield, Illinois, and cultivated the friendship of loyal Methodists throughout the area.[25]

He returned to Los Angeles in September, however, to find himself "frozen out" of Peniel Hall, to use the blunt phrase of the *Los Angeles Times*. Friends of Dr. Bresee claimed, so the *Times* reported, that although he was ostensibly in charge of the mission, he had been excluded from the councils which controlled the movements of the workers. Now the proprietors asked him to withdraw. Since he had no financial interest in the property, he had no other choice but to comply. The man who had forsaken the pulpits of Methodism to minister to the poor was now without a place to preach at all.

But, like Moses on the desert side of the Red Sea, Bresee remained true to his calling. It seemed providential that during the summer Dr. Widney had changed his plans and was remaining in Los Angeles that year. With characteristic decisiveness, these two fast friends determined to form a new organization in which their program of a church home for the poor might be fully carried out.

They announced a service for Sunday, October 6, in Red Men's Hall, a short distance from Peniel. A *Los Angeles Times* reporter, it happened, gave us the only extant firsthand account of this meeting. The leaders, he wrote, announced that although no name had been decided upon for the new denomination, its work was to be chiefly evangelistic and its government congregational. Bresee preached in the morning from the text, "Thus saith the Lord, Stand ye in the ways, and see, and ask for the old paths, where is the good way, and walk therein, and ye shall find rest for your souls." He declared that the only thing new in the movement was its determination to preach the gospel to the needy, and to give that class a church they could call their own. Gone was the snobbish idea that a mission was good enough for the poor.

Two weeks later, 82 persons united as charter members of the Church of the Nazarene. Within a short time their number had grown to 135. Among them, in addition to the Bresee and Widney families, were other substantial Methodists: Mr. and Mrs. W. S. Knott, Mrs. A. P. Baldwin, sister to Mrs. Knott, Mr. and Mrs. Leslie F. Gay, and Gardner Howland, a retired paper manufacturer who had been prominent in the holiness movement in New York state. Mrs. Mary J. Willard, an Episcopalian lady of considerable talent who had been sanctified at Peniel Mission, led Colonel Duncan, a wealthy southerner, and others from her denomination into the fold. Most of the membership, however, was made up of recent converts from the poorer sections of Los Angeles.

On the day of organization Dr. Widney preached on the words of Christ, "Follow me." He pointed out that the essence of Christianity was not to receive a creed or to observe church forms and rituals, but simply to accept the Christ life, to make Christ himself the Lord of one's heart. After an interesting reference to the novelist Tolstoy's recent decision to abandon his high position and go to serve the peasants of a Russian village, Widney attempted to explain why a new denomination was required. The reason, he said, was that the machinery and the methods of the older churches had proved a hindrance to the work of evangelizing the poor.

Dr. Widney also explained the choice of a name for the church. The word "Nazarene" had come to him one morning at daybreak, after a whole night of prayer. It immediately seemed to him to symbolize "the toiling, lowly mission of Christ." It was the name which Jesus used of himself, Widney declared, "the name which was used in derision of Him by His enemies," the name which above all others linked Him to "the great toiling, struggling, sorrowing heart of the world. It is Jesus, Jesus of Nazareth, to whom the world in its misery and despair turns, that it may have hope."[26]

The first piece of Nazarene literature ever printed, a little flyer advertising the meetings at Red Men's Hall, bore much the same message. Headed with the words of Jesus, "Come unto me, all ye that labour and are heavy laden," the announcement ran as follows:

> The Church of the Nazarene is a simple, primitive church, a church of the people and for the people. It has no new doctrines, only the old, old Bible truths. It seeks to discard all superfluous forms and ecclesiasticism and go back to the plain simple words of Christ. It is not a mission, but a church with a mission. It is a banding together of hearts that have found the peace of God, and which now in their gladness, go out to carry the message of the unsearchable riches of the gospel of Christ to other suffering, discouraged, sin-sick souls. Its mission is to everyone upon whom the battle of life has been sore, and to every heart that hungers for cleansing from sin. Come.
>
> "His yoke is easy, his burden is light.
> I've found it so, I've found it so. . . ."

On the back of the flyer was a listing of the services of the church. Sunday morning began with a young men's prayer meeting at 9:00. Sabbath school followed at 9:45; then, in turn, preaching at 11:00 by Dr. Bresee, a Bible reading at 3:00 by J. P. Widney, called "Walks with the Nazarene," and evangelistic services at 7:30. A street meeting preceded both the Sunday and the Wednesday evening meetings. The young people's gathering was Friday at 7:30 p.m. Also, on the back of the flyer, the deaconesses were listed as follows: Miss Arabella E. Widney, Miss Emma Stive, Mrs. M. E. Kroft, Mrs. J. W. Ernest, and Mrs. W. S. Knott. Underneath was a note of great interest:

We endeavor to supply medical attendance for those who are unable to provide it for themselves. Please notify the pastors or deaconesses of such need.

Partially worn clothing is solicited for the poor. Please bring to the church, or notify the deaconesses where it may be had.[27]

The reaction of the Methodists to the organization of the new church was surprisingly mild. The article in the *California Christian Advocate* which reported the event bore no rancor toward the founders. Dr. Widney was allowed to explain their aims to the Los Angeles Methodist preachers' meeting. At the end of his report, resolutions were adopted expressing great appreciation for Widney's services to Methodism. The next week the conference organ carried an editorial which began thus:

> The *Advocate* is pained to learn that Dr. P. F. Bresee, for many years an honored member of the Southern California Annual Conference, has, with J. P. Widney, M.D., an influential lay worker in Los Angeles Methodism, decided to withdraw from our church and establish an independent organization. We deem the movement unwise. These brethren are no doubt sincere. They mean to do good. But the Methodist Episcopal Church is doing precisely the kind of work they propose in the new organization. . . . Our people will not oppose this new organization in honest efforts to save men. But we cannot admit the necessity for such divisions of the church of Jesus Christ.[28]

Dr. Bresee would only have pointed to the rapid growth of his congregation—350 members in a year, 1,500 members and a swarm of other churches in eight years—as proof that the new organization was indeed necessary.

Characteristics of the Early Nazarenes

Looking backward on the circumstances surrounding the birth of the Church of the Nazarene in the West, we can understand very well why Bresee always regarded it as a providential event. Certainly very little advance planning preceded the undertaking. Doctrines, rules of discipline, practices of worship, methods of evangelism, and even a name were formulated after the decision had been made to form a new church. For this reason the developments of the first three years are especially significant. We are fortunate indeed that E. A. Girvin, first pastor of the church in Berkeley, California, and clerk of the California Supreme Court, has preserved his and Dr. Bresee's memories of this period.

What kind of people were these earliest Nazarenes? What was their form of government and discipline, their way of worship, their framework of belief? The answers to these questions are of interest to all.

First of all, *the government of the church was thoroughly democratic.* This is surprising in view of the Methodist background of the founders. True, Bresee and Widney were named "general superintendents." But their power was more personal than legal. A church board, composed of trustees and stewards, shared full responsibility for the temporal side of the work. Numerous deaconesses, as we have seen, labored among the poor. Ministers were ordained by vote of the congregation, with the proviso only that the general superintendents must approve the ordination before it became final.

Dr. Bresee refused from the outset to allow money-raising methods which in any way distinguished those who were able to give generously. There were no pledges, no collections of tithes, no records of individual gifts. Whenever large sums were needed the pastor simply announced well in advance a day for special sacrifice. When the time for the offering came, members of the congregation marched around the altar and placed their contributions on an open Bible. Bresee urged individuals never to let others know what they gave. "This is a church of poor people," he would say, "and I want the poorest to give without being embarrassed and the richest to come without being begged." By 1903, when the permanent house of worship was constructed, Bresee was able to raise $10,300 in cash in one such offering.

The original constitution specifically recognized the right of women to preach. Mrs. W. S. Knott was the first one so ordained. Her first ministry was to the young women of "Company E," scores of whom she helped win to Christ. She and her husband also founded the Mateo Street Mission, later organized into the Compton Avenue Church.[29]

The chief aim of the church was to preach holiness to the poor. This fact is evident from every page of the literature which they published. The first stationery bore at its head the scripture verse, "Inasmuch as ye have done it unto the least of these my brethren, ye have done it unto me." Year after year the Nazarenes protested fine and expensive church buildings, "tending necessarily," as Dr. Bresee wrote on one occasion, "to drive the poor from the portals of the so-called house of the

Lord." "We don't need forts and barricades," he added; "we need a marching, conquering army." The first *Manual* announced the church's determination to win the lost "through the agency of city missions, evangelistic services, house-to-house visitation, caring for the poor, comforting the dying." The founders declared themselves convinced that their mission was "to go into the poorer parts of the cities and into neglected places and by the power of the Holy Ghost create centers of fire.[30]

In an editorial written in October, 1898, Bresee endeavored to explain the relation between social work and evangelism. Speaking of the days when the church was first organized, he wrote:

> We were convinced that houses of worship should be plain and cheap, to save from financial burdens, and that everything should say welcome to the poor. We went feeling that food and clothing and shelter were the open doors to the hearts of the unsaved poor, and that through these doors we could bear to them the life of God. We went in poverty, to give ourselves—and what God might give us—determined to forego provision for the future and old age, in order to see the salvation of God while we were yet here. God has not disappointed us. While we would be glad to do much more, yet hundreds of dollars have gone to the poor, with loving ministry of every kind, and with it a way has been opened up to the hearts of men and women, that has been unutterable joy. The gospel comes to a multitude without money and without price, and the poorest of the poor are entitled to a front seat at the Church of the Nazarene, the only condition being that they come early enough to get there.[13]

The strong stand against fine church buildings undoubtedly grew out of Bresee's experience at Simpson M.E. Church, Los Angeles. But it was reinforced by the difficulties which the Nazarenes had in securing a place of worship. The congregation moved from first one rented hall to another, in part as a result of complaints that the services were too noisy for the neighbors. Bresee prayed one day for money to build a church. But the answer he believed God gave him was, "I have given myself to you."

The pastor set out at once to lease a lot and construct a cheap building. In the spring of 1896 the congregation moved to the famous old "Board Tabernacle," located on Los Angeles Street between Fifth and Sixth. Here Bresee was to preach for the next seven years. The rough simplicity of this building combined with the obvious respectability of the pastors and key laymen to create an atmosphere in which rich and poor, high and low, came to feel wonderfully united and at home.

Evangelizing the destitute obviously did not imply wholesale denunciations of the rich. Bresee urged the well-bred ladies of his congregation not to think that "the poor woman will be chilled because your dress is better." She has more sense and keener insight, he said, than "to care so much about that fruit of the worm. It is your face she looks at, your heart she feels."³²

All of which brings us to a third aspect of the young church: *its discipline depended primarily upon the work of the Holy Spirit.* Dr. Bresee always thought that if men and women were really sanctified wholly they would of their own accord follow a narrow path. He and his people believed fully, of course, in the historic concept of a disciplined church fellowship, and in the Methodist idea of stating the standards of personal behavior which were required of all. The first Nazarene *Manual* set forth a simplified version of the "General Rules" which the *Discipline* of the Methodist churches had contained for decades. Several provisions were omitted, such as the prohibitions of usury and slaveholding. The only new rule forbade voting for the licensing of liquor establishments. The more important departure, however, was that the Nazarenes incorporated their statement into the ritual for the reception of church members, making each such ceremony a reminder to all of the vows they had taken on joining. This step no doubt dictated the effort to beautify and simplify the language of the rules. New members pledged to walk in "hearty fellowship" with the church, and not to rail against its doctrines and usages. And they promised to manifest their desire "to be saved from all sin,"

First "By avoiding evil of every kind, such as,
"(1) The taking of the name of God in vain.
"(2) The profaning of the day of the Lord, either by unnecessary ordinary labor or business, or by holiday diversions.
"(3) The use of intoxicating liquors as a beverage, or the trafficking in the same, or giving influence, or voting for the licensing of places for the sale of the same.
"(4) Quarreling, returning evil for evil—gossiping, slandering, spreading surmises injurious to the good name of others.
"(5) Dishonesty, taking advantage in buying and selling, bearing false witness, and like fruits of darkness.
"(6) The indulgence of pride in dress or living, the laying up of treasures on earth.

"Secondly, By doing that which is enjoined in the word of God.

"(1) By being courteous to all men.

"(2) By contributing to the support of the Church and its work, according to the ability which God giveth.

"(3) By observing carefully the teachings of the Word of God, which is both our rule of faith and practice.

"(4) Songs, literature, and amusements that are not to the glory of God. The avoidance of such places as the theater, the ball room, the circus and like places, lotteries and games of chance, looseness and impropriety of conduct.

"(5) By loving God with all the heart, mind, and strength, a faithful attendance upon all the ordinances of God, and the means of grace; such as the public worship of God, the ministry of the Word, the Sacraments, searching the Scriptures and meditating thereon, family and private devotions.

"(6) By seeking to do good to the bodies and souls of men. Feeding the hungry, clothing the destitute, visiting the sick and imprisoned, and ministering to the needy, as opportunity and ability are given.

"(7) By pressing upon the attention of the unsaved the claims of the Gospel, inviting them to the house of the Lord, and trying to compass their Salvation.

"(8) By being helpful to those who are of the household of faith, in love forbearing one another."[33]

In some matters, however, Bresee believed that advice and exhortation would be sufficient. Hence membership in secret orders and the use of tobacco were the subject of strict admonition, rather than specific prohibition. Dr. Bresee particularly discouraged preachers from making too much an issue of the way church women dressed. He sometimes told friends that from the day he had received the baptism of the Holy Spirit he had not mentioned that subject in the pulpit. His aim was not to make well-to-do people dress poorly, but to inspire them to love and service. Both rich and poor, he believed, must learn to worship and work and pray together in the joyous unity which Pentecost could bring. Thus in 1899 an article in the *Nazarene* on "Holiness in Relation to Adornment" warned of the sinfulness of pride in style and fashion and love of the world. But, the writer continued, "we believe every Christian should settle this question of personal adornment in harmony with the Word of God, as the Holy Spirit directs . . . , with a willing heart, and dress only to please God, as you would be found of Him at His coming." Bresee's editorial called "Broadness," in the issue for December 6, 1900, declared that "holiness looks out through eyes of faith and love, and is necessarily broad. Sectarianism, churchanity, and fanaticism are . . . likely to have shortness of vision and to be governed largely by personal interests or prejudices." An undue emphasis upon nonessentials, he warned, can ruin any church.[34]

Bresee's position in such matters often led to misunderstanding. When, in 1904, he visited Portland, Oregon, seeking a nucleus for a congregation there, people from one small holiness group attacked him for alleged compromises on the questions of adornment and secret society membership. Bresee replied that the clothes which he and his wife wore were the best defense of their stand on adornment. As for secret societies, he reported later, "I had to confess that I was a member of two societies, one in some sense a secret society, it being somewhat exclusive, and composed only of my wife and myself; but the other was open to all good people, it being the Church of the Nazarene." In commenting on the incident Bresee went on to say:

> One of the elements of fanaticism seems often to be a feeling of necessity for those thus affected to impose their own notions about social and economic things and methods on everybody, and to regard everybody as heathen who does not exactly think and do according to their shibboleth.[35]

Furthermore, *the church's creed was brief and made the doctrine of perfect love central.* The confession of faith required of all who joined read simply as follows:

We believe:
1. In one God, the Father, Son, and Holy Ghost.
2. In the inspiration of the Holy Scriptures as found in the Old and New Testaments, and that they contain all truth necessary to faith and practice.
3. That man is born with a fallen nature, and is thus by nature inclined to evil and that continually.
4. In the sure loss of the finally impenitent.
5. That the atonement through Christ is universal, and whosoever hears the word of the Lord and repents and believes on the Lord Jesus Christ is saved from the condemnation and dominion of sin. That a soul is entirely sanctified subsequent to justification through faith in the Lord Jesus Christ.
6. That the Spirit of God bears witness in the human heart to justification by faith and to the further work of the entire sanctification of believers.
7. In resurrection of the dead and life everlasting.[36]

A glance at the longer statement of doctrine which appeared later in the *Nazarene Manual* will reveal many points which this earlier confession of faith passed over without comment. This was no accident. The undogmatic tenor of Widney's teaching is evident from the sermon he preached at the organization of the church, described above. As for Bresee, the cornerstone of his doctrinal policy to the end of his days was liberality in all matters not in his view absolutely essential to salvation.

For example, Bresee welcomed to his Los Angeles pulpit preachers who stressed the premillennial view of Christ's second coming, though he did not himself accept this doctrine. W. E. Shepard, once a preacher in the Holiness church and an ardent premillennialist, preached often at the old tabernacle and wrote frequently for the *Nazarene*. Mrs. Knott was thoroughly converted to his views. Yet Dr. Bresee resisted any attempt these or other persons made to impose premillennialism upon all of the church. He was determined not to raise up a denomination in which the doctrinal statement was merely a collection of latter-day dogmas. Christian perfection, on the other hand, seemed to him the main channel in the stream of gospel truth. He intended that the Nazarenes should sail upon it.[37]

A fifth and most important characteristic of the original Los Angeles congregation was that *its worship was joyously free*. Sundays at the old tabernacle were a kind of holy holiday. Families drove in from all over the city, bringing a basket dinner and preparing to spend the day. After the morning service, usually closed with an altar call, everyone ate together. They then joined in an afternoon service of praise, often conducted like a camp meeting love feast. Visitation among the poor nearby and a street meeting occupied the hour before the evening service. When the church building was erected in 1903, provision was made for Sunday dinners to be served in the basement downstairs. Occasionally meals were prepared while Dr. Bresee preached in the auditorium above. Many a hungry boy, we may be sure, had difficulty keeping his mind on the sermon. More important, many a needy family, hungry for something better than bread, found a sense of belonging in the fellowship that came at noon.

Nearly every public holiday likewise became a momentous occasion. The "Christmas Love Feast," which Dr. Bresee had conducted in Pasadena or Los Angeles Methodist churches for many years, became a Nazarene institution. Likewise New Year's, Memorial Day, and the Fourth of July were spent in spiritual celebration.

Dr. Bresee early began to make the Sunday school picnics a high point of the year. The church board would often charter a special train and carry several hundred members to Long Beach. After a morning spent in recreation, the crowd would gather under the pavilion for dinner. The meal was followed by testimonies, songs, and preaching by Dr. Bresee. Nearly every year seekers would crowd the makeshift mourners' bench before time to take the train back home.

Little wonder that an early news leaflet distributed by the church noted happily that "the voice of prayers and hallelujahs trembling on the lips" and "the shouts of those who conquer" were frequent at the Church of the Nazarene. "Evangelical faith brings Pentecostal glory," the leaflet continued.

> The presence of the Lord is often so manifest as we are gathered together, that not only do our hearts burn within us, but our tongues are tuned to praise, and triumphant hallelujahs fill the house—to Jesus be all the glory.[38]

Producing this powerful sense of God's presence, or "getting the glory down," as Dr. Bresee put it, was in his eyes the most important aim of every service. Though he instructed I. G. Martin and other musicians who assisted him to keep off the platform any singers who would "make a show," Bresee knew that simple choruses and popular hymns helped to create a sense of emotional expectancy. Since he himself could not carry a tune, he fell into the habit of clapping his hands slowly while the people sang. The audiences soon picked up the custom of clapping through the chorus of nearly every song. Far from halting such direct and simple expressions of feeling, the pastor encouraged them. After all, he was building a church for plain people.

But "getting the glory down" was not simply a matter of working up emotions. God's presence could be real, he believed, only when it stemmed from the declaration of the great promises of the gospel. Dr. Bresee's preaching illustrates this fact well. He was one of the first men of his generation to use consistently the conversational style of pulpit delivery. Looking directly at his audience, he talked as though he were speaking to each person alone. Every paragraph, nearly every sentence, was packed with truth which spoke to the deepest needs of men. Such preaching could not but set in motion strong currents of feeling. The good doctor would often have to restrain the "amens" and "hallelujahs" so as to be able to complete his message. Toward the end of each sermon, however, he would tie together his thoughts with a succession of such powerful sentences as would nearly lift the people out of their seats. Then the walls of old First Church would echo with the people's joy.

This, to Dr. Bresee, was indispensable. The glory of the Lord must fill His house. But that glory was a revelation of the good news which was the gospel—of the truth which answered to the hungers and hopes of all mankind.

Other aspects of Bresee's conduct of the pastorate helped to keep the tide of feeling running high. For example, he rarely preached more than once on any Sabbath. Most Sunday evenings the platform was occupied by one of a dozen or so special speakers who were his favorites. Evangelists from the East and officials from various other holiness churches were always welcome. Revivals were called "Home Camp Meetings." Special Sundays like Easter and Pentecost were high points of the year.

Dr. Bresee had a natural instinct for publicity. In May of 1900, Rev. Augustus B. Pritchard was ousted from the pastorate of the First Presbyterian Church, Los Angeles, because of his earnest preaching upon "the work and power of the Holy Ghost." Bresee at once arranged for him to preach at the tabernacle the following Sunday, and the people turned out in droves. This seemed far more profitable to him than doctrinal hairsplitting.

Some of the pastor's personal peculiarities became important symbols. For example, he used never to go to the rear to bid people good-by at the close of a service. He claimed that he was so ashamed of his poor preaching that he could not face them. Actually, this plan left him free to speak at length with those who came forward with real problems. But before each service Bresee would stand at the door and welcome every worshiper. If a man came in poor clothing and with obvious embarrassment, the pastor would put his arm around him and usher him to the best seat in the house. Whenever he greeted anyone, at whatever time of day, Bresee said, "Good morning." It was always morning for the Christians, he said, for their eyes were fixed on heaven. He refused ever to back up a buggy. In this world and the next he was interested only in going forward. Although he often carried money with him as he started out on his pastoral calls, he never brought any back. He could not turn away men who really needed help.[39]

The growing frequency of services of great emotional power at the tabernacle became at last too much for J. P. Widney; he decided to return to the Methodist church late in 1898. There is no evidence at all of any hard feelings between Bresee and Widney. Their parting was most friendly. It happened that one night, after a great "outpouring of the Spirit," some of the most prominent members of the church went to the altar. Several were overcome completely, and a good deal of noise and confusion resulted. Widney, a quiet-mannered man, decided that he could not be happy any longer amidst such scenes. In October, 1898, delegates from the various churches voted to accept the resignation of the two general superintendents from their lifetime tenure, and to limit the term of office to one year. Widney dropped out, and Bresee became the sole superintendent.[40]

The infant denomination which Widney left, however, was soon to grow by leaps and bounds. Bresee's congregation became every year more a church and less a mission. In a summary statement published in the first regular issue of the *Nazarene,* in January, 1898, Dr. Bresee wrote:

> It is now somewhat more than two years since, under a peculiar yet unmistakable call of God, the Nazarenes, putting the old things behind them, went out to follow in the footsteps of Him whose name they bear—to bring comfort to the sorrowing, help to the downcast, a message of help to the brokenhearted, and to carry the gospel of peace to lives burdened with sin. They went out as a feeble band to a new and untried field of labor, taking as their especial work the neglected quarters of our city—yet soon finding that there are hungry hearts and neglected lives in homes that the world does not call poor, and so the work has broadened out beyond the field originally selected, until now they feel that the call is to go wherever lives are burdened with sin and hearts are crying out, "What shall I do to be saved?" Surely the seal of Divine approval has been upon the work. From the first day in that hall upon Main Street, a revival fire has kept burning that has spread and broadened, until now the Nazarenes are organized, and have their places of worship, on Los Angeles Street in Elysian Heights; in East Los Angeles; in South Pasadena; and in Berkeley at Oakland. Only the lack of available leaders has delayed the opening of the work at other points from which a call has come.[41]

We must turn now to the story of the expansion of the movement in the ten years between 1897 and 1907—north along the coast, and east across the Rocky Mountains, into the plains and prairie cities of the American Middle West.

CHAPTER VI

The Nazarenes Become a National Church

If one scans a dozen issues of Dr. Bresee's weekly paper, the *Nazarene Messenger,* for 1900, and then picks up a sheaf of those published in 1905, he will quickly realize what large changes these five years made in the young denomination. The directory for the latter year listed twenty-six organized congregations: four in Los Angeles, six elsewhere in southern California, three in the northern part of the state, five in Washington and Idaho, three in scattered areas across the plains states, and five in Illinois.

More important than numbers is the fact that the key congregations were located in cities: Los Angeles, Oakland, Berkeley, Seattle, Spokane, Boise, Salt Lake, Omaha, and Chicago. The tenth assembly, held in Los Angeles in October, 1905, reported 3,195 members in all, of which the Los Angeles congregation alone accounted for over 1,500. By that time also, a remarkable group of pastors and evangelists had cast their lot with Bresee and the Church of the Nazarene. Among them were L. B. Kent and Isaiah Reid, patriarchs of the holiness movement in Illinois and Iowa; J. B. Creighton, formerly prominent in the Church of God (Holiness); C. V. LaFontaine, who had been pastor of the First Methodist Church in South Chicago before becoming Bresee's assistant in Los Angeles; C. W. Ruth, a young evangelist from the Holiness Christian church; C. E. Cornell, Friends lay evangelist from Cleveland, who was now pastor of the First Church of the Nazarene in Chicago; and W. C. Wilson, formerly a Methodist evangelist in Kentucky but one day to be a Nazarene general superintendent.[1]

These five years, and especially the crucial one of 1903, were the happiest in Phineas Bresee's long life. One Friday night in early spring, 1903, Bresee and Evangelist Cornell led the Los Angeles congregation in a "hallelujah march" to their new brick church on Wall Street. The new "tabernacle," as it was still called, was large enough to accommodate great conventions, yet simple enough for the poor to feel at home. A week later the congregation laid $10,300 in cash on the altar to help pay the bills. In April, Charles J. Fowler, president of the National Holiness Association, came with "Bud" Robinson and Will Huff to conduct a two-weeks convention. The spiritual tide of these meetings swept away what remained of the mistrust which the national association had earlier fostered against Bresee's work. The growing fame of the Los Angeles congregation had in fact combined with a new crisis over the "church question" in the holiness movement to thrust upon Bresee the responsibility for the building of a national denomination.[2]

Bresee had not been anxious to be the founder of a new denomination. He had left his Methodist connections principally to preach holiness to the poor. The organization of the Church of the Nazarene had been a means to that end. He had avoided every kind of ecclesiastical machinery which was not necessary to the spiritual life of his people, and had for many years ignored or neglected calls to add a far-flung chain of congregations to his following. But heroic challenges and bold ventures had always attracted him. Bresee moved, therefore, naturally and with vigor into his new role.

Looking backward across these years, we wonder what happened to the inner life of the Nazarenes as their movement expanded. What new institutions emerged to serve their larger needs? By whose toil and prayers were the first organizations established in the cities of the Rocky Mountain region? And how did the denomination first gain a foothold in the Midwest, the heartland of American Methodism? The answers to these questions comprise a story of absorbing interest.

The Dawn of the Idea of a National Holiness Church

As early as July, 1899, one of Bresee's pastors declared in the *Nazarene Messenger* that the holiness movement in America had reached its zenith under the "iron-clad government" of the popular churches; now, he wrote, "something must be done to conserve the fruit of years of labor." Bresee came to the same conclusion the next month, when he returned after an absence of four years to preach at the Illinois "state camp meeting" at Springfield. He found the influence of this gathering pitifully diminished. The leading ministers of the city no longer attended, and an interdenominational association had become necessary to protect the freedom of the sponsors. "The great sad question" that pressed upon his mind was, "Who shall care for those who have been converted, feed them and lead them on?"³

The aging L. B. Kent, long-time leader of the holiness Methodists in Illinois, visited Bresee in California the following winter. Soon after, Kent wrote the *Christian Witness* that the Los Angeles congregation might be God's pattern for the future of the holiness movement. Bresee welcomed the ensuing discussion, declaring that the policy of loyalty to the older churches was bankrupt. Though he carefully rejected the "come-outism" which the editors of the *Witness* had been at pains to denounce, Bresee pointed out that "the desire to please a church that is not pleased with holiness comes very near being willing to be the friend of the world."⁴

The sharpened tones in which Bresee thereafter attacked Methodist compromises on the issues of holiness and prohibitionism helped to dramatize his new convictions. He bluntly rebuked the northern bishops for suggesting that the witness of the Spirit, rather than entire sanctification, was the central doctrine of Wesleyanism. He heaped scorn on Bishop John H. Vincent's conduct of a revival in Trinity Church, Denver—a "revival" in which the good bishop invited no seekers to the altar, stressed cultivation more than conversion, and denied the reality of heaven and hell. When a friend reproached Bresee for speaking thus of his "mother," Methodism, the Los Angeles pastor retorted publicly that Wesley's church was "not an old lady to be coddled in the corner, and protected from public gaze." She had in fact failed of her mission and become "a dangerous place for the souls of men and women."

Bresee's language was sharp and effective. He was plainly, and by design, destroying all his lifelong ties with Methodism. He pointed to the history of the church's attitude toward the Salvation Army, the Keswick movement, and the holiness associations as proof that "Methodism puts its hand . . . to destroy the work of holiness" wherever it found opportunity. Unless it should speedily reverse its course, friends of that doctrine must find shelter elsewhere. "Life is too short and the interests at stake are too vital," he said, "to deal with these things in any uncertain way."⁵

At about the same time Dr. Bresee converted his congregation into a prohibition church. The head of the state party, Dr. Stephen Bowers, became a member in 1900. Soon after,

Bowers told a questioner in the *California Voice* that there was no need to organize in Los Angeles a denomination dedicated to fighting the liquor traffic, for one was already established there. "The Church of the Nazarene . . . is emphatically a prohibition church," he declared; "holiness and prohibition are two of its leading tenets." Occasionally Bresee turned his Sunday evening service into a prohibition rally, with a heavily advertised special speaker. At the close of such meetings, in place of the altar call, the pastor would give a rousing exhortation and ask every man present to stand to his feet and take the pledge to fight the liquor business to the death.[6]

In Los Angeles County this issue was a hot one. Southern California was a key center of the national prohibition crusade in the years between 1895 and 1910. While cities in the eastern half of the United States were filling up with Catholic immigrants from southeastern Europe, those of the Far West were welcoming newcomers from the small towns and prairie farms of the Midwest. The latter group were Protestant, evangelical, and thoroughly temperance-minded. They were also deeply disillusioned with both major political parties—an aftermath in part of the failure of William Jennings Bryan's unsuccessful campaign for the presidency in 1896. Since in California both Republican and Democratic organizations opposed the "dry" position in local option campaigns, large numbers turned to the Prohibition party. These were the very people whom Bresee was seeking to win.

When, therefore, the Methodist General Conference of 1900 failed to denounce President McKinley for refusing to discontinue the sale of liquor in army canteens, Bresee explained the matter thus: "The present administration is not only Republican but the president is a Methodist, a man who has been highly honored by the church. He has proved himself to be a most intent and active friend of the liquor traffic, both as a public official and a private citizen." A few weeks later Bresee wrote:

> The *Nazarene Messenger* is not a political paper. It goes deeper than all politics, and seeks the salvation of man from sin. Its banner . . . is *Holiness through the blood of the Lamb;* but this fact makes it the enemy of the saloon and the earnest advocate of the destruction of the liquor traffic. It seems clear that the Church in America can never go on to victory until this gigantic enemy of all good is slain.[7]

In vain did the Methodists in California respond to these charges. A renewed emphasis upon the doctrine of holiness during 1901 in their newspaper, the *California Christian Advocate*, did not silence Bresee. The *Advocate* reported the "Pentecostal Camp-meeting" at Beulah Park, California, so fully that an officer of the camp felt it necessary to ask the editor to explain to his readers that the "California Pentecostal Association" was an interdenominational group, not simply a Methodist one.[8] Bresee knew, however, that Methodist leaders outside of California, even more than in that state, were moving away from Wesley's doctrine. He reviewed for the readers of his paper a Boston University professor's recent explanation of the way in which the denomination had rejected the founder's belief in entire sanctification. He recounted fully the refusal of the bishops to intervene when a Pennsylvania conference tried and expelled the prohibitionist editor of the *Pennsylvania Methodist*. And he deplored the agitation of influential Chicago Methodists for removal from the Methodist *Discipline* of rules against dancing, card playing, and theatergoing. "There is scarcely a connectional Methodist paper," Bresee wrote in 1903, "that clearly teaches and insists on the second definite work of grace whereby converted people are sanctified holy."[9]

Thus the need to shelter the converts won by the holiness movement combined with what Bresee believed were the compromises of Methodism to influence him to refashion the Church of the Nazarene into a national denomination. Another factor was the outbreak of a new wave of fanaticism in the holiness ranks which, by contrast with that in the 1880's, appealed chiefly to the urban poor.

The General Holiness Assembly, held at the First Methodist Church, Chicago, in May, 1901, helped to highlight all these factors. It convinced many others besides Bresee that the day for a national church organization had come. Leading members of practically all wings of the holiness movement were present. Six Methodist bishops and one each from the Free Methodist, African Methodist Episcopal, and United Brethren churches gave their names in endorsement of the meeting, along with leading editors, college presidents, and mission workers in the holiness movement. C. J. Fowler served as chairman. Yet this body, clearly dominated by men who had previously advocated loyalty to the older churches, wound up giving firm support to those who, in various parts of the country, had found it necessary to organize independent churches.

The "General Address" of the Chicago assembly declared that "wherever practical, every saved man and woman should be connected with some church. . . . Professors of holiness are not excusable in voluntarily surrendering their church privileges for trivial causes." However, the address continued,

> if oppressive hands be laid upon them in any case by church authority, solely for professing holiness, or for being identified with the work of holiness, depriving them of the privileges of Christian communion or public testimony and service, they should then, in whatever way seems best, adjust themselves to circumstances. . . . Our advice to such would be in all cases to seek affiliation as Christian people who believe in and are committed to holiness.

Interestingly enough, three of the seven authors of this pronouncement—A. M. Hills, a Congregationalist; E. F. Walker, a Presbyterian; and L. B. Kent, a Methodist—eventually became Nazarenes. One of the remaining four was W. E. Shepard, Dr. Bresee's representative, who had come to Chicago with deep misgivings but at last rejoiced in the convention's work.[10]

For those who had not yet broken with their churches the assembly endorsed the organization of local "bands." It directed these groups to accept a uniform constitution and statement of doctrine, however, and urged them to affiliate with county and state holiness associations. The bands were declared to be "in no sense churches" but simply organizations for Christian purposes similar to the Y.M.C.A., the W.C.T.U., and the missionary unions. Such groups were nonetheless in the twilight zone between loyalty to the older denominations and formation of the new. They required doctrinal leadership and discipline in all aspects of the Christian gospel, not simply sanctification.

For years the National Holiness Association had forbidden the discussion of "divisive" themes like divine healing or the Second Coming, on its camp meeting platforms or in the columns of the *Christian Witness*. The only result had been the emergence of fanatical extremes in the preaching of both doctrines, and even greater divisions over them. The Chicago assembly, however, spelled out forthrightly the belief of its members "in the personal return of the Lord Jesus Christ for the final redemption of his saints" and in the doctrine "that the sick may be healed through the prayer of faith." As Isaiah Reid noted during the sessions, earlier national assemblies—at Jacksonville in 1880, and Chicago in 1886—took place in an atmosphere of confidence that the older churches would soon come back to the way of holiness.

In those meetings, therefore, the main stress was upon the clarification of the doctrine of perfect love. "No one in those assemblies had any thought of advocating the addition of any other issues to the holiness movement," he declared. "No one felt called to preach on the second-coming or to call an altar service for bodily healing. Doubtless there was not a soul there who did not believe in both, but not one considered these doctrines any more a part of the holiness work than the matter of water baptism or the creation of the world." Now, however, such declarations were needful, both to guide the faithful and to restrain the radical.[11]

But the radical party was not easily bridled. Seth C. Rees, John Norberry, Duke Farson, and J. T. Hatfield, the last-named fresh from a series of revivals in Bresee's churches, conducted services which competed with the Chicago assembly, in the chapel of the same building, the First Methodist Church. They first refused to unite with the larger body on the grounds that the Second Coming and divine healing were to be excluded subjects and that the leaders seemed determined "to pet up the existing denominations." Even after the assembly had adopted its statement of belief in the disputed doctrines, however, the radicals rejected a renewed invitation to join forces.

Soon after, Farson and E. L. Harvey organized the Metropolitan Church Association, with headquarters in Chicago. W. E. Shepard, who had served previously as Dr. Bresee's assistant pastor, eventually joined the Metropolitan church. So, for a time, did F. M. Messenger, a mill superintendent from Connecticut who had sponsored revivals which disrupted the peace of the Association of Pentecostal Churches in New England, and Arthur Ingler, a gospel singer associated with the latter group. The Metropolitan leaders seemed to glory in the kind of emotional demonstrations which brought unfavorable notice from the police and the newspapers. They waged a bitter warfare upon the more conservative holiness workers, both in their pulpits and in their magazine, the *Burning Bush*. They publicly denounced members of the associations who belonged to secret orders, insisted that all divorce and remarriage was sinful, and rejected labor unions as the work of the devil. In 1905 they read Mrs. Alma White, of Denver, out of their fellowship, on the divorce issue. She thereupon organized the Pillar of Fire church, gathering in many of the parent group's followers in the Colorado foothill towns.[12]

Here, then, was an urban radicalism springing out of the holiness movement which was quite as bitterly opposed to the churchly objectives of the "loyalist" party as the rural extremists of an earlier period had been. Its leaders felt no restraint about organizing a national denomination. Small wonder that many conservatives called for tighter discipline of bands and associations and took a second look at the idea of forming a national holiness church. Inevitably, such men gravitated toward Bresee and the Nazarenes.

One of the young evangelists present at the Chicago assembly was C. W. Ruth, of Indianapolis, Indiana. He was a member of the very small Holiness Christian denomination, centered in eastern Pennsylvania. Someone recommended Ruth to Dr. Bresee, and the latter invited him to Los Angeles for the "home camp meeting" in October, 1901. The congregation liked Ruth so well that Bresee decided to recommend his election as assistant general superintendent in the assembly which followed. Bresee intended for the younger man to assume a large part of the care of the Los Angeles congregation, so as to give the founder time to attend to wider challenges. Their actual roles, however, turned out to be the opposite. In January, 1902, Ruth went to Spokane, Washington, and organized the People's Mission into a Church of the Nazarene. He returned by way of Berkeley for special meetings, and in the spring answered a call to conduct a camp meeting and organize a church in Illinois. The following August, Bresee announced that Ruth would be engaged for another year in order to help answer the calls from independent bands springing up all over the country. These calls, Bresee said, were proof that there was "no measuring the possibilities that are before this new movement."

Perhaps no man saw these possibilities more clearly than did C. W. Ruth, and none was better suited to take advantage of them. He was conservative by temperament. Skilled in the common-sense exposition of Bible passages on holiness, he showed almost no interest in other themes, particularly "divisive" ones. To Ruth, the policy of unity in essentials and charity in all else was vital to the task of unifying the holiness movement; and he set himself to this task. By March, 1903, he felt so strongly "the divine impulse to push the work in other places" that he asked for a two-months leave of absence, later extended indefinitely. "He is now to continue as assistant general superintendent," Bresee announced, "giving his time largely to what might be termed evangelistic work, organizing the work of the Church of the Nazarene in such places as it shall seem providential to do so."[13]

Thus by April, 1903, when Fowler, Robinson, and Huff arrived for their convention in the new house of worship, the basic decisions were already made. Although Fowler and many of his associates did not join Bresee's church, they made it plain that they would encourage its growth just as they had that of the Association of Pentecostal Churches in New England.

The next month C. W. Ruth set out on his first long evangelistic tour of the East, serving as an advance scout for the Church of the Nazarene. He organized a church in Salt Lake City, and with Bresee's consent appointed I. G. Martin as its pastor. He helped gain a foothold in Chicago through a sweeping revival at the Methodist church in North Harvey, Illinois. He then proceeded to Danville for the annual camp meeting of the Eastern Illinois Holiness Association. Here he worked with the future General Superintendent E. F. Walker, and with the laymen who were later to found Olivet Nazarene College. Even more important, Ruth established contact at two Pennsylvania camp meetings with his old friends in the Holiness Christian connection and with the company of vigorous young men who had welded the Association of Pentecostal Churches into a thriving New England denomination. From Allentown, he wrote Dr. Bresee that William Howard Hoople, H. F. Reynolds, and C. Howard Davis led a "plain, fire-baptized, Holy Ghost people" who conducted "about the noisiest and 'shoutinest' " camp meeting he had ever attended.[14]

Bresee spent that summer at home with his Los Angeles congregation. His sermons and editorials during these months expressed clearly the vision which was to dominate the rest of his life. Let the Nazarenes establish "centers of holy fire" in all the great cities of the nation. Let them actively recruit both ministers and key laymen from those who were losing heart in the crusade to bring back the older churches to the faith of the fathers. Let them extend the largest possible fellowship to every congregation and association of holiness people. Let them stand foursquare against fanaticism, legalism, and sectarianism, even while seeking out and evangelizing the poor. And the glory and glow of their work would attract young men, strong and true, who would help build holiness churches in every corner of the land.[15]

By November, 1903, Bresee could report to the annual assembly that new churches had been added at Maples Mill and Pekin, Illinois; Omaha, Nebraska; Boise, Idaho; and Salt Lake City, Utah—all of them coming at their own request. "We have never sought to push this work as an ecclesiasticism," he said.

> Our lack of funds—going forth as we have more especially to the poor people—has been such as to preclude our entering many doors which otherwise would have been open to us. . . . Nevertheless, we have joyfully entered such doors as have been clearly opened . . . , using such agencies as in the providence of God have been by Him raised up. . . . I am impressed that God wants us to occupy, to strongly occupy, the great centers.

A light would soon be kindled in these centers, Bresee believed, which would shine out into towns, villages, and countryside and quicken the spiritual life of the whole nation.[16]

Thus it was that in his sixty-fifth year Phineas Bresee undertook a task which would have staggered other men half his age. He had no illusions that it would be easy. The previous twenty years had seen the holiness movement hammered into splinters, twisted by the strength of the opposition without and the force of fanaticism within until her most optimistic leaders were tempted to despair. But this preacher had been tested in many trials, and despair was not in the vocabulary of his soul. "The sun never sets in the morning," he said. However late the hour of the day, he greeted all comers with the words, "Good morning." A Christian, he declared, cannot be a pessimist.

The Growth of the Church in California

The story of the early expansion of the Nazarene movement in California illustrates the most important element in Dr. Bresee's method of leadership: he was so democratic that he often seemed to follow rather than lead the people. He never assumed responsibility for any venture until he was certain of full support, certain that the "providential" time had come. Nearly every new mission or church and every major institutional development except the newspaper owed its beginning to someone other than Bresee. The Los Angeles laymen even had to take the lead in the movement to construct their new church building. For seven years they had met in the old board tabernacle, on land they did not own. The explanation is simple: Bresee feared high-pressure financial schemes and the people were engrossed in mission work.

The interest of both pastor and people in evangelizing the poor of their own community also explains why they often passed by opportunities to establish churches elsewhere. In the winter of 1900-1901, for example, John T. Hatfield, known as "The Hoosier Evangelist," spent three months working with the various churches and missions. His revival campaign in Pasadena inspired the formation of a "band" which met regularly thereafter in the G.A.R. hall. Not until 1905, however, did Bresee organize the Pasadena church. J. W. Goodwin, recently from New England and an ordained minister in the Advent Christian denomination, became their first pastor. Elsewhere, S. S. Chafe organized congregations at Cucamonga and Upland, at the foot of the mountains in east Los Angeles County, while the youthful A. O. Hendricks pioneered the work at nearby Ontario. In 1903, W. C. Wilson, a Methodist evangelist from Kentucky who had been disciplined for holding meetings for the Baptists, joined the Nazarenes. He moved to the West Coast the next year and conducted a month-long tent revival at Long Beach, out of which came the Nazarene church there. Wilson stayed on as pastor for a time, then moved to Upland.[17]

The first congregation in the San Francisco Bay area, at Berkeley, had been organized much earlier. Ernest A. Girvin, "phonographic reporter" for the State Supreme Court, was chiefly responsible. He professed sanctification in 1888, joined the Trinity Methodist Church, received a local preacher's license, and became teacher of a Bible class. Court duties often took Girvin to Los Angeles, where he began attending Bresee's services, first at Peniel Hall and then at the Nazarene tabernacle. He persuaded Dr. Bresee to go to Berkeley for a ten-day meeting in 1897. At its close Bresee organized a church and appointed Girvin pastor. The congregation worshiped for a time in rented halls. Girvin himself donated the lot on which a permanent building was later erected.[18]

For seven years Dr. Bresee made little effort to expand this northern California beachhead. Late in the fall of 1904, a year after the idea of a national church had crystallized, Robert Pierce, who had recently brought his group at Boise, Idaho, into the denomination, came to Oakland and began gathering a substantial nucleus of converts. Bresee conducted a tent meeting there the following July, by which time the Oakland membership had reached forty-three. The general superintendent also arranged to rent a building on city hall square, San Francisco, where services began the same summer. Meanwhile P. G. Linaweaver, who had joined the denomination at the new church in Chicago, accepted Bresee's appointment as Girvin's associate pastor in Berkeley. Linaweaver was a most capable and aggressive man and was expected to lead that tiny congregation out of the doldrums; but larger plans loomed. Bresee set apart northern California as a "missionary district" and appointed Linaweaver its superintendent just prior to the General Assembly of 1905.[19]

Both the mother congregation at Los Angeles and the new organizations elsewhere developed during these years a program of activities which gave substance to the notion that the poor should have a church and not just a mission. Religious rituals grew up which enshrined rather than restrained emotional freedom. Sunday school and youth programs flourished. A weekly newspaper gained in popularity and usefulness, the Pacific Bible College began regular sessions, and an enlightened program of social work continued full blast. In all these developments, laymen played key roles.

Evangelism remained the central Nazarene concern, of course. The emotional fervor which from the first had attracted the poor was characteristic of every service. One observer noted that Bresee allowed his "happy congregation" an "unrestrained freedom." The people, he said, "laugh, clap their hands, shout 'amen' or 'hallelujah', [and] walk to and fro." He had seen "a colored sister execute in her joy the most beautiful dance we ever beheld." It was not thought disorderly "to 'demonstrate' in a natural way the gladness of the heart in the Nazarene Church." A local newspaper commented on the "jubilee services" of 1908 as follows:

> It is no secret in Los Angeles that the Church of the Nazarene has in times past provoked much comment. . . . By many Methodists, of which denomination Dr. Bresee was a former presiding elder, the "new sect" was regarded as too free in religious expression. Dr. Bresee told his parishioners yesterday: "We glory in the spirit

of religious freedom." . . . The meetings all day were joyous in the extreme. . . . Dr. Bresee, amid his faithful followers, sang, taught, exhorted, waved his song book, shouted for joy, and showered blessings right and left. There were great choruses of "Amen!"[20]

Nevertheless the new denomination gave surprising attention to rituals and sacraments. The first church *Manual*, published in 1898, devoted nine of its forty-six pages to stated ceremonies, including the reception of members, baptism, the Lord's Supper, matrimony, and the burial of the dead. Later editions increased this proportion. Dr. Bresee conducted baptismal services regularly, using whichever mode the candidate desired. The Lord's Supper came once a month, on Sunday afternoon. It alternated at biweekly intervals with the monthly love feast, which combined the freedom of camp meeting testimonies with the old Methodist rite of breaking bread. Sabbath afternoon thus became a high moment in the spiritual life of the congregation. Seekers often bowed at the altar at the close of both the love feast and Communion services. In such an atmosphere, emotions ran deep and powerful, and commitments were strong.[21]

The Nazarenes also gave careful attention to religious education and organized youth work. The reader will remember that, while at Peniel Hall, Bresee had been willing to risk serious controversy in order to carry on the youth program he believed necessary. He established a Sunday school the day the Church of the Nazarene was organized, and faithfully promoted its work across the years. The record of succeeding annual assemblies shows how large was the heritage from Methodist Sabbath school traditions. Reports of attendance and of conversions resembled those in the parent denomination. The school had the usual group of officers, including especially an active librarian. The *Nazarene Messenger* carried a weekly children's column, which spiced up expositions of the Sunday school lesson with testimonies of youthful religious experiences from the youngsters themselves. Plans for the new church building constructed in 1902-3 called for "large rooms for young men and young women" to be used as needed "for social meetings," as well as for a "comprehensive and complete" Sabbath school department.

Two young people's societies, Company E for girls and the Brotherhood of St. Stephen for boys, early became a vital part of the life of the church. Each was the handiwork of enthusiastic laymen. Their activities were intensely evangelistic, of course, whether coming under the heading of "social" or "spiritual." C. W. Ruth wrote in 1903 that the Nazarenes in Los Angeles, with over two hundred active young people in the membership, had proved that entertainments, festivals, and church frolics were not necessary to hold the young. The group there, he declared, "ask no better entertainment than a good live prayer-meeting . . . and a happier lot of young people cannot be found anywhere." On the other hand, contemporary accounts of the annual Sunday school picnic show that the church was not afraid for its young people to enjoy themselves. Usually the congregation chartered a special train and went for a day to Long Beach or Playa del Rey. At the latter place in 1904, over 1,000 were present. "Boating, bathing and a good picnic did good service to the outer man," the account ran, "while a genuine Nazarene service refreshed the spirits of all. At 2:30 P. M. the pastor called all together in the large tent and after singing, prayers, and many spiritual testimonies an altar call was given for seekers and three young ladies responded. . . . This is the real way of having a picnic, as is customary with the Nazarenes."[22]

As churches came into existence up and down the Pacific Coast, complete Sunday school organizations and new units of Company E and the Brotherhood appeared. Mrs. Lucy P. Knott, who was chiefly responsible for Company E, became pastor of the Mateo Street Mission, later a church, in Los Angeles, and kept a live-wire company going there. The annual assemblies gave enthusiastic support to the youth work. The one held in 1904 urged that young people be given responsible positions on the official boards of the church and that they assume full responsibility not only for their own meetings but occasionally for the regular church services as well. Nazarene young people, the assembly declared, must have something more than worldliness on one hand or formal religion on the other. The assembly of the next year repeated these recommendations, only cautioning that young people's societies "inaugurate no movement contrary to the judgment of the church or without consent of the pastor in charge."[23]

Both pastor and people continued to take seriously during these years their obligations to minister to social needs. Dr. Bresee was president of the board of the Florence Home, Los Angeles branch of the Crittenton chain, which ministered to unwed mothers. His son, Paul, was an attending physician there, and First Church laymen provided continuous support. The Brotherhood of St. Stephen operated an employment bureau for a time. A laywoman, Mrs. A. F. McReynolds, promoted Nazarene missions and schools among Spanish-speaking Indians and Mexicans, in both the city and the county of Los Angeles. Other lay persons sponsored missions in Chinese and Japanese communities. The outburst of anti-Oriental feeling on the West Coast seems not to have affected the Nazarenes at all. By 1912 the Japanese mission church at Upland, California, under Miss Ethel McPherson, was practically self-supporting, and a Japanese member of the Oakland congregation conducted a school for thirty children of his nationality. When the San Francisco earthquake of 1906 sent refugees pouring into Los Angeles, Dr. Bresee called a special meeting of the official board and set up a temporary shelter in the church. The Sunday school rooms and the church basement were cleaned, stocked with food, and equipped with bedding and furniture to meet their needs.[24]

On the crucial subject of labor's rights, however, Bresee shared the conservative views typical among Wesleyan clergymen of the period. "In the conflict—where there is a real conflict—between capital and labor," he wrote in 1902, "Christian thought is naturally on the side of the laborer." Nevertheless he believed that strikes deprived employers of their right to hire whom they pleased, and laborers of their right to work. Bresee's solution of the labor problem was universal submission to the golden rule. Moreover, he doubted that the moral influence of good men, which Charles M. Sheldon stressed in his famous book *In His Steps,* could take the place of entire sanctification in enabling people to live up to that rule. Only a revival of personal holiness would protect America from social upheaval, the *Christian Witness* declared. "A holy Christianity, saving men from selfishness, greed and all sin, is the need of the hour." Bresee agreed with this sentiment fully.[25]

The growth of the church also brought changes in the *Nazarene Messenger.* Dr. Bresee began publishing this paper as a monthly in July, 1896, with the help of lay volunteers. Mrs. L. L. Ernest, who served as office manager, lived in the Bresee home. The *Messenger* became a twelve-page monthly in 1898 and the next year appeared as a weekly. Early in 1900, $5,000 in capital stock was issued for the Nazarene Publishing Company, with the church holding a majority interest. The usefulness of the paper in education and discipline, as well as in the task of unifying and directing the organization, was immeasurable. Its columns provided young people with specific instructions upon the harmfulness of "worldly indulgences" such as tobacco, card playing, and "French" dancing, and tutored new converts carefully in the doctrine of Christian perfection. The paper kept an increasingly widespread membership fully informed of events at First Church. Naturally, evangelists in different parts of the country began to read it regularly and to report their own revival campaigns through its columns. Joseph Jamison, W. E. Shepard, Herbert and Lillie Buffum, and many others of these soon united with the church. Thus again, a device Dr. Bresee had intended as a means of helping his own people became a factor in preparing them for wider leadership.

Beginning in July, 1901, the *Nazarene Messenger* employed a layout obviously intended to appeal to a national audience. Two full pages carried news and quotations from other holiness papers across the country, and two were devoted to reports from Nazarene evangelists and pastors in distant cities. An entire page of editorials gave Dr. Bresee a chance to comment on both local and national issues. After August 8, 1901, a complete summary of the pastor's sermon the previous Sunday provided holiness people everywhere with an introduction to the vision and the spirit of this good man. The effort to unite the movement in a national church would have failed without the help of this and other weekly papers published in various sections of the country. That the Los Angeles congregation understood this fact well is evident from the large cash offerings they gave to keep their paper alive in days when they were straining every resource to construct their new church building.[26]

In the founding of the Pacific Bible School, parent institution to Pasadena College, laymen again led the way, persuading a reluctant Bresee to support the venture. Interestingly enough, the leaders were women, as had been true also in the missionary, youth, and publishing work.

Some time prior to 1901, Mrs. A. L. Seymour, Miss Leora Maris, and Mrs. Herbert Johnson felt themselves called to organize a training school for Christian workers in Los Angeles. They were not at the time members of Dr. Bresee's church. Early in 1902, however, they united with the Nazarenes and laid their plans before the founder. Bresee consented rather grudgingly to the venture, but promised little or no assistance. Undismayed, Mrs. Seymour and Mrs. Johnson prevailed upon their husbands to give approximately $4,000 to cover a major portion of the cost of an elegant old house and several lots at 28th and San Pedro streets. Despite the heavy burdens of their own building program, the First Church congregation assumed the remaining debt of $3,000. Mary A. Hill, a missionary to China, appeared in time to be appointed principal. She persuaded a group of the most pious and cultured members of the congregation to serve as a faculty and announced a half dozen courses for the fall.

The announcement stressed that the school was to be distinctly a *Bible* college. Since Dr. Bresee had flatly rejected the idea of having it named for him, they called it the Pacific Bible College, and declared that it was not to be sectarian but "in the broad sense Christian, being under the control of the Church of the Nazarene." Forty-two students from seven states and ten religious denominations registered the first year. Religious enthusiasm ran high—so high, in fact, that Miss Hill easily persuaded the cream of the first year's class to give up further education and follow her across the Pacific with the "China Band." Three of them died in the Orient before as many years had passed.

The extent to which female piety and persistence made the school possible is plain from the list of faculty assignments for the second year. Leora Maris was principal, a post she held for many years. Bresee taught homiletics, scriptural theology, and Bible holiness one day a week. Mr. Seymour, who was a medical doctor, offered Old Testament, and Evangelist Joseph Jamison led the class in Old Testament history. The remaining members of the faculty were all women: Mrs. A. P. Baldwin, Mrs. A. T. Armour, Mrs. Leoti McKee, Mrs. Lilly Bothwell (responsible for "Memory Drill" and "Philosophy of the Plan of Salvation"), and Mrs. E. J. Kellogg, who gave "Lectures from a Layman's Standpoint."

Inevitably, under such leadership, the principal activities centered in missionary and evangelistic bands. One cannot but admire the zeal of students who spent summers and other vacation periods among the Spanish-speaking Indians in the mountainous districts of Riverside and San Diego counties, and week nights during school terms in the Chinese or Mexican missions in Los Angeles.

In his annual report to the assembly of 1904 Dr. Bresee said plainly that the schoolwork had been "entered upon with some misgivings." The Nazarenes were "a young and small people," hence "the attendance could not be expected to be large." However he rejoiced that "an excellent faculty" had attracted a gratifying number. Best of all, the school had been "greatly blessed with outpourings of the Holy Spirit."[27]

Bresee was slow in overcoming his reluctance toward the idea of the church operating a college. Perhaps he remembered his difficulties in trying to help J. P. Widney make the University of Southern California a center of piety ten years before. A series of tub-thumping and quite sectarian pronouncements by educational committees of the General Assembly, declaring that only a Nazarene school could train Nazarene ministers, left him unmoved. He was not always certain that education was the training which his preachers needed anyhow. On one occasion when speaking of the subject he said, "God led Moses rather to a burning bush, to a consuming fire."[28]

In May, 1906, Mr. and Mrs. Jackson Deets, of Upland, California, gave $30,000 to erect new buildings for the Bible school. Dr. Bresee thereupon joined enthusiastically in the plans to develop a "Nazarene University," comprising an academy, a college of liberal arts, and the Bible school, now renamed in honor of Deets. The first $10,000 of the gift was used to purchase a new seven-acre campus, with the inevitable additional building lots intended to be sold at a profit. The next year, when this transaction was completed, Deets offered to give $20,000 more for buildings if the Nazarenes could repay the $10,000 used for the land. He also announced that he had provided a $100,000 endowment for the college in his will. The real estate company which sold the land also had homesites for sale near the campus. In June, 1907, a picnic and dedication service on the new site, jointly sponsored by the church and the real estate men, stirred enthusiasm for both the new "university" and the building lots as well.

The financial campaign bogged down, however. One year later a new associate pastor at First Church, A. L. Whitcomb, led a secession movement which carried away many of the women who were leaders in the Bible college. Bresee's earlier fears seemed vindicated. At this juncture, however, he decided over the objections of J. W. Goodwin and others to buy the magnificent tract of land which Pasadena College now occupies, and to establish in the City of Roses a much more ambitious educational venture, the first actually known as "Nazarene University."

Looking backward in 1915 at the sunset of his life, Bresee finally agreed that God had called the Nazarenes to college work. In an address at the education service of the district assembly he observed that "many things have been accomplished which only could have been accomplished by the overruling of divine providence." He had recently made the youthful H. Orton Wiley president of the school and placed the powerful revivalist Seth C. Rees in charge of the "University" Church. Bresee believed that he had thus guaranteed that the college would remain a center of "holy fire." Happily, he did not live two years more, to see it become a center of dissension.[29]

Thus as the church in California grew, the developing needs of the Nazarene community—needs which laymen often saw more clearly than did their leaders—decisively determined the pattern of the denomination's life. Bresee is one of the few outstanding examples of democratic leadership in American church history. Faith in "providential" guidance was the central theme of his work as superintendent. Moreover, the church which he and his people built doesn't fit very well into contemporary theories about the origins of the "small sects" of America. True enough, the Nazarenes arose among the poor. But they enunciated no new doctrines and abandoned no Methodist sacraments or rituals. They promoted education as heartily as any of the "churches" of their time, and linked their heavenly hopes with a continuous ministry to the needs of men in the world around them.

Nazarenes in the Northwest

The holiness movement reached Methodists in Oregon and Washington in the 1880's through the same instrumentalities as elsewhere. Evangelist William Taylor appeared in Portland in 1881 and led Pastors T. L. Jones and T. L. Sails into the experience. In 1885, at the request of the Oregon Conference, Bishop John M. Walden gave the latter two permission to serve as conference evangelists for a year. They held numerous camp meetings and revivals. Several of their converts joined Taylor in

Africa, and a wealthy layman gave $34,000 to support Taylor's mission there. In the following years news of holiness camp meetings and revivals came from every section of the Columbia River and Puget Sound conferences.[30]

H. D. Brown, who had earlier served with Phineas Bresee in the Iowa Conference, was presiding elder of the Olympia, Washington, district between 1887 and 1890. His annual reports stressed the "special attention" which he gave to the doctrine of entire sanctification. Later he transferred to north Nebraska, where, at the Nebraska State Holiness Camp Meeting for 1895, he renewed his acquaintance with Bresee. Brown returned to Seattle as pastor of the Battery Street Methodist Church in 1896, and thereafter kept in close touch with the Los Angeles pastor.

Evangelists of the Free Methodist church began organizing congregations in Oregon and Washington during this period also. Frank and Harry Ashcraft, originally from Texas, and the young T. P. Ferguson, who later founded Peniel Mission, came to Sunnyside, Oregon, for revivals in the early 1880's. Other meetings followed, and a state holiness association was founded. The denomination established Seattle Pacific College, on the shores of Puget Sound, as early as 1891, and by 1903 had organized five annual conferences to serve the two states.[31]

Around 1900, a group of independent evangelists began to range the towns of the Great Northwest, preaching in missions, churches, or camp meetings as they were able. Isaiah G. Martin, a Methodist lay preacher and song evangelist, was especially active. He held meetings in Seattle about 1900, first at the Free Methodist college, then, with sensational success, at the First Methodist Church in the city. Martin soon joined Bresee at the Los Angeles tabernacle as song leader and "platform manager." William Lee, who later founded the Lee Missions in Colorado, one nucleus of Nazarene work in that state, served his apprenticeship in city missions in Washington and Montana also. Lee's father and his uncle, Jason Lee, had been the pioneer Methodist missionaries to the Northwest.

In 1901, Martin and Lee helped organize at Spokane the Washington State Holiness Association, from which came the first Church of the Nazarene in the Northwest. The association opened the John 3:16 Mission in the saloon district of Spokane, and placed it under the superintendency of William Lee and Mr. and Mrs. DeLance Wallace. The little band invited C. W.

Ruth to be evangelist for a convention held at their mission hall in January, 1902. At the end of a week Ruth had persuaded them to form a Church of the Nazarene. He enrolled fifty charter members and appointed Mrs. Wallace pastor in charge until Dr. Bresee should come in the summer. This laywoman had rapidly developed into a fearless and persuasive preacher, but she was not yet ordained. Circumstances were compelling, however, and Ruth did not hesitate. Mrs. Wallace's first letter to Dr. Bresee requested four dozen church *Manuals* and asked suggestions for literature for the Sunday school which she planned to open at once.[32]

Up to this time Bresee had been more hopeful of a start in Seattle. He had conducted a revival at the Union Holiness Mission there during September, 1901. H. D. Brown attended, of course; but Seattle Methodists, save for members of a small Swedish M.E. church, ignored the meeting. Nonetheless Bresee returned home convinced that the city needed "a strong, vigorous Church of the Nazarene, under able leadership." Possibly he had tried to persuade Brown, who was just then closing his pastorate at the Battery Street Church, to head a new congregation. If so, he did not succeed. Brown decided instead to take up full-time work with the Washington State Children's Home Society, an orphanage movement which he had founded in 1896. Not until December, 1904, when Dr. Bresee organized the Northwest District and offered his old friend appointment as superintendent, did Brown join the Nazarenes. Even then he continued to serve the orphanage society on an almost full-time basis for two more years.[33]

Bresee readily accepted, therefore, the "providential" organization in January, 1902, of the church at Spokane. He consented to go to the Washington State Holiness Association camp meeting at Elberton, the next summer, as co-worker with Evangelist M. L. Haney, of Illinois. The small crowds and cold, rainy weather dampened Bresee's spirits. However, at this camp he met Robert Pierce, who soon brought his congregation at Boise, Idaho, into the denomination. Also H. D. Brown agreed to accept the vice-presidency of the association and to arrange a camp meeting near Seattle the next year.

Bresee proceeded to Spokane in answer to Mrs. Wallace's urgent call that he come and shepherd his "youngest lambs." He was pleased to find that the congregation there was "made up of clear-headed, anointed workers." At the general superintendent's suggestion, they asked officially that Mrs. Wallace be appointed their pastor, and elected her to elder's orders. Bresee presided over her ordination on the Sabbath. In this courageous lady he found a worthy addition to the company of devoted woman ministers on whom he so often relied. And in her congregation's dedication to the poor he heard an echo of the call which had pulled him into mission work seven years before.

Bresee returned home by way of Seattle, preaching one night in the Battery Street Church, and another at the Free Methodist camp meeting nearby. But no prospect of other Nazarene organizations in Washington state appeared until 1904, when a small congregation was brought together at Garfield, near Spokane.[34]

By that time, as we have seen, Bresee had fully committed himself to building a national church. He spent December, 1904, in the Great Northwest, laying plans for the future of the work there. He found the church at Spokane in thriving condition, though located "in the darkest place in the city—in a block almost literally filled on its four sides with saloons and places of wickedness." The only other churches were at Boise and Garfield. Bresee set off a separate Northwest District, comprising the states of Oregon, Washington, Idaho, and Montana, and appointed H. D. Brown district superintendent. He returned home by way of Seattle and Tacoma, hoping in each place to interest friends in a church organization. A little band was formed in Seattle, but that was all.[35]

In 1905, L. B. Kent, now a Nazarene, joined the Wallaces and others in a tent revival at North Yakima, Washington. J. B. Creighton, who had once been Kent's associate in the Illinois Holiness Association, had retired to that city in ill health, after a period spent as a pastor in the Church of God (Holiness), in Missouri. Kent encouraged Creighton to join the Nazarenes and to accept the pastorate of the new congregation in North Yakima.

Kent then proceeded to Seattle, where he joined Dr. Bresee in a large tent campaign. The meeting gained only indifferent success. The Seattle "band" was organized into a church, however, with H. D. Brown as pastor. Bresee then went to Spokane for the district assembly, and returned home by way of Walla Walla, Washington, and Portland, Oregon, in each place visiting small bands of Nazarenes. The Portland church was organized in 1906, but remained for some time heavily dependent upon the good will of the Friends congregation in the city. Small organizations were also reported that year in Ashland and Milton, Oregon, and Monroe, Tipso, and Plainview, Washington. H. D. Brown continued to serve as district superintendent of all these churches, as well as pastor in Seattle, but the church in the latter place grew very slowly.[36]

The key to the Nazarene work in the Northwest, therefore, was Spokane. But the congregation there still operated primarily as a mission. Until 1906, services were held in their hall every night. Drunken and impoverished transients were their chief concern, although the Sunday school and youth organizations flourished too. H. D. Brown began urging the group to purchase a church home soon after his appointment as district superintendent, but they paid him little attention. Providentially, as Dr. Bresee would say, the owners of the mission hall gave them notice of eviction just a week before the district assembly was to meet there in July, 1905. Clinging stubbornly to their original purpose, however, the congregation rented a blacksmith's shop and voted late in August in favor of "the continuance of the work as at present—as a mission." Nonetheless, they listed for sale a lot they owned downtown and looked at possible sites for a church building. When it became evident that the proposal for a church was winning out, several families announced their intention of organizing a separate group to continue mission work.

At a climactic board meeting on February 12, 1906, Brown spoke at length on the subject of "going into church work," urging the group to locate "somewhere among the residents of the city." Brown said it was his impression that church work had become the objective of the Nazarenes in Los Angeles, in Berkeley, and, he believed, in the new organization in Chicago. The board heeded his advice and purchased soon after a new location at the corner of Monroe Street and Sharp Avenue. Thus, on the eve of the national unions of 1907-8, the pioneer congregation in the Northwest decided that it was to be not just a mission but, as Dr. Bresee once put it, a church with a mission.[37]

How Bresee's Church Came to the Mississippi Valley

The greatest concentration of Methodists in the United States is in the Middle West, in a triangle whose northern line runs from

Nebraska to northeast Ohio and whose southern point is Memphis. The upper Mississippi Valley was the circuit rider's most permanent conquest. The growth of the small Wesleyan denominations in this section was, therefore, inevitable. The Free Methodists, the Wesleyan Methodists, and the Ohio Yearly Meeting of Friends, all of whom clung to the spiritual traditions of rural Methodism, had gained footholds there by 1900.

In general, however, Methodists who believed in the doctrine of holiness remained loyal to their church longer in this section than elsewhere. Midwestern Methodist leaders were less receptive to the new liberal theology than those in the East, and their people were more closely bound to traditional church ties than those in the newer communities farther west. For these reasons the small Wesleyan denominations grew slowly in the corn and wheat belts until after 1910, and made rapid progress only after 1920. In 1907, when Bresee's Church of the Nazarene united with the Association of Pentecostal Churches from New England, only fifteen of their congregations were located in the area between the northern Rockies and Pittsburgh.

All of these were, moreover, recently organized Nazarene churches rather than outposts of the eastern organization. This too is understandable. Few easterners had very deep or meaningful contacts with the Midwest. But the great majority of Californians had come to the coast by way of the plains states, and many of them still maintained personal contact with churches and kinsfolk back across the mountains. Quite naturally, therefore, the return visits which Bresee's preachers and converts made to their earlier homes spread the fame of the Church of the Nazarene over plains and prairies.

When young evangelists decided to cast their lot with the Nazarenes in Los Angeles, they inevitably turned their faces toward their old homes in the Middle West and sought to extend the movement there. Bresee himself had been the first to do this, in visits to Iowa, Nebraska, and Illinois in 1895 and 1899. While on the second trip he invited the president of the Illinois Holiness Association, L. B. Kent, to come to Los Angeles for meetings at First Church in February, 1900. The result, as we have already seen, was that Kent joined the Nazarenes and raised publicly the question whether all holiness people might eventually find their home in this or a similar organization.

Herbert and Lillie Buffum held revivals throughout Kansas, Missouri, and Oklahoma in 1901 and 1902. When their meetings were in "friendly" Methodist churches, the Buffums were often content to organize simply a county holiness association. Where no local church was willing to accept their converts, they would form what was called a "class," receiving members officially into the faraway Los Angeles congregation, and electing lay people to be leaders of local Sunday and weekday services. In some places, as at Wichita, Kansas, where the pastor of the First Methodist Church was president of the state holiness association, they did not raise the question of organization at all.[38]

W. E. Shepard, who was for a time Bresee's unofficial assistant pastor, spent the greater part of 1900 and 1901 in similar evangelistic work, first in Texas and then in the corn-belt states. At the Scottsville Camp Meeting in east Texas, Shepard found that a great number of the preachers present had withdrawn or been expelled from the M.E. Church, South, and were now members of the northern branch of Methodism. In Texas, the latter was "frequently called the holiness church," he wrote; "would to God it might properly be called that everywhere." In Iowa the next year, Shepard refused to leave his converts to the care of northern Methodist pastors. At a meeting in Bloomfield he revived the county holiness association, arranged to return for a camp meeting the next summer, and established a regular Tuesday night prayer meeting "to conserve the work," despite predictions that his action would split the Methodist church. Following a camp meeting at Albia, Iowa, Shepard held meetings in several Friends churches. There he met Edgar P. Ellyson, Friends minister in charge of the Bible school at Marshalltown, who in 1908 became a Nazarene general superintendent. Next this "Nazarene" evangelist filled engagements at the Christian and Missionary Alliance camp at Cleveland, Ohio; at a Methodist church in Chicago; and, finally, at a Disciples of Christ church in Berea, Kentucky, blessed with "a sanctified pastor and sanctified members."[39]

Others of Dr. Bresee's followers returned to the Midwest with definite plans to establish Nazarene congregations. William Allison went to Kansas City, Kansas, in the spring of 1900, hoping to organize a small band which had been meeting for some time in the home of a laywoman. The work did not prosper, so Allison proceeded the next spring to San Antonio, Texas, where another little-known minister in Bresee's congregation had been trying to gather a group of "God's poor" into a Nazarene mission. By fall, Allison had decided it would be wisest to begin by forming the San Antonio Holiness Association. This body rented a hall and announced the opening of the Union Mission of San Antonio. While engaged chiefly in the city, Allison organized the first Nazarene congregation in Texas at the nearby town of Schiller in November, 1901. By May of 1902 he wrote Bresee that the constitution of the Union Mission had been altered to make possible its transformation into a Church of the Nazarene, but the name used in public was still simply the City Gospel Mission. Some financial support had to be sacrificed to take even this step, he noted, "but religiously and spiritually we have suffered no decline." Another church and a mission or two were established in the community round about. But the distance from Los Angeles and the absence of the kind of leadership which was necessary for thorough planning greatly weakened the San Antonio movement. Apparently these congregations all died before the unions of 1907 and 1908.[40]

In January, 1902, J. A. Smith, a Methodist minister of Pekin, Illinois, decided to unite with the Church of the Nazarene and to organize a congregation in that city. He began weekly meetings in Peoria, fifteen miles away; but there the sponsors of the holiness mission bitterly resisted the idea of a church organization. The following year Smith set in order a congregation of fifty-two charter members at Maples Mill, Illinois, a rural community whose Methodist church had recently been denied its usual privilege of having a pastor who preached holiness. C. W. Ruth wrote about this time from Danville that the Eastern Illinois Holiness Association contained many people who felt that just such a church as the Nazarenes were building was "needed in every city" of the state. Farther west, Mr. and Mrs. J. A. Dooley, who had conducted mission and church work at Omaha, Nebraska, for the previous five years, decided in August of 1903 to merge their First Pentecostal Mission Church with Bresee's movement. A few months later the Dooleys resigned the pastorate at Omaha and went to Minneapolis, Minnesota, to open another mission, which became the first Nazarene congregation in that state.[41]

By far the most important outpost in the Midwest, however, was Chicago First Church, established in 1904. Both in its origin as a mission to the poor, in its spontaneous and lay-directed growth, and in its role in igniting lesser "centers of fire" in cities and towns nearby, this congregation was an exact copy of the one in Los Angeles and a concrete demonstration of Bresee's design for denominational growth.

A holiness prayer meeting which began in Chicago in January, 1900, under the leadership of a Methodist woman evangelist, soon blossomed into a holiness mission, one of many in the city, directed by Rev. S. Rice. In 1903, Rice moved to St. Louis, and left a layman, Dr. Edwin Burke, as superintendent. One of the workers, Jack Berry, a tea and coffee salesman, met Dr. Bresee on a trip to Los Angeles the same year and returned home determined to persuade his associates in Chicago to become Nazarenes. The group invited M. L. Haney and I. G. Martin for a revival in the fall. Partly as a result of this meeting the South Side Mission, as it was then called, greatly multiplied its membership and rose to front rank among the holiness groups in the city. Edwin Burke, Jack Berry, and J. W. Akers also became the most prominent lay members of the Illinois State Holiness Association, organized in January, 1904, under National Association auspices. This brought them into contact with many Methodist pastors who favored holiness, but raised conflicts with some of their own pastors who did not. Their decision to inaugurate a full program of Sunday morning and evening services at the mission hall increased the opposition so much that it became apparent they must either sever their church relations or abandon the mission.

I. G. Martin returned for a second revival in March, 1904. Since the hall would no longer accommodate the crowds, the group moved in early summer into a tent at Sixty-second Street and Lexington Avenue. About this time they decided to ask Dr. Bresee to come for a ten-day meeting in August "with the ultimate purpose of organizing a Church of the Nazarene." Bresee made his usual fine impression upon the holiness leaders of Chicago. When he opened the charter of membership on August 28, 1904, the one hundred persons who came forward represented three distinct groups: five well-known Methodist ministers and their families, not previously associated with the mission; the middle-class Christians like the Burkes and the Berrys, who had sponsored the work originally; and numbers of their converts from among the poor.[42]

The new church called I. G. Martin as their pastor immediately. A few days later Jack Berry's horse made an unexpected

THE NAZARENES BECOME A NATIONAL CHURCH 149

turn and stopped in front of a vacant church. A sign, "For rent or for sale," was on the door. Berry decided that God had directed him to the spot. He climbed through a basement window and into the empty sanctuary, where he shouted himself hoarse. Within a week the Nazarenes were in possession of the building. Of the wonderful days which followed, one of them wrote later:

> People came from far and near, brought their lunches and stayed for the services, all day Sunday, beginning with Sunday school at 9:30; the morning preaching, with altar services often running into the afternoon meeting; the great afternoon mass meetings with altar services running on until 5:00 or 6:00 in the evenings; the rousing street meetings; the Young Peoples meetings; and closing the day with an Evangelist service with altars filled and re-filled and lasting far into the night.[43]

During its first year, the Chicago First Church grew to four hundred members; one thousand seekers bowed at its altars. Laymen of the church meanwhile provided the chief local support for the Illinois State Holiness Association camp meeting at West Pullman. A bit later their pastor began writing a regular column for the *Christian Witness*. Thus the congregation became almost the officially approved route by which Chicago holiness people who found themselves hard pressed in older churches made their way into a new denomination. Certainly here was no place for religious loafers. By August, 1906, the congregation was operating three different missions to the poor, one of them for Swedish immigrants; it sponsored various prison and rescue-home endeavors and supported a group of deaconesses who not only made calls on needy families, but distributed clothing, bought coal, groceries, and medicine, and paid hospital and doctors' bills as well. By this time, too, these self-reliant laymen had also fully paid for their church building, and had purchased for $10,000 a lot at nearby Sixty-fourth Street and Eggleston Avenue—all with no dishes to wash and no oysters to fry, as one of them put it.

Although the general superintendent was three thousand miles away, they nonetheless asked for a change of pastors at the end of their first year. They arranged for an interim ministry by G. A. McLaughlin, editor of the *Christian Witness;* organized their membership Methodist-fashion into classes; and called as their pastor a Friends layman, C. E. Cornell, to whom they gave his first minister's license! Cornell accepted with delight and pushed the work wholeheartedly. He was happy, as he put it, to lead a congregation with no place for "the ecclesiastical frills of salaried 'high art' in the choir, 'higher criticism' . . . in the pulpit and 'highest social circles' . . . in the pew." Drunkards, thieves, gamblers, common sinners, respectable sinners, and men, women, and children from all walks of life, he wrote in September, 1906, had "bowed at the altar seeking a common Savior." Awful conviction had rested upon the people, "at times until some were swept off their feet and fell prostrate to weep and pray until deliverance came."[44]

Meanwhile, smaller congregations were springing up all over the area—at Stockton, Kewanee, Canton, and Auburn, Illinois; and at Hammond, Indiana. Dr. Bresee conducted the district assembly at Chicago in July, 1906, and helped raise the vision for new "centers of holy fire" in St. Louis, Indianapolis, and Des Moines. The strong church at Hammond was an offspring of the Chicago organization. A. T. Harris laid down his blacksmith's hammer in September, 1906, and went to Hammond to open up mission work. At the end of the first year Harris counted 129 conversions, and reported 155 had professed sanctification at his altars. T. H. Agnew, whom Dr. Bresee appointed district superintendent of the midwestern work late in 1906, held meetings for Harris, encouraged him to move into a better building, and in March, 1907, organized a church with 89 members.[45]

Thus it was that even before the merger with the Association of Pentecostal Churches of New England in October, 1907, the Church of the Nazarene became a national denomination. Through a combination of what Dr. Bresee would have called providential circumstances, the congregation which started its life in the old board tabernacle at Los Angeles became the nucleus of a spreading movement destined to give spiritual shelter to holiness people everywhere and especially, in succeeding years, to those in the inland states of the American Middle West.

CHAPTER VII

From the Cumberland to the Rio Grande: The Heritage of Holiness in the Old Southwest

The Civil War left a deep scar on the soul of the South. The economic hardships and social conflict which that section endured during the long reconstruction period added new bitterness to the memory of defeat. When recovery came at last, in the 1880's, northern investors reaped most of the profit. The southern farmer and townsman remained for long decades on the ragged edges of poverty.

About 1890 a genuinely democratic farmer's movement began. But political bosses crushed this "revolt of the rednecks" by encouraging racial strife between whites and Negroes and writing "Jim Crow" laws on the statute books of every state. Cities grew, meanwhile, as in the North, but here from a population more often driven by despair than drawn in hope. Those who wished to avoid the city headed west, usually to Texas, though some ventured on to the dreamland called California.

Whatever frontier the migrant southerner occupied during the next fifty years, however, whether mill village, city, or prairie farm, he turned for personal strength and comfort to some new version of what he believed was "the old-time religion." His social experience was certainly not conducive to the religious optimism, to the hope of building a better world so prominent in the North. Nor was the idea of "immediate sanctification by faith" easy for him to accept. Although revivals remained the usual method of winning converts in the dominant Baptist, Presbyterian, and Methodist churches, southern evangelism continued to represent an older, rural tradition. It was more responsive to law than to love, and more inclined to a premillennial than to a socially optimistic postmillennial view of the second coming of Christ.

The minority denominations in the Old Southwest differed strikingly from those which held second rank in other sections of the country. Here were the strongholds of the Cumberland Presbyterians and of the two branches of the Church of Christ, one of them called Disciples, or simply Christians. The latter groups had originated in the hill country of Tennessee and Kentucky during the period of the Great Western Revival, after 1800. They spread south and west as the people spread. Congregations of both branches governed themselves independently, ordained their own ministers, baptized converts by immersion, celebrated the Lord's Supper every Sunday, and accepted the New Testament as a complete rule of faith and practice. The Cumberland denomination retained the Presbyterian form of government, but rejected the requirement that ministers must be able to read the Bible in the original languages. More important, its preachers were Arminian in theology and fervently evangelistic in spirit. By the 1880's many Cumberland Presbyterian pastors were stressing the doctrine of the baptism of the Holy Spirit as a second work of grace and supporting holiness camp meetings and revivals in their communities.[1]

The chief factor which made the history of the holiness movement in the Old Southwest different from that in other sections of the country was that large segments of the Methodist Episcopal Church, South, were never committed to the doctrine of entire sanctification. In the 1890's, as holiness associations grew, presiding elders resisted them heartily, especially in Texas, Tennessee, and Kentucky. The result was a series of local crises in which individual preachers found themselves ousted from their charges and unable to continue in the ministry except on an independent basis. Matters came to a climax after the General Conference of 1894 adopted a rule forbidding any Methodist preacher or evangelist to hold meetings within the bounds of another's charge against the local pastor's will. This action led directly to the formation of a small congregation known as the Church of Christ of Milan, Tennessee, the oldest of the southern churches which in 1908 united with the Nazarenes.

Robert Lee Harris and the New Testament Church of Christ

In 1890, Robert Lee Harris, a west Texan known as "the cowboy evangelist," returned to America from an independent mission work which he had conducted for a few years at Monrovia, capital of Liberia. C. W. Sherman, of the Vanguard Mission in St. Louis, and S. B. Shaw, at that time a Free Methodist leader in Michigan, had sponsored Harris' venture in Africa. They also helped to get him started in evangelistic work when he returned. Harris soon joined the Methodist Episcopal Church, South. The summer of 1893 found him conducting numerous meetings in west Tennessee, including one at the country town of Milan. In this meeting Mr. and Mrs. R. B. Mitchum were converted, and a widely publicized debate with J. N. Hall, a Baptist preacher, gave Harris considerable notoriety.

In November, 1893, the West Tennessee Conference of the Methodist Episcopal Church, South, passed resolutions which declared the work of "unauthorized, self-styled evangelists" to be "in the main an evil of great magnitude." The conference urged its members to refuse either financial support or the use of their church buildings to such preachers. Harris thereupon published a pamphlet which announced his withdrawal from the Methodist church. He attacked the "fashionable and worldly" congregations, filled with card players and theatergoers, and announced his intention to seek a true "New Testament" church fellowship.[2]

Harris was meanwhile slowly succumbing to tuberculosis. He accepted the invitation of Mr. and Mrs. E. H. Sheeks to share their home in Memphis, and there began publishing a small religious paper called the *Trumpet*. The following spring Sheeks formed a partnership with R. B. Mitchum to conduct a store business in Milan. The entire household thereupon moved to the little farming community some ninety-five miles away, carrying the printing press for the *Trumpet* with them.

Harris began conducting prayer meetings at Milan, and in the summer had a tent erected in which he held revival meetings for three months. He encouraged several of the women, including especially Mrs. Mitchum and Mrs. Harris, to preach on occasions when he was ill. Even after he had to be carried to the tent, the evangelist delivered a series of sermons on the "church question" which alleged all sects and denominations to be unscriptural. Harris' declaration that pouring was the proper mode of baptism provoked a second debate, this time with a Church of Christ minister. On the evening of July 9, 1894, the evangelist "set in order" a congregation of fourteen members, which he called the New Testament Church of Christ. Those who had previously been immersed, including the Mitchums, were rebaptized by pouring. The group worshiped under the tent for a time, then moved in the fall to the Cumberland Presbyterian meetinghouse, and finally to a rented hall. Harris died on November 26, 1894. Not until March, 1896, however, were his followers able to complete the little chapel which became their church home.

Before the founder passed away he published a pamphlet describing *The Government and Doctrines of the New Testament Church*. The Church of Christ, Harris wrote, was not a legislative but an executive body. Its laws were to be found in the New Testament. This scriptural constitution, he believed, made local congregations fully autonomous. They had the right to expel members who had fallen from grace, to send out missionaries without consulting any other ecclesiastical body, and to ordain their own "bishops," or elders. They were also empowered to elect lay deacons who, in addition to caring for the secular needs of the church, might serve Communion as needed. All these teachings had been for years characteristic in the older "Christian" denomination. To these Harris added baptism by pouring; the Methodist doctrine of sanctification as a second work of grace; and the renunciation of all forms of "worldliness": sinful amusements, extravagance in dress, the wearing of jewelry, membership in secret societies, and the use of opium, tobacco, or intoxicating drinks.

Harris' "New Testament Church" fitted some definitions of the word "come-outer." It stood isolated not only from the older churches but from the organized holiness movement as well. Yet its laws and its doctrines were simply a new alloy, forged of Methodist piety and Disciples churchmanship.[3]

From 1894 to 1901 the small group spread slowly through west Tennessee, Arkansas, northern Alabama, and sections of Texas, under the leadership of women preachers whose ordination knew no apostolic succession. Mrs. Mary Lee Harris, widow of the founder, returned to her native west Texas for revival meetings as early as 1895. In the following years she traveled back and forth between Texas and Tennessee, holding meetings with Mrs. R. B. Mitchum, and encouraging Mrs. Sheeks and other women to begin active ministry. Whenever they thought it advisable, the women organized new congregations. Mrs. Harris held revivals and organized three groups in her native county in Alabama in 1897. That year the ladies divided into first two and then three teams. They conducted tent meetings throughout the territory in the summer, and when winter came turned to halls and rented churches.

In the fall of 1898, J. A. Murphree, of Waco, Texas, joined the congregation at Milan and made his paper, the *Evangelist,* the semiofficial organ of the New Testament churches. Murphree conducted a missionary training school in Waco, along with a rescue mission and a woodyard where he gave employment to tramps. Since many of the most recent settlers of the west Texas frontier had come from Tennessee, it was natural for Murphree and his associate, William E. Fisher, to join Mrs. Harris in revivals and camp meetings out on the plains two hundred miles away. By 1900, a dozen-odd little congregations had been organized in towns south and west of Abilene. Mrs. Harris that year married a cowboy named H. C. Cagle, of Buffalo Gap, and settled down to pastor the church and promote the annual camp meeting in that town. Murphree's training school soon moved to Buffalo Gap, and the congregation there became one of the few substantial ones in the group.[4]

The women who carried on this independent gospel work seem to have combined piety and practicality to a remarkable degree. Between revivals they maintained a normal and apparently stable family life, if the few surviving letters may be taken at face value. Their husbands joined happily in their meetings when they were near home and accepted periods of separation without much protest. Only one of the women seems ever to have gone to extremes of religious emotionalism, and on that occasion the sound common sense of the others shook her out of it. Mrs. Harris was an especially forceful individual, able to wield a strong influence over the holiness movement in the Southwest long after men had taken over actual direction.

Inevitably, of course, questions concerning the propriety of women preachers arose, in part from the intense prejudice against them in Cumberland Presbyterian and Church of Christ circles. The ladies usually accepted whatever challenges came to debate the issue. Mrs. Fannie McDowell Hunter published a volume in

1905 entitled *Women Preachers,* in which a dozen of them presented their defense in autobiographical form. Practically all of the group had at first believed that their "call" was to *foreign* missionary work, at that time the only public ministry in which women were actually welcome. All insisted that "providential" circumstances had thrust them out into the ministry, first as "home missionaries" and rescue workers, then as evangelists and, in some cases, pastors. W. B. Godbey, the quaint but scholarly evangelist of the holiness movement in the South, had defended them from the start. Woman is morally stronger than man, Godbey declared; Satan would win a great victory if he could paralyze the "larger, truer, and more efficient wing" of the Christian army. Give the women a chance, he wrote,

> and they will rob Satan of his whiskey, confront him on every ramification of the battle field, fill the saloons and brothels of Christendom, and the jungles of Heathendom, with blood-washed and fire-baptized missionaries, march to the music of full salvation to the ends of the earth, belt the globe with the glory of God, and transform a world long groaning in sin and misery into a paradise.[5]

The Beginnings of Denominational Organization

The leaders of the New Testament Church of Christ maintained a steady opposition to legislative changes which would infringe upon congregational independency. The story of the development of the annual "councils" in west Tennessee and west Texas clearly illustrates this fact.

In December, 1899, a business meeting of the church at Milan, under the chairmanship of R. B. Mitchum, took up several questions which were obviously of general interest to the entire movement. The first one was, "Should we make immersion a bar to fellowship in the congregations of the Church of Christ?" After three days of discussion and "much prayer and fasting" those present agreed that they could not afford to turn away on account of the mode of their baptism those whom God seemed to accept. The second question was, "How shall we best supply our congregations with pastors? And see to the support of said pastors?" The next, provoked by recent editorials in J. A. Murphree's *Evangelist,* which seemed to the Tennessee people too liberal on the question of divorce, was, "Has a man any scriptural right to put away his wife and marry again?" The answer, arrived at in similar fashion, was, No, save on the

New Testament ground of infidelity. The final question asked whether women were eligible for ordination. Again, much prayer and searching of the Bible brought them to an affirmative answer. Thereupon the group examined and ordained Mrs. R. L. Harris, Mrs. E. H. Sheeks, along with Mr. G. M. Hammond, a convert of theirs who had already taken a pastorate.[6]

In the ensuing year, as new congregations were organized and new ministers recruited, the need grew for united consideration of these questions. When the Milan group assembled for its second annual meeting, representatives were present from most of the other congregations. R. B. Mitchum explained carefully at the outset that the object of the gathering was simply mutual encouragement through "talking freely among ourselves as to the teaching of God's Word on such questions as might be suggested." The council was not a legislative body, Mitchum said, for Christ and the apostles had set forth all the laws and rules necessary. Their task was simply to study the Bible together and learn the laws given to them.

A delegate from Jonesboro, Arkansas, insisted upon knowing at once, however, whether "the actions of this conference should be binding on other congregations." After some discussion, the original record tells us, "it was settled in the minds of all present that the congregations of the Church of Christ were according to the teachings of God's Word, local in government. Hence the action of one congregation had nothing to do with other congregations." Technically, the "council" thus chose to regard itself as simply an annual meeting of the Milan church.

Nonetheless the body went back over the identical questions of baptism and pastoral supply dealt with the previous year. Though the answers were the same, the reconsideration by representatives of all the churches gave them greater weight. At the close of the conference I. A. Russell, a newcomer to the preachers' group, presented a motion, heartily endorsed by all, that each congregation should be represented at succeeding annual meetings "and thus come in touch with the Elders of the Church." G. W. Mann, pastor at Jonesboro, Arkansas, stated that his congregation had instructed him to invite the next council to their community. Obviously, a group of aggressive men were replacing the women evangelists as the real leaders, and were moving as fast as possible toward the development of stronger denominational ties. During the next two years Methodist, Free Methodist, and independent preachers, both male and female, united with the church, usually placing their membership in the Milan congregation until they were settled in a pastorate elsewhere.⁷

By the time the annual council met at Jonesboro in October, 1901, the new men were clearly in charge. Especially prominent were Joseph Speakes, from Arkansas, O. W. Rose, leader of a city mission in St. Louis, G. W. Mann, I. A. Russell, G. M. Hammond, and the former Mrs. Harris' new husband, H. C. Cagle, from Buffalo Gap.

Quite naturally, preachers with families, who were giving their full time to ministerial work, were more deeply concerned than the women had been for adequate pastoral support. The previous councils had discussed this matter but had not taken any significant action. Now the question was, "Is it scriptural for a person to promise a stated sum per year for his pastor?" At the end of a long discussion, the council declared that such a promise was "not unscriptural." Although the resolution on the subject left every pastor free to "work on the finance line" as he believed God's Word taught, a great ecclesiastical boundary line had been crossed. The laws of the New Testament Church were no longer confined to specific scriptural decrees. They might thereafter be developed rationally, to meet unfolding needs, so long as their features were not *contrary* to the principles of the Bible.⁸

Meanwhile, in west Texas a similar development of council organization was taking place. The two key differences here were that all of the pastors save Mrs. Cagle were men; and the most important ones were greatly interested in social work and city missions. Among these were J. A. Murphree, William E. Fisher, and J. T. Upchurch, founder of the Berachah Rescue Home at Arlington, Texas.

In December, 1902, in response to numerous suggestions, Mrs. Cagle sent out a call to the different congregations to send representatives to a general meeting at Buffalo Gap. Eleven churches sent sixteen ministers and eight laymen to this conclave. Fisher served as chairman. Those present seemed noticeably less anxious than their eastern brethren to protect congregational independency. The delegates readily agreed to publish both a statement of doctrine and a "guide" for the direction of all the congregations. They were more preoccupied with laymen's rights, however; all the officers elected for the new year were laymen except Mrs. Cagle.

At succeeding annual councils in 1903 and 1904, William E. Fisher and B. F. Neely, a young preacher who was Mrs. Cagle's close friend, exercised commanding influence. In the latter year Fisher led the way toward union with the Independent Holiness church, and the whole question of congregational sovereignty versus council leadership had to be thrashed out anew. Before the dust had settled, the union with the Nazarenes replaced council leadership with a full-fledged superintendency.[9]

The Holiness Movement in Eastern Texas

The congregations of the Church of Christ which Mrs. Cagle and William E. Fisher shepherded in west Texas grew up quite independently of a much older and more significant holiness movement in the eastern part of the state.

Beginning in the year 1877, when, as we have seen, Evangelist Hardin Wallace brought a band of workers from Illinois to hold meetings in Beaumont, Denton, Gainesville, and Ennis, the doctrine of "entire sanctification by faith" had won substantial support from Methodist, Methodist Protestant, Cumberland Presbyterian, and Baptist churchmen. A Texas Holiness Association, organized in the fall of 1878, conducted annual camp meetings in the triangle between Corsicana, Dallas, and Waco. The Free Methodist church soon established a foothold in this area. Among Methodists, the Northwest Texas Holiness Association flourished for a time after 1885.

Camp meetings grew in number every year. The most notable of the permanent encampments was at Scottsville, in deep east Texas. Colonel William T. Scott, founder of the town which bore his name and first president of one section of the Southern Pacific Railway, donated a site on his estate in 1887, shortly after he had professed sanctification. In the years which followed, most of the outstanding southern evangelists of Wesleyan persuasion and some of the Methodist bishops as well appeared on the platform there. Scottsville camp was no middle-class summer resort; the throngs came to pray and witness and seek a higher Christian life. And so it was at twoscore other such centers across the eastern counties of the state.[10]

As elsewhere in the South, however, the Methodist leadership soon began to resist the growing force of the holiness revival. In 1894, J. T. Smith, Methodist pastor at Marshall, near Scottsville, protested "the vicious teaching, that is constantly heard, that our preachers who claim no higher experience than that of regeneration are not qualified to preach the gospel to the sanctified." Though he praised some of the "second blessing people" as "loyal and true Christians," Smith insisted that "there will be no peace while some abuse the church, our bishops, and presiding elders, and preachers, and members in general, and accuse them of fighting holiness."

What the historian of Methodism in Texas called the "tremendous controversy" of the 1890's was, in the eyes of John H. McLean, who had helped oust young Bud Robinson from the Methodist ministry, not "a difference in doctrine, but in the theory of a doctrine." McLean in later years insisted he could not accept the idea of a second blessing because his initial experience of Christian grace brought him the ecstasy of a "full salvation." "I believe in growth," McLean wrote, "spiritual progress, going on to perfection, and I know of no perfection, save being made perfect in love."[11]

No amount of preaching or pressure, however, could bring the holiness revival to a halt. W. B. Godbey was in Texas for meetings in 1886. He no doubt brought with him the recent *Address by the Southern Holiness Associations* on the subject of Christian perfection, which renounced "come-outism" and insisted that the various state leaders were the most loyal of Methodists. A campaign was already under way, however, to silence or drive out of the ministry the most fervent of the holiness preachers in Texas. Those ousted in addition to Bud Robinson were R. L. Averill, who became a Free Methodist presiding elder; J. W. Lively, who later filled a like position for the Northern Methodist church; and E. C. DeJernett, who founded the Texas Holiness University at Greenville.[12]

The M.E. Church, North, which had been seeking a foothold in Texas since the Civil War, welcomed these homeless preachers and actively sought to recruit members from among those converted in their revivals and camp meetings. In 1897, for example, the Gulf Mission Conference of the northern church received James W. Lively and Frances J. Browning, the latter of whom had been Colonel Scott's pastor. Early in the sessions Bishop John M. Walden asked Browning to conduct a "Pentecostal service." "The altar was filled with seekers," the conference secretary wrote, "and a wonderful revival season of grace and the outpouring of the Holy Ghost came like an anointing upon the people." Although Browning wound up a Baptist, Lively became presiding elder in northeast Texas. R. L. Selle, presiding elder in the San Antonio area and later a pastor and camp meeting leader at Denton, helped Lively to seek out "wholly sanctified men" to be the pioneers of Northern Methodism in the Lone Star State. Bishop Willard F. Mallalieu, who was stationed at New Orleans during this period, lent his influence in support of their efforts.[13]

Thus by 1898 the holiness preachers in east Texas faced three alternatives. They could join one of the new "small sects": the Holiness Church Association, the Free Methodist, or the Methodist Protestant church. They might unite with the M.E. Church, North. Or they could organize a new interdenominational association to protect and nurture the work until providential events revealed some better solution of their problem.[14]

The Holiness Association of Texas: Peniel

In the year 1894, E. C. DeJernett, pastor of the Southern Methodist congregation in Commerce, Texas, requested a release from his conference obligations in order to give full time to evangelistic work. He settled at nearby Greenville and bought the hills on the north side of town for a permanent camp meeting site. Here grew a small community named Peniel, its residents attracted by the building lots which DeJernett sold to help pay for his land. In a few years Peniel was to boast a college, a publishing firm specializing in holiness literature, an orphanage, and one of the largest camp meetings in the area. Perhaps most important, it was the home and the heart of the Holiness Association of Texas.[15]

DeJernett was ousted from the M.E. church in 1898 for conducting a revival in a Northern Methodist church at Atlanta, Texas, over the protest of the pastor of the local Southern congregation. Believing, like many other leaders of the movement in Texas, that a broad swing toward a new denomination was imminent, he and a young layman, C. B. Jernigan, summoned a convention to meet in connection with a camp meeting which Henry Clay Morrison and Bud Robinson were scheduled to conduct at Terrell that year. Their announced purpose was to consider steps "to provide a home for homeless holiness people of the South; or at least to organize them into an association for mutual protection." Although a large and representative group appeared at the gathering, those who hoped for decisive action were disappointed. The majority supported a recommendation that all should "maintain their present church relationship . . . , enduring patiently the slights or open persecutions of their fellow members and their pastors." Those who for one reason or another were without a church were urged to join one of the existing denominations. Morrison helped to confuse the situation by proposing a state "Holiness Union," to be affiliated with similar organizations in other southern states, all of whose members were required to belong to some local church.

A small group of pastors and evangelists thereupon joined the Northern Methodist church. C. B. Jernigan noted later, however, that as soon as local congregations were well established "the Southern-raised holiness boys" were replaced by Yankee pastors of a "different political faith," some of whom opposed the doctrine of sanctification. Northern Methodism was in these years a firmly Republican organization; and, as Jernigan observed, Texans of that era had a difficult time being Republicans.

The same was true of the Free Methodist communion, which a few others joined. Perhaps a more important objection to the Free Methodists, however, was their ban on instrumental music. Jernigan complained also that in Texas in those days a "large share of their preaching and testifying was devoted to talking against cravats, rag roses, and other externals." He felt that the Free Methodists of the Lone Star State were too sectarian, too uninterested in co-operating with holiness people outside their own communion.[16]

Early in the year 1899 a young minister named B. A. Cordell bought and donated land for a college at Peniel. Within three months DeJernett had gathered a board of trustees from among the holiness leaders of the Southwest. On the recommendation of Cordell, this group elected as president A. M. Hills, an Oberlin College graduate and Congregationalist evangelist then teaching at Asbury College, Wilmore, Kentucky. W. G. Airhart, another young preacher, was chief among those who scraped up money for the first simple buildings. In September the Texas Holiness University welcomed its first student body of twenty-seven pupils.

That fall DeJernett and Jernigan summoned a second conference to consider the problem of a church or other organization for the holiness people. Delegates from all over east Texas met in the hall of the mission then being conducted at Greenville. Although at the beginning sentiment was much stronger for a new denomination than at Terrell the previous year, J. W. Lively made a great plea on behalf of the Northern Methodist church. "Come home, boys, to your Mother," he said.

> Methodism is the Mother of Holiness. Come home and we will do as they used to do: give you a horse to ride, and a pair of old fashioned saddle bags, with a Bible on one side and a Methodist Hymnbook on the other; and put some money in your pockets, and send you out to preach holiness.

Although as Jernigan noted later "the boys would not come home," the voices of moderation were sufficiently powerful to cause this second convention to adjourn without action.[17]

As the meeting closed, Dennis Rogers, leader since 1886 of a group of tiny congregations in Collin County called the Holiness Church Association of Texas, came to Jernigan saying, "Since the big folks won't do anything, why can't we little folks get together and do something?" That very night in a meeting at Jernigan's house Rogers joined C. M. Keith, editor of the *Texas Holiness Advocate,* then being published at Peniel, and C. A. McConnell, a layman who represented a new group of holiness bands around Sunset, farther west. They decided to call another convention to meet one month later, December 23, 1899, for the purpose of forming the Holiness Association of Texas. They hoped that this new body, half church and half association, would combine McConnell's group, known as the Northwest Texas Holiness Association, with Rogers' Holiness church group and attract as well many of the individuals and bands in the area from Greenville eastward.[18]

The brief story of McConnell's bands illustrates the special debt which the Nazarenes in Texas owe to the Cumberland Presbyterian church. R. L. Averill conducted meetings at Sunset in January, 1898, in which John Stanfield, a Cumberland Presbyterian pastor, and McConnell, then editor of the local newspaper, professed sanctification. Stanfield began immediately to preach the Wesleyan doctrine, and his presbytery at once suspended him. Undaunted, he proceeded to organize the converts at Sunset and at a half dozen nearby places into holiness bands and offered to serve them on a circuit basis as their pastor. He also laid out a campground at Sunset. At the first meeting there in August, 1899, thirteen bands answered Stanfield's call and organized a second Northwest Texas Holiness Association, not to be confused with the earlier Methodist one disbanded in 1892.

The *Form and Plan of Local Organization* published by the new group predicted that the bands would soon become churches, and pointed out that a number of ministers of several denominations who had recently experienced the "second blessing" would make excellent pastors. For the time being, the constitution made each local organization free to establish its own rules, to select its own pastor, and to form with two or more other local groups such arrangements for co-operative action as they desired. However, the association adopted a uniform statement of doctrine and declared itself competent "to ordain ministers of the gospel, both pastors and evangelists, in accordance with the Holy Scriptures."[19]

When Rogers, Jernigan, McConnell, and a few associates met in Greenville in December, they decided to move slowly so as to recruit the widest possible support. The first step was to meet the next April in connection with the annual gathering of the Holiness Church Association at their campgrounds in Collin County. Successful here, they moved on west in November, 1900, to Sunset, in Brother McConnell's territory. There, with the spirit of union sealed, they appointed a committee to prepare a constitution and statement of doctrine. This document was presented and ratified at yet a fourth meeting, held at Peniel in May, 1901.

The long doctrinal statement, which began with a recital of the Apostles' Creed, provided careful checks against the fanaticism which had earlier thrived on weak organization. The constitution made no provision for the ordination of ministers, no doubt a concession to Methodist scruples. But the association claimed the right "to license or recommend evangelists, pastors, or workers who come duly recommended by the local bands, unions, county and district associations, and local churches." Members of any denomination who were willing to accept the statement of doctrine and who "professed or earnestly were seeking the experience of sanctification" were welcome to join.[20]

The Holiness Association of Texas gathered strength from the rapid expansion of the college and community at Peniel, as well as from the spreading influence of C. M. Keith's *Texas Holiness Advocate*. McConnell moved to Peniel to become managing editor of this paper and remained on after Keith sold his interests to a stock company in 1905. B. W. Huckabee, the new editor, renamed the paper the *Pentecostal Advocate*. He promoted interdenominational fellowship and expressed optimistic hopes for the improvement of the world spiritually, educationally, and socially. Christianity, Huckabee declared, which had destroyed slavery and ushered in democracy, was building a new world "through the natural evolution of the gospel."

Meanwhile President Hills attracted a young but dedicated faculty to Texas Holiness University. In the sound tradition of the American frontier school, the curriculum combined small amounts of classical education with large doses of practical training in mathematics, bookkeeping, business methods, and music, as well as in theology and Bible. From the very beginning, teachers and students came from the North as well as the South, thus helping greatly to break down the Mason and Dixon line dividing the holiness movement. By June, 1906, numerous frame structures surrounded a new $16,000 classroom building, and the college reported that 340 students had been enrolled during the year.[21]

Successive revival campaigns of unusual power helped to advertise the Peniel institution. After his meeting in 1902, Seth C. Rees published an appeal to parents to "stop at once and take your children out of Christless schools and send them to this holiness university." The community itself attracted many parents, especially evangelists, who wished to rear their youngsters away from the evil influences of the city. Bud Robinson established his home there in 1900 and began his lifelong custom of aiding needy students.

Especially interesting was the attempt made after 1903 to organize the civic life of the town on a Christian basis. A constitution adopted that year aimed to put the teaching of holiness "to the practical test of a government where the impelling force should be love and not fear." The document provided that the penalty for infractions of the law should be only "the expressed disapprobation of the community." All persons eighteen years of age or older who were "willing to be governed by the law of Christian love and service," and who subscribed to the constitution, might be citizens. The town council of ten members had one representative chosen by the faculty, one elected by the students, and two from each of the four sections of town. Taxes were very low; individual residents were expected to contribute voluntarily to make up the difference between assessments and actual needs. A monthly "mass meeting" of citizens passed on all important laws. "We are not trying to make each man share his labor equally with his less energetic neighbor, or any such impractical socialistic scheme," the town fathers wrote; "we are simply trying to live together in brotherly love and mutual helpful acts." Two years later the community seemed well satisfied with the experiment and decided to continue it.[22]

For many years there was no church organization in Peniel. Finally, about 1907, a local society of the Methodist Episcopal Church, North, began meeting in Bud Robinson's home. The interdenominational tone of the community is evident from the fact that when A. M. Hills resigned to head a nonsectarian holiness college at Oskaloosa, Iowa, the board elected as his successor E. P. Ellyson, a Society of Friends clergyman, who had recently been principal of a Bible College at Marshalltown, Iowa. The *Pentecostal Advocate* printed the news of independent holiness associations alongside that from pastors working inside both old and new denominations, and rejoiced in the establishment of holiness colleges at Plainview, Texas, Vilonia, Arkansas, and Des Arc, Missouri. The paper also promoted all of the annual camp meetings held in Texas, whether denominational or nonsectarian. By 1906, those at Sunset, Waco, Milan, Noonday, Blossom, and Denton were, like Scottsville, well-established institutions. Each channeled students to the college at Peniel.[23]

The Holiness Association meanwhile encouraged the organization of local bands throughout the area. In 1907, however, the editor of the *Advocate* wrote hopefully that the growing number of congregations in older denominations friendly to the experience of holiness made possible a new view of the function of these lay organizations. Properly managed, a band would not be a hindrance but a blessing to the church which was willing to receive its members into fellowship. "The Association was never so strong as now," C. A. McConnell wrote in November, 1907.

> It has reached a place its founders scarcely dared dream of, and its future usefulness can only be measured by God. . . . Some of the churches who even hold to our doctrine have been a little shy of us, but this year they came to the annual meeting apparently with no doubt but that they belonged among us. Imagine the pleasure it was to us to have a bishop preach to this body of interdenominational workers with all the liberty and fire and gumption of a backwoods brush arbor evangelist before his own crowd.[24]

The Independent Holiness Church: Pilot Point

Within the fellowship of this broader association, however, independent holiness congregations appeared, usually in response to special needs. A revival at Van Alstyne, Texas, in 1901, produced so many homeless converts desiring an organization of their own that C. B. Jernigan helped form a church there and consented to become its pastor. "Not a man in the whole number of charter members was a land owner," he wrote later; they were "poor renters" who could not even afford money to print the new church manual. Jernigan soon found himself organizing other congregations.

Henry Clay Morrison came to Peniel for the spring revival in 1902 and rebuked Jernigan publicly for these measures. Seth C. Rees, however, encouraged him. Jernigan and A. G. Jefferies joined Rees's new Apostolic Holiness church in order to secure a "proper" ordination. While conducting a revival in Paris, Texas, in October, 1902, Rees advised the formation of an annual council of the Independent Holiness church. Jernigan became president of the new group, and a youthful evangelist named James B. Chapman was named secretary. Chapman had promoted the organization of independent congregations from the beginning of his ministry. "I joined the Independent Holiness Church at Van Alstyne, Texas, in 1901," he sometimes said, "and since then I have let the church do the joining."[25]

Naturally, the organization of a federation of independent churches by persons who still maintained membership in the Holiness Association of Texas raised some concern among those in the latter group who were anxious to extend their influence in the older denominations. When delegates from twelve such churches appeared at Greenville, in November, 1903, for their annual council, the Peniel community virtually snubbed them. Jernigan had to entertain the whole company in his own home. They had planned to have Rees come down from Cincinnati to discuss union with the organization he headed there, but opposition to this move was so strong that Rees was asked not to come. Significantly, the leaders of the Independent Holiness church were chiefly young evangelists, who had little hope of achieving national standing like that which Bud Robinson and Hills enjoyed. They were more concerned for the fate of their converts than for traditional ties. All of them remained active in the Holiness Association of Texas, however, viewing it as a way station on the road to a new denominational organization, not an auxiliary of the old-line churches.²⁶

Meanwhile the development of a rescue home, orphanage, and prospective school at the little community of Pilot Point, sixty-five miles to the west, produced a new center to which the leaders of the Independent Holiness church readily gravitated. The "Hudson Band" of evangelists, who had helped get the Sunset camp meeting started, founded an orphanage at Pilot Point around 1900. To this institution in 1903 came J. P. Roberts, an Oklahoma evangelist who had recently felt a call to rescue work as a result of a sermon which Seth C. Rees preached at Oklahoma City. During a season of fasting and prayer at the Pilot Point Holiness church, Roberts "fell into a trance," as Jernigan's account reads, "and there appeared to him in a vision some ten girls from the slums, kneeling just outside the door of the building that he was in and begging him to help them get out of their old life of sin, and give them another chance in life." The following day, at a public service, Roberts described his vision to the congregation. The audience immediately pledged $3,250 to purchase for a rescue home a large residence and six acres of land at the edge of the village. Rest Cottage was established immediately. During the next fifteen years it gave shelter and medical care to 750 unwed mothers during the hardest hours of their lives. It remains to this day the only social service institution sponsored by the Church of the Nazarene.²⁷

The Rising Star Union of 1904

The annual council of the Independent Holiness church did not live long enough to develop any permanent organizational structure. Its founders looked upon their new venture as a means to the larger end which they had been seeking since 1898— the establishment of an enduring denominational home for the holiness people of the Southwest. They eagerly accepted, therefore, the opportunity for union with the New Testament Church of Christ, an event in which C. B. Jernigan played the key role.

Jernigan's contacts with the Eastern Council of the New Testament Church came through his friendship with J. D. Scott, an evangelist from the Indian Territory, who attended Texas Holiness University in 1900 and 1901. Scott left Peniel for a "nation-wide" evangelistic tour in the latter year, but got only as far as Jonesboro, Arkansas. Here he and Allie Irick joined the New Testament congregation, and received the same night ordination to the ministry. In the two years following, Scott founded New Testament churches at Grannis and Old Cove, Arkansas, and established a Bible school at the latter place. He also organized a Southwestern Arkansas Holiness Association and then, in 1904, the Arkansas Holiness Association. Wherever he pastored, Scott invited Jernigan to come for revival meetings at the first opportunity.[28]

Meanwhile, at the annual meeting of the Holiness Association of Texas for 1903, Jernigan became acquainted with William E. Fisher, leader of the west Texas branch of the New Testament church. They discussed the church question at length, and found such little difference between their two movements that they agreed to try to bring about a union. The Independent Holiness group, which by that time numbered twenty-seven congregations, gathered in council at the village of Blossom on October 5, 1904, and approved the proposal for union with enthusiasm. They elected Jernigan, Chapman, Dennis Rogers (who was still serving as president of the Holiness Association of Texas!), John F. Roberts, and M. J. Guthrie as delegates to the Western Council of the New Testament Church of Christ, scheduled to meet at Rising Star, Texas, the next month.

A little less than two weeks later, on October 15, the Eastern Council of the New Testament church met at Stony Point, Arkansas. A committee appointed to draft a constitution, composed chiefly of former Methodist ministers but including Mrs. Cagle, who was present to represent the western churches, promptly brought in a recommendation that its work be deferred pending the outcome of the "union" negotiations. L. L. Gladney then moved that representatives be appointed to confer not only with the Independent Holiness church, but with like delegations from the Pentecostal Mission of Nashville, the Pentecostal Union (Morrison's new all-southern association), the Union Mission Association, and any other holiness organizations interested in "the consolidation of these churches into one body." R. B. Mitchum, R. M. Guy, G. M. Hammond, and C. W. Sherman were named to this committee. They were empowered to act independently of the note on baptism in the church's *Manual*, but were admonished to contend both for its statement of doctrine and for the principle that "in all matters of polity, the local congregation is an independent republic and is sovereign in itself, hence the church in its government is congregational strictly."

Little instruction was necessary on the last point, certainly. Mitchum had begun the session, as in previous years, with the declaration that

> we have not met here to organize a church, nor to make laws to govern a church. The Church of Christ is not a legislative but an executive body. She makes no laws, but accepts laws which Christ and the Apostles have already made. We are not here to bind ourselves up in red tape, formalism, and parliamentary usages, but to be controlled by our great executive Head, the Holy Ghost, who is to guide us into all truth. We are assembled together for mutual help and encouragement, to better understand each other, and the needs of the world.

A short while later the council headed off a motion by E. H. Sheeks to appoint a committee to examine candidates for ordination. It resolved "now and forever" to "accept the congregational form of government in the Church of Christ, and leave each local church a sovereignty in itself." And it rescinded an order adopted the previous year requiring ordained ministers to report directly to the council rather than to their churches, warning that "as we are congregational in government, we must steer clear of episcopacy."[29]

No doubt a chief factor in their successful transition from such intense congregationalism to an eventual acceptance of superintendency was the mediating role played by the lay leader and charter member, R. B. Mitchum. Practically every minister in the New Testament church was in Mitchum's debt, for hospitality enjoyed for periods short or long at his Milan home. About 1900, Mitchum had become a traveling salesman, marketing especially his patented "churnless butter process." As he journeyed over the Old Southwest, this good layman visited churches, missions, and camp meetings, and came into frequent contact with the leaders of other holiness groups. In principle wedded to congregational independency, he came eventually to see the necessity of enlarging and more thoroughly organizing the work. On his shoulders was to rest much of the responsibility for the decisions for union, first at Rising Star, and then with the Pentecostal Church of the Nazarene, at Pilot Point.[30]

When the delegations met at Rising Star, however, the issue most sharply in debate was not superintendency but water baptism. Apparently some of the Independent Holiness churches had allowed persons to become members without being baptized at all. The New Testament church had known differences of opinion on the *mode* of baptism, many prefering immersion to pouring; but none had ever allowed the rite to be ignored altogether. Mrs. Cagle and B. F. Neely made it plain that they could not and would not join a church that failed to require baptism of all its members. The observance of this sacrament, they pointed out, was one of Christ's clearest commands. On the other hand, W. J. Walthall, of Texarkana, Arkansas, leader of the Holiness Baptist churches in that state, refused to join the union unless immersion was required of all members. This the assembly could not prescribe without giving offense to the former Methodists and Cumberland Presbyterians among Jernigan's group. Walthall then withdrew, and the convention was left free to require baptism of all but to leave the mode up to the choice of individuals or congregations.

A joint committee was then appointed to frame a manual and a statement of doctrine to serve as a basis for union. The committee's report, ratified the succeeding year at Pilot Point, provided for a name which combined those of the two original groups, the Holiness Church of Christ. The doctrinal statement was simple and laid the usual stress upon the experience of sanctification. Congregations retained their sovereignty over calling and ordaining ministers and over the conduct of their business affairs. Laymen were assigned important roles in both local churches and councils, of course; but this policy owed no more to the traditions of the New Testament group than to the discontent of the east Texans with the tendency of the Holiness Association of Texas to become a ministers' organization.[31]

The Holiness Church of Christ, 1905-8

The most important task of the Holiness Church of Christ was to provide for the education of preachers and rescue workers. Certainly the need was great. A committee of the Eastern Council complained in 1905 of the "painful lack of education on the part of our preachers in general, many not being blessed with the privilege of early schooling." The group rejoiced to note, however, that "the educational tide" was rising. "Full salvation schools" had been established over the land and both laymen and ministers were taking advantage of them.[32]

By 1906, the denomination was supporting three Bible schools, located at Buffalo Gap, in west Texas; at Vilonia, Arkansas; and at Pilot Point. Mrs. Cagle's school at Buffalo Gap was always small, and ministered chiefly to the churches nearby. Mrs. Fannie E. Suddarth, formerly a social worker in Fort Worth, was principal for many years. Arkansas Holiness College at Vilonia had likewise been a local project. It was under Free Methodist auspices until 1906, when J. D. Scott took charge after a fire destroyed his school building at Old Cove. E. H. Sheeks, Joseph N. Speakes, and other members of the Arkansas Council were added to the board at this point. However, the actual operation of the college was for many years farmed out under contract to President C. L. Hawkins; it remained technically independent of denominational ties. Many pastors and evangelists later prominent in the Church of the Nazarene, including Lewis and D. Shelby Corlett and J. E. Moore, Sr., received their initial training at Vilonia.[33]

The Bible institute at Pilot Point was established by the same council which met there in 1905 to ratify the Rising Star union. R. M. Guy, a rough-hewn but respected evangelist, was placed in charge. Guy had long been interested in the problem of providing a theological education which would not rob young preachers of their zeal and loyalty to the old-time religion. J. B. Chapman, who was then pastor of the Pilot Point congregation, promoted the school in many ways. The first session, held in the fall of 1905, lasted only four weeks but enrolled fifty students. A six-week term was scheduled the following spring and longer ones thereafter. An ambitious plan to purchase the property of a defunct private college in Pilot Point and to add a "literary course" to the offerings fell through. But the Bible institute helped to make the little railroad town the unofficial headquarters of the Holiness Church of Christ until 1908. When in that year the leaders of the college at Peniel cast their lot with the Church of the Nazarene, the smaller school became superfluous, and soon passed out of existence.[34]

For a time religious periodicals threatened to multiply in the young denomination as rapidly as Bible schools. In February, 1906, W. E. Fisher began publishing at Peniel the *Missionary Evangel*. A paper printed at the headquarters of the Holiness Association of Texas, however, could not really serve an organization whose center was Pilot Point. Another periodical named *Highways and Hedges* soon appeared at the latter place, with C. B. Jernigan as editor. Jernigan's salutatory declared that his magazine would be devoted to spreading scriptural holiness, to the systematic organization of church work, to carrying the gospel into the slums, and to "the maintenance of a Bible school run strictly on the faith line, where all of God's poor can get the necessary preparation for the work of the ministry to which God has called them."[35]

Significantly, both Mrs. Cagle and R. B. Mitchum opposed the designation of either publication as an official organ, fearing the concentration of power which would result. "I think the greatest danger ahead of us," Mitchum wrote in 1906, "is that of becoming sectish, the very thing we stand boldly against —the church of the New Testament is not a sect." Nevertheless, the annual council which met at Texarkana that year agreed to assume the small debt of both Fisher's and Jernigan's papers and to issue its own official journal under the title the *Holiness Evangel*. Jernigan was made editor, however, and the platform of his maiden editorial in *Highways and Hedges* became the program of the church.[36]

Both the paper and the schools were designed to support the particular kind of evangelism which the Holiness Church of Christ stressed during the three years of its history: rescue and city mission work at home, and "self-supporting" missions abroad.

The church directly sponsored Rest Cottage, at Pilot Point, and endorsed two other homes for unwed mothers, one at South McAlester, Oklahoma, and the other at Arlington, Texas. A column on rescue work appeared in practically every issue of the *Holiness Evangel*. Sensational accounts of "Nights in the Slums," some of them exhibiting both wisdom and heroism, fired the zeal of the church. A Home Mission Commission, of which R. B. Mitchum was chairman, reported in December, 1906, that one of their number had become matron of yet a fourth rescue home in Little Rock, Arkansas, and that city missions had been established in towns from San Antonio to Memphis. By November, 1907, Arkansas folk under Mrs. Sheeks's direction had raised over a thousand dollars to support the Little Rock home.

The evils which Christian workers discovered in the red-light districts intensified their concern for puritan standards of dress and behavior. At the Arkansas council meeting for 1907, the committee on rescue missions urged that "we do some preventive work on the line of family government and home training." In an admonition against undue familiarity between the sexes, the committee urged ministers to insist that women "dress themselves and their children in modest apparel, as God in his Word commands, and forever abandon short sleeves, low necked dresses, [and] gauze waists." Such dress, the committee declared, "invites insult from the opposite sex and is the cause of many of our precious girls going down in sin and shame."[37]

The ambitious effort which the young church put forth to establish a mission in Mexico grew naturally from such zeal. John and C. E. Roberts conducted for several years an annual "missionary campmeeting" at Pilot Point, which featured both foreign and domestic work. In an editorial for October 1, 1906, C. B. Jernigan called both for early organization of "a chain of missions in all of our larger cities" and for the launching of a foreign venture as well. "The door of Mexico stands wide open," he wrote; "the hands of the brown man, our nearest neighbor, are stretched out to us calling for help." Jernigan noted that S. M. Stafford and a band of workers were ready to depart for that country at once. Their plan was to operate among the Indians living along the Pan-American Railway, establishing a mission station, securing farm lands, and achieving both self-support and the organization of a native church as early as possible. Although some expressed fears of investing too much in foreign missions, R. M. Guy staked his own ministry and the existence of the Bible school at Pilot Point on the promotion of the Mexico project.[38]

Preoccupation with mission and rescue work reached such intensity in the year 1907 that it seemed almost to exhaust the capacity of the movement to fulfill its original purpose of establishing holiness congregations. In Little Rock, one of the few new groups organized that year actually worshiped in a chapel erected by the matron of Crittenton Home. Though no church at all existed in Memphis, Mr. and Mrs. Sheeks agitated for the establishment of a mission home there. The *Holiness Evangel* was filled with stories and editorials on rescue work, carrying such titles as "The Single Standard" and "Sin, Hereditary; or

From the Fireside to the Scarlet District." The Rest Cottage Association published a flaming book, *The White Slaves of America,* in which J. D. Scott recounted experiences in the slums dating back to his service in 1894 at the Texas Woman's Industrial Home, in Fort Worth. Scott pointed out that even among Christian workers a double standard sometimes prevailed. A "rescued" woman was sent away to shame and seclusion while the father of her child, redeemed from an equally wicked condition, was often "led to the platform and introduced to the audience with a brief rehearsal of his black, dirty life, and asked to tell the people what God had saved him from."[39]

Between 1905 and the union with the Nazarenes in 1908, therefore, the Holiness Church of Christ added only fifteen new congregations to the seventy-five in existence in the former year. A few of those established earlier—at Buffalo Gap, Pilot Point, Greenville, Jonesboro, and Vilonia—were strong enough to provide decent support for their pastors. But most of the others were very small.[40] One new area of expansion was in eastern Tennessee, far beyond Nashville, where J. O. McClurkan's Pentecostal Mission held the field. Chapman and Jernigan conducted meetings at Pelham and Monterey, Tennessee, in 1905, organizing churches in both places. The next spring Chapman returned for a revival at Tracy City, where he organized a third church and helped found a council which met annually thereafter, adding several congregations and missions to its fellowship. The spread of the movement into this new area not only increased contacts with McClurkan's Pentecostal Mission but quickened the desire for union among all the holiness churches in the South.[41]

The expansion of both foreign and home mission work required supervision, publicity, educational training, and a centralized program of financial support. Inevitably, therefore, the young denomination rapidly developed a polity which preserved the forms of congregationalism but accepted the practical necessities of a superintendency.

At the Pilot Point council of 1905, R. M. Guy and other leaders of the former New Testament church had taken great pains to explain the nature of the congregation's sovereignty, particularly its exclusive power to ordain and discipline its clergy. But within a year Jernigan was calling for a "General Council Committee," composed of "at least three safe and competent persons," to examine candidates for license or ordination. A few months later the Arkansas council appointed three officers whose duties foreshadowed a district superintendency. G. M. Hammond was made council evangelist; Mrs. E. H. Sheeks, rescue home agent; and J. D. Scott was elected missionary secretary and treasurer. It was agreed that Hammond should record his income and expense and, in case of deficiency, draw from the general funds in the home missions treasury.

A lengthy discussion, in which every leading member of the group participated, preceded the passage of the motion for Scott's appointment. Then the question immediately arose whether the churches were to be "compelled to send their missionary money" to the new officer. The answer was, of course, negative, since, as Chairman R. B. Mitchum pointed out, the denomination was congregational in government. Nevertheless, he added, "all our churches are kindly advised to send their missionary money through this council." A very practical reason lay back of the council's further decision to adopt a uniform system of quarterly reports and to print a list of preachers and officers: the railroads issued regulations in 1906 requiring that a minister's name must appear on such a list before he could receive "clergy" rates.[42]

That same fall, 1906, R. M. Guy was elected to a one-year term as president of the General Council. He announced a plan to visit as many of the congregations as possible, preaching two or three days at each place. Thus Guy hastened at the general level the process by which, within each council, leaders of ability came to exercise a practical superintendency: Hammond and Joseph Speakes in Arkansas; Jernigan and Chapman in east Texas; and Mrs. Cagle and B. F. Neely in the west Texas field.[43]

Such leaders soon recognized that the chief prerequisite for more rapid growth of local congregations was the development of a corps of effective pastors. In the fall of 1906, Speakes and Scott called this "the greatest problem that now confronts us in the home field." J. B. Chapman wrote about the same time that the woods were full of evangelists, but more good pastors were badly needed. "Most any person, if he can be anything at all, can be an evangelist," Chapman declared. A pastor, on the other hand, "has to stay by the flock in time of trouble, and live down and pray out of the bother that he or the devil may stir up."

There was no shortage of preachers, certainly. One hundred and fifty-six ordained elders, beside missionaries and licensed preachers, were listed in 1906. The church at Pilot Point counted twenty-three ministers of various ranks and seventeen missionaries among its one hundred members. Congregational independency had produced an abundance of preachers, but had not solved the problem of placing men in charges which they felt bound to keep at the peril of their souls.[44]

Growing dissatisfaction with a sectional and a sectarian solution to the church question and a renewal of cordial relations with the Peniel community helped pave the way for the union of the Holiness Church of Christ with the Nazarenes. Significantly, the men whose natural capacities for leadership had thrust them into an unofficial superintendency accepted the idea most readily. For example, when in 1906 Henry Clay Morrison, editor of the *Pentecostal Herald,* called for a national consolidation of holiness forces, Jernigan wrote: "We want to say amen! Loud enough to reach clear across this American continent. Holiness churches have come to stay; they are no longer an experiment. So let's all get together in one body. . . ."

A little later, news of the successful steps toward union between the Nazarenes and the Association of Pentecostal Churches reached Texas. Jernigan commented that the interdenominationalism characteristic of both local bands and regional associations had failed to conserve the fruits of Wesleyan evangelism. The reason was that most of the people were too poor to pay two pastors, "one to build up the holiness work, and another to tear it down." R. M. Guy heartily agreed, professing to fear the "radical interdenominationalists" as much as those who were willing to see the Church of Christ become a sect. "I am both inter- and super-denominational," Guy wrote.

> I am ready to and do fellowship every good man, and woman, and work and enterprise. . . . I have no respect for religious bigotry. . . . Nothing tends [as much] to narrow the spiritual horizon, circumscribe religious effort, and paralyze worldwide evangelism as a strict and unyielding *denominationalism.*

To all of which J. B. Chapman answered, "I am for the union of all Holiness churches who are straight in doctrine and clean in life, the world over. Amen."[45]

That these professions of brotherly love could be put to practice in the group's relationships with the leaders of the Holiness Association of Texas was commendable. Many of the latter were still bent upon an interdenominational solution to the church question. The laymen and most of the ministers still belonged to Northern and Southern Methodist, Free Methodist, Methodist Protestant, and Cumberland Presbyterian congregations. Both parties realized, however, that the Texas Holiness University, the *Texas Holiness Advocate,* and the anual meetings of the association helped preserve a unity essential to the future of the entire movement.[46]

Both association and church faced serious problems. Evangelists operating along interdenominational lines were as much concerned about the shortage of "sanctified" pastors in the older communions as were Jernigan and J. D. Scott in the new. Both groups were deeply interested in city mission and rescue work and were equally committed to the idea of foreign missions. Especially after 1906, the *Advocate* recognized these common bonds by giving full publicity to the activities of the holiness churches. When C. A. McConnell succeeded B. W. Huckabee as editor in June, 1907, he brought Dennis Rogers and William E. Fisher to his staff. Meanwhile the leaders of the association appeared regularly at Church of Christ councils and were welcomed to all the privileges of regular members.[47]

These facts help to explain the appeals which the editors of the *Holiness Evangel* made to the community at Peniel to join in the union with the Pentecostal Church of the Nazarene. Recounting the history of the relationship between the two Texas groups, Jernigan declared in 1907 that he had never asked people to join his church, but had "stood willing and ready to make any sort of concession necessary, where vital doctrine was not involved, to get all of the holiness churches into one body." He rejoiced that the *Advocate,* while still interdenominational in policy, now championed any church which dared to preach a full gospel. He also agreed to a point on which eight years earlier the cosmopolitan group at Peniel had anticipated him; the holiness movement, Jernigan now declared, knew no Mason and Dixon line. J. B. Chapman's essays on the church question about this time carried the same message. A national denomination was necessary both to multiply and strengthen the sentiments binding holiness people together, as well as to fence out the fanaticism which had frequently threatened the movement from within.[48]

These appeals lay directly back of Phineas Bresee's success in April, 1908, in bringing a solid portion of the Peniel community over to the Church of the Nazarene. This event, which took place six months before the union assembly was to gather at Pilot Point, made the Nazarenes heir to the whole of the holiness movement in the Southwest. But before we can understand the story of that union we must consider one other parent branch of this church, one which for a time refused to acknowledge its parenthood at all—the Pentecostal Mission, of Nashville, Tennessee.

CHAPTER VIII

The Pentecostal Mission in Tennessee, 1898-1915

The movement to organize the holiness people in the southeastern part of the United States centered in one man—J. O. McClurkan, a Cumberland Presbyterian evangelist who made his home in Nashville. Methodist preachers who professed the second blessing were able in some parts of this section to establish tolerable relationships with their church's leadership. They managed eventually, indeed, to exert wide influence in the Georgia and Kentucky conferences. This was not the case, however, in the Central Tennessee Conference, which embraced the headquarters of Southern Methodism.

Around Nashville, therefore, the field was left clear for McClurkan. He organized and developed a mission movement which, by stopping short of formal church organization, provided a haven and a field of labor for holiness people of many denominations. Some of these forsook their old allegiances while others maintained them. McClurkan welcomed all alike. In both doctrine and organization, therefore, the Pentecostal Mission was somewhat different from other parent bodies of the Church of the Nazarene—sufficiently different, in fact, to delay its union with them until 1914.

Two factors thus explain the relatively late growth of the denomination in the southeast Atlantic states. Methodist advocates of holiness slowly won a place for themselves and their converts in Wesley's church. And a stout champion of the nonsectarian mission idea led the only important separate organization.

The Holiness Movement Comes to Middle Tennessee

B. F. Haynes, a former presiding elder and editor of the *Tennessee Methodist,* professed sanctification in a revival held in Nashville about 1894. He championed the second blessing thereafter with such fervor that, as we have seen earlier, his conference disowned the paper. Haynes continued it under the title *Zion's Outlook,* however, giving wide publicity to the holiness awakening which was spreading through the churches in nearby cities and towns. In 1897 the embattled editor was assigned the Methodist pastorate at Lebanon, Tennessee. A general revival broke out, giving rise to a permanent annual camp meeting there. At the next conference, however, Haynes and several associates were sent to "hard scrabble" circuits. In the years following, the Methodist churches which maintained their witness for Christian perfection in central Tennessee had to brave the bishops' wrath and to look for help from evangelists from outside the state, especially Kentucky.

When Sam P. Jones held a city-wide campaign in Nashville in 1897, he broke his customary silence on perfectionism by noting that preachers and laymen who fought holiness seemed powerless and worldly. Perhaps the highest praise of which Jones felt himself capable was his statement that he had "never seen a holiness man that wasn't a prohibitionist from his hat to his heels." Until after 1900, however, Methodist preachers tended to hide whatever feelings of sympathy they had for the second-blessing movement.[1]

The holiness Methodists were delighted, therefore, when J. O. McClurkan appeared in Nashville in 1896 and began leading his Cumberland Presbyterian brethren into the higher life. McClurkan had been licensed to preach by the Charlotte, Tennessee, Presbytery, about 1879, his eighteenth year. He soon moved to Tucuna, Texas, where he attended the local college and, after returning to Tennessee to marry Martha Rye, alternated pastoring with teaching school. He moved to California in the late 1880's. After brief terms as a pastor in Visalia and Selma, he wound up in 1893 in charge of a Cumberland congregation at San Jose. Here, in a revival at the Methodist church, this mountaineer on the move heard Evangelist Beverly Carradine preach on entire sanctification. McClurkan sought and found the experience. He set out in 1895 on a long evangelistic tour. After a year, however, the ill health which he fought for the remainder of his life forced him to settle down in Nashville.

He soon began to conduct revivals, both in churches and in a large gospel tent. The time was well chosen. Presbyterian

Evangelist J. Wilbur Chapman's book, *The Surrendered Life*, which appeared in 1897, signaled a new interest in the subject outside Methodist ranks. One Cumberland pastor, in reviewing the volume for his denominational paper, exhorted his brethren to "not be afraid of the doctrine of sanctification, of the Baptism of the Holy Ghost, of a holy life in Christ and in God. We need that life here and now. For lack of more holiness we are shorn of our power and fruitfulness."

Inevitably, Cumberland Presbyterians who accepted the doctrine drew inspiration as much from Oberlin as from the Methodists. They also responded favorably to the view of sanctification popular at the Keswick Convention in England. But in central Tennessee they made common cause with the Methodist preachers when the latter were under fire. McClurkan, certainly, remained Wesleyan through and through, despite his friendship and respect for many who clung to a more "Calvinistic" view of the experience.[2]

In midsummer, 1898, McClurkan invited representatives of the holiness people of the area to join him in an association designed to preserve the fruits of their labors. Interested persons met at the Tulip Street Methodist Church, in Nashville, on July 18 and 19, and organized the Pentecostal Alliance. The first executive committee included three laymen, one of whom was John T. Benson, later prominent as a publisher. Of the four ministers, two were Cumberland Presbyterians and one a Southern Presbyterian; the only Methodist was B. F. Haynes. The committee announced that they planned no new denomination but simply a "banding together of the holiness people" for mutual support and union in foreign missionary ventures. Two years later seven members of the Alliance bought Haynes's interest in *Zion's Outlook*, and made McClurkan editor. For the next fourteen years his influence outside Nashville was to be chiefly exerted through the columns of this journal.[3]

The Nashville group soon established close relations with A. B. Simpson's Christian and Missionary Alliance, in New York City. They invited Simpson to a missionary convention in March, 1900, at which arrangements were perfected for the Tennesseans to send both money and prospective missionaries to his training school in New York. Officials of Simpson's organization appeared at the annual convention in Nashville the following fall, and Christian and Missionary Alliance ministers from the cities of Atlanta, Richmond, and Columbia united with McClurkan's organization, apparently in expectation of its formal affiliation with the national body.

The early associations with Simpson's group helped to plant zeal for foreign missions deep in the life of the Pentecostal Alliance. These were the years when, thanks to the Spanish-American War and the acquisition of Hawaii and the Philippines, the average American was rapidly developing great interest in the world beyond our shores. For earnest Christians, that interest inevitably expressed itself in the support of overseas evangelism.

The Pentecostal Alliance never lost sight of missionary needs at home, however, a fact which is illustrated by its work among Negroes. J. T. Brown, a colored evangelist, reported his meetings frequently in *Zion's Outlook,* and by 1901 was planning the establishment of an affiliate mission and rescue home for his people. In an editorial for February 7, 1901, McClurkan declared that the holiness movement was becoming a major force in eliminating sectional prejudices from the southern churches. "Thank God that holiness is the great resolvent of this problem," he wrote.

> The sanctified heart is absolutely cleansed of all war or race prejudice. Holiness deepens and sweetens and broadens the nature until every man of all and every section and nationality and color and condition is loved as a brother. There is no North, no South, no Jew, no Greek, no Barbarian to the sanctified. . . .[4]

Despite its founder's Presbyterian background, the doctrinal position of the Alliance was unquestionably Wesleyan. McClurkan early made plain his rejection of the notions of immutable perfection and of the sinfulness of the body. Like the Methodists, he taught that the "inbred corruption" remaining in believers "must be extirpated, the whole tap-root of sin excised." That he always wrote charitably of the Keswick and kindred movements merely demonstrated his determination to put in practice the conviction that "religion is love and . . . without love any and all religion is but a name." The Keswick teachers, McClurkan said, had failed to distinguish between "the good and the bad self," between the sinful and the human nature. Hence they could not comprehend an experience which promised to eradicate the roots of sin. To McClurkan, however, "the whole trend of Scriptural teaching" aimed at "the putting off of the old man, *the cleansing of the heart from all sin.*" He urged his followers "to stress this point: *the utter eradication of all evil in the heart.*"⁵

The doctrinal statement proposed for the Nashville group in fact differed from those of other Wesleyan associations only in the absence of certain cautionary phrases about divine healing and in its uncompromising stand on the premillennial second coming of Christ.⁶ McClurkan thus disagreed sharply with the policy under which the leaders of the National Association for the Promotion of Holiness had sought to restrain discussion of these so-called "side issues." The holiness movement had suffered from too much narrowness, he believed. It should proclaim a "full gospel" in which sanctification was but the center of a constellation of important latter-day truths.

The emphasis upon healing, of course, accorded with that of A. B. Simpson, who maintained that the atonement had provided restoration to health for all Christians who could pray the prayer of faith. Both McClurkan and Simpson found it necessary, however, to reject publicly the doctrines of John Alexander Dowie. In 1901, *Zion's Outlook* declared Dowie's healing missions in Chicago to be unscriptural, sectarian, and based on the religion of the Old Testament rather than the New.

McClurkan's stress upon premillennialism continued without qualification until his death in 1914. In the early years the *Outlook* carried a weekly column under the title "Behold, He Cometh," and advertised repeatedly the solid Mennonite treatise on premillennialism by J. A. Seiss. He carefully defined the implications of the doctrine for social and political theory in many editorial columns. Thus in the issue for April 18, 1901, McClurkan condemned alike the rich for their unjust exploitations of the poor, and organized labor for uniting workingmen on a platform of greed and strife. True, he agreed, the poor man had little chance in a nation held in the grip of those who had purchased power with money. To the middle-class Protestants who were supporting Theodore Roosevelt's progressivism, he wrote: "Reform politics if you can, it is a great and good work." But only the return of Jesus could really remedy political and economic evil. Then the poor would have their rights, and both millionaires and labor unions would go out of style.⁷

An Undenominational Path, 1901-7

By the spring of 1901, leaders of the Nashville group had become discontented with their affiliation with the Christian and Missionary Alliance. The reasons are obscure. If they were doctrinal, no evidence of this fact appears in the literature which has survived, save that a succession of committees had failed to produce a manual of faith and practice satisfactory to the group. A good guess is that the differences arose as much over ways and means of organizing the work at home as over the appointment and support of missionaries abroad.[8]

Certainly the evangelization of the poor and individual freedom in the solution of the church question became prominent issues in the columns of *Zion's Outlook* during the early part of this year. In February, 1901, McClurkan praised the Volunteers of America highly, not only for their ministry to the underprivileged, but for the fact that they left the question of church membership entirely to the option of the individual. Some holiness associations, he noted, made the mistake of requiring their members to belong to a church.

McClurkan's own Nashville Holiness Tabernacle, established the same year, had no such requirements. Instead, he offered to all comers a full schedule of three Sunday services and weekly young people's and prayer meetings. Faith and activity, rather than church membership, was the basis of fellowship. He urged the creation of similar missions for the "neglected masses" in other cities, as well as in rural areas of Tennessee. At the same time he began more actively to promote rescue work, particularly the Door of Hope mission in Nashville.[9]

The end of May, 1901, found the editor urging his followers to exercise great care before making any decisions about church membership. Although he believed that a majority of the holiness people would, for the time being, maintain their present church relationships, the "little independencies" springing up all over the land indicated that a general realignment was at hand. He warned readers against attacking the latter groups, lest they "lay hands on the Ark." He hoped, however, that the holiness people would never attempt to unite all in one body, for such a step would result in "a great big ecclesiasticism," of which the country already had enough. "None of us," he added, "can corral the holiness movement."[10]

In August the executive committee of the Nashville Alliance met at the Murphreesboro campground to confer with J. M. Pike, of Atlanta, on the question of organizing the holiness forces of the southeastern states separately from the Christian and Missionary Alliance. The annual convention which followed in November adopted proposals to change the name of the Tennessee group to the Pentecostal Mission and to place its management entirely under a local board of 25 members. The 125 delegates who attended this meeting came from several states and a half dozen denominations. But they seem to have agreed readily upon a confession of faith which affirmed the "verbal inspiration" of the Bible; the "vicarious atonement" of Christ; the "total depravity" of the human race; a future of blessedness for the saved and of "unending conscious suffering" for the lost; justification and entire sanctification; divine healing "in answer to the prayer of faith"; and "the Pre-Millennial Coming of our Lord and Savior Jesus Christ to reign on earth as King."[11]

In retrospect, the Pentecostal Mission, like Peniel Mission in Los Angeles, seems to have differed from such organizations as the Holiness Association of Texas only in its predominantly urban cast. McClurkan's group invited "individuals, societies, prayer circles, missions, or churches" to affiliate as members, on the sole condition that they agree with the doctrinal statement. He stressed the fact that the organization was "strictly undenominational," and went out of his way to explain that it was no longer affiliated with the Christian and Missionary Alliance. The group had changed its name precisely to avoid that impression, he declared, though they still felt "close kinship to and love for that devout people."[12]

From this point forward, the expansion of the Pentecostal Mission work in home fields received as much attention as ventures overseas, if not more. By the time of the October, 1903, annual meeting, at which Presbyterian Evangelist E. F. Walker was the speaker, twenty-six missions were reported in the state of Tennessee, as well as one each in the cities of Atlanta, Georgia, and Columbia, South Carolina. Nashville laymen, especially John T. Benson, Tim H. Moore, and A. S. Ransom, were the most prominent members of the executive board.[13]

Foreign missions were by no means neglected, however. On the contrary, the Nashville group seems to have over-extended itself, in part through the adoption of the principle that those sent overseas must go in faith, without a stated salary. By 1903 nine persons represented the mission in Cuba; Mr. and Mrs. R. S. Anderson and two associates were laying foundations for the present Nazarene work in Guatemala; and five were under appointment to India. Work in India began early in 1904, in the beautiful mountain town of Igatpuri, later a headquarters for Nazarene missions in the Asian subcontinent. All the missionaries, as required by the rules adopted in 1901, professed to have "received the Holy Spirit in His sanctifying power"; and they pledged to keep their work "strictly undenominational." Monthly collections averaging between two hundred and four hundred dollars, and large special offerings at camp meetings and conventions, provided their support.[14]

Both home and foreign missions demanded workers specifically trained in holiness evangelism. As in other sections of the country, therefore, a Bible institute and eventually a college arose in Nashville.

McClurkan's followers might have relied upon other institutions, especially the East Mississippi Female College in Meridian, Mississippi. J. W. Beeson, a member of the mission and a staunch friend of holiness, was president there. By 1901 this institution enrolled two hundred boarding students from fourteen states. Holiness evangelists conducted frequent revivals. The curriculum seems to have been principally vocational: teacher education, stenography, bookkeeping, dressmaking, and practical nursing. In addition, a "Chair of Bible" provided training for Christian workers and an "Industrial Home" gave cheap lodging to girls of slender means. Glowing reports in *Zion's Outlook* undoubtedly attracted many students from the various Pentecostal groups. In 1903, Beeson renamed his school Meridian Female College and boasted that it had the largest enrollment of any private college for young ladies in the South. His brother, M. A. Beeson, had meanwhile established Meridian Male College only one-half mile away. Like other holiness schools, the men's institution excluded intercollegiate sports and secret societies, and adopted the compulsory military training which was a feature of so many private colleges in the South.[15]

McClurkan, however, felt the need of a training center in Nashville. As early as March, 1901, when the separation from the Christian and Missionary Alliance was foreseen, he announced plans for a Bible institute. He secured in May a brick building which, from its appearance, was originally a factory, and announced that classes would begin in the fall. Although English, history, mathematics, Greek, and Hebrew would be taught as needed, he wrote, the chief subjects would be Bible and evangelism. Students were to supplement their classroom experiences by actual participation in mission and open-air services. Twenty-five students registered on November 5, and *Zion's Outlook* appealed for contributions for the support of young people who wished to attend but had no money.

The school grew slowly. In 1906, McClurkan secured a new location which afforded facilities for both institute and tabernacle church, as well as living quarters for him and the faculty. The curriculum still combined simply a "common English" education with practical training in missions and evangelism. But a few outstanding teachers made both classwork and field work exciting. Henrietta Matson, a retired missionary who had been educated in Scotland, taught mathematics at Fisk University by day, and gave the rest of her time to McClurkan's institute. Miss Fannie Claypoole, beloved as an English teacher and indispensable as office editor of *Living Water*, invested her whole life in the cause. Eighty students from fifteen denominations were enrolled in 1906. Tuition was free to all who could not pay. To a young man from Louisiana who wrote of his call to preach and his lack of money for an education, the Nashville pastor wrote simply,

> Dear Brother L——,
> Come along. Bring your bedding.
> Your Brother in Christ,
> J. O. McClurkan[16]

N. J. Holmes, head of a Bible institute in Atlanta, cast his lot with McClurkan's group in 1901. Holmes soon organized a similar educational venture at Columbia, South Carolina, in connection with the Pentecostal Mission there. In March, 1905, Holmes reported that his new school had attracted some thirty students, who lived together with the faculty as one household so as better to engage in gospel "apprentice" work of various sorts. Meanwhile, another affiliate mission sponsored the Elhanan Training and Industrial Institute for poor children and young people at Marion, North Carolina.[17]

In many ways the mood in which this missionary, evangelistic, and educational work took place was a more important index to the independent tendencies of the Pentecostal Mission than were its stated policies or doctrines. About 1900 a volume by F. L. Chapell appeared, entitled *The Eleventh Hour Movement*. The book depicted as signs of the last days the emergence of nondenominational evangelistic Bible school and city mission ventures in England and America. McClurkan's group immediately identified themselves with this image. The first editorial calling for the establishment of the Bible institute in Nashville pictured it as a necessary adjunct to any "Eleventh Hour Movement." In the following years the *Outlook*, renamed *Living Water* in 1903, used the phrase to describe the entire work of the mission, as well as to solicit support for Holmes's school in Columbia.[18]

Such a mood was neatly tailored to loosely organized nonsectarianism. It also helped to sustain McClurkan's broad toleration of the Calvinistic system of theology, despite the fact that he, a Cumberland Presbyterian, had embraced Wesleyanism. By 1905 he was stressing the fact that the Bible institute was committed to neither the Calvinistic nor the Arminian system of theology. In 1909, McClurkan reorganized the institute as a college by adding advanced courses in literature and history and a "normal course" for public school teachers. He chose to name the new school Trevecca in memory of the institution which Lady Huntingdon founded in eighteenth-century England, where she hoped the followers of Whitefield and Wesley might study together and bury their disagreements over grace and free will.[19]

Nevertheless, McClurkan also saw that little and poor organization could hinder the spread of holiness. In an editorial for May 12, 1904, entitled "Feed My Sheep," he deplored the tendency of the mission's workers to overrate evangelism at the expense of the pastoral ministry, and thus throw their sheep to the wolves. "Running around over the country, stopping here and there, staying ten days or two weeks, running a high pressure revival," he said, "then leaving the people to get along the best they can, without . . . a single teacher to instruct or care for them" was definitely not the gospel plan. The policy of establishing local Pentecostal Mission centers and of forming these into districts under regular ministerial supervision seemed to him to provide the minimal organization necessary. "We are not especially wedded to this plan," he wrote, "but it is the best we have yet seen for preserving the work. . . . The people are left free on the church question. We neither take them out or put them in, but let each decide the question for himself." Nevertheless, he stood ready "to join heart and hand with anything better, should it come along."

A little later McClurkan reiterated the point that, although the Pentecostal Mission did not at its beginning think the founding of a new church desirable, yet it had organized itself to provide instruction, discipline, and encouragement to converts. "Very few seem to have any well-defined conviction as to how far the matter of organization can be pressed without hampering the spontaneity and freedom of this remarkable movement," he wrote. He was anxious that "narrowness and littleness" not overtake his people in any rash solution of the church question. Obviously, however, McClurkan was dealing with the same problems which in other sections of the country had driven persons once wedded to congregationalism toward the adoption of stronger denominational bonds.[20]

Thus it was that he entered into correspondence with Phineas Bresee and considered seriously and at length uniting with the Church of the Nazarene. The story of how and why that union was postponed until after McClurkan's death provides a fascinating insight into early Nazarene history.

The Postponement of Union with the Nazarenes

The Pentecostal Mission had from the beginning been in touch with the leaders of those holiness movements in Tennessee, Arkansas, and Texas which finally cast their lot with the Church of the Nazarene. The Tennessee leader was one of the evangelists at the Waco, Texas, camp meeting in 1901. Here he began a lifelong friendship with B. W. Huckabee, based upon their mutual interest in foreign missions. McClurkan praised the Texans whom he met in Waco for the absence of any "argumentative, bitter, censorious spirit," despite the severe trials through which they had passed. Thereafter C. B. Jernigan and R. M. Guy began sending frequent reports to *Zion's Outlook,* and A. M. Hills wrote occasional articles. Guy, who lived for several years at Meridian, Mississippi, was one of the few evangelists whose schedule the magazine regularly listed.

In west Tennessee, meanwhile, members of the New Testament Church of Christ read McClurkan's paper and sent money for his missionaries. In 1905, fraternal delegates from the Pentecostal Mission appeared at the meetings of the Arkansas Council of the Holiness Church of Christ, voicing sentiments hopeful of union. The R. B. Mitchum family moved to Nashville in 1906 and began attending McClurkan's tabernacle. Alike in basic doctrines, heirs of the same tradition of independency, and faced with the same need for organization, McClurkan and Mitchum might well have united to promote the merger of their two churches. But such was not to be.[21]

A widespread legend attributed the failure of the first efforts at union between the Nazarenes and the Pentecostal Mission either to McClurkan's laxity on membership in secret orders and the use of tobacco, or to his Calvinistic doctrines. Substantial evidence from contemporary sources indicates that both explanations are untrue.

In a pamphlet published as early as 1899, McClurkan stressed the dangers of tobacco, secret societies, and "gay worldly attire" to those who would follow a holy path. "Men active and prominent in lodges are seldom very spiritual," was his blunt comment. He recognized the folly of extremes, of course. *Zion's Outlook* carried in March, 1901, an article by A. M. Hills which denounced those "professed holiness people" who seemed "to glory in their boorishness and to trample with a relish upon all the instinctive refinements of civilized, Christian society." But students who attended the Bible institute during the early years never forgot McClurkan's strong stand against worldliness of all descriptions.[22]

Nor did the Nashville founder at any time modify his acceptance of the Wesleyan belief that the experience of sanctification cleansed the heart from "inbred sin." True enough, the *Outlook* carried numerous articles in the early years revealing a debt to the mystic tradition of holiness which had come down from the French Catholics through T. C. Upham and certain other American Congregationalists. Moreover, by 1905, as we have seen, McClurkan was insisting that his paper and his school must seek to draw the best from both the Arminian and the Calvinistic views of theology.[23] Nevertheless, a succession of editorials and articles every year left no doubt that he rejected "Keswick" views. Most effective, perhaps, was a comic piece in German dialect, entitled "Hans Don't Like the Suppression Theory":

> I haf me mine mide up. Der is someding midtin me wrong—ungovernable—someding uncondrolable . . . I haf found me oudt vat der matter mid me is. It is dot undesired, unmanageable, ungentlemanly, unkindt, unholy old man midtin. He must outcast be. I haf me mine made up to lead him to der electrocudtor's chair vonced vhere he must die. I haf tried to "keep him under," but ven I looks not for him, oudt he comes up yusht ven I don'dt vant him. I haf tried to "subbress" him, vat Mr. Kesvick vould say; but ven I see mine neighbor's pigs in der garden midt mine kraut make havoc, he gets off die cellar-door vhere I keeps him subbressed, undt schpoiles die beautiful subbression theory. I am sorry for Mr. Kesvick.24

In his book *Wholly Sanctified,* McClurkan made very plain what he was driving at. He was attempting to clarify the distinction between sinfulness and human frailty, between purity and maturity. The cleansing of the heart from all sin was, he said, "the very bedrock of the work wrought in sanctification, and therefore of the most vital importance." In this experience, the sinful self was destroyed. The natural self, however, must continue to "die daily." In the higher Christian life, McClurkan insisted, "the 'ego' or creature life still exists, and the displacement of the natural self by the incoming of the Christ life is . . . accomplished in these deeper crucifixions."

Only against this background can we place in proper perspective the memories old-timers have of doctrinal controversies between the Nashville leader and other Wesleyans. At a conference at Meridian, Mississippi, for example, McClurkan expressed to the assembled leaders of the holiness movement in the South his anxiety that in preaching the eradication of the carnal mind they might fail sufficiently to stress the human frailties of those who enjoyed this exalted grace. Henry Clay Morrison, so one account has it, interrupted and took McClurkan sharply to task. The reproof went on some time. At its end, the Nashville pastor, famous above everything else for his gentleness, rose quietly, pointed to Morrison, and said, "Brethren, *that* is exactly what I mean."25

McClurkan himself seems in fact to have made the first overture looking toward possible union with the Church of the Nazarene. In a letter to Dr. Bresee written January 1, 1907, he explained the growing need to turn the loosely organized missions into churches, so as to preserve the work. In looking around for a kindred organization with which to unite, he said, "The Church of the Nazarene comes nearer our ideal than any other . . . , yet there may be difficulties that would not be easily removed in the way of our union." He felt sure that "a movement of sufficient breadth to include all the varied work of the Holy Spirit and in polity stand about halfway between Congregationalism and the Episcopacy would be the very thing." The "difficulties" which he noted in this letter seemed unimportant: the length of the denominational name, and the desirability of locating the foreign mission headquarters of the united church in Nashville. Possibly the two men exchanged other letters before Bresee's reply of August 1, 1907, the only one extant. In any case, Bresee stressed the point that the doctrinal basis of belief should be "very simple, and embrace what is essential to holiness." Nonessentials should be relegated to "personal liberty," a phrase which Bresee said referred to a person's right to hold a belief, and his obligation "to recognize the same right in another to believe differently, without fussing about it. We have and do hold," Bresee went on, "that any truth about which there can be two theories, and a person can be holy and believe either theory, may be safely, and should be, relegated to individual liberty." This, he understood, was the gist of what McClurkan had said, and it was the platform of the Nazarenes.[26]

This exchange of letters revealed no differences at all on the issue of church government, and in fact none developed. In a general letter of September 6, 1907, to representatives of Nazarene and Pentecostal churches on the eve of their meeting at Chicago, McClurkan again repeated his desire for a stronger organization. The loose forms which in their early days had helped to widen the fellowship of the holiness movement were now weakening it. "Independentism is exposed to too many dangers," he wrote; the holiness people needed "both spurs and bits." Although congregational polity had once served a useful purpose, "a movement of such immaturity and intensity" required a stronger discipline. The "modified Presbyterian polity" which he proposed resembled exactly the framework of government agreed upon at the Chicago assembly.

On the doctrinal issue, McClurkan explained carefully what he meant by the oft-repeated admonition to avoid the "extreme statements" of Calvinism and Arminianism. "Our candid judgment is that the holiness movement as a body would be strengthened by a little more emphasis being put upon grace," he wrote. But a "perfect heart" was the heritage due all God's children. The chief lack was that there had "not been enough teaching as to what follows sanctification, and as a result many sincere and devout people are confused as to the distinction between humanity and sin."[27]

A strong delegation from the Pentecostal Mission attended the Chicago assembly. They received a hearty welcome, and prospects for their union with the new movement at Pilot Point, Texas, the next year seemed bright. The representatives who attended the Pilot Point assembly, however, seem to have uncovered difficulties not suspected earlier. The Nazarenes, they reported, were "not sufficiently committed to the doctrine of the Lord's premillennial coming to justify us in organic union as yet." Moreover, the ordination of women, as distinct from their freedom to participate in religious services, seemed unscriptural. Why, this late in the negotiations, did the Nashville group raise these issues?

No two subjects could have been found upon which the Nazarenes would have been less willing to compromise. Premillennialism ran counter to the personal views of Bresee and H. F. Reynolds, and to those of countless Methodists who honored the tradition of their church on this question. Moreover, every parent body from which the church sprang owed much to the work of consecrated women in the pulpit. All had adopted provisions for their ordination in the earliest days of their work; two had been ordained at the Chicago assembly of 1907. Rose Potter Crist, a woman evangelist, had served as Bresee's assistant pastor in Los Angeles during part of the same year. For that matter, McClurkan's own wife had become, with her husband's steady encouragement, one of his movement's finest preachers, though she remained, of course, an unordained one. Did other more troublesome issues lie back of the delay?

In any event, negotiations were not broken off. A standing commission of Nashville leaders was empowered to conclude a union if it could work out with a like commission from the Nazarenes a compromise of the two major questions. But an alternative plan grew in favor, with McClurkan's blessing: to strengthen the bonds among the Pentecostal Mission groups themselves, and remain independent of other denominations. In September, 1909, the annual convention considered the union question again. The delegates voted down a proposal to organize their own work more thoroughly, after lengthy discussion. At that point they would probably have approved union had not McClurkan presented in writing a motion urging them to defer action.[28]

The Last Years of the Pentecostal Mission

The discussion, and the frustration, reached a climax in 1910. At the annual meeting that year, McClurkan's followers resolved, despite his continued reluctance, to invite the Nazarene commissioners to come to Nashville at once, with as many of the general superintendents as could make the trip. H. F. Reynolds, P. F. Bresee, C. E. Cornell, and E. P. Ellyson arrived in a few days. The convention voted specifically to request J. O. McClurkan "to make a statement to the Commission in reference to women's ordination as would be satisfactory to him" and toned down their previous insistence upon premillennialism to a simple declaration that "they greatly preferred" this view.

During the deliberations which followed, no differences at all appeared over matters of church government. Dr. Bresee and the Nazarenes readily agreed to locate the missionary headquarters in Nashville. Far from advocating, as some have thought, a more liberal policy on lodges and tobacco, McClurkan's group insisted that strict prohibitions be written into the "General Rules." Bresee agreed that this could be arranged. The Nazarene founder did not, however, think that the statement on ordination of women could be changed, or that the doctrine of the Second Coming could be narrowly defined, for "a man could be either premillennialist or postmillennialist and be a holy man."

At the end of a full day of further discussion, McClurkan declined the request of his own members to state whether he would go with them into the Church of the Nazarene. Unwilling to move without their leader, the Mission's executive committee thereupon voted twenty-one to five against the proposed merger, and nineteen to three in favor of organizing among themselves. Nevertheless, they invited the Nazarenes to come to Nashville for their General Assembly the next year, and so kept alive hopes for union.[29]

A few weeks later, however, McClurkan wrote a four-page letter to General Superintendent E. P. Ellyson explaining that

> after our meeting adjourned and we had time to quietly consider the matter further, it occurred to us that perhaps it would be better for you to come to Nashville without any official recognition of us at all; just meet here like you would in any other city. We would provide for your entertainment and look after all matters of that kind, . . . and let you in no sense be obligated to us. You remarked in our first meeting last summer that you would not again go to a place on trial, and perhaps this is wise.

On first sight, this letter seems an obvious effort to delay and confuse plans of union. Anyone acquainted with Brother McClurkan's personality and modes of operation, however, might well see in it only his familiar caution. Later on in the letter he suggested that if the Lord desired to bring the two churches together perhaps it could be done more efficiently if both were left "absolutely free for the present." He noted that his own people showed little enthusiasm for closer organization among themselves. If the assembly did meet in Nashville and the Pentecostal Mission did not unite with the Nazarenes, he added, "the brethren wanting the organization would unite with you anyway."[30]

The general superintendents were indeed loath to accept an invitation extended under such circumstances. When they were on the point of deciding to go elsewhere, however, McClurkan urged Reynolds to come to Nashville to talk the matter over. After extended negotiation, Reynolds finally organized, with McClurkan's blessing, the Clarksville District of the Church of the Nazarene in western Tennessee. He appointed J. J. Rye, until that time a Cumberland Presbyterian, superintendent. Reynolds and Ellyson then decided to take the General Assembly to Nashville, despite Dr. Bresee's reluctance, and despite the fact that McClurkan's group still refused to promise to bring the Nashville congregation into the union.

Edward F. Walker, a Presbyterian evangelist well known to McClurkan's people, had recently united with the Church of the Nazarene. Walker preached the first Sunday of the assembly, and swept the congregation off its feet with his eloquence. On Thursday he found himself elected a general superintendent, replacing E. P. Ellyson, who had accepted the presidency of the college at Pasadena. This and many other actions of the Nazarene assembly reflected the effort to conciliate the Pentecostal Mission, among them, the inclusion in the General Rules of statements which unmistakably forbade lodge membership and the use of tobacco. Nevertheless, the assembly adjourned with union still beyond its grasp.

The General Foreign Missionary Board continued in session in the city, however, and engaged in further conferences with the Nashville laymen. E. F. Walker proposed that the Nazarenes should not assume responsibility for the foreign work of the Mission unless the congregation of the Nashville Tabernacle agreed to unite with the denomination. The next day John T. Benson informed the board that his associates were unable to agree upon this decision. He suggested that the Nazarenes proceed to make their appropriations for foreign missions without considering the overseas work of the Tennessee group. If the Nashville congregation should decide upon union later, they would support the missionaries they had sent out until better arrangements could be made.

Devotion to their leader thus triumphed over the practical concern the laymen of the Mission felt for the increasing financial difficulties facing their home and foreign work. The property of the Mission, including the paper and Trevecca College, was in the hands of individuals. The liabilities inevitably were shared by men such as Benson, Tim H. Moore, Ransom, and others.[31]

The Nazarenes, however, had long since begun to organize their own work in the territory where Morrison's Holiness Union and McClurkan's Pentecostal Mission had provided the chief leadership. A Kentucky and Tennessee District was laid out as early as 1908. C. A. Bromley, pastor at Louisville, and his successor in that charge, W. A. Eckel, served in turn as district superintendents. County holiness associations and holiness unions as well as local units of the Pentecostal Mission provided nuclei for Nazarene congregations. As McClurkan had predicted in 1910, those of his people who desired closer bonds of church fellowship soon formed the backbone of the work in Tennessee. Nor did the Nashville founder oppose this trend. He had made concessions at the time of the Nashville General Assembly which, as an early statement in the district minutes put it, caused the Nazarenes properly to feel that "the land is ours for the taking." At the assembly which marked the end of J. J. Rye's first year as district superintendent in Tennessee, Mrs. McClurkan addressed an open-air meeting and her husband shared the preaching with Dr. Bresee.³²

Meanwhile, General Superintendents Reynolds and Ellyson promoted the growth of another Nazarene center at Donalsonville, Georgia. Here a good church, supported chiefly by the T. J. Shingler family, had grown from seed sown through previous years by the Georgia Holiness Association. The group had joined the Holiness Church of Christ in 1907. In the fall of 1910, Shingler gave forty acres of land and the lumber to erect a Bible school in the town. Reynolds blocked out a plan for a college, proposing to sell the twenty acres nearest the village to finance the construction of school buildings. "We must not let this proposition cool off," he wrote Ellyson. Shingler and his business associates had just put up a cottonseed-oil mill, and the town was soon to boast a hotel and two railroads. He hoped that Ellyson would consider moving there if ever he planned to leave the college at Peniel.³³

In September, 1914, J. O. McClurkan lay near death at his home in Nashville. Recent years had multiplied his burdens beyond bearing. The foreign mission work he loved showed a mounting deficit, and the paper, *Living Water,* was losing $2,000 a year. Income to Trevecca College was, as usual, not meeting running expenses. The patient warrior talked to his wife of the event he knew was near. "Papa, what will we do about the Mission?" Mrs. McClurkan asked. His answer was that they should unite with the Nazarenes. Within a few days he passed away. For a moment the leaders of his adopted city paused to mourn their loss.

Within a month the annual convention appointed a committee of five, including John T. Benson, Tim Moore, and C. E. Hardy, to arrange the details of union. They promptly requested the Nazarenes to provide a pastor for the Nashville congregation and a leader for the school and to assume responsibility for the home and foreign work of the Mission. They noted that only $4,000 of the $9,000 annual cost of the foreign missionary venture regularly came from the Nashville membership; friends who had in the past provided the balance would probably cease their contributions once union with the Nazarenes was completed.³⁴

Negotiations proceeded swiftly. Objections from the Nashville congregation were silenced by Benson's frank explanation of their financial situation. General Superintendent H. F. Reynolds appointed R. B. Mitchum, Foreign Missions Secretary E. G. Anderson, and J. A. Chenault, Tennessee district superintendent, to confer with the Nashville group. In the articles of agreement drawn up in February, 1915, the leaders of the Mission declared themselves to be "in hearty agreement and sympathy with the *Manual.*" Their local units, save for the Nashville Tabernacle, were free to join or remain independent. The Nazarenes agreed to recognize all ministers' credentials. All the Mission property was to be turned over, but the denomination would not assume responsibility to continue the foreign work except in India, where it was well established. On these terms, union was concluded. On April 15, 1915, the Pentecostal Mission became a part of the Church of the Nazarene.[35]

The Progressive Movement in American Religion

The present and preceding chapters describing the emergence of the new Wesleyan denominations in the years between 1890 and 1910 leave one further question begging an answer. What was the relationship of these movements to dynamic forces at work in American society generally?

What one historian has called the "psychic crisis" of the 1890's lay in the background of the great events of the first twenty years of the twentieth century, known as the "progressive period" in American history. Professor Richard Hofstadter's view is that this intellectual crisis arose from the passing of the frontier, fears of the consequences of mass immigration from Europe, the clash of new ideas in science and religion, and the conflicts between farm and city, between laborer and employer. But even more important, in his opinion, were the revolution in the status of social classes which the rise of big business produced, and the challenge which the city posed to the way of life of a people used to rural and small town customs. Many historians now agree that the political and social reforms initiated during the period when Presidents Theodore Roosevelt and Woodrow Wilson occupied the White House were the work of a middling class of Americans—bankers, editors, teachers, clergymen, and lawyers. Such men felt the bite of the "status revolution" which had placed newly rich industrialists at the head of American society. Members of the old Protestant native families resented the rise of the multimillionaire industrialist class as much as they feared socialism's growth or the organization of labor unions among masses.

Many of the "progressive" leaders, as Professor George E. Mowry has shown, had recently come from small town and rural places to the city, and were shocked by the corruption, the poverty, and the cynicism which they found. They supported the reform of municipal government, discussed ways to "Americanize" the immigrant, engaged in social work in the urban slums, and fought for prohibition, the graduated income tax, and the enfranchisement of women. The prohibition crusade was as symbolic of their concern for old standards of morality as their attack upon monopolies was an expression of their desire to go back to the simple conditions of free competition in business.[36]

It has long been known that a parallel movement in religion gave rise to what was called the "social gospel," led by such men as Walter Rauschenbusch and Lyman Abbott. Some of its program of reform looked forward to revolutionary changes in the structure of society. But the basis of its appeal was a stern application of the old standards of morality to the new abuses of wealth and the new evils which many thought stemmed from urban slums and Roman Catholic immigration. Likewise, as we are now coming to understand, the progressive movement in education was scarcely revolutionary. Its stress upon vocational training for the children of the poor, upon the honest administration of school funds, and upon "education for democracy" was inspired as much by the desire to preserve traditional values in an age of change as by any plan to plot a new or radical course.[37]

What has hitherto escaped notice is that persons of solid middle-class background launched a multitude of popular spiritual ventures designed to help underprivileged families in the years after 1890. They aimed to preserve traditional religion by adapting it to new conditions. The institutional churches which older denominations established among the poor represented only a small part of this "progressive" movement in religion. The founders of the Christian and Missionary Alliance, Peniel Missions, the Pentecostal Mission, the Door of Hope Rescue Homes, the Church of the Nazarene, the Apostolic Holiness Union, the Volunteers of America, and the Salvation Army, as well as the pastors of a host of independent missions and "people's tabernacles," also labored to solve the problem of the masses. But they approached the problem on a spiritual rather than a sociological plane. All of them acted out of a passionate desire to preserve the old-time faith in a new kind of society.

The new denominations which emerged from these varied activities provided churches *for* the disinherited. The leaders, not the converts, set the pattern. Their puritan standards of personal behavior comprised no poor man's code, drawn up by people who could not afford the luxury of rich men's sins. They exalted, rather, the same virtues which Baptist deacons and Methodist class leaders had taught to a previous generation. Crystallized into specific rules and enforced by intense religious sanctions, these codes helped converts from among the poor to resist the powerful temptations which the city produced.

The doctrines of these new sects were not new, either, as we have seen. The most "radical" one of all, Christian perfectionism, endured principally by reason of its well-advertised historic authenticity. Phoebe Palmer and an earlier band of Methodist preachers had so simplified and clarified the way of holiness that, as Isaiah's prophecy put it, the wayfaring man, though unlettered, need not err from it.

The loyalty of all of the holiness leaders to the prohibitionist platform is an obvious illustration of one aspect of the "progressive" mind at work. Thus the union assembly of the Pentecostal Church of the Nazarene charged in 1907 that the liquor interests had "taken possession of the ruling powers in politics and in the official life of the nation." The Standard Oil Company, the beef trust, and other kindred trusts seemed to that gathering "angels in comparison to this black demon of hell." The saloon, they declared, in a passage which ignored two centuries of native American alcoholic history, was the "rallying place" of Roman Catholic immigrants, whose contributions to political corruption, pauperism, and crime seemed to need no documentation.

But the religious commitment to social betterment was pervasive, even in rural east Texas. Early in 1907, J. D. Scott told readers of the *Holiness Evangel* that "the greatest need of the American people . . . aside from the cleansing blood of Jesus Christ" was "a political reform." Power bought with money, he declared, was ruling the world; politicians were "selling their principles, their honor, and their country, like Judas sold his Lord." Christians must do their best to correct these evils, but their hopes ultimately rested on the return of Jesus to "set up His personal, material kingdom." At nearby Peniel, C. A. Mc-

Connell printed the same year a long article which linked praise for the growing spirit of interdenominationalism and internationalism with a call for Christian leaders who would work for human brotherhood. The times demanded men "large enough to ignore caste," brave enough to respect manhood and womanhood without regard to prestige or money, and willing to "clasp hands across race boundaries," across "seas and oceans and continents."38

The rescue missions, the street meetings in the slums, and the rest homes for unwed mothers represented the same religious drive. The Bible institutes and the colleges aimed to elevate through education those who had been converted from the poorer classes, and to build into them the habits, attitudes, and ideals of the older generation. Such schools as Pentecostal Collegiate Institute, Deets Pacific Bible College, and the Missionary Training Institute in Nashville organized their curriculums in ways which, with a little imagination, appear "progressive": they stressed vocational training, centered their teaching upon students' needs and interests, believed in "learning by doing," and gave relatively little attention to the classics.

As the number of converts and ordained ministers in these movements multiplied, the loose forms of organization first adopted seemed no longer adequate. The more responsible and better educated leaders developed a superintendency to maintain discipline and restrain fanaticism. Each successive union, in whatever section of the country, strengthened the bonds of church order and weakened independency. Interestingly enough, the denominations which most freely admitted converts from the lowest class into active leadership, the Salvation Army and the Volunteers of America, employed from the outset a rigid, semimilitary discipline, with control exercised firmly at the top.

Within the parent bodies of the Church of the Nazarene, moreover, an inner conflict also characteristic of the wider "progressive" movement soon became evident. A sharp divergence appeared between those who hoped to fashion a better future for society and those who despaired of anything more than a holding action until the Second Coming. Thus as early as 1904 the committee on missions of a Nazarene assembly flatly rejected the theory that American civilization had become too highly organized to be affected by the gospel. They declared that "centers of holy fire" planted among the poor in every city would help to stem the tide of social evil. Three years later, at the union assembly of 1907, the committee on the "state of the church" expounded the same theme more fully:

> Our divine call has been to erect the old standards and spiritual landmarks, to restore to the people the Apostolic faith, to preach the gospel of full salvation with the Holy Ghost sent down from heaven. . . . Our people are mostly in the lowly walks of life and of very modest means, but they love God and have an intelligent understanding of His great plan of salvation in Jesus Christ. . . . The time is near at hand when He will shake this continent and manifest Himself to his people. . . . Indeed, He has commenced to do it already. The great reforms which have recently taken place in our political and commercial institutions, the wonderful and sweeping advance of prohibition, the outpouring of the Holy Spirit in Wales, India, and Korea, the steady growth of the holiness movement, all unite in proclaiming that this is true.

McClurkan's group, as we have seen, took a dimmer view of the future, as did the southern people generally. The outbreak of World War I, and continuing disillusionment with measures of moral reform, attracted many others to this view. By the late 1920's, as we shall see, it had become the dominant one.[39]

For nearly a generation, American scholars have interpreted the rise of the small Wesleyan denominations in terms of social protest. They have thought these movements were religious revolts, geared to the spiritual needs of the exploited masses. The sociologists of religion have supposed that the new sects made radical departures from traditional ways of churchmanship, abandoned education, ignored sacraments and rituals, created rigid rules of behavior, and developed radical new doctrines to express their alienation from the more privileged classes. After some decades, so the theory runs, rebellious sects either began slowly to accommodate themselves to acceptable patterns of church life, or else formalized their rebellions in cult practices which permanently separated them from the society of which they were a part.[40]

If the foregoing chapters are correct, most of these new "sects" in fact displayed an opposite tendency. Loyalty to old patterns, in doctrines, rules of behavior, forms of church organization, sacraments, and Sunday school and youth activities, was their hallmark. What was new was chiefly their willingness to adopt experimental methods of achieving their essentially conservative ends: the rescue band, the mission, the tabernacle church, the ordination of women, congregational government, and the "liberty of the Spirit" in praise and evangelistic services.

In the second generation of these denominations, to be sure, leaders who had known little of the churchly tradition tended to accept more readily innovations which distinguished their groups sharply from the older churches. But the truly revolutionary changes took place, not in the new, but in the old, denominations. Throughout the first fifty years of the twentieth century the great churches of America adapted their worship, their theology, and their social programs to modern conditions. They abandoned on a broad scale the doctrines, rules of behavior, and free forms of worship they had inherited from the past in favor of those allegedly suitable for an industrial and scientific age. The notion of sectarian rebellion from a churchly "norm" merely serves to obscure this fact.

CHAPTER IX

Union and Liberty—
One and Inseparable

If the appearance of separate holiness denominations seemed to their leaders a mystery explainable only in terms of providential guidance, the subsequent union of several of these to form the Church of the Nazarene was a miracle indeed. Years later, J. B. Chapman pointed out that merging groups of holiness people "separated by geography, human leadership, [and] ecclesiastical background, and yet collectively and individually driven by well-developed prejudices and inwrought convictions," was a task commonly believed to be impossible. Moreover, many opposed the effort, thinking God's plan was to scatter the influence of the sanctified among all the churches.

The story of the success of the merger suggests that the inner similarities of the regional bodies may actually have been greater than their apparent differences. In any event, where differences did exist, the tendency within each group to tolerate variations of opinion was strong enough to tide over the proposals for union. The spirit of sectarianism turned out to be not nearly as strong as the bent toward churchliness. Early in the year 1907, B. W. Huckabee wrote that the holiness movement as a whole had "never been more non-sectarian than now. . . . It is God's voice to the denominations, and if ever heart union comes to the Christian world, it will come through the preaching of a non-sectarian movement."[1]

The new organizations taken together, moreover, were the heirs of a revival which had been basically national in scope. Regional alliances grew up only because most of the national leaders had chosen to stay with the older denominations. The independent congregations and the denominations which they created thus arose out of local conditions. Once they had established themselves, however, they sought naturally to restore the bonds of nationwide fellowship, cherished in their memories and now challenging to their hopes.

First Steps Toward the Union of East and West, 1906-7

The initial contact between the Association of Pentecostal Churches of America and Bresee's Church of the Nazarene seems to have come from easterners. Deacon George Morse, sponsor of Douglas Camp Meeting, visited Los Angeles in 1896 and gave $100 toward the construction of the old board tabernacle. C. W. Griffin, one of the charter members of the church at South Portland, Maine, moved to California in 1904 and thereafter encouraged Dr. Bresee's interest in events back east. Another New Englander, J. W. Goodwin, moved west in 1905. Soon after, he published in Bresee's paper his impressions of the similarities between the Church of the Nazarene and the Pentecostal churches. Goodwin stressed especially their "broadest charity" on the "nonessentials" of Christian doctrine. "It may . . . be in the Divine order," he added, "that these two movements for organized holiness unite their forces somewhere in the Middle West in the near future."

We do not know whether this first printed reference to the possibility of union indicates the existence of other contacts and correspondence. But as early as January 17, 1906, the Missionary Committee of the Association of Pentecostal Churches instructed their secretary to invite Dr. Bresee to their annual meeting in April. The Los Angeles pastor did not come, but his letter of response helped prepare the way for the events which followed.[2]

C. W. Ruth visited New England in the summer of 1906. He arranged to conduct a revival for E. E. Angell at John Wesley Church in Brooklyn, and to accompany the latter to the Grandview Park Camp Meeting, near Haverhill, Massachusetts, where the Missionary Committee was scheduled to meet. Ruth and Angell took the boat from New York to Boston, as was frequently done in those days. During the long night's ride the two discussed the possibility of union between east and west. On Wednesday afternoon, June 27, Angell asked Ruth to present the idea to his associates. Although unable to speak as an official representative of Dr. Bresee, Ruth urged the committee to send a delegation to the Nazarene General Assembly in Los Angeles that fall. After a brief discussion they voted unanimously to send J. N. Short, H. N. Brown, and A. B. Riggs, and to pay their expenses from the foreign missions treasury, on the grounds that "such a union if culminated would materially help our missionary work."

When news of these developments reached Los Angeles, Dr. Bresee was delighted. He noted Ruth's description of "the close similarity" of the two denominations "in preaching and testifying to holiness, avoiding sidetracks," and in "organizing . . . for aggressive service." Bresee prophesied that if such a union came about, it would provide "a rallying place into which might come . . . all organizations who seek the same ends," and marshal forces which could soon establish "a center of fire in every great city in America."[3]

No better emissaries of union could have been sent than the three whom Dr. Bresee almost immediately dubbed the "Wise Men from the East." Riggs, Short, and Brown were all former Methodist preachers, inclined by habit to seek order and discipline in church work. They had nonetheless felt enough of the iron of episcopal wrath to fear an unlimited superintendency. They were, moreover, humble, earnest, and intelligent preachers. Their trip to Los Angeles, made at a leisurely pace, turned out to be a triumphal procession through the Nazarene churches. They stopped first at Chicago, where C. E. Cornell reported they preached and exhorted "with Holy Ghost fire and earnestness." Then they proceeded to Spokane for a four-day meeting with Mrs. DeLance Wallace, and onward to the Nazarene bands at Seattle, Portland, and San Francisco. H. Orton Wiley, pastor at Berkeley, California, was so impressed with Brown's preaching that he encouraged his congregation to have the easterner back for a revival soon after. Meanwhile, in Los Angeles, enthusiasm over the union rose rapidly as the time for the General Assembly drew near.[4]

This meeting proved to be the last general gathering of the western wing of the church. Public expressions of emotion at the services welcoming the Pentecostal delegates were matched by the ease in which private negotiations proceeded. Bresee, Ruth, and W. C. Wilson represented the Nazarenes on the committee assigned to seek a basis of union. Dr. Bresee was quick to highlight the areas of agreement, but he also identified at once the point really at issue.[5]

Surprisingly enough, that issue was not the question of superintendency, but of the right of a congregation subsequently to withdraw from the church and carry its own property with it.

Both denominations actually operated under a limited superintendency. Eastern leaders, in fact, had recently been pressing harder than those in the West for an increase of supervisory power. Dr. Bresee's authority as general superintendent rested more on personal than legal foundations. It had evolved slowly out of a polity which originally gave much power to the laity. The *Manual* for 1898, for example, provided that local groups were to ordain their own ministers; the general superintendent, who was elected annually, was responsible only to approve and sign their credentials. Although this original constitution authorized the general officer to appoint ministers to new congregations, as soon as these were established they gained the right to elect their own pastor, subject only to the superintendent's approval.[6] The assembly of 1903 had with his blessing further restricted Dr. Bresee's power. It subjected the arrangement of new assembly districts and the appointment of evangelists and district superintendents to the approval of an "advisory board," composed of two elders and two laymen elected annually by the General Assembly.[7]

H. D. Brown, district superintendent in the Northwest and the first man actually to serve in this capacity, tried to persuade the assembly of 1905 to increase the authority of district superintendents over the appointment and transfer of ministers and other matters. The proposal got nowhere. The General Assembly provided rather that, once called, a pastor's term in office might continue indefinitely in the absence of formal action by the local church.[8]

In the West, therefore, even before the union with the Association of Pentecostal Churches, the Nazarenes had hammered out what they believed was a "middle course" between episcopacy and congregationalism, a course which the twin drives toward freedom and unity required. The actual outcome of their experimentation did not differ widely from the framework of government which, as we have seen, Reynolds and others were trying to develop in the East.[9]

Little wonder, then, that the special committee on church union at the Los Angeles assembly accomplished its work "without a discordant note." Their report declared that the two churches were already "one in doctrine, basis of church membership, general superintendency, basis of ownership of church property, and especially in the all-embracing purpose to spread scriptural holiness over the land." They unanimously recommended union of the two branches, declaring frankly that the *Manual* of the

Church of the Nazarene adequately set forth the general principles upon which they were agreed. Even minor customs, rules for the ordination of ministers, rituals, and "Christian advices" seemed to them so much in harmony that adjustments could safely be left to the action of the united church. The mission, publishing, and educational ventures were so nearly balanced in both sections that they posed no special problems.[10]

The only real issue, that of a congregation's sovereignty over its property and its pastoral arrangements, was held over for discussion at the annual meeting of the Association of Pentecostal Churches at Brooklyn the next year. Bresee felt this question was a crucial one. Was the new denomination, taken as a whole, to be a church, or merely an association of churches, with each congregation ultimately a law unto itself? To decide the latter, he felt, would threaten the success of the nationwide evangelistic crusade which was the chief reason for the union. Riggs, Brown, and Short seem to have agreed with him, but they knew that others in the East would have to be persuaded.[11]

In the first of a series of midwinter editorials on the question, the Los Angeles pastor declared that "no great aggressive movement, wherein all are joined and new churches are founded through their united effort," would be possible if individual congregations retained the right of secession. Men of judgment, he believed, would not "put their time and money and themselves into the building of institutions that a whiff of wind may blow down." Back home in New England, Hiram Reynolds shared this sentiment fully. He had come to believe that independency and congregational sovereignty served simply to enable people to shirk responsibility.[12]

Bresee moderated this position somewhat in March, in response to a protest in an independent journal which H. B. Hosley published in Washington. A long editorial declared his willingness that each local church should be free to select its pastor, manage its local affairs, and hold its own property for the use for which it was intended, provided that

> the whole body should have such power as is possible to prevent an individual church—as a church—from going wrong, turning away from the truth and devoting its possibilities to evil. . . . It should not have the right to go off on lines of fanaticism or higher criticism, or any other evil way, if it can be prevented. We say, the largest liberty in righteousness, but as little license toward misusing the gathered forces or property as possible.[13]

Forging the Links of National Fellowship

Dr. and Mrs. Bresee, Rev. and Mrs. H. D. Brown, and E. A. Girvin were the western delegates to the annual meeting of the Pentecostal churches, held at John Wesley Church, Brooklyn, in April. The occasion echoed in every way what had happened in Los Angeles the previous fall. A committee of nine from the East met with the three Nazarene leaders. After two days of discussion, the group unanimously adopted a basis of union which contained a compromise of the congregational sovereignty issue but otherwise varied only in terminology from that prepared at Los Angeles. It provided that any congregation already a member of the Pentecostal Association which felt it "imperative to do so" might continue to hold its property in its own name. Those organized later, however—the fruit of combined endeavors—would be bound forever to the denomination.

The statement reiterated the agreement of the two churches upon "the doctrines considered essential to salvation," especially entire sanctification, and upon "the necessity of a superintendency" to "foster and care for churches already established" and to "organize and encourage the organizing of churches everywhere." It promised, however, that superintendents should never have authority to "interfere with the independent action of the fully organized church" in calling its own pastor and in managing its own affairs. Dr. Bresee wrote J. O. McClurkan in August that these "slight modifications" suited the notions of the "extreme Congregationalists" so well that they had become "the most enthusiastic of all" for the union.[14]

More important than agreement on polity was the achievement of spiritual unity through shared experiences of great emotional power. The formal reception for the westerners was delayed until the report of the committee on union was ready. It provoked tremendous enthusiasm. Brown, Girvin, Bresee, and C. W. Ruth all spoke. Then the whole audience called upon William Howard Hoople for a speech. The Brooklyn founder responded by describing how "he and Brother H. D. Brown had had to *gulp a good deal down* in order to make union possible," since they represented the two extremes in governmental ideas. But they had submerged all "secondary matters," Hoople said, in favor of the more important one of a "combined attack on the powers of hell and darkness."

The next day the resolutions for union were presented formally and unanimously adopted, "amidst tears and laughter and shouts and every other possible manifestation of holy joy." Despite the "strong convictions of strong men" upon matters of church government, one observer wrote, "the unity was one of love and this triumphed over all differences of opinion."[15]

On the following day the delegates authorized their moderator to join Dr. Bresee in publishing a proclamation making the union official, under the name Pentecostal Church of the Nazarene. They invited all holiness bodies interested in joining them to send representatives to the first General Assembly of the united church, to be held in Chicago the following October. They also passed a resolution which declared anew that the Church of the Nazarene *Manual* was the "working basis" of the merger, and urged the Pentecostal churches in the East to suggest such additions or changes in that document as they thought desirable. A commission composed of seven men from each branch was ordered to assemble before the Chicago meeting to work out the details of necessary revision.[16]

The zeal which the new movement showed for evangelism helped to rally the support of Dr. C. J. Fowler, president of the National Association for the Promotion of Holiness, and Henry Clay Morrison, leader of the interdenominational Holiness Union in the South. Fowler's *Christian Witness* observed that the Brooklyn merger "should rejoice the hearts of all lovers of holiness. There have been too many holiness sects. In union there is strength. Those who love holiness ought to welcome any plan that will make its forces more efficient and aggressive."[17]

The chief work of the assembly which met at Chicago in October, 1907, proved to be the strengthening of the cords of spiritual union, rather than legislation. At Los Angeles and Brooklyn, delegates from the host denominations had met only a small company of their future associates. Now, for the first time, the rank and file of ministers and leading laymen from both sections met together for work and worship. The opening day was crowned with what observers called "Pentecostal glory." As expected, many other holiness groups had sent fraternal delegates who, when introduced, rejoiced to find, as one of them put it, that "the Pentecostalers and the Nazarenes could shout as loud as the holiness folks in Texas." Again and again Dr. Bresee had to call the people back to the business which had been interrupted by testimonies, singing, praise, and shouts of joy. In between public sessions, 15 different committees, with 236 members, dealt with the problems of education and temperance, evangelism and *Manual* revision, publications and Sunday schools, young people's and missionary societies. The committees proposed few legislative innovations, but they gave opportunity for men and women to form friendships destined to last a lifetime.[18]

Dr. Bresee's report as general superintendent stressed, however, the close relationship between good supervision and successful organization. Calls to organize new churches were appearing rapidly, he said. Only by electing an efficient corps of superintendents, at both general and district levels, could the Pentecostal Nazarenes take full advantage of their opportunities. "Nothing short of planting this work in every considerable city in this country," Bresee declared, "and doing it as soon as possible" would fulfill the church's mission.

After at least one "warm session" in the committee on superintendency, the delegates adopted a framework of government almost exactly like that set forth in the earlier Nazarene *Manual* for 1905. One change bestowed upon the general superintendents exclusively the powers which Dr. Bresee had formerly shared with a general advisory board. The latter group was done away in favor of *district* advisory boards of two ministers and two laymen. A General Missionary Board of twenty-four members, responsible for both home and foreign ventures, assumed the functions of the Missionary Committee of the Association of Pentecostal Churches and the Missionary Board of the Church of the Nazarene. Individuals previously active on the regional units assumed key positions in the new national body.

The drift of events made almost inevitable the election of Hiram F. Reynolds as the second general superintendent. This humble but stalwart organizer seemed to his associates just the man to fill a position whose burdens were incredibly heavy but whose powers many feared. After the assembly closed, the General Missionary Board elected Reynolds its executive secretary as well, a position similar to the one he had held so long in the East. This dual appointment solved the problem of his support. The assembly had voted no salaries at all for general superintendents; Dr. Bresee drew his from the church in Los Angeles, and the missionary treasury provided for Reynolds.[19]

For the two men thus elected to lead the united forces of "organized holiness," the year 1907 brought profound changes. Reynolds, young and vigorous, with more than twenty years of active general superintendency ahead of him, had to pull loose from some of his New England ties. He gave thereafter care and energy without measure to fashioning on a national scale the cohesive church organization which, through many years of frustration, he had dreamed of for the East alone. Reynolds above all others understood that the business of union was barely begun.

Bresee, who stood nearer the close of an active life, found this year of union balanced evenly between hope and memory. After the April meeting in Brooklyn he spent a few days in the hill country of northern New York, his boyhood home. In the two churches where he and Mrs. Bresee had been converted fifty years before, he wrote,

> the occupants of the pews were strangers, the pastor a stranger, all things strange. All we can do is to find our way to the altars where we knelt so long ago, and with tearful memories and holy trust, and heaven-lit hopes, worship and adore, and preach the word. As we closed our eyes how the vanished forms seemed to fill the pews again, and the loved faces to smile anew.... It was a joy, though shaded by many sorrows, to kneel again where the eternities dawned in divine love and pardon.

Bresee was never long in backward looks, however. A man's birth, he said, was a "setting up of new forces," a "pushing off on the boundless sea of being an immortal soul." Here, in these storied hills, he had been born a "living being in the eternities of God."

That fall on his return journey from the Chicago assembly, Bresee passed through San Antonio and El Paso, Texas. Again he wrote an editorial filled with memories. He had decided to go to Los Angeles in 1883, rather than to San Antonio, because he did not want to fight the prejudice against northerners. As he approached El Paso, he remembered that here alone, among strangers, died Joseph Knotts, the Iowa Methodist preacher and business promoter who was the best friend he ever had.[20]

At home, a year of troubles awaited him. Both the new pastor appointed for Los Angeles First Church and the new district superintendent of the Southern California District proved unwise choices. A secession at the college and the church were but the beginning of the trials Bresee had to endure, and overcome, in the first year of his general superintendency of the national organization.[21]

Bresee and Reynolds found their greatest challenge for the immediate future, however, in the extension of the movement for church union to the South. Indeed, this had been their prime objective from the moment they realized that the merger between East and West would be successful.

Erasing the Mason-Dixon Line

Shortly after the Los Angeles assembly of 1906, representatives of both Bresee's group and of the Association of Pentecostal Churches wrote C. B. Jernigan and other leaders of the Holiness Church of Christ inviting them to send delegates to the meeting at Brooklyn in 1907. The General Council was unable to pay expenses for such a long trip, so no one went.[22] Jernigan welcomed this invitation enthusiastically, however, and began at once to agitate in favor of such a merger. But he insisted that "real union" could be achieved only if all were really one in doctrine. "Post and pre-millennialism will not mix," he declared. "Tobacco chewers and clean men would not unite. We can not afford to get tangled up with godless secret societies in a holiness church." He thus highlighted the issue of law *versus* Christian liberty which was to dominate efforts to unite North and South.[23]

By the time representatives from the East and West gathered at Chicago it was apparent that the principal new legislation that body would adopt would be aimed at paving the way for union with the Holiness Church of Christ. Jernigan, J. D. Scott, J. P. Roberts, Joseph N. Speakes, and Mrs. E. H. Sheeks were fraternal delegates from the South. With them came T. J. Shingler of Donalsonville, Georgia, who had recently brought his congregation into the southern denomination, and S. M. Stafford, their missionary to Mexico. A rousing reception, with speeches by each of the visiting delegates, took place the second night. "The flood of holy joy," wrote Secretary Robert Pierce, was "for many minutes . . . impossible to restrain." Brother Scott said he had expected to find things stiff, but was happily disappointed. All declared "they had forgotten that there was a Mason and Dixon line."

Jernigan later reported proudly to the readers of the *Holiness Evangel* that the southern delegation was "put on the legislative committee to help frame the doctrine and polity" of the new denomination. "They gave us all that we asked for," he declared. "Holiness of heart and life was made the basis of union, with liberty to all on non-essentials." Significantly, Jernigan's editorial quoted entirely the new articles on the second coming of Christ and divine healing which had been added to the *Manual*. He also printed the rephrasing of the "special advices" on tobacco and secret societies. These were now so strongly put as to carry almost the same force as the General Rules. From "we advise our people to abstain," the words became "we insist that our people abstain from membership in or fellowship with worldly, secret or oath-bound lodges and fraternities." The flat declaration followed that "the spirit and tendency of these societies are contrary to the principles of our holy religion."24

The adoption of these changes made the southern delegation so confident of the eventual outcome that the Chicago assembly arranged to appoint only sixteen of the twenty-four members of the General Foreign Missionary Board, leaving eight to be elected later from the Holiness Church of Christ. Bresee and Reynolds were authorized to name a third general superintendent from that group also. Many hoped that a second assembly would not be necessary to ratify the union.

Jernigan, Speakes, and Scott returned home expecting to convince the annual meetings of the various councils to implement the merger at once. These men, like the leaders from the East, had had their fill of congregational independency. Their formal report to the councils praised especially the "better system of pastoral work" which the united church would provide, since the district superintendent of each area would "visit each congregation at least once a year, and secure pastors for churches needing one."25

Speakes apparently encountered no difficulty at all at the Arkansas council. The manuals of the two churches were read publicly and compared, after which Mrs. Sheeks presented the motion for union. "The saints sang and shouted all over the church while the vote was being taken," Speakes reported; the decision was unanimous. The resolution ordered that the *Manual* of the Pentecostal Church of the Nazarene be put into force immediately among the various congregations, save that the name and the officers of the council should be left unchanged until a General Assembly ratified their action.26

Jernigan and Scott found the western council harder to persuade. This group contained many strong leaders, such as

J. T. Upchurch, J. B. Chapman, B. F. Neely, and Mrs. Mary Cagle. At the annual meeting held in November at Oak Cliff, in South Dallas, they spent two full days discussing the report of the Committee on Church Union, and comparing their own with the Nazarene *Manual*. H. D. Brown had come along with Jernigan to this gathering. Reports differ as to whether his presence helped matters, however. Some Texans had little use for former Methodist presiding elders, especially those whose concept of the Nazarene district superintendency grew out of their experience in the parent denomination. In any event, the council voted to request that the articles pertaining to tobacco and divine healing in the discipline of the Holiness Church of Christ be substituted for those adopted at Chicago. It also approved a motion that the provision in the Nazarene ritual for the use of a ring in the marriage ceremony be stricken out. The delegates set the next annual meeting for Pilot Point, Texas, in October, 1908, in expectation that the General Assembly would meet with them there.[27]

Possibly the Texans had been made wary by reports that at the Chicago assembly some of the Nazarene sisters had worn "too many frills and feathers." Robert Pierce's pointed explanation in the *Nazarene Messenger* that the gathering had kept the strict "advices" on tobacco and secret societies out of the General Rules so as to leave them "for the individual conscience to settle under the light of the Word and the Holy Spirit" did not help. It posed, rather, the question whether the southern delegates had, indeed, as Jernigan had reported, gotten all they asked for at Chicago. Pierce's conclusion had been quite the opposite. The chief accomplishment of the Chicago assembly, he wrote,

> was to convince all that holiness people can come together and organize on the basis of gospel essentials, and with perfect love grant freedom and liberty in those things which do not pertain to or hinder the salvation of the soul.[28]

In the months preceding the Pilot Point assembly, leaders on both sides sought to minimize these issues. The early Nazarene *Manuals* carried the general rules of the old Methodist *Book of Discipline* in their full rigor, to be sure. Nevertheless, Bresee reprinted in 1908 an article entitled "Legalism Overdone," which explained that young Christians must find the experience of holiness before they could be expected to conform to strict standards of dress. The author warned preachers against "plucking the bird before it is dead." Mrs. Cagle visited Los Angeles the following spring and went out of her way to point out that the atmosphere at Deets Pacific Bible College was "deeply spiritual," and that not one student wore gold and no girls' dresses had short sleeves.[29] On the eve of the assembly, J. N. Short wrote in all church publications "an open letter" reminding the South that at Chicago their delegates had been taken "into heartiest fellowship and counsel" and had helped to frame "a code upon which we could all unite." Since individual views varied, Short stated, none had expected the *Manual* to set forth his particular beliefs, or to interpret the whole Bible. The simpler it was, in fact, the better. All were fallible in judgment. The church must therefore grant "some elasticity to thinking men on some beliefs not essential to salvation."[30]

The year's delay in the ratification of the union gave Dr. Bresee time to take advantage of an unexpected opportunity to bring into the merger the interdenominational community at Texas Holiness University, together with scores of the holiness bands which supported it. President E. P. Ellyson opened the door by inviting C. W. Ruth to Peniel for the midwinter revival in January, 1908.

From the time of his arrival at Peniel as a professor in 1906, Ellyson and his wife, also a Friends minister, had cultivated the friendship of the Pilot Point leaders. As soon as he became president of the school, Ellyson led it rapidly away from the "interdenominationalism" which President A. M. Hills and the now-discredited B. W. Huckabee had promoted.[31] C. A. McConnell, who replaced Huckabee as editor of the *Pentecostal Advocate*, was of the same mind. McConnell, like Ellyson, had been born and reared in the North. In a maiden editorial in October, 1907, he declared that holiness people could "sit on the Caanan bank of Jordan and cry 'sanctification' until the new wine turns to vinegar," but only the cultivation of a "broader love" among them would break down the "walls of prejudice" which hindered the progress of a national awakening. Ruth's ministry therefore, which one described as "the clearest, closest, most thorough Bible preaching that many of us ever heard," was exactly what the situation required.[32]

At the same time Ruth was at the college, Bud Robinson, Peniel's first citizen, was conducting a revival for C. E. Cornell at Chicago First Church. Afterwards, the Texas evangelist made his way west by way of the Nazarene congregations at Seattle and Portland to a great "Southern California holiness convention," held March 19 to 29, 1908, at Dr. Bresee's church in Los Angeles. The outcome of these various contacts was Ellyson's invitation to Bresee to preach a few days at Texas Holiness University on his way to the spring and summer assemblies in the East. Since Bresee was already scheduled to stop at nearby Pilot Point to arrange the details of the proposed General Assembly, the announcement of this new plan occasioned no surprise.[33]

The result, however, created a sensation. Bresee preached just four sermons in the college chapel at Peniel. Then, on Tuesday evening, April 7, 1908, a full six months before the union assembly at Pilot Point, he called for all those ready to unite with the pioneer Church of the Nazarene in Texas to meet him at the altar. One hundred and three persons, including President and Mrs. Ellyson and the entire faculty, stepped forward. Among the younger charter members was Henry B. Wallin, a student in the college who was one day to occupy Bresee's pulpit in Los Angeles. In a few moments' time, they appointed a church board and, with Dr. Bresee's approval, called Mrs. Ellyson to be their pastor. What had made possible such an event?

Professor Z. B. Whitehurst explained to the readers of the *Pentecostal Advocate* that the Peniel community contained members of so many different denominations that for many years they had agreed simply to worship together in the college chapel without organizing a church. This had laid them open, however, to charges of neglecting their Christian duty. It also deprived their families and young converts of regular pastoral guidance.

Bud Robinson became so concerned about the problem that he organized a class of the M.E. Church, North, which met for a time in his own home. He persuaded several of the younger preachers, including young Professor R. T. Williams, to worship with him. Confused memories of this event gave rise in later years to the legend that Robinson had opposed the movement to unite with the Nazarenes. The evidence indicates the contrary. "Uncle Bud" preached at the afternoon service in Peniel the Sunday Bresee's meeting began there. He told the college community, to which he had given such faithful support, that he had been long enough without a church home, and would prefer to move from the town rather than to endure this privation longer; he was heart and soul for immediate union.[34]

The day after the organization of the church at Peniel, Bresee proceeded by train to Pilot Point. He found the little town soaked in rain, which meant, even in that country, ankle-deep in mud. He inspected the school, the rescue home, and the printing press, and preached several nights at the church of which J. B. Chapman was pastor. As usual, several persons sought the experience of perfect love at the altar. Only then, when he was sure that the leading representatives of both branches of the holiness movement in Texas were ready for union, did Bresee announce officially that the General Assembly would gather at Pilot Point in October. He realized, no doubt, that a great meeting there might help to sweep the entire Texas holiness movement into the Pentecostal Church of the Nazarene.[35]

With a light heart Bresee made his way eastward, first to Indianapolis, Indiana, where C. W. Ruth met him and introduced him to the newest urban "center of fire," and then by way of new and prospective churches at Seymour, Indiana, Louisville, Kentucky, and Johnstown, Pennsylvania, to Hosley's church in the nation's capital. He conducted the district assembly of the Washington District at the new church in Harrington, Delaware, preached a few days for the Holiness Christian group in Philadelphia, and then joined Reynolds at the New York and New England district assemblies. He found each area ablaze with enthusiasm for the pioneering of new churches. H. F. Reynolds had urged this journey as the first step of a campaign to eliminate the idea of a sectional superintendency. For the same reason Reynolds accepted Bresee's invitation to visit and preside at the western district assemblies later in the same summer.

On their way to the West Coast, the two men had their first chance to become well acquainted. They stopped off at Greeley, Boulder, and Denver, Colorado, to lay the groundwork for major accessions there. Then followed in turn assemblies and camp meetings on the Northwest, Northern California, and Los Angeles districts. This "grand tour" of the two general superintendents, the only one they ever made together, symbolized concretely to the whole church the high promise of their union. The trip provided both men, moreover, with an insight into local conditions which made it easier for them to decide judiciously by correspondence the thorny issues they were to face during the next seven and one-half years.[36]

And so at last the October day came when weary travelers from four corners of the nation climbed off the trains at Pilot Point and headed for the big tent beside Brother Roberts' rescue home. The links of their fellowship had been forged on many anvils, yet tense moments of debate must temper them again before they could be joined. At one point in the proceedings, discussion of such matters as wedding rings and tobacco became so heated that H. D. Brown rose to suggest that if union could be had only at the price of multiplying rules the Nazarenes should let the southerners go. His speech, repeated several times, was finally reduced to the words, "Mr. Chairman, let them go." Dr. Bresee, his hand upraised, responded each time, "We cannot let them go, Brother Brown; they are our own folks." Like so many other leaders in both North and South, Bresee had caught the vision of a national holiness denomination, which should set ablaze a line of churches and missions in every city of the nation.

Under the grip of this simple, evangelistic impulse, the southerners agreed to accept the consecration they could see in place of the legislation they desired. The delegates agreed to spell out in full in the "general rule" on modesty and simplicity the scriptural references to woman's dress in I Timothy 2:9-10 and I Peter 3:8. They reworded slightly the "advice" on tobacco, and dropped the ring ceremony from the marriage ritual. But that was all. What won out over argument was brotherliness; love prevailed over law. And so the Nazarenes became one people, North and South, East and West.[37]

The Meaning of Pilot Point

On October 13, 1958, several thousand Nazarenes joined in a second "pilgrimage to Pilot Point" to celebrate what they called the fiftieth anniversary of the birth of their church. Many who were present asked the question why that assembly should have been chosen for remembrance over the other union gatherings which preceded and followed it. They remembered that individual congregations in all parts of the country had celebrated their golden anniversaries years before the reunion in Texas. What, then, was the historic meaning of that first assembly at Pilot Point?

It signified, first, a broad acceleration of the trend away from associations and independent churches toward a fully organized denominational fellowship. Throughout the country, and particularly in the great valley of the Mississippi River, the nonsectarian holiness associations dominated the Wesleyan movement right down until 1908. These groups encouraged their members to remain connected with the old denominations; where no local holiness church existed, their rules made this mandatory. They hoped thus to revive the work of Christian perfection in the main-stream Protestant churches of America. Many of the Texas evangelists, especially those who lived at Peniel, had supported this plan, among them Bud Robinson, J. B. McBride, and Allie Irick.[38]

At the Pilot Point assembly, the two groups of Texans, so long divided on the strategy of holiness evangelism, united with one another in the same action by which they joined the Pentecostal Church of the Nazarene. Both Pilot Point and Peniel were thereafter Nazarene centers. Dr. Ellyson, who had actively promoted the union of both the local and the national forces, was elected the general superintendent from the South despite the fact that several men in the Holiness Church of Christ seemed to have a prior claim. The selection of this former Quaker made it clear that the fear of episcopacy had vanished in the general zeal to evangelize the nation. The assembly in fact perfected the organization of eighteen districts. And some of those chosen to be district superintendents were men who formerly had advocated congregational sovereignty: William Howard Hoople, H. B. Hosley, William E. Fisher, J. D. Scott, and R. M. Guy.[39]

The Pilot Point meeting is further memorable for its affirmation of the church's unity in essentials, and its determination to maintain liberty in all other things.

A great doctrinal unity existed in the parent bodies of the Church of the Nazarene long before their union. Moreover, time and experience, as we have seen, had erased the chief differences which originally characterized their views on government and superintendency. But varying emphases in rules of personal behavior, even in small matters, could pose stubborn problems in a holiness church, which considered harmony a trustworthy thermometer of spiritual health.

As we have seen, Dr. Bresee and his western group thought

the baptism of the Holy Spirit a far better guarantee of discipline in the church than legislation. His church's *Manual* contained strict rules, of course, most of them borrowed from the *Methodist Book of Discipline.* Earnest "advices" covered subjects not dealt with in the rules. As though in anticipation of the future, these advices had been strengthened in 1905. But Bresee's emphasis was still upon the discipline of the Spirit. He especially resisted enforcement of the strictures on women's dress in I Timothy 2:9 and I Peter 3:3, unless those passages were "properly understood." Easterners generally seem to have shared this position. But the Holiness Church of Christ had long forbade by rules what others had simply advised their people to shun.[40]

The compromise finally worked out required each group to give a little, one as a pledge to the purity, and the other to the liberty of the way of holiness. Whatever our judgment of the compromise, it established a balance between puritan and perfectionist, between law and liberty, which has characterized the Church of the Nazarene from that day forward. Those who in later years sought to upset the balance by multiplying or ignoring rules have usually overlooked this fact.

Pilot Point also signified the establishment of the Church of the Nazarene on a *national* basis. The casual observer might assume that the union at Chicago, the year before, where East and West joined forces, had achieved this goal. But the lines dividing the holiness movement had always separated North and South much more sharply than they did East and West.

Two Methodist denominations existed in those days, one northern and the other southern, a consequence of the controversy over slavery decades before. As the revival of entire sanctification swept across the country, the National Association for the Promotion of Holiness drew together chiefly preachers from the northern body. Southern advocates of the doctrine usually formed their own associations and leagues, culminating in 1904 in Henry Clay Morrison's Holiness Union. The leaders of the two groups which united at Chicago in 1907 had nearly all formerly been Northern Methodists, and adherents of the National Association for the Promotion of Holiness as well. Moreover, most of them represented the urban wing of the movement, with its characteristic moderation upon "side issues." The southern associations contained a much larger proportion of rural churches and preachers.

Sectional, social, and religious prejudices thus divided North from South, whereas men of the East and West had shared a basically common experience. What bridged the chasm was concern for church-centered holiness evangelism, in the nation and in the world at large.

Many old-timers who attended the assembly at Pilot Point remember how, after the unanimous vote for union had been announced, a wiry little Texan started across the platform saying, "I haven't hugged a Yankee since before the Civil War, but I'm going to hug one now." At once Brooklyn's William Howard Hoople, his 275 pounds adorned with a glorious handlebar mustache, leaped up from the other end of the platform and met the Texan near the pulpit. Their embrace set off a celebration. The gap between North and South was closed forever.

Some pure genius of a Yankee had prepared for just this moment a song of holiness union. A similar one, sung at Chicago the year before, used the tune of "The Battle Hymn of the Republic." But that would never do in Texas. This one was set to the music of "Dixie." As the chorus rang out, spiritual and brotherly emotions struck a major key.

> *With forces all united*
> *We'll win! We'll win!*
> *We'll preach a gospel o'er the land*
> *That fully saves from sin.*
> *Praise God! Praise God! Praise God!*
> *For Full Salvation!*
> *Praise God! Praise God! Praise God!*
> *For Full Salvation!*[41]

Pilot Point was, indeed, the birthplace of the Church of the Nazarene.

CHAPTER X

Some Unheralded Accessions, 1908-15

The First Fruits of Union

Public attention excited by the news of the unions completed at Chicago and Pilot Point helped to attract to the new denomination a number of individuals and congregations whose importance to its early growth is often overlooked.[1] In the East, Deacon George Morse, founder of Douglas Camp Meeting, joined the communion and deeded to it a church building he owned at Putnam, Connecticut. Isaiah Reid, founder and for many years president of the Iowa Holiness Association, and Evangelist L. Milton Williams, who lived at Oskaloosa, Iowa, site of an interdenominational holiness college, united with the movement at the Chicago assembly and set in motion a chain of events which soon made Iowa an open field for Nazarene work.[2] Reid returned with Dr. Bresee to Los Angeles, where he taught for a time in the Bible school.

There he found veteran preachers of many persuasions ready to affiliate with the new denomination. Among them were A. P. Graves, a well-known Baptist evangelist, and Walter C. Brand, former editor of the official organ of the Holiness Church of California. Another was Lewis I. Hadley, a birthright Quaker and former editor who had been a superintendent in two midwestern yearly meetings of Friends. Hadley was pastor from 1906 to 1908 of a Friends congregation at Portland, Oregon, which he placed in league with the Nazarene group there. He accepted the pastorate of the Pentecostal Nazarene church in Whittier, California, a predominantly Quaker city, in 1908.[3]

Edward F. Walker, a Presbyterian evangelist long famous for his preaching of the higher Christian life, accepted a call to pastor the church in Pasadena immediately following the Pilot Point union. He was at that time moderator of the Indianapolis Presbytery. Walker had been converted at San Francisco in 1872 in a meeting sponsored by the National Association for the Promotion of Holiness, and professed soon after the grace of sanctification. In the following decades he preached the doctrine faithfully in his own as well as in other communions, and wrote widely in the holiness press.[4]

Equally as important, a number of independent congregations around the country cast their lot with the Nazarenes. Several sent their pastors or lay leaders to the Chicago assembly of 1907. Among them was Dr. M. F. Gerrish, a physician who had directed the establishment of first a mission and then a church at Seymour, Indiana. In the following nine months ten such congregations, containing in all over six hundred members, united with the denomination. Several of these, like the one at Harrington, Delaware, owned their church buildings free of debt.[5]

The same story was repeated after the General Assembly of 1908. H. F. Reynolds and E. P. Ellyson went directly from Pilot Point to Des Arc, Missouri, and brought the Bible school there and four related churches into the fold. The next month Reynolds read the vows to a substantial congregation of forty-eight members in Warren, Pennsylvania, originally organized to conserve the results of a revival which L. Milton Williams held three years before.[6]

In Kansas and Oklahoma, meanwhile, the newly appointed district superintendent, C. B. Jernigan, reaped a harvest where others had sown. He early established contact with the Apostolic Holiness Church of Hutchinson, Kansas. This congregation was the fruit of a Tuesday holiness meeting which Mrs. Mattie Hoke began in 1898. A little band, chiefly women, met weekly for six years, sometimes in the homes of "the very poor and lowly" and "often with the sick and dying," as Mrs. Hoke remembered it, and at other times "in the county jail, at the county poor farm, on the street, in brothels, in the home of the banker and businessman, in the downtown office, in groves, in schoolhouses, in some of the churches, and in hotels and tents." They stressed divine healing from the beginning, and after extensive Bible study, adopted the premillennial view of the Second Coming.

In October, 1904, the ladies opened a mission, complete with a Sunday school and other regular services. It appealed especially to persons who had recently moved to Hutchinson from other cities or from the surrounding countryside, where local holiness associations flourished. Within a few months twenty charter members united in the organization of a church. They soon purchased a substantial residence to house a Bible school, and moved the church to the new location. They also conducted an annual camp meeting which became an adjunct of the school and its chief source of support. By October, 1906, at the beginning of the institution's second year, a new forty-room building, comprising a dining room, a large chapel, and a dormitory for women, was ready for use.[7]

In October, 1909, Jernigan received the Hutchinson congregation, with their campground and school, into the Pentecostal Church of the Nazarene. What was then called Kansas Holiness College was later renamed for Bresee. C. B. Widmeyer, one of the teachers, persuaded a similar "mission church" in Newton, Kansas, of which he was a member, to join the next year. Joseph Speakes of Arkansas became pastor of this congregation; it had been organized in 1906 among former Mennonite families who had received the teaching of Christian perfection. Before the end of Jernigan's second year in office, Kansas contained enough Nazarene churches to be organized as a separate district. Speakes was the first superintendent. A. S. Cochran, a scholarly Methodist clergyman who had recently cast his lot with the Nazarenes, succeeded him early in 1911.[8]

The Kansas District grew rapidly thereafter. At the General Assembly of 1911, Cochran reported 22 churches with 561 members. He was runner-up in the balloting which named E. F. Walker a general superintendent. Some of the new churches in the Sunflower State, like the one at Dodge City, sprang from revival meetings conducted by county holiness associations. Evangelists and district superintendents dug out others in home mission campaigns. Wichita, Kansas, First Church, now one of the largest congregations in the denomination, was born in a four-weeks tent meeting which Cochran and R. E. Gilmore conducted in May, 1912. The 16 charter members worshiped for a year in a rescue home in the city, and afterward in a frame tabernacle.[9]

Jernigan's success in Oklahoma was greater even than in Kansas. He needed no introduction to the state holiness association there, for this body was an affiliate of the paper and school at Peniel. Eight of its bands were ripe for organization at once. In Oklahoma City, Mattie Mallory operated under the association's general sponsorship the Beulah Heights Academy and Bible School, and a rescue home as well.[10] By March, 1909, Jernigan had persuaded Miss Mallory to lead her group into the denomination and to lend him $5,000 with which to close a deal with the Oklahoma Railway Company for 160 acres of land a few miles to the west. She also turned her rescue home property at Beulah Heights over to a Nazarene board, of which Jernigan was chairman. He promptly sold it and invested the proceeds in the new land also. In a few weeks the eager superintendent had laid out a town called Bethany. He announced that Miss Mallory would conduct an orphanage and Mrs. Jernigan a rescue home there, and that he would devote himself to establishing Oklahoma Holiness College.

In the good tradition of the American pioneer school, Jernigan listed for sale 200 lots ranging in price from $85.00 to $175.00, the income from which was to pay for the erection of a college building. H. H. Miller, a Methodist minister recently prominent in the educational affairs of his conference and also a past president of the Oklahoma Holiness Association, accepted appointment as head of the embryo institution. By late spring, Jernigan had pitched his tent in the "black jack forest" at Bethany. He built a barn into which he moved his family in June, and then constructed the first house in the town. During the next two years he alternated promotion of land sales and supervision of the erection of the college building with revivals and tent meetings all over the state. The Bethany church was organized under the shade of a tree in August, 1910.[11]

By the time of the General Assembly of 1911, the Oklahoma District reported 63 churches, with 1,756 members, an achievement which prompted the delegates to pause for a special prayer of thanksgiving. The next year the state became the first one outside of California to support two districts. The college at Bethany grew slowly but substantially. It eventually outdistanced and absorbed the schools at Hutchinson, Kansas, Peniel and Hamlin, Texas, Vilonia, Arkansas, and Des Arc, Missouri. Bethany became the Nazarene center for the whole Southwest.[12]

Many were the fascinating tales of evangelism among the Indians of Oklahoma which Jernigan's preachers later told. At a council of converted Poncas, Chief White Eagle, called the "silver-tongued orator of the Ponca," is reported to have given the following account of the revival which Jernigan and I. G. Martin held among his people:

> The white man come along and take our children away from us all the week and make them go to white man's school, read white man's books, live in white man's houses, eat like a white man with knife

and fork, do housework and farm like a white man, but white man don't know that Indian has a black heart. He sprinkle water on his head, make him learn books with his head. He all the time doctor his head. But the Indian's head not bad—trouble in his heart. Then come the Methodists and build big church, put up a big bell that we hear every Sunday morning. Mr. Simmons preach heap big sermon—say heap big words—Mrs. Simmons sing mighty fine song. Sing like a bird. Play piano good—fine music. Mr. Simmons don't know that Indian has black heart. Then come Nazarenes—put up big brown tent—sing, clap their hands, look happy. Mr. Martin preach hot words. Tell Indian he no good—go to hell or be better—Indian feel bad. Come to mourner's bench, get on his knees, PRAY, CRY, shed tears—talk to great Spirit—soon he jump up, face shine—shake hands with everybody, look good. Be happy. Say Amen! Everybody cry. Then he go home—no more smoke a pipe, no more drink whiskey, no more eat mescal bean—read a Bible and pray. Good Indian—heart changed. Come on, Nazarenes, come on![13]

The enthusiasm which animated Jernigan aroused district superintendents in other parts of the country as well. On the Northwest District, for example, H. D. Brown reported seven new churches at the assembly held in June, 1908, including promising ones at Salem, Oregon, Walla Walla, and Everett, Washington, and at several places in the Snake River Valley of Idaho, where Clyde T. Dilley and J. G. Rogers had conducted revival meetings.[14] Mr. and Mrs. DeLance Wallace moved that year from Spokane to Seattle, where they put the church upon a permanent if not flourishing basis. At the assembly of 1909, Mr. Wallace, who had been ordained only twelve months before, was elected district superintendent, after a close race with others, including his wife. Dr. Ellyson later appointed her to the office of "district evangelist." These two stalwarts, one the nominal head but the other the heart of the work, set the Northwest towns ablaze with home mission revivals. In 1914 alone, on the Northwest District, Wallace organized seven new churches. He had already set off the state of Idaho in another district, the Idaho District, in 1913.

H. D. Brown meanwhile spent the year 1911-12 in Alberta Province, Canada, scouting out possibilities for Nazarene work there. W. B. Tait, a Methodist layman, had begun a holiness mission in Calgary in 1906. He combined forces in 1910 with a holiness association which met weekly in the homes of interested families. Thomas Bell, a Methodist conference evangelist, joined the group in the spring of 1911. When L. Milton

Williams and I. G. Martin organized a Church of the Nazarene in Calgary, at the close of a tent revival in August, 1911, Bell became the first pastor.

Dr. Bresee promptly authorized Brown to set up and take charge of a district organization. Most of his attempts to establish churches during the following year, however, proved unsuccessful. Bresee came to Calgary in 1912 for a district assembly, at which W. B. Tait was ordained and appointed superintendent. En route, Bresee organized a congregation at Victoria, British Columbia, eventually placing it and other nearby bands under the supervision of the Northwest District.

During the following years, Thomas Bell established a church at Red Deer, future site of a Bible school and college, and he and Charles E. Thomson, a young Methodist student minister, joined L. Milton Williams in an evangelistic tour from which several congregations sprang. Another recruit from Methodism, C. A. Thompson, became superintendent of the Manitoba-Saskatchewan area in 1914. Progress throughout western Canada was slow, however. Scarcely a dozen congregations existed in all that vast country by 1917, and only the one at Calgary was flourishing.[15]

These accessions, together with a mushroom growth of the church in the midwestern portion of the country, to be discussed later, were overshadowed in the religious press by reports of the efforts to bring about mergers with other holiness denominations. The remarkable fact is, however, that in the three years between the Pilot Point and Nashville assemblies the Pentecostal Church of the Nazarene doubled its membership and almost tripled its Sunday school enrollment without help from any major union. Individual initiative and enthusiasm was the chief factor in the expansions of these early years.[16]

Success and Failure in Other Merger Efforts, 1908-15

At the close of the General Assembly of 1908, Phineas Bresee thought it a "foregone conclusion that the holiness forces of the country" would unite very soon in one organic body. The movement had been so "providentially led," he wrote, that each "incoming wave" seemed to prepare the way for another.[17] His prediction, however, proved groundless. From that hour onward, in fact, despite occasional successes, the movement for consolidation ground slowly to a halt. Simply to tell the story makes the reasons clear. But, in any event, each attempt to bring in other groups produced significant inner changes in the character and tendency of Nazarene fellowship.

On many occasions before 1907, C. W. Ruth had urged his former associates in the Pennsylvania Conferences of the Holiness Christian church to join the Nazarenes. He was delighted, therefore, when the conference voted to send its leader, Horace G. Trumbauer, to the Chicago assembly. Trumbauer was pleased with what he saw, and returned home to push the union through.

His task was relatively easy, for this group had experienced the same development of church polity as other parent bodies of the new denomination. Five men and women banded together in Philadelphia in 1882 to evangelize the Pennsylvania Dutch country. They conducted revivals in halls, tents, and groves, and met annually for a conference which in 1894 took the name Holiness Christian Association. The previous year a second conference had been established in Indiana. Three general assemblies were held, in 1897, 1900, and 1904.

When Trumbauer reported his trip to Chicago to a ministers' meeting in December, he found 80 per cent of the pastors already in favor of union. The group decided to submit the matter to the next quarterly meeting of each church. Practically all of these voted favorably by the time of the annual conference in March, 1908. The Indiana group meanwhile proved unwilling to take the same step, so the eastern conference asked and received a brotherly release. Bresee visited Philadelphia in June and preached to several congregations, including one which was wavering on the question.

A special session of the Pennsylvania conference, held in connection with a ten-day holiness convention at Philadelphia in September, agreed by an almost unanimous vote to present their fifteen churches to the Nazarenes. H. F. Reynolds and the two neighboring district superintendents, H. B. Hosley and William Howard Hoople, were present to receive them officially. Reynolds organized and appointed Trumbauer superintendent of a new Philadelphia District, taking territory from both the others. Before many years had passed, the new district had outstripped its neighbors and absorbed the Washington District as far south as Arlington, Virginia. John Thomas Maybury, ordained at the union conference in Philadelphia, served as district superintendent in all but three years of the period from 1915 to 1929.[18]

What might have become an equally significant accession of a troop of William Lee's mission churches in Colorado is less well known. To understand what happened, we must weave together strands from the history of three different movements: the Colorado Holiness Association, the pioneer Nazarene congregations in Greeley and Boulder, and the Lee Holiness Mission centered in Colorado Springs.

The settlements along the base of the Rockies, from Pueblo on the south to Fort Collins on the north, had been for years a favorite field for independent holiness evangelists. The continued expansion of large-scale mining in the mountainous districts after 1890 brought numerous workingmen to the state, while the irrigation of the valleys below attracted farmers from the drought-ridden plains of Kansas. Many of both classes wound up in the poorer sections of the foothill towns, the social no man's land between the mining and the agricultural frontiers.

From the year 1900 onward, the Colorado State Holiness Association held annual camp meetings and conventions at Greeley, Denver, and Colorado Springs. The Metropolitan Church Association meanwhile sponsored a series of sensational conventions which divided the movement and paved the way for Mrs. Kent White to organize the Pillar of Fire Church. Her coterie insisted upon strict standards in dress and behavior, and unfettered emotion in worship.[19]

In such a "burned-over" district, some persons inevitably heard about the new holiness denominations. J. W. King, previously a Congregational pastor in Denver and Greeley, organized a group of his followers at Greeley into a Church of the Nazarene early in 1907. The same year a tiny band in nearby Boulder affiliated with the Holiness Church of Christ. Whether the latter was the same congregation which L. E. Burger, King's assistant at Greeley, reorganized the next year under Nazarene auspices is not clear. In any event, when Bresee and Reynolds journeyed from New England to the West Coast in June, 1908, they visited both of these churches. They also conducted a brief convention in Denver under the sponsorship of the Colorado State Holiness Association, whose secretary, Alpin Bowes, had been at Deets Pacific Bible College the preceding spring. Bresee refused to organize a church in Denver on this trip, however, fearing lest he should introduce further division into a work which had had its fill of it.[20]

Reynolds returned in August to dedicate new church buildings at Boulder and Greeley, and to conduct a second brief meeting at Denver. Thus was laid the groundwork for the holiness convention which Dr. Bresee held at the state capital on his way to the union assembly at Pilot Point. At its close he organized a church with forty charter members, and appointed Bowes pastor.[21]

Meanwhile, at Colorado Springs, seventy miles to the south, William H. Lee had been pastor since 1901 of the People's Mission Church, originally formed to conserve the results of a revival held by I. G. Martin. Lee was a nephew of Jason Lee, pioneer Methodist missionary to Oregon. He had earlier collaborated with Martin in the establishment of the People's Mission at Spokane, Washington, the original nucleus of our church in the Northwest. By 1906, when Martin returned to Colorado Springs for a second revival meeting, Lee's band had become what Martin called an "institutional church." They maintained a workingmen's home, a free reading room, an employment agency, a large store of supplies for relief of the poor, and a rescue home, and sponsored branch missions in several nearby towns. Like Bresee, Lee wrote of "going to the neglected fields in city, village, and country," seeking out those whom the churches had failed to reach.[22]

Travelers from both the East and the West who were acquainted with Lee's work visited Colorado Springs frequently. A. B. Riggs spent a happy Sabbath there on the way home from Los Angeles in 1906. Lucy P. Knott and Mr. and Mrs. Leslie Gay stopped off on their return from the Chicago assembly the next fall. Little wonder, therefore, that not long after the Pilot Point assembly Lee wrote a report to Dr. Bresee's paper extending "the hand of Christian love and fellowship" to the Pentecostal Church of the Nazarene. "We are with you in the holy war," he declared; "we rejoice in your victories and sympathize with all your plans. . . ."[23]

Lee took a trip to Los Angeles late in 1910 and discussed at length with Dr. Bresee the desirability of a merger. He returned home to find his people receptive to the plan. By early January, Bresee had mailed to General Superintendents Reynolds and Ellyson proposed articles of union with the People's Mission church. He suggested also that the General Assembly of 1911 be held in Colorado Springs, rather than at Nashville, where McClurkan's resistance to union was becoming an embarrassment. In his enthusiasm, however, Dr. Bresee had failed to consult with L. E. Burger and other Coloradans already in the denomination. This seemed to Ellyson and Reynolds "a little hasty action." Nevertheless they ratified the agreement in April, despite indications that the churches in the northern part of the state were unhappy about it.

At the next assembly in Colorado, Reynolds set off the seven new congregations into the Southern Colorado District, and made Lee the superintendent. Those in Denver, Boulder, and Greeley remained a part of the Rocky Mountain District. In May, Reynolds and Ellyson decided, over Dr. Bresee's continued objections, to take the General Assembly to Nashville after all. They reasoned that by going to Nashville the Nazarenes might encourage a great number of the Pentecostal Mission people to unite with the church, even though McClurkan and others stood aloof. Lee gracefully agreed to the change, and brought his delegates to the gathering in the Tennessee city. On January 6, 1912, however, he and his preachers wrote Dr. Bresee that they desired to withdraw from the denomination. They gave as their reasons their inability "to perfect the union in spirit which was intended," and the fact that the "distinctively congregational form of government" in the Church of the Nazarene was not suitable for a work so "pioneer and aggressive" in character as theirs had been. All efforts to patch up matters failed, and only a small band in Colorado Springs remained loyal to the church.[24]

Disagreement over the precise terms of the compromise on "rules" adopted at Pilot Point three years before undoubtedly hindered all the various union negotiations. Certainly it complicated the Nashville assembly's climactic effort to bring in the Pentecostal Mission. At that meeting stirring debates again took place on the issues of tobacco and secret societies. Representatives of the Texas and Oklahoma districts now claimed that their understanding in 1908 was that the *Manual* statements on these subjects were to be considered a test of membership. "When they learned that this was not the case, but that the matters referred to came merely under the head of Special Advices," E. A. Girvin wrote, they determined that the assembly must place these paragraphs in the General Rules, "thus making them obligatory, instead of advisory." The only compromise the southerners would allow was that local churches desiring to do so might adopt a probationary system for members not yet up to the standard. That they won their point was in large measure due to insistence upon the same changes by men prominent in both the Pentecostal Mission and the Louisiana Conference of the Methodist Protestant church.[25]

The interest of the latter body in union with the Nazarenes is a forgotten chapter in the history of the Nashville assembly. In 1910, leaders of the conference secured through General Superintendent Ellyson the appointment of a joint commission to work out the basis for a merger. When the General Assembly convened, the youthful R. T. Williams, a native of Louisiana, presented the commission's report. It touched off a general debate, not only on the questions of tobacco and secret societies, but on the nature of the superintendency as well. The Methodist Protestant pastors desired that all actions of district and general superintendents be made subject to respective vetoes by district and general assemblies. The report was finally referred to the committee on *Manual* revision, which, after further discussion, incorporated into the law of the church all the requested changes save the one which implied that labor unions were secret orders. A floor debate made it plain to everyone that many labor organizations did not bind their members with a secret oath.

The president and several officers of the Louisiana conference were present and took part in the discussions, along with visitors from the Mississippi conference of the same denomination. Hopes ran high for a very large addition to Nazarene strength in these states. But the articles of union were never ratified. Nor, as it turned out, did McClurkan's Nashville congregation fall into line until after their founder's death in 1914. During the twenty years following the 1911 assembly only two other mergers took place, one with the Pentecostal Church of Scotland and the other with the Laymen's Holiness Association of North Dakota. Neither increased the membership of the denomination as much as 3 per cent. The secret of the great expansion of those two decades was evangelism.[26]

The Midwest Becomes the Nazarene Heartland

Far more significant than any union which took place after 1908 was the rapid growth of the Church of the Nazarene in the states of the upper Mississippi Valley—Ohio, Kentucky, Indiana, Illinois, Michigan, Missouri, and Iowa. When combined with the plains states of Nebraska, Kansas, and Oklahoma, these contained in 1920 over 40 per cent of the total Nazarene membership, nearly half of the estimated value of church property, and four of the denomination's colleges.[27] The Nazarene headquarters, located at Kansas City, where no church existed in 1911, now lay in the midst of the church's greatest field. Why, we may ask, did the Nazarenes grow so rapidly in the Midwest after getting off to such a slow start?

One answer is that the withdrawal of holiness preachers from the older denominations in this territory was slower than elsewhere in the country. Most Methodist conferences there gave favorable treatment to ministers who preached the "second blessing" right down to 1910, thanks partly to the great influence which the National Association for the Promotion of Holiness exerted from its Chicago headquarters and publishing house. Any who became discontented earlier had the option, moreover, of joining the Free or Wesleyan Methodist churches, well established in the Midwest, or of uniting with the Ohio Yearly Meeting of Friends, the Holiness Christian Conference of Indiana, the Mennonite Brethren in Christ, the Anderson, Indiana, Church of God, and the Church of God (Holiness) in Missouri.[28]

In the years after 1910, however, a nationwide controversy between "fundamentalism" and "modernism," engulfed the Methodist as well as other churches. It intensified greatly all the issues dividing rural and urban America, and drew a sharp line between men who sought new religious horizons and those who clung to the old-time faith. Within Methodism, the doctrine of holiness soon lay at the center of the argument. The new Nazarene pastors and district superintendents in the Midwest exploited fully the opportunity this situation provided to identify their communion with the "true" Wesleyan tradition. Their enthusiasm for the national program, moreover, suffered no inhibition from prior loyalties to a regional organization. They had come directly from the older churches, in most cases by personal choice. Their aggressiveness soon became proverbial.

The Chicago Central District, the first organized in this section, encompassed at its beginning practically all the country between Pittsburgh and the Rockies. L. B. Kent, pioneer leader of the Illinois State Holiness Association, joined the Nazarenes in 1905 and became the first district superintendent. Almost at once young independent congregations began to transfer to the denomination, including important ones at Stockton and Auburn, Illinois, and Seymour, Indiana.[29]

T. H. Agnew, an evangelist and member of the Rock River Conference of the Methodist Episcopal church, joined C. E. Cornell's group in Chicago in February, 1907. Soon after, at the request of several ministers on the district, Dr. Bresee appointed him superintendent. For the next five years Agnew ranged the country from Ohio to Iowa seeking out holiness bands and missions willing to be the nuclei of Churches of the Nazarene. Within a year he had organized twelve congregations, including substantial ones at Indianapolis and Terre Haute, Indiana; Columbus, Ohio; and Louisville, Kentucky, where C. A. Bromley, a prominent evangelist in the Methodist Episcopal Church, South, accepted the pastorate.[30]

In Indianapolis the Nazarenes were heirs of the Young Men's Holiness League, an organization which in recent years had counted 3,000 persons at its altars. Some of the members became discouraged by their inability to conserve these gains, however, and evangelist L. Milton Williams persuaded them to organize a church. C. W. Ruth, then living in Indianapolis, served temporarily as their minister. Later on, John M. Wines, Methodist "conference evangelist" in northern Indiana, joined the denomination and accepted the pastorate there.[31]

The month of May, 1908, found Agnew at Oskaloosa, Iowa, attending a National Holiness Association camp meeting at the site of Central Holiness University, where A. M. Hills was president. Agnew wrote Dr. Bresee that he had sold out his supply of church *Manuals,* so great was the interest. "Iowa is soon to have many open doors for organized holiness," he continued, but "there must be no conflict between the 'holiness association' and the Pentecostal Church of the Nazarene." In August he organized the first of the denomination's churches in the state, at Marshalltown, at the close of a meeting held under the auspices of the state association. In 1911, when the Chicago Central District elected J. M. Wines superintendent in preference to Agnew, the general superintendents approved a division which set off Iowa and Nebraska as a new field for Agnew to cultivate.[32]

Rapid growth on the eastern end of the territory had by that time resulted in the organization of two other new districts, also. A former Methodist evangelist, C. A. Imhoff, conducted a revival meeting at New Galilee, Pennsylvania, in the summer of 1907. At its close Agnew came and organized a church of thirty-four members. They rented a hall at first but constructed a church building within a year. Early the following spring, eighty-five persons professed conversion in a meeting which Imhoff held at East Palestine, Ohio, and sixty-one of them became charter members of the Nazarene congregation. They were people of "intelligence and high standing in the city," the evangelist wrote, and "as true and devoted to God and holiness as any we ever saw."

Imhoff accepted temporary appointment as pastor of the fledgling church in Indianapolis in April, 1908. This left the field clear for the election of John Norris as the first superintendent of the newly organized Pittsburgh District. Norris helped establish congregations in Newark, Columbus, and Lithopolis, Ohio, and at several points in eastern Pennsylvania. C. W. Ruth meanwhile made the first contacts in Cleveland.[33]

In 1909 the Pittsburgh assembly elected Imhoff to return as their leader. By October, 1911, the superintendent reported that the district had 18 churches with 951 members and 1,517 Sunday school scholars. This was but a foretaste, however, of the growth which was to come. Nine years later the new Ohio District, now separate from Pittsburgh, contained 1,207 members. Indiana at that time counted 2,512 communicants and Michigan, 984. Dr. Bresee had agreed to the establishment of the latter two as separate districts in 1914.

County holiness associations and "independent" Methodist missions provided the nuclei for many congregations in the central and northern parts of Ohio and Indiana. Typical of these was the charter group which Imhoff organized at East Palestine. Their leader, John Gould, left the potter's trade to become a minister, and later served as superintendent of the New England District. To the south, in the rolling country above the Ohio River, God's Bible School and camp meeting in Cincinnati prepared the way for the Nazarenes as well as other young Wesleyan denominations. J. M. Wines meanwhile helped to establish the first Nazarene church in Dayton, parent to a score later founded in and around that city.[34]

Thus it was that the Midwest, where the denomination began latest, became the center of its chief strength. Although the

Nazarenes correctly insist that their communion did not begin as a secession from any other, but rather as a union of people already outside the established churches, there can be little doubt that their growth in the Midwest was closely related to discontent within the Methodist fold. As elsewhere, however, that discontent expressed itself first in holiness associations. In the beginning, these operated within a framework of loyalty to the old denominations; but they soon developed religious activities and programs which pointed to the new.

The Pentecostal Church of Scotland

The story of the origins of the Church of the Nazarene in Scotland is inseparably bound up with the life of George Sharpe. A native of Craigneuk, in the iron-manufacturing region of Lanarkshire, Sharpe was converted in 1882, at the age of seventeen. He resisted for several years what he felt was a call to preach, and finally accepted instead an invitation to go to Cortland, New York, to train as an industrial foreman in a business planning to establish a branch plant in France. On his arrival, however, he took such an active part in the Methodist church that within a matter of weeks he was asked to become pastor of a small church nearby. The young Scotsman's zeal and uprightness so impressed the Cortland congregation that they raised money to enable him to attend a Methodist preparatory school and college. In 1890, Sharpe accepted a pastorate in northern New York. A powerful awakening there prompted the bishop to appoint him to Hamilton, New York, the seat of Colgate University.[35]

Transferred to Chateaugay, New York, in 1898, Sharpe continued his usual emphasis upon evangelism by inviting L. Milton Williams, then a major in the Salvation Army, for a revival. The whole countryside was stirred; five hundred seekers appeared at the altars. First Mrs. Sharpe and then her husband sought and obtained the "second blessing." E. F. Walker came along a little later for a convention which fully established the doctrine of entire sanctification in the church and community, and in the lives of the pastor's family.[36]

In 1901, on one of their occasional trips to Scotland, Sharpe felt called to return to preach holiness in his own country. A Congregational church at Ardrossan, near Glasgow, extended him an unexpected call, and he accepted. He began preaching on Christian perfection there with some trepidation, however. In October, 1904, he invited Evangelist Williams to come to the British Isles for a revival at Ardrossan. This meeting initiated the holiness movement in that section of Scotland. It also prompted the opposition to Sharpe's preaching which led him to accept a call in September, 1906, to the Parkhead Congregational Church in Glasgow.

Now in the prime of life, the pastor determined to preach holiness uncompromisingly at Parkhead from the very beginning. In less than thirteen months his sermons on the subject, particularly a series which he began on the Sermon on the Mount, so enraged the deacons that they called the congregation into session to oust him. The meeting broke up in riotous disorder. Robert Bolton, one of the deacons, stood up and cried, "All who still want this man to be your preacher come underneath the gallery." Eighty persons responded. Someone turned out the church lights, but in the darkness they sang and prayed and appointed a committee to secure a hall for services the next day, Sunday, September 30.

Thus began the work of the Parkhead Pentecostal Church. For a year and a half they worshiped in the Great Eastern Roads Hall in Glasgow, making it the scene of continuous revival. A fine church building, constructed by dint of much local sacrifice as well as with aid from American friends, was dedicated in 1907. Mission and evangelistic work, chiefly by the young people of the church, soon resulted in the organization of congregations at nearby Paisley, Uddingston, and Blantyre.[37]

On May 7 and 8, 1909, representatives of these groups gathered at Glasgow and organized the Pentecostal Church of Scotland. The declaration of faith of the Parkhead Church was made the standard for all. Disciplinary rules forbade immoral and imprudent conduct, and "special advices" urged abstinence from strong drink and tobacco. The delegates specifically endorsed the "action of other holiness churches" in extending to women the right of ordination, and adopted a resolution calling for the establishment of holiness churches throughout the British Isles. "The weakness of the holiness movement has been that it is fragmentary," they declared. So long as Pentecostal workers confined themselves to "leagues, missions, small societies, associations, independent churches" and "holiness bands," they could never hope for permanence for their work. Little wonder that when Dr. Bresee found the record of this assembly in an English periodical he reprinted it in full in the *Nazarene Messenger*.[38]

Indeed, every major holiness paper published in America carried some account of Sharpe's work between 1907 and 1909. Evangelist and Mrs. Bud Robinson met him at a camp meeting in New York state in 1907, and introduced him to the readers of the *Pentecostal Advocate*. In December of the same year L. D. Peavey, a lay member of the Pentecostal Church of Malden, Massachusetts, wrote Dr. Bresee suggesting that the Nazarenes should ally themselves with "this work across the sea." Olive M. Winchester, a teacher at the Pentecostal Collegiate Institute, went to Scotland in 1908 to help with Sharpe's new Bible school and to attend Glasgow University. A. M. Hills, former president at Texas Holiness University, visited Scotland in 1908 and 1909. He preached at the meetings which preceded the organization of the churches at Paisley and Uddingston, and may have helped inspire the calling of the first assembly.[39]

The Nashville General Assembly adopted a resolution offered by William Howard Hoople that the general superintendents appoint American representatives to be present at the next annual meeting of the Pentecostal Church of Scotland to seek their union with the Nazarenes. Strangely, however, three years passed before the motion bore fruit. In March, 1913, Olive Winchester wrote Dr. Reynolds a long letter urging immediate action. Reynolds circulated the letter to the members of the General Foreign Missionary Board, and thus awakened the interest which led to the merger of 1915. The National Association for the Promotion of Holiness, Miss Winchester reported, had tried to recruit Sharpe's support for their missionary work, but the effort had gone awry. At the recent district assembly in Glasgow she had convinced the delegates that they should affiliate their missionary program with that of the Nazarenes. They had elected her president of the newly organized missionary society with the full understanding that she was committed to this goal.[40]

Miss Winchester urged Dr. Reynolds to come to Scotland for several months and help win over the people to union. He must secure his expense in the homeland, however. "The people are poor," she explained; "the average wage for a labouring man is $7.50 per week. . . . and the rule has been here as elsewhere that it has been the common people that have heard the message gladly." Since "the first step . . . has been taken by the churches on this side," she concluded, "should not our people do everything in their power to foster this union?"[41]

The General Foreign Missionary Board sent General Superintendent Edward F. Walker to Scotland in the spring of 1914. Dr. Walker found Miss Winchester preparing to return to New England to teach theology at Pentecostal Collegiate Institute. She had just completed her work for the first bachelor of divinity degree ever awarded to a woman at Glasgow University. He also learned, however, that a recent conference had unanimously directed Superintendent Sharpe to have each church vote on the question of uniting with the Nazarenes before June 30.

Walker's presence and preaching were exactly what was needed to encourage favorable action on this proposal. He spent part of his time, however, visiting other branches of the holiness movement in the British Isles. His reports to the *Herald* described the missions clustered about Star Hall, Manchester, where Dr. A. M. Hills was then teaching, and those which David Thomas led in the London area, later organized into the International Holiness Mission. He found Sharpe's people more like the Nazarenes than any of the others, however. They had recently established new churches at Ardrossan, Perth, and Edinburgh, in Scotland, and at Morley, England, and were, in fact, the only one of the holiness groups committed to denominational order. By the time Dr. Walker left the country in May, so many congregations had voted for union that he and Bresee assumed the merger was settled. He wrote Reynolds, then in India on his first trip around the world, that the prospects were bright.[42]

Reynolds thereupon informed the missionary board that he would visit the annual assembly of the Scottish churches on his way home from Africa. On July 14, however, a Serbian patriot shot Archduke Franz Ferdinand of Austria at the little town of Sarajevo, in what is now Yugoslavia. The first World War began a few days later, causing Reynolds to miss the assembly. He was aboard a German steamer in the south Atlantic when he heard the news. The vessel made for a neutral port in Brazil. Undismayed by the possibility of German naval action in the Atlantic, the missionary superintendent caught a British ship going directly to Liverpool. He regretted only that he had to omit a planned visit to the Cape Verde Islands.

Soon after his arrival in Scotland, Reynolds discovered

that the merger faced real hurdles still. Few of the people were thoroughly acquainted with the Nazarene *Manual*. The Parkhead congregation were loath to adopt the term "steward" as the title for the lay leaders whom Scottish churches had for ages called "deacons." The requirement that they be elected annually, instead of for a lifetime, was even more distasteful. Moreover, Sharpe had promised the people they would have another chance to vote on the union before it became final.

A "provisional committee" appointed by the assembly met with Reynolds on Friday evening, October 2. The general superintendent insisted that the questions at issue be referred again to the churches. Throughout that long week end, he and Sharpe visited one congregation after another. By Tuesday, October 6, the day before Reynolds' scheduled departure, all had acted favorably but Parkhead, where over a third of the infant denomination's membership was enrolled. After some further discussion they, too, voted by a large majority to go along. Some of their reluctance sprang from the knowledge that part of the price would be the loss of their pastor to full-time work as district superintendent. Reynolds went rushing off by the midnight train to catch his boat at Liverpool, and to head home across the same dark waters where seven months later the "Lusitania" fell prey to a German submarine.[43]

The accession of the Pentecostal Church of Scotland was not ratified finally until the General Assembly met at Kansas City the next year. By it there came to the Church of the Nazarene something more valuable than merely the 8 churches, 665 members, and the property to which they assigned a net worth of $27,000. In this merger was conceived the vision of an international holiness communion. True, the relative poverty of the Scottish churches prompted the General Foreign Missionary Board for some years to appropriate the full amount and more of the offerings received from them to support their own district superintendent. But after a time the Nazarenes of Scotland became an example to the entire connection in their zeal for missions. Two of their young people, Dr. David Hynd and his wife, Agnes Kanema Sharpe, both graduates of Glasgow University, joined Harmon Schmelzenbach in Africa in 1924 to give their lives to building the famous Fitkin Memorial Hospital in Swaziland.[44]

CHAPTER XI

Achieving the Inner Reality of Union

Unfinished Business

The official merging of the eight groups which made up the Church of the Nazarene took place within a period of only seven years. This process inevitably outran the adoption of measures necessary to knit the rank and file of laymen and ministers into a cohesive Christian community. The unfinished business of the union assemblies, therefore, was the transfer to the national body of the loyalties which had for many years been sectional in their scope. This required recruiting and training a generation of pastors whose outlooks were national, and the establishment of respect for the authority of the general superintendents greater than that accorded the native sons who occupied the corresponding district office. It also called for the unification of foreign mission, publishing, and educational activities around general objectives, if not under a single administration. The movement to nationalize "connectional interests" made rapid progress, as a matter of fact, everywhere except in educational work. Even there, a remarkable degree of integration had been imposed from the top by 1920.

The birth of the spiritual fellowship necessary for the hard tasks of legislative and administrative integration took place in the union assemblies themselves, as we have seen; and the early tours of the general superintendents throughout the country kept it alive. Evangelists from each section meanwhile crisscrossed the continent for revival meetings in which untraveled lay people caught the spirit of their brothers far away. A few key pastors migrated to new sections of the church, too: C. Howard Davis, from Brooklyn to Spokane; C. E. Cornell, from Chicago to Los Angeles; H. H. Miller, from Oklahoma City to San Francisco; and, in 1915, evangelist R. T. Williams, from Peniel to McClurkan's congregation in Nashville.

Such an interweaving of human and spiritual relationships could not, however, take the place of direct action. The very first General Assembly felt compelled to curb the employment of revivalists who encouraged their converts to stay in the older denominations. The delegates recommended that the church commission only those evangelists who were "not ashamed to be known as members of the Pentecostal Church of the Nazarene, and who in declaring themselves" would "do so without apology."

Some of the early pastors, moreover, turned out to be of such an independent disposition that they could not wear the harness of unity. By January, 1910, H. B. Hosley, district superintendent in Washington, D.C., was reviving his old complaints against H. F. Reynolds. The missionary secretary, he charged, was promoting foreign work to the detriment of home missions, and was collecting a salary and expenses so large as to give him an unfair advantage over the other general superintendents. Hosley published independently the *Pentecostal Era*. In February, 1910, he announced in that journal that Washington First Church had placed its property in the hands of three trustees who were leaders of the interdenominational wing of the holiness movement: C. J. Fowler, Will Huff, and H. F. Kletzing. Although he remained superintendent of the Washington District for three more years, Hosley left the denomination in 1913 and carried most of the congregation in the nation's capital with him. His new group declared itself "Wesleyan in doctrine" but "independent and congregational" in government.[1] Similar dissent cropped up in Florida, Pennsylvania, and elsewhere. In Texas, as we shall see, two former leaders of the Holiness Church of Christ nearly ruined the mission in Mexico by a strange scheme which appeared to combine a land speculation with evangelism.[2]

Most serious, and most embarrassing, were the troubles which rocked the Southern California District in the period just before and just after the Pilot Point assembly. Bresee's quickness to forgive a prominent young minister for indiscretions which some felt were evidence of a moral lapse produced great unrest. A. L. Whitcomb, who had resigned the presidency of the Free Methodist college at Greenville, Illinois, to take over Bresee's old pulpit, joined the dissident group within six months after his arrival in Los Angeles. He led a secession from First Church into a new congregation, then asked that it be admitted to the district. The controversy deeply affected the Bible college. Practically the entire faculty had to be replaced during the year 1908-9. The new dean, W. W. Danner, for many years an officer of the Iowa Holiness Association, lasted only nine months. E. F. Walker, who succeeded Whitcomb at Los Angeles First Church, was soon carrying heavy responsibilities at the college as well.

The district assembly elected John W. Goodwin superintendent in August, 1908. After some months of deliberation, Goodwin determined to accept Whitcomb's new Trinity Church into regular standing on condition that its leaders should withdraw in public print their charges that the general superintendent had been "covering up sin." Bresee, still deeply hurt, disagreed with Goodwin's plan; "nevertheless," he wrote, "I shall find some way to approve your action." The whole matter was finally thrashed out on the floor of the district assembly of 1910, with Dr. Bresee in the chair. Goodwin spoke for two hours, closing with a moving appeal for unity. The revered founder then adjourned the meeting with a prayer in which the spirit of reconciliation prevailed. Goodwin was unanimously re-elected district superintendent, as we shall see in a moment, and remained Dr. Bresee's most loyal friend.[3]

That some friction should have arisen during the period of consolidation was to be expected, of course. When each of the three general superintendents became directly and personally involved, however, matters looked grave indeed. That they succeeded thereafter as well as they did in establishing the power and stature of their office was a tremendous achievement.

The Early History of the General Superintendency

If Bresee's public leadership had made the first unions possible, Hiram Reynolds' passion for detail and devotion to duty during the next seven years made them permanent. These two, in fact, played mutually complementary roles. Aging and in ill health, and beset with a towering crisis in Los Angeles, Bresee was not as free as Reynolds to seize upon the work of episcopal visitation. Reynolds, on the other hand, held in the office of general missionary secretary a mandate to raise funds on any district or in any church where he thought it wise. In 1909, for example, his announced itinerary called for visits to churches on the Arkansas, Oklahoma, Dallas, Kentucky, and Southeastern districts in late winter; then in the spring to those in the Washington, Philadelphia, New England, Newfoundland, and Nova Scotia superintendencies; and finally, in the summer, to the Chicago, Rocky Mountain, Northwest, and California territories. He planned to come back again by way of Texas and Oklahoma to the annual meeting of the General Missionary Board at Chicago in October. The reports of this long year's work, published weekly in the *Nazarene Messenger,* show that Reynolds counseled with pastors, met with district superintendents to go over "plans for the work," raised missionary funds, visited colleges, ordained ministers, and scouted out prospective mergers with other denominations, all in addition to the more routine matter of conducting district assemblies.[4]

Both Bresee and E. P. Ellyson seem to have been taken aback by this outburst of episcopal energy. In March, 1909, the former urged Reynolds not to visit southern California, on the grounds that the economic crisis there forbade any additional expense. He had not received any salary at all since his resignation at First Church on January 1, Bresee explained, and ill health had made it impossible for him to travel among the western churches. As for the missionary offerings, he added, "Brother Gay very efficiently looks after this matter." Later in the year, when Reynolds insisted that all the general superintendents should attend the missionary board meeting in Chicago, Ellyson wrote from the Hollow Rock campground in Ohio that he did not see how he could afford to come. He had already scheduled several district assemblies during the fall, despite his primary obligation to the college at Peniel. "What living I get comes from the school," he wrote. "The Sup'tcy as yet hasn't paid expenses. If I neglect the school work I cannot expect full pay, and I hardly receive enough now to live on. What can I do? I greatly desire to be with you but do not see how I can afford either time or money."[5]

Bresee and Ellyson both finally managed to make it to the Chicago conclave. Encouraged somewhat at the improvement in his health, Bresee made plans, at Reynolds' insistence, to visit the eastern assemblies again in the spring of 1910. He took the southern route, by way of Ellyson's home at Peniel. Reynolds met him there, for what was one of the only two meetings these three ever held apart from sessions of other boards and committees. They reviewed plans for the acceptance of Texas Holiness University as a Nazarene institution, discussed ways to make the *Pentecostal Advocate* a denominational paper, and took steps to deal with major problems facing the missionary work in Mexico.[6]

In the spring of 1911, Ellyson chose to abandon the office of general superintendent in favor of the presidency of the new "Nazarene University" at Pasadena. Reynolds also considered resigning, and decided definitely to give up the secretaryship of the missionary board. With Bresee in increasingly poor health, it looked for a time as though the church might be deprived of all these key leaders.[7]

It helped none at all that, on the very first day of business at the General Assembly in Nashville that fall, E. F. Walker proposed and the gathering adopted a resolution designed to "correct any interpretation" that the church's government was episcopal in form. "We are not an episcopal church in the common sense of that term," the statement ran.

> Our system of superintendency does not contemplate episcopal oversight. We would deplore and discourage any tendency in that direction. Our pastors are the overseers of their particular charges. Our superintendents are mainly for the oversight of pastorless churches, the work of evangelism, and the organizing and encouragement of organizing of churches, where there seems providential opening and call.

Six days later the delegates elected the author of this resolution a general superintendent, along with Reynolds and Bresee. When the result of the ballot was announced, Walker rose to suggest that the three of them kneel together in a circle, with hands clasped, so that the elders of the church might gather round and lay hands upon them. They did so at once. The prayer of consecration which hallowed the observance fell from the lips of the most stalwart congregationalist of them all, William Howard Hoople![8]

Such acts of self-effacement may actually have strengthened the hands of the superintendents. The same assembly adopted a plan to provide regular support for each of them. Although the delegates transferred from the General Missionary Board to the districts all responsibility for work in the United States, they explicitly endorsed its "centralization policy" for foreign missions. A new provision that the missionary secretary be elected by vote of the assembly served only to force Reynolds' critics to show their strength. He won handily, over opposition only slightly greater than in the balloting for general superintendent. Thus vindicated, Reynolds humbly accepted both offices.⁹

During the next four years the chief responsibility for general leadership in the church rested upon Hiram Reynolds' shoulders. He visited practically every congregation in the denomination, and conducted assemblies at least twice on almost every district. As missionary secretary, he kept detailed records of gifts from individuals, prepared receipts for local missionary treasurers to record, and wrote literally hundreds of letters calculated to give laymen a personal tie with the general interests of the church. As a presiding officer, his winsome spirit disarmed those who feared that general superintendents might become ecclesiastical tyrants. J. B. Chapman later remembered that when he once objected to Reynolds' ruling in a district assembly the good doctor publicly withdrew it, simply in order to avoid embarrassing the young preacher.

Despite such displays of humility and patience, discontent with the general leaders continued strong in some quarters. On the eve of the assembly of 1915, I. G. Martin suggested that the church be divided into four great sections, each of which would elect its own superintendent at a biennial conference. The General Assembly then would choose only a moderator, who would head a general cabinet, composed of the superintendents of the four regions. This, Martin hoped, would eliminate any further tendency toward centralized authority.¹⁰

Dr. Bresee, weak and on the very verge of death, watched these developments from his home in Los Angeles with growing concern. Despite the orders of his physician, he determined to attend the General Assembly at Kansas City in 1915, and to read there the first quadrennial address of the general superintendents. Characteristically, Bresee made no direct appeal in that pronouncement for a strong superintendency. Leadership in a Christian community, he knew, rested not so much upon law as upon the ability to persuade men to accept spiritual challenges and to preserve brotherly commitments.

The years since the Pilot Point union had seen the churches "put into the melting pot together," he began. The real question now was "whether the holy fire of the glory which Christ has given, would be able to melt us into the sacred unity for which He prayed." Noting the many controversial issues scheduled to come before the delegates, Bresee urged them in a voice which trembled with both age and compassion to humble themselves, to join him in making sure "that there is no selfish way in us, . . . that no word or act of ours shall be a hindrance or stumbling-block in the way of any human soul." If in anything they should not see eye to eye, they must still "abide heart to heart," patiently waiting to be led by Him who would glorify himself in the unity of their love to God and to each other, and in their devotion to the work to which He had called them. All who professed holiness must remember, he continued, "that humility and regard for the best judgment of others becomes us." It is always a pitiable sight, he said, "for any one to stand out and oppose, or forsake the fellowship of his brethren, because he is, in his own judgment, better or wiser than they."[11]

The issues were thrashed out in the committee on superintendency, headed by John W. Goodwin, who but for Dr. Bresee's provision might have missed the assembly altogether. The committee firmly rejected Martin's suggestion of a Presbyterian-like polity. They recommended that the missionary board be empowered to name one of the general superintendents to spend his full time supervising the foreign work. They also proposed increasing the number of general superintendents to four, directed that each local church raise fifteen cents a member annually for their support, and suggested that these leaders reside in different sections of the country, but not preside exclusively there. When time for the balloting came, Bresee spoke strongly in favor of the proposal for a fourth general superintendent, noting that only one able-bodied man, Dr. Reynolds, remained in the office. The assembly elected Bresee, Reynolds, Walker, and Ellyson. Dr. Ellyson declined, however, and W. C. Wilson, district superintendent in southern California, was named in his place.[12]

Dr. Bresee died on November 13, 1915, just thirty-three days after the General Assembly adjourned, and his friend Wilson passed away five weeks later. Dr. Walker's health was meanwhile failing rapidly. The district superintendents chose John W. Goodwin and Evangelist R. T. Williams to fill the vacancies. Williams, who had been a college teacher and administrator and more recently pastor of Nashville First Church, wrote his friend and mentor, C. A. McConnell, asking what to do about the election. Thirty-two years was too young for the office, he believed, and he was in any case very anxious lest administrative work cut off his preaching. Yet he hesitated to say "no" to his brethren. He did accept, and by midsummer, 1916, the young evangelist was wrestling with the greatest crisis the church had yet faced.[13]

Ten more years were required before the new general superintendents were able actually to exert the kind of authority the denomination needed, but they had made a good beginning. The multiplication of the powers and functions of general boards, which at first seemed to diminish their role, finally produced a host of problems which only strong and respected leaders could solve. That story, however, belongs to a later chapter.

The Organization of Foreign Missions

No area of the church's activity needed central direction as much as foreign missions. All four of the principal parent bodies of the denomination had established outposts on foreign soil. In each case the complexities of finance and administration had almost overwhelmed the original sponsors. Although union seemed at first only to enlarge the difficulties, it produced the zeal and determination necessary to put the missions on their feet.

In the East, the Association of Pentecostal Churches had established a missionary committee and approved a woman's foreign missionary auxiliary at the time of their first organization in 1895. The office of missionary secretary was added in 1897. Although the committee was responsible for both home and foreign work, its funds came chiefly from appeals for the missions to India, launched in 1897, and to the Cape Verde Islands, begun in 1900. By the time of the Brooklyn annual meeting in 1907, five persons maintained three stations in India: in Berar province, northeast of Bombay; at Buldana and Mulkapur; and at Igatpuri. All of the property, including thirty acres of land at Buldana and substantial buildings there and at Igatpuri, was free from debt. The women's society supported two of the missionaries directly, however, and the salaries paid to the whole group totaled only $1,793 for the entire year.[14]

The foreign enterprise of the Nazarenes in California developed much more slowly, due chiefly to the fact that Dr. Bresee was reluctant to undertake work overseas when so many calls pressed for attention at home. In 1902, Mary A. Hill recruited a band of students from the Bible school to reopen at South Chih-Li,

Shantung Province, China, a faith mission closed during the Boxer Rebellion. But the church never officially adopted the project. Two years later, however, Mrs. Mary McReynolds established a Spanish mission in Los Angeles which secured immediate and enthusiastic support.

In a report to the General Assembly of 1905, which was typical of the statements he made on the subject throughout his life, Bresee insisted that the primary task of the Nazarenes was "to Christianize Christianity" and thus "to save America . . . as a center of religious life to the world." He approved efforts to convert "heathen" immigrants, however, since these might raise up persons specially fitted to bear the gospel to their kinsmen abroad. The assembly's committee on missions, headed by Leslie Gay and Mrs. McReynolds, took direct issue with their general superintendent. The church's acceptance of the great commission could not be delayed, they declared. The establishment of one hundred strong Nazarene churches in America would only increase the demand for "more than all the workers available and more than all the money in sight" to meet the challenge at home. The assembly agreed and urged each congregation to begin at once giving a tithe of its total income for foreign endeavors.[15]

The next spring Dr. Bresee himself presented to Gay's "home and foreign missionary board" what he thought was a providential opportunity to sponsor an orphans' and widows' home in Calcutta, India, known as Hope School. Mrs. Sukhoda Banargee and Mr. P. B. Biswas, Indian natives, had come to America the previous fall seeking financial help for the venture they had recently begun on faith alone. Mrs. E. G. Eaton, a woman evangelist from Oregon, took them to Dr. Bresee. The board enthusiastically agreed to raise eighteen hundred dollars a year for general expenses and twenty-five dollars for each widow or child housed in the institution.[16] By 1907, Hope School was supporting sixty widows and orphans, but the problems of administration had not been solved. Bresee meanwhile continued to bombard the missionary board and the General Assembly with pleas for more support for the church's "first and special field," the cities of America.[17]

The Holiness Church of Christ and McClurkan's Pentecostal Mission had erred more on the side of enthusiasm than of restraint. Both conducted their foreign missions on the "faith" principle, which relieved the church at home of responsibility to equip and support the missionaries beyond the income which the Lord sent in. The resulting permissive approach to administration allowed individual congregations to initiate ventures which later required help from others if they were to survive. By 1908 as many as twenty persons in Japan, India, and Mexico claimed to represent officially the Holiness Church of Christ, though that group's missionary board had authorized only S. M. Stafford's "self-supporting" mission in Mexico. What Stafford meant by self-support was not clear, either. He appeared at both the Chicago and Pilot Point union assemblies and at many subsequent meetings of the denominational missionary board to solicit aid, and began writing regular columns to the *Nazarene Messenger* months before the union with the South was complete.[18]

A Los Angeles layman, Leslie F. Gay, and General Superintendent H. F. Reynolds deserve perhaps chief credit for the establishment of a centralized program for the support and administration of these manifold missionary enterprises.

Gay's long report as chairman of the committee on missions at the Chicago Assembly was no model of brevity, and the plan he outlined was not a simple one. It called for separate boards at each level—general, district, and local—and specified at great length their powers and forms of organization. The important recommendation, however, was to consolidate the former regional missionary administrations in a General Missionary Board, with headquarters at Chicago, the geographic center of the church. All "documents, deeds, bequests, legacies, applications for help," and "calls for helpers," with "all moneys, pledges for missions, accounts, bills, . . . statements of present system of collecting and disbursing of funds, contracts with missionaries or workers, officers, etc.," were to be turned over to the new group at once. The board was authorized to employ an executive secretary and to pay his salary and expenses out of missionary funds, and to promote the "envelope system" of raising money in the local churches. It was to consist of "not less than sixteen" members, two from each district, there being at that time four districts in both the East and the West. When union with the Holiness Church of Christ was completed, the plan was for four districts to be organized there as well, increasing the membership to twenty-four.

ACHIEVING THE INNER REALITY OF UNION 253

Here, then, was a thoroughgoing integration of foreign missionary efforts. The delegates adopted the program readily and elected outstanding men from both sections to the new board. At their first meeting the group named Gay treasurer and Reynolds executive secretary, and empowered the general superintendents to act on their behalf in the intervals between meetings.[19]

Within a few months the "money panic" of 1907 began to constrict missionary giving. Reynolds published a plea for funds which significantly asked both easterners and westerners not to refer any longer to "your work, your churches, your paper, your preachers," but to speak of all as "ours." The denomination must develop a "deep feeling of joint heirship," he wrote, which would "obliterate all former boundary lines." The members of the Pilot Point General Assembly agreed fully with this idea. Their committee on missions urged all persons who were supporting orphans, native workers, and missionaries overseas to channel their giving through the General Missionary Board, and appealed directly to the operators of independent missions to turn them over to that body. The committee also proposed combining the three different missions in operation in India under one administration as soon as possible, and gave the envelope system, appealing to all of the church, priority over fund-raising by women's missionary societies.

At the close of the assembly, however, the newly elected missionary board ran into difficulties. The unorganized condition of the southern group's Mexican work made the united body hesitant to assume responsibility, yet the southerners could scarcely desert the men and women they had so recently sent out. The board deemed it wise, therefore, to allow the former congregations of the Holiness Church of Christ to continue to support these missionaries on their own. But it directed them to assign each a definite monthly salary, to remit all funds through the central treasury, and to allow no direct appeals from the field to the churches at home. Further discussion indicated that these stipulations were not entirely satisfactory. Dr. Bresee thereupon proposed that the General Missionary Board divide into three sections: one each for the East, the West, and the South, each to operate with its own secretary and treasurer under the chairmanship of the general superintendent elected from that zone. When this motion carried, Reynolds, already re-elected general secretary, saw the danger at once and "spoke to the board of the necessity of his traveling at large in the Church to better perform the functions of his office."

Within twelve months, Dr. Reynolds had worked so hard to raise funds and secure accurate information on the condition of the various fields as to make himself indispensable to the "subboards" in all three regions. The General Missionary Board abolished the sectional divisions at its annual meeting for 1909 and returned to the original plan of a single secretary and treasurer. A southerner, E. H. Sheeks, was elected treasurer. He and Reynolds agreed to move to Chicago if at all possible. No doubt the improvement of financial conditions during the preceding year contributed to this decision. The western division raised $8,023; the southern, $3,162; and the eastern, $5,287—a total of $16,472. The board adopted a budget of $20,000 for the next year, one-half for foreign and one-half for home missions, and carefully distributed the responsibility for raising it among the various districts. The sum was oversubscribed. At long last the church commanded resources sufficient to keep alive the missions which its parent bodies had begun with such unchastened zeal.[20]

The General Assembly of 1911 strongly supported the centralized administration of foreign work. Significantly, it set up as a basis of representation on the general board six "missionary divisions" which cut across both the new district boundaries and the old lines of sectional allegiance. A sign of the times was the fact that Dr. Bresee himself moved to begin the mission in Japan, the first new field to be entered since the union of 1907. In the following years Dr. Reynolds fell to his dual task as missionary secretary and general superintendent with a zeal surpassing even that he had shown before. He inaugurated the "field reports," which required each missionary to answer each year a long questionnaire covering every conceivable aspect of the material and spiritual condition of his station. The central board thus secured for the first time an unvarnished picture of the work abroad. The hard truth was necessary, however, before effective supervision could begin.[21]

The trouble in the Mexican mission in 1910 and 1911 underlined the urgency of getting the facts straight. It also showed how unsystematic administration of foreign missionary programs could complicate the development of a national policy for educational and publishing ventures at home.

For over a year after the union assembly of 1908 the two schools in east Texas, at Peniel and Pilot Point, and the two papers, the *Pentecostal Advocate* and the *Holiness Evangel,* continued to operate side by side, along with the much smaller Bible institute at Buffalo Gap, farther west. Late in 1909, business and real estate promoters of the west Texas town of Hamlin offered to subsidize the establishment of a Nazarene college there. Leaders of all three institutions seemed to have agreed to combine the Pilot Point and Buffalo Gap projects in the new Central Holiness University at Hamlin.

Dr. Ellyson believed, however, that the *Holiness Evangel* should go out of business entirely. He objected strongly, therefore, when a group of Hamlin businessmen offered to buy and move the *Evangel* press to their city and to continue J. D. Scott as its editor. As an alternative, Scott and Dennis Rogers proposed that the General Missionary Board purchase the printing plant and ship it with them to Tonala, Chiapas Province, Mexico, where they hoped to establish a new mission field and publish a missionary paper for the entire denomination. Some alleged that they planned to engage in ranching and land speculation on the side. Ellyson and C. A. McConnell were so anxious to be rid of the competing paper, however, that they agreed to support the proposition and to make the *Pentecostal Advocate* an official Nazarene organ if the agreement went through.[22]

When Hiram Reynolds received Ellyson's summary of this wild scheme, he refused to approve it. He brushed aside the Peniel president's exhortation to trust the Lord for the money with the statement, "We well know the Lord will help us, but He will not help us if we enter into any unwise and injudicious arrangement."[23] A compromise was finally worked out under which the General Missionary Board accepted the *Evangel* press, but assumed no legal responsibility for the purchase price of $4,000 and made no promise to support the former owner, a Brother Ball, in his plans to go to India. The southern people were to be asked to buy stock to finance the transaction.

Late in February, however, Scott and Rogers packed the type and presses aboard a railroad boxcar and departed with their families for Mexico, all without authorization and over Ellyson's objections. Then they claimed to be officially appointed representatives of the General Missionary Board. Neither Reynolds nor Ellyson could accept this, especially in view of Scott's letter of February 17, 1910, indicating that he thought the agreement was only a matter of form. "The only thing I want," Scott had written, "is to have the freedom and liberty to work for God unmolested, and of course we will be so far away from you folks, that you know Dennis and I will do as we please anyway." Although the two men later denied that they were involved in a land promotion, their refusal to accept discipline or direction from headquarters was intolerable. A year of increasing disorganization followed. The General Assembly of 1911 finally patched up a compromise of sorts but the revolution which broke out in Mexico the following year forced all the missionaries home.[24]

An equally serious crisis soon faced the work in India. In October, 1913, the General Board of Foreign Missions asked its treasurer, Elmer G. Anderson, to go to India and unify the administration of the three missions in operation there. Anderson delayed his acceptance, however. The next spring found Hiram Reynolds in Calcutta, shocked at the discovery of improper relationships at Hope School, and grieved by the severe illness of Mr. and Mrs. E. G. Eaton, the principal American missionaries there. In this emergency Dr. Reynolds brought L. S. Tracy from Berar province to Calcutta and appointed him temporarily superintendent of both the eastern and western India districts. He wired Kansas City urging Anderson not to sail until he reached home. Reynolds wished to explain to him among other things a plan to provide converts from among the Garo tribe with loans at low rates, to relieve them of the 85 per cent annual interest they were paying on money borrowed to purchase seed for their crops. He urged the board, moreover, to concentrate on one or the other of the Indian stations. This, he said, would reduce the wholesale sacrificing of the missionaries' health and usefulness which resulted from keeping so small a working force at one place.[25]

At the urging of the general superintendents, Anderson finally decided not to go to India at all. To L. S. Tracy fell the task of integrating the Berar and Calcutta projects and of fusing them with the strong work in the Bombay territory inherited from the Pentecostal Mission the next year. Roy G. Codding, head of the latter venture, was most co-operative. He became superintendent of the entire work in India in June, 1915. He and Tracy drew up a statesmanlike policy designed eventually to develop full autonomy and self-support in the national

ACHIEVING THE INNER REALITY OF UNION 257

church, and meanwhile to give the Indian converts a larger voice in the decisions of the district assembly. This policy, somewhat amended, later became the rule for all missions of the Church of the Nazarene. Governing the Calcutta field from western India proved impracticable, however. In 1916 the board sent George J. Franklin for what was in the long run a futile effort to make Hope School a going concern.[26]

Much yet remained in the task of fashioning an effective missionary program for the united church, but a beginning had been made. The General Board of Foreign Missions had established its authority, as much by necessity as by legislation, and had inspired the church to increasingly generous giving. Offerings for the four years between 1911 and 1915 averaged over $28,000 annually. Under Reynolds' prodding, the board had also developed orderly procedures for the recruiting, appointment, and governing of missionaries in foreign fields. These were commendable achievements, in view of the loose organization of the "faith missions" which the church had inherited seven years before.

The Harmonizing of Educational Activities

At the time of the union of 1907, the leaders of the church felt little need for national direction of the educational program beyond encouraging generous support of the two institutions then in existence. Since the laws of California forbade any change in the corporation which governed Deets Pacific Bible College, it seemed fitting to leave the old educational committees in charge both there and at Pentecostal Collegiate Institute.

When, however, in 1908, the Bible institute at Pilot Point, the Texas Holiness University, and Arkansas Holiness College at Vilonia were added to the list of institutions having a claim on the church's support, a general policy seemed necessary. A committee of which E. P. Ellyson was chairman and E. E. Angell secretary recommended that the General Assembly establish a "General Educational Board," with power to handle the property and to supervise the work of all the schools. Since the Pilot Point institution had already offered its property to the denomination, the committee suggested that it should be the first to fall completely under central control. They had in mind, however, the yet unannounced agreement of the trustees of Texas Holiness University to turn over their school to the denomination as well; the general superintendents had decided to keep the plan confidential for a time, so as to avoid an immediate break with patrons in other denominations. Ellyson's committee simply noted, therefore, that the Peniel institution was "closely affiliated to our Church in spirit and interest," and recommended it to Nazarene young people who desired a full college course.[27]

Few realized that this was but a beginning of the multiplication of educational institutions which was to follow in the wake of union with the South. Reynolds and Ellyson secured Missouri Holiness College to the denomination the very next month. Instead of giving way as some thought it would to nearby Texas Holiness University, the Bible institute at Pilot Point moved west to become Central Holiness University at Hamlin, in 1910. C. B. Jernigan, as we have seen, added two other institutions, at Hutchinson, Kansas, and Bethany, Oklahoma. And J. B. Chapman helped make Arkansas Holiness College a Nazarene school in 1911. The trustees at Vilonia tried repeatedly, as their minutes bluntly put it, to bury the "church question" so deep that no one "could ever scratch it up again." But the Nazarenes finally managed to crowd out the Free Methodists, who had actually been first on the ground.[28]

In Nashville, meanwhile, all those who anticipated an early union with the Nazarenes looked forward to incorporating Trevecca College into the denomination's educational program. Farther to the southeast, at Donalsonville, Georgia, T. J. Shingler dreamed of establishing a great holiness institute which would both strengthen the church in that section and increase the population of the town in which he had substantial business and real estate interests. In 1911, H. F. Reynolds asked Dr. Ellyson to consider the presidency there, rather than at Pasadena, so as to be able to remain a general superintendent representing the southern states.[29]

Dr. Ellyson seems to have been the first to see the need for centralized direction of the church's educational program. In February, 1911, a month before his election to the presidency of Pasadena, he sent to Hiram Reynolds a detailed plan which he hoped would curb institutional rivalries, promote the wise investment of available resources, and encourage higher academic standards. He proposed that the General Assembly establish at once the board of education envisaged at Pilot Point, and empower it to oversee all educational endeavors. It should be authorized to grant official recognition to schools, to classify them as either academies, colleges, universities, or theological seminaries, and to see that the curriculum in each lived up to the standards implied by its name. Although each district might properly sponsor an academy, Ellyson wrote, the church "must not approve the multiplication of colleges beyond our needs and our ability to equip and sustain them." Three "universities," one for the East, one for the West, and one "in the South Central part of the United States," should be "thoroughly equipped and sustained" before any others were allowed.[30]

The committee on education of the next General Assembly adopted most of Ellyson's suggestions, and issued a public warning against multiplying the number of institutions at the expense of their quality. The assembly ratified the agreement of the general superintendents to make Texas Holiness University a Nazarene enterprise, and provided that the new Board of Education should name its trustees. Significantly, however, the delegates did not agree to restrict the number of schools claiming the rank of university, an eminence already staked out on the west Texas plains by the promoters of the venture at Hamlin.[31]

The Chicago Central District was by then also anticipating a move to bring "Illinois Holiness University" into the denomination. Laymen of the Eastern Illinois Holiness Association had persuaded L. Milton Williams and A. M. Hills to help them establish this institution in 1909. It was located at the village of Olivet, on the edge of the prairies fourteen miles south of Danville. The school early attracted a large part of its students and its financial support from the growing midwestern section of the Church of the Nazarene. The farmer-trustees constructed a fine administration building, which they financed in part from the sale of lots in their village Zion. Overwhelmed both with debt and administrative problems, however, the board voted in February, 1912, to offer the college to the Chicago Central District. In June they elected General Superintendent Walker president. By October, when the district accepted the gift, the sixteen trustees were all members of the denomination. The next year's assembly set up terms of office for them, and took other measures which allowed the board to continue to function under its old charter while at the same time making it amenable to the desires of the school's new owners. When two new districts, Michigan and Indiana, were set off in 1914, Dr. Bresee insisted that they must share the power to elect trustees and to control the college property. Thus emerged the system which, despite the resolutions of two previous general assemblies, eventually placed all the colleges under regional rather than general boards and made them answerable only to the district assemblies which supported them.[32]

Olivet seemed from the outset a vigorous new competitor to Peniel and Pasadena for educational leadership in the church. E. P. Ellyson resigned his post at Pasadena and became Walker's vice-president at the Illinois school late in 1913. By 1915, student enrollment had reached 234. However, the succession of distinguished leaders who occupied the president's office proved unable to reduce the large debt. Only the steady growth of the Nazarene congregations in midwestern towns and cities enabled the college to survive the repeated crises of the next two decades.[33]

Bresee was meanwhile almost crushed beneath a grinding succession of problems at the Nazarene University. Few knew the grief which lay back of the public announcement in the fall of 1909 that the Hollywood property, recently purchased with the Deets gift, had been sold and the school moved to Pasadena. Bresee himself decided upon the relocation at the height of the Whitcomb secession, over the strenuous objections of Jackson Deets and District Superintendent J. W. Goodwin. Fred C. Epperson, a young minister on the Los Angeles District who was engaged primarily in the real estate business, secured an option on the Hugus Ranch, consisting of 134 acres at the foot of the mountains in northeast Pasadena, at a price of $165,000. The college board took up the option, in Bresee's name. They realized $25,000 from the sale of the Hollywood plot, and agreed to make regular payments of $25,000 each six months thereafter to complete the purchase. They expected to raise the money through the subdivision and sale in residence-size lots of that portion of the land nearest the city. The large and ornate house, since known as the "Gay Mansion," seemed adequate for the college classes until new buildings could be erected.[34]

By March, 1911, the holder of the notes gave notice of his intention to force a foreclosure of the mortgage on the property. Sales of lots had been slow, in part because the city had for a time believed it was not responsible to supply water to the area. Dr. Bresee, anxious to the point of illness lest a scandal doom the work, readily accepted the aid of his loyal friend, Goodwin.

Within a week the district superintendent had badgered and persuaded friends, including Jackson Deets, to sign new notes covering the money due. Bresee thereupon resigned the presidency of the school and recommended that the board elect Dr. Ellyson in his place. But he could not withdraw from "the business," as he called it, since the titles and the mortgages were all in his name. The financial burden thereafter fell upon Goodwin's shoulders. He resigned the district superintendency the following September and, with J. F. Sanders, gave the next two years of his life to raising money, securing a street railway connection, and selling lots. Bresee made out deeds transferring all of the property except thirty acres reserved for the college grounds to a new corporation, but the latter group found it unwise to accept the deed. He thus remained for many months thereafter personally liable for the debts.[35]

Evangelist Seth C. Rees was the preacher at the first camp meeting held on the new campus, in 1911. He accepted soon after the pastorate of the new University Church. Meanwhile, the youthful Dean H. Orton Wiley mapped out a four-year curriculum for the "College of Liberal Arts." The faculty, however, showed little scholarly improvement over previous years. In 1911-12 President Ellyson was responsible for instruction in three fields, theology, astronomy, and geology, and Wiley in two, philosophy and education. Recent graduates taught such subjects as history and biology. Mrs. Ellyson was dean of the Bible school. Ellyson resigned after only two years, and Wiley was elected to replace him.

What the church heard more about was the series of great revivals, led first by President Ellyson and then by Seth C. Rees, pastor of the University Church. "Our purpose is not primarily educational," Ellyson had said in his inaugural address, "as this word is commonly used. We are to be a real training school to prepare men and women for true life. In this work education is an important incidental, but it is only an incidental." Character building, he declared, was their first and supreme objective— "holy character and useful life for goodness and efficiency."[36]

Meanwhile, at the village of North Scituate, Rhode Island, twenty miles north of Providence, E. E. Angell and J. C. Bearse wrestled with the almost impossible task of financing the academy and Bible school known as Pentecostal Collegiate Institute. In order to help needy students pay their way, Angell decided in

1908 to set up a small manufacturing shop. He studied carefully the extensive literature on industrial education then appearing. He decided upon a broom factory, however, because the primary necessity was a marketable product. By 1910, this department had bought broommaking machinery and printing and sewing equipment, and was incorporated under the name Pentecostal Trade Schools. As years passed, the faculty gave more serious attention to the idea of industrial education and introduced commercial and stenographic courses in the academy curriculum. But the hope expressed in the catalogue of 1910 for instruction in skilled trades, partly to train leaders for "Industrial Missions" overseas, was never fulfilled.[37]

Despite the humble terms in which they described their work, the eastern school had reason to be proud of its faculty. J. C. Bearse, who succeeded Angell as principal in 1914, had attended Brown and Boston universities. That year Olive Winchester, fresh from the completion of her bachelor of divinity degree at Glasgow University, returned to teach theology. Bertha Munro, head of the academy, was an honor graduate of Boston University, and Stephen S. White was attending graduate classes at Brown. "If we only could have fires to keep us warm, and food to eat that was paid for," Bearse wrote, "it would seem almost like heaven. . . . The struggle to meet our bills is a real test of blood and nerve."[38]

Miss Munro began her graduate work at Radcliffe College the next fall. Her experiences there helped to raise her educational sights for P.C.I. The difficulties in the way of establishing a liberal arts college were greater in the East than elsewhere in the country, she agreed, because of the very high educational standards which prevailed in that section. This fact could, however, be turned to advantage, since Nazarene scholars could teach in the denominational institution while pursuing graduate studies nearby.

A major financial problem had to be solved first, however. J. E. L. Moore came from Hamlin, Texas, to be principal in 1917, and promoted what he called a "whirlwind campaign" to liquidate the debt and equip the school for college work. The eastern churches oversubscribed the $50,000 required before December, 1918. Lowell gave $7,500, Lynn, $4,000, Malden, $3,670, and so on. In the midst of the campaign the trustees voted to change the name to Eastern Nazarene College and to begin a full four-year college course. Fred J. Shields, a Pasadena graduate, was elected president and the educational committee moved the institution to a new campus in Wollaston, on the shore just south of Boston proper. Here students readily found employment afternoons, and faculty members took the noon train to town for the advanced study they must do if the college was to reach the standards it desired.[39]

In retrospect many of the measures designed to fashion a uniform national program of higher education for the denomination accomplished little. Personal and economic factors, and the primary responsibility which trustees and district leaders felt for the institution in their own section, overrode plans for central control. The only point really established was that the Nazarenes were determined to build in every section colleges which were worthy of the name.

In the general superintendents' address at the assembly of 1915, Dr. Bresee insisted that the church must attend to the higher education of its own young people. Spiritual religion, and especially that which testified to the grace of heart holiness, he said, was no longer welcome in the nation's centers of learning. If the young people of the church were to "go forth to our pulpits, our counting houses, our farms, and our homes, full of the hallowed fire of the indwelling Spirit," they must live "under the shadow of the Almighty in the classroom, chapel, and social life of their college years." Just a month earlier, in his last address at the Nazarene University, he had insisted that devotion and learning were not enemies, but allies. "We have not forsaken the old classics," he declared. "We do not fear philosophy. We delight in mathematics. We cultivate the sciences." But in all of these matters, the rule of life was the Word of God. "It is appealed to, honored, studied," he said. "It is the standard of experience, morals, life."[40]

The Establishment of a Central Publishing House

Unifying the four church papers in circulation in 1908 turned out to be somewhat easier than centralizing the educational program. Neither the Chicago nor the Pilot Point assemblies made any effort to consolidate the two major weeklies, Bresee's *Nazarene Messenger* and the *Beulah Christian*, organ of the eastern churches. The *Pentecostal Advocate*, at Peniel, enjoyed a larger circulation than either of these, but in 1908 its managers agreed with Ellyson and Bresee that the paper, like the college, should remain interdenominational for a time. J. D. Scott's *Holiness Evangel*, published at nearby Pilot Point, could scarcely have survived the competition, even if its press had moved to Hamlin instead of Mexico. As it turned out, however, Scott's abortive scheme helped crystallize in Dr. Reynolds' mind, if not in the minds of others, the idea of a single journal to promote the missionary program. "I wish we were able to have our central printing plant at Chicago and have one large denominational paper and one missionary paper," he wrote Ellyson; "would the Advocate Company favor coming here?"[41]

The General Assembly of 1911 found it difficult to deal directly with this matter. A special committee on publishing interests recommended in an early session that the *Beulah Christian*, the *Nazarene Messenger*, and the *Pentecostal Advocate* continue to be recognized as "official organs" of the church. The committee also proposed, however, that the assembly elect immediately a new board of publication, and empower it to establish and operate a central publishing house which would provide church and Sunday school literature for the entire denomination. The delegates promptly approved this suggestion and elected as members of the board Will T. McConnell, L. D. Peavey, and C. J. Kinne, associated respectively with the Peniel, Providence, and Los Angeles periodicals. Others representing the church at large were DeLance Wallace, A. S. Cochran, W. M. Creal, and B. F. Haynes.

The new group met at once, and named Haynes president and McConnell secretary. The next day the board announced to the assembly that they had selected Kansas City for the location of the publishing house and employed C. J. Kinne to be its manager. They asked the gathering to authorize an immediate campaign to raise $50,000 to consolidate the various companies. Bud Robinson rose at once and pledged his $4,200 worth of stock in the *Advocate* company; others present subscribed nearly $11,000 more. Before the assembly had adjourned the board was deep in negotiations for the purchase of the three plants.[42]

The group determined to press matters to an early conclusion, even though the campaign for funds made little further progress. At a meeting held at Peniel November 21, 1911, Kinne announced that the stockholders of the Nazarene Publishing Company were giving their entire property to the church. His financial statement, however, indicated that their liabilities exceeded assets by $1,189. By contrast, the owners of the *Pentecostal Advocate* believed their company's net worth to be substantial. After three days' deliberation, the board agreed to pay them $12,250, the exact amount of the listed assets of the business, $5,598 in cash, and the remainder by assumption of liabilities of $6,652. The board then agreed to begin publishing at Kansas City on April 1, 1912, a new paper entitled the *Herald of Holiness*. They named B. F. Haynes editor and C. A. McConnell his assistant.[43]

F. A. Hillery and his associates in the company which printed the *Beulah Christian* proved unwilling to risk the assets of their firm in the joint undertaking. As early as November 3, 1911, Hillery wrote Kinne that his group could not think of handing over their fine plant merely for a contract for purchase, with no money in sight. The directors backed Hillery up in December with a vote to hold out for cash. They knew, of course, that the limited resources of the Board of Publication made this impossible. They proceeded, therefore, to complete a merger with H. B. Hosley's *Pentecostal Era,* and insisted that the General Assembly had granted the eastern churches full discretion to continue the *Beulah Christian* as their organ. With the appearance of the *Herald of Holiness* in the spring, however, Hillery received notice that his paper was no longer an official publication of the denomination. It was a bitter blow when, months later, H. F. Reynolds himself confirmed this ruling. In February, 1913, the Board of Publication felt sufficiently entrenched to publish a resolution asking Nazarenes everywhere to refrain from "establishing or circulating local papers which would interfere in any way with the *Herald of Holiness*."[44]

As the General Assembly of 1915 drew near, a lead editorial in the *Herald* called for a greater "spirit of connectionalism, or of real loyalty to the Church and her institutions." The assembly's committee on publication heartily agreed. They noted the "four years of financial leanness," which the central publishing house had endured, its capital consisting "not so much in money as in good will." Only the business of printing Sunday school literature had earned a profit. The service which the new missionary paper, the *Other Sheep,* rendered had justified a loan from the Foreign Missionary Board large enough to save the undertaking from collapse. Now it must have solid support from the church.

The committee proposed that each congregation make it a rule that every Nazarene should "receive the church paper as a right of church membership, and that the subscription price be made a part of the annual budget to be raised in the same manner as other church expenses."

But the assembly made no provision for the more pressing needs: adequate working capital and an effective program of cost accounting. Nearly ten years were to pass before the church assumed fully the financial responsibilities implied by its decision to establish a central publishing firm. One group deserves honorable mention at this point, however. The Tennesseans who joined the denomination in 1915 became immediately the most loyal supporters of the *Herald of Holiness;* their own paper, *Living Water,* quickly passed out of existence.[45]

A Churchly Way of Life

If "churches" are to be distinguished from "sects" by their emphasis upon a trained ministry, by devotion to Christian education in Sunday school and youth activities, by the recognition that ritual, hymnody, and sacraments are means of grace in divine worship, by a sense of responsibility for the welfare of the society outside the church, by the development of efficient and responsible administration of missionary and publishing ventures, and by a willingness to recognize other denominations as members of the family of faith, then the Church of the Nazarene has never been a sect.

To be sure, many of the early pastors were laymen who had been ordained without the benefit of much formal education. But this was true also of many prominent but self-educated Methodist and Baptist clergymen of the time. Dr. Bresee himself is a case in point. A survey of his editorials in the *Nazarene Messenger* will readily confirm E. A. Girvin's judgment that Bresee made constant use of the exceedingly wide selection of Biblical and historical materials in his library, including, surprisingly, works by Horace Bushnell and Washington Gladden.[46]

Moreover, as we have seen, every branch of the young denomination established a school for the education of preachers and lay Christian workers. The national consolidation produced a strong demand for the improvement of academic standards at these institutions. The tendency of uneducated preachers to desire evangelists' commissions early brought about a rule subjecting them to a four-year course of readings and examinations. The General Assembly announced in 1911 a home study curriculum for candidates for ordination which resembled in scope and quality that provided by the Methodist *Discipline*. The list of books emphasized classics on the subject of Christian perfection handed down from Methodist antecedents, of course. But on it also appeared John S. Miley's theology, John Dewey's psychology, and Albert Bushnell Hart's *Essentials in American History*.[47]

In every section the new denomination emphasized from the very beginning religious education for its youth. The Chicago Assembly of 1907 adopted resolutions which called for methods which would teach children "through the eye as well as through the ear," and urged every Sunday school to institute a "normal class" for prospective teachers. The General Assembly of 1911 made similar recommendations, adding to them one establishing a commission to prepare a catechism for the church's children. The Nazarene Publishing Company in Los Angeles began issuing a full line of Sunday school literature in 1907, including lesson helps and journals for teachers, and quarterlies for students. Rural congregations of the Holiness Church of Christ in Arkansas and Texas began using this material months before the union at Pilot Point. Statistical records demonstrate, moreover, that the denomination's rank and file took Sunday school work seriously. In 1907, when East and West united, the church membership of 6,198 exceeded the Sabbath school enrollment by more than 10 per cent. By 1920, however, the latter had reached 56,876, 50 per cent more than the membership of the church.[48]

True, a national organization for the young people's societies was not instigated until the General Board honored R. T. Williams' plea on their behalf in 1921. But larger congregations of the western branch had maintained active local units from the beginning. The largest for many years was at Cornell's church in Chicago. C. B. Jernigan encouraged them heartily in Kansas and Oklahoma also. By 1915, 3,162 young people belonged to local societies around the country. Although the General Assembly of 1911, mindful, as their resolution put it, of "the importance of keeping our young people intensely spiritual," advised against introducing social events into the program, the societies flourished from the beginning through a combination of zeal and fellowship.[49]

A tradition dating from the earliest years of the eastern churches eventually led to the establishment of a national Woman's Foreign Missionary Society. On the eve of the union of 1907, the officers of what was by then called the Woman's Foreign Mission Society of the Association of Pentecostal Churches urged their "Western sisters" to join them in forming a national organization. Every denomination, they noted, had seen the necessity of such a corps. The Chicago assembly decided, however, in the words of one of the western women, to make "the entire membership a missionary body." Although this plan may have been "apostolic in its simplicity," it did not satisfy the desire of the ladies for an activity of their own. The two succeeding General Assemblies, however, merely endorsed the work of such local auxiliaries as existed. Finally, in 1915, the delegates at Kansas City adopted resolutions which recognized woman's "unique adaptability" to missionary work and approved the formation of a national body. The General Board of Foreign Missions appointed Mrs. John T. Benson, Mrs. Ada F. Bresee, and Mrs. Susan N. Fitkin to prepare the first constitution.[50]

Nazarene services, whether "worship" or "evangelistic," were always open to demonstrations of praise or zeal, of course. Even in ritual and sacramental observances their customs allowed for a "freedom of the spirit" unknown in churches of liturgical background. When away from their home church, at camp meetings and district assemblies, and especially at national gatherings, the people's enthusiasm often broke all bounds of prescribed order. There can be no doubt that the leaders regarded such liberty as a strength rather than a weakness of the movement. Responsiveness and commitment, they believed, went hand in hand.

The sacraments were of vital importance to them, however. One of the oldest traditions of the General Assemblies is the reverent observance on the opening Sabbath of the Lord's Supper. Despite their toleration of differences of opinion on the mode of baptism, all the congregations insisted upon the rite in some form. Significant also was the early and sustained agitation for a church hymnal, reflecting the memory which most of the founding fathers had for the orderliness of the Methodist service. One of them wrote in 1907 that "the way of worship at the great service in the sanctuary" should be "stately and divinely magnificent." Nazarenes approved a form of worship, he said, but not a merely *formal* observance. "The Holy Spirit," he added, "will inspire our careful thought and preparation much more surely and fully than our careless neglect."[51]

The surviving pictures of the buildings which congregations both small and poor constructed remove all doubt that after 1907 the Nazarenes intended to establish at their new outposts churches, not simply missions. In the older centers, the movement from mission to church work, and from exclusive preoccupation with the poor to a general ministry to the whole community, proceeded rapidly. As early as 1906, Bresee wrote that the great advance in the value of real estate around Los Angeles First Church was driving his people out to the suburbs, where cheap lots and lower rents were available. The kind of family which chose this among other alternatives, however, did not remain poor very long. The same thing happened in Spokane. In describing the new church building there, Mrs. Wallace noted that "many young men and women rescued from Satan's power" in the mission hall now had "homes and families." The church, she said, had to move out of the saloon district with them. The Nazarenes were not merely disgruntled members from other churches, she added; "we are bringing up our own children, *born in our own family*." Pictorial surveys showing buildings occupied by churches founded both before 1915 and after 1935 reveal in fact no greater tendency to begin in store-front structures in earlier days than later. They always regarded rented halls as temporary shelters; the construction or purchase of a fitting house of worship was a primary goal.[52]

The tradition of Christian social work which was characteristic in each section persisted in the national organization also, though it eventually gave way to more "connectional" concerns. General Assembly committees on rescue work repeatedly denounced both the liquor and the white slave traffic, and urged every district to sponsor rescue missions and homes in the larger cities in their territory. By 1915 the church operated homes for unfortunate girls at Wichita and Hutchinson, Kansas; Bethany, Oklahoma; Pilot Point, Texas; and Oakland, California; and endorsed others at Lynn, Massachusetts; Nashville, Tennessee; and Arlington, Texas. The General Assembly that year voted to establish both a General Board of Rescue Work and a General Orphanage Board, and to press for support of such ventures in every section.[53] Much evidence indicates, in fact, that the subsequent decline of these activities resulted from the demands which other more "churchly" enterprises laid upon the resources of the denomination. "Are we getting so much machinery inside the church," a committee at the Northwest district assembly asked in 1914, "that we have no time for any of this kind of work . . . ?" They insisted that to fold one's arms and sing, "Rescue the perishing, care for the dying," was no substitute for reaching out in honest love to help lost men.[54]

The story of Jack F. Sanders illustrates how the church was torn between social service and the promotion of its other institutions. A convert from the earliest days of the Spokane mission, Sanders moved to Los Angeles to assist C. J. Kinne in the Nazarene Publishing Company. He next joined J. W. Goodwin in the business of disposing of the land belonging to the college in Pasadena. When he completed that task, Sanders took charge of the new Fifth Street Mission which a group of Nazarenes had organized in Los Angeles. During 22 months, he saw 2,200 people at the altars, and enjoyed perhaps the happiest period of his life. He answered a summons to Kansas City, however, in 1915, to pilot the new central publishing house through its most difficult days. He then went in turn to Northwest Nazarene College and Pasadena. The financial campaigns Sanders conducted helped save these institutions from bankruptcy, but they took his life. His body lay in state for a day at the Fifth Street Mission. The record states that "in the evening the service was crowned with salvation and several souls prayed through to victory beside the open casket."[55]

If sectarianism is defined in more traditional terms, as exclusive preoccupation with the internal life of one's denomination, then the educational and missionary agencies, the publishing house, and the schools so often regarded as hallmarks of churchliness seem in fact to have nourished it. Witness the chorus of pleas which these interests inspired at the General Assembly of 1915 alone. The Board of Publication called for more of the "spirit of connectionalism," and the delegates responded with the stark declaration, "We look with suspicion upon any preacher holding membership in our church who circulates other religious papers to the impoverishment of our own." The group surveying problems of Christian education naturally felt it proper to insist that all churches use "our own Sunday school literature." The hymnal committee warned that

Nazarene congregations were having "to procure their hymnals from other denominations." And the committee on education heartily seconded Bresee's warning that the church would "soon find itself robbed of its best inheritance" if it turned the higher education of its youth over to others. The founder told a Pasadena student body that fall that the college's nonsectarian platform did not prevent the development of "a strong, pure, healthy denominationalism." He continued thus:

> We have no sympathy with the twaddle ... that all people [should] be of one denomination. We believe that such is neither providential nor desirable. We are lovingly, earnestly, intensely denominational. If anyone wishes to criticize his own denomination, this is a poor place for him to do it.[56]

Yet the earlier declarations against sectarianism were more than propaganda intended to attract as many groups as possible into the various mergers. They were an authentic expression of the broadness which Bresee, Ellyson, McConnell, and McClurkan then felt toward other communions, and which many others later shared. Bresee's editorial of 1908, which condemned "any narrowness, either ecclesiastical or personal, that would think ours or mine the 'only' way" or hinder "the broadest love and co-operation with every agency in pushing the work of full salvation," is echoed in the quadrennial address of the general superintendents for 1960, which declared, "We do not claim to be the Church of Christ in any exclusive sense, but we would identify ourselves as a vital part of His great Church. . . . Our hearts are open to all people of like precious faith."[57]

The struggle between broadness and bigotry, between the gospel of the church and the spirit of the sect, was, in fact, just beginning in 1915. In the Nazarene denomination, at least, the pressure toward sectarianism characterized the second more than the first generation, and stemmed directly from the institutional activities which in retrospect seem to have been necessary to the life of the communion. The passing of an older generation of leaders, steeped in Methodist and other churchly traditions, encouraged this tendency. The reins of authority passed to young men who had known neither bishops nor councils, nor a church broadly responsible for the welfare of society. And the situation was incredibly complicated, as we shall see, by the religious upheaval called fundamentalism, which reached its apex at the close of the first world war.

CHAPTER XII

The Transition to a New Generation

A Crisis of Leadership

Two of the four general superintendents elected by the General Assembly of October, 1915, P. F. Bresee and W. C. Wilson, died within sixty days after that body adjourned. The whole church was shocked but few understood how really serious a crisis their passing created.

Of the two survivors, E. F. Walker was in failing health, and was preoccupied with the presidency of Olivet College, while H. F. Reynolds was engrossed in plans to spend most of his time in the promotion and administration of foreign missions. These two, moreover, rarely understood each other. When Dr. Bresee died in early November, Dr. Walker refused to approve the election of a replacement, and insisted that he and Wilson alone were responsible to arrange for the jurisdiction of the "home work." Wilson's death altered this stand. In January, 1916, the district superintendents elected R. T. Williams and John W. Goodwin to the church's highest office. Walker, however, found an excuse not to attend the session which Reynolds planned for the four men in Kansas City early in February.[1] Yet he requested and received assignment to reside in the California area, despite the fact that outstanding lay and ministerial leaders there had wired pleas for Dr. Goodwin to remain among them.[2]

Goodwin stayed in southern California until September, 1916, while Walker wound up his affairs at Olivet. They were unhappy months for the new general superintendent. A personal debt, arising from an unwise business venture, kept him strapped in poverty throughout this and the succeeding year. Moreover, he could not escape involvement in the storm which was brewing at Pasadena College. By the end of April, Goodwin was imploring Reynolds to come to Pasadena for the annual commence-

272

ment sermon in May, to help calm things down, and warned, "We are in great trouble."[3]

As the tumultuous events of the next twelve months unfolded, it became clear that Dr. Bresee's death had coincided with the outbreak of serious conflict between those who saw the hope of the Nazarenes to lie in churchly order and a strong superintendency, and a group of independent-minded men zealous for "spiritual freedom." As long as he lived, Dr. Bresee had been able to keep this conflict under control. He was no sooner in his grave than the Nazarene community in southern California began to come apart at the seams. By a kind of chain reaction, the trouble spread to other sections as well.

A factor complicating the crisis was the haphazard division of responsibility between the general superintendents on one hand and the denominational boards of publication, home missions, foreign missions, and education on the other. These boards were answerable directly to the General Assembly. Moreover, they had the advantage of a regular organization, while the superintendents exercised their authority only as individuals. Had there been no defection at Pasadena, this problem of administrative responsibility would still have remained, to be solved by a group of churchmen who were working under great handicaps.

Reynolds, the only experienced hand at the helm, had learned through long years of apprenticeship among eastern independents the virtues of patience and forbearance with those who sought to trim his prerogative. J. W. Goodwin thought the powers of general superintendents were primarily spiritual, a view for which he was indebted both to Bresee's example and Reynolds' advice. However useful such attitudes had been in the days when the denomination was being formed, they were inadequate to deal with men who now threatened to tear it apart. Two younger men, R. T. Williams and H. Orton Wiley, saw clearly that in the future courage must be married to humility in the exercise of the highest offices of the church.

Liberty Versus Unity

Evangelist Seth C. Rees, whose biography by his distinguished son, Paul, was titled *The Warrior Saint*, had figured in many a stormy controversy before he joined the Church of the Nazarene. Originally an evangelist in the Society of Friends, he became well known among all holiness groups through his interest in city missions. In 1897 he and Martin Wells Knapp, founder of God's Bible School, Cincinnati, organized the International Holiness Union and Prayer League. Rees served as president of this organization for five years, then launched out in successive mission and evangelistic ventures of his own. The group he had helped to found, however, gradually took on denominational form. It was reorganized in 1913 as the International Apostolic Holiness church. In 1919 the remnants of the Holiness Christian church in Indiana joined the movement. Two years later, when Rees brought his California followers in, the communion adopted its present name, the Pilgrim Holiness church.[4]

In 1911, Evangelist Rees joined the Nazarenes and became pastor of the new University Church, at Pasadena. General Superintendent Ellyson accepted the presidency there the same year. Apparently the two men got on well. Rees won an especially loyal friend and admirer in the youthful dean of the college, H. Orton Wiley. Wiley succeeded Ellyson as president in 1913. He soon brought to the faculty as professor of Bible A. J. Ramsay, a graduate of the Union Theological Seminary in Richmond and formerly a Baptist minister. Many believed that a great day had dawned for the school, and for the churches which supported it.[5]

Wiley's birthplace was a sod house on the Nebraska prairies; the date, November 15, 1877. His family moved first to California and then by stages to Medford, Oregon, in the beautiful Rogue River Valley. While attending the Oregon State Normal School at Ashland, Wiley worked in a drugstore and became a registered pharmacist. He served for a time as a minister in the United Brethren church, and then enrolled as a student at the University of California. He soon united with the Church of the Nazarene in Berkeley and became its pastor, serving from 1905 to 1909. During these years he finished his undergraduate work at the university and earned a divinity degree at the Pacific School of Religion. Then, in 1910, he accepted a call to Pasadena. A spiritual firebrand, a sound scholar, and in later years a firm and resourceful administrator, Wiley willingly accepted a secondary role during his early stay at Pasadena, deferring first to Ellyson and then to Seth C. Rees.[6]

THE TRANSITION TO A NEW GENERATION   275

In January, 1914, a tremendous revival broke out on the Pasadena campus. It began in a week of prayer following the New Year's Eve watch-night service. Pastor Rees announced on Tuesday, January 6, that a "judgment day meeting" was to convene the next evening. All were to prepare for it by making such confessions to one another as they would if they knew that Christ would return that night. Deep and solemn conviction accompanied the making of restitutions. On Friday morning the excitement was so intense that classes broke up and faculty and students gathered at the chapel. Shortly, so a friendly account tells us, more than two hundred were on their feet at one time, "shouting and weeping and leaping and marching," while others lay prostrate on the floor. Many professed experiences of conversion or sanctification.

Dr. Bresee came out to the college Sunday morning and preached from the text, "The sun shall be turned to darkness, and the moon into blood, before that great and notable day of the Lord come." People began streaming to the mourners' bench before his sermon was finished. He preached again at night and the same thing happened. On Monday, recitations again gave way to prayer meetings. Throughout the week emotional tides ran high. Most of the services were unplanned. "Dying out" was the keynote of such short sermons as Rees, Wiley, and others preached. Student leaders were in the forefront, among them Ralph Hertenstein, Floyd and Orval Nease, Fred J. Shields, and Weaver Hess. This group developed an abiding admiration for the two leaders, Wiley and Rees, a fact of great importance in understanding their reaction to the confusing events of 1916-17.[7]

As the revival faded away, trouble developed between Rees and Wiley on one hand and, on the other, Professor Ramsay and A. O. Hendricks. Hendricks was pastor of First Church in downtown Pasadena, and was both a student at the college and a member of the board of trustees. The laymen of his congregation were rapidly gaining social status in the community. They may, like Ramsay, have found distasteful the "freedom of the Spirit" in which Rees and Wiley rejoiced. By the spring of 1915, Dr. Wiley had decided that fundamental theological issues were at stake. In a series of chapel lectures that fall he denounced Ramsay for his doctrinal errors. Rees at once took a similar public stand. Dr. Bresee, who was no enthusiast for Ramsay's premillennial views, came out to the college repeatedly for board meetings called to heal the rift. A committee appointed to investigate the professor's theology cleared him with but one dissenting vote—that of Seth Rees. Even Dr. Wiley seems to have been satisfied.[8]

Rees countered, however, by suddenly filing charges against a leading young minister who had been for many years a close associate of the Bresee family. The accused man surrendered his credentials at once, but the University Church pastor publicized the matter fully, apparently in an effort to expose alleged compromises with sin in others. Later, when retaliatory charges of a different sort were preferred against Rees, Dr. Bresee quashed them.[9]

District Superintendent W. C. Wilson, who had previously supported Rees, became convinced at this point that the college pastor's actions were irresponsible and contrary to the law of the church. He gave up the superintendency in June to take charge of the congregation at Upland, and, with C. E. Cornell, pastor of Los Angeles First Church, became a firm friend of Professor Ramsay. The district assembly, therefore, had to elect a new superintendent amidst all of the excitement these issues had raised. The two principal candidates were Howard Eckel, a bitter foe of Rees, and the former superintendent, J. W. Goodwin, who was, if anything, a friend. When Goodwin received fewer votes on an early ballot, he persuaded his supporters to unite in electing Eckel. Under the sudden glare of newspaper publicity, the assembly voted to sustain the appeal of an evangelist whom Rees had sought to oust from membership in his congregation, and, after a sharp debate, closed the Hillcrest Home for Fallen Women, which Rees had founded.

It was a worried and divided group, therefore, which boarded the train late in September, 1915, to attend the General Assembly at Kansas City. "Rees stays to himself," Sue Bresee wrote in her diary, and "does not come to visit Papa much—did for about three minutes today but seemed to be in a rush to get away." He might well have shown more appreciation of Bresee's faithfulness. Before their departure, the founder had delivered at Pasadena First Church what proved to be his final sermon there. The text was I Corinthians, chapter 13. Quite obviously he directed his remarks to Rees's opponents, who now had the upper hand. Ramsay and W. C. Wilson attended together, and agreed afterward that Dr. Bresee's long-standing policy was right—to act with love and forgiveness, and keep people in the church. The General Assembly, however, rejected sharply Rees's appeal from the action of the Southern California District, which had reinstated the evangelist ousted from University Church. And, as we have seen, the delegates elected W. C. Wilson a general superintendent.[10]

A month later Dr. Bresee lay at the point of death in his home in Los Angeles. He sent an urgent request for Wiley to come to see him. In his parting words he begged his young friend to "stay by the college." But Bresee was no sooner gone than Rees revived his old attacks on Ramsay, and Wiley determined to leave the college if he could not free himself from constant interference from the board of trustees. The young president resigned in March, 1916. Soon afterwards he announced that he would return to the pastorate of the little congregation at Berkeley and enroll as a candidate for a master's degree in theology at the Pacific School of Religion. He had scarcely gotten settled there, however, before the trustees of the infant college at Nampa elected him their president, granting him, however, the privilege of remaining in Berkeley a full year.[11]

Meanwhile, General Superintendent Goodwin was presented with a new set of formal charges against Rees. Pursuant to the *Manual*, a trial was arranged late in May, 1916, at Los Angeles First Church. Such trials are always closed to the public, but the embattled pastor arrived with two hundred members of his flock, all of them called as "character witnesses," and demanded that the doors be thrown open to everybody, including newspaper reporters. The clamor became so great outside the building that the trial committee deemed it wise to admit the people to the church auditorium, though not to the proceedings themselves. The charges were principally the ones which Dr. Bresee had refused to entertain the year before. The jury of five elders was unable to agree, so Rees was acquitted. Goodwin, heartbroken at the folly of the district leadership in allowing the charges to be presented, saw that the result could only be great harm to the church and the college. But he was unable to do anything, and in September relinquished his place in southern California to General Superintendent E. F. Walker.[12]

The Rees Dissension

Matters came to a head in the winter of 1916-17. A. M. Hills occupied the chair of theology that year at Pasadena. Thinking to help young people wrestling with spiritual problems, he stressed faith as the way to sanctification in seeming contradiction to Pastor Rees's emphasis on "dying out." Early in February a group of students circulated a petition, declaring their objections to having persons on the faculty who did not believe in holiness. A few days later a score or more of them withdrew from the college and announced their determination to enroll at once at Nampa, where Wiley was serving as president *in absentia*. At this point Seth Rees returned from conducting revival services at Kansas City First Church. He had found the pastor there, John Matthews, waging a private war on the Nazarene Publishing House for allowing employment to postmillennialists and union members. Although a meeting of the general superintendents made short work of this attempt of the local pastor to dominate the publishing affairs of the denomination, and specifically forbade making requirements for employment beyond the standards set forth in the *Manual*, Rees had gained an ally in John Matthews. Thereafter he could and did claim to have inside information on "spiritual compromise" at the national headquarters of the church.[13]

Ostensibly to reduce tensions on the Pasadena campus, the congregation of the University Church had meanwhile decided to move from the college chapel to a building of their own. They hurriedly erected a tabernacle on a nearby lot, and made plans to occupy it the first Sunday in March. On their last Sabbath in the old building, however, Howard Eckel, district superintendent, appeared in the pulpit to announce that, under the authority he believed granted him by the most recent Nazarene *Manual*, he was disorganizing the University Church. The congregation was further stunned to learn that General Superintendent E. F. Walker had given the action his approval.

An open letter, printed and distributed by Rees the very next day, informed Nazarenes far and wide of the event. The southern California newspapers carried full details, including the story of the resignation of several faculty members and of the almost physical struggle over the furniture in the college chapel which members of Rees's congregation felt belonged to

THE TRANSITION TO A NEW GENERATION 279

them. H. Orton Wiley, as ever fearing no man, came down from Berkeley to preach the first sermon in the new tabernacle, and I. G. Martin began a revival meeting the same night. Eckel issued on March 8 a printed flyer which defended his action, chiefly by reciting facts which he believed demonstrated Brother Rees to be "unruly" and "rebellious." Rees eventually launched a periodical entitled the *Pilgrim*. In the first number, I. G. Martin, J. B. McBride, Bud Robinson, and Arnold Hodgin refuted at least some of the charges made against him, and sought to rouse the congregationalism latent in many sections of the denomination.[14]

The controversy threatened, as one of Rees's friends at Nampa put it, "to burst the Church wide open from end to end." The Nazarenes had only recently achieved national unity. They had established an effective superintendency in the face of a strong tradition of congregational independence. The disorganization of a flourishing church, however, was an exercise of powers that no one until that moment believed superintendents possessed.

H. F. Reynolds' correspondence for the period from March to June, 1917, reveals beyond all doubt that the crisis was a great one and that the dismemberment of the denomination was barely avoided. From the East, James W. Short, district superintendent of the Pittsburgh area, pleaded for immediate action. William Howard Hoople wrote that the only basis under which he would continue to stay in the church was that he be released from all he had formerly agreed to "in the line of Superintendency." He would thereafter "privately and publicly advocate away with all Superintendents." A few months later, Hoople gave up his work in Brooklyn to join a Y.M.C.A. team which accompanied the American Expeditionary Force to France. In Donalsonville, Georgia, E. P. Ellyson and C. A. McConnell, who were laboring to establish Shingler's new school, expressed similar concern. Bud Robinson, a member of University Church who at first believed the act of disorganization placed him legally outside the denomination, sent from an Arkansas revival campaign a picturesque complaint, which asked why all the other general superintendents had been as "Mum as Clams." "When I was turned out of the Methodist Church," Uncle Bud continued, "they did give me a tryal."[15] The scores of appeals which reached

Reynolds' desk from southern California showed the loyalties of the leading members there about equally divided.[16]

In mid-April, Harry Hays, pastor at San Diego and, like Rees, a former member of the Society of Friends, began taking steps to lead his congregation out of the denomination. He was quickly summoned to trial and expelled. This action served only to confirm the conviction of many former Friends ministers in the Nazarene fellowship that the cause of spiritual freedom was at stake. At Nampa, where Hays had recently been pastor of the college church and where G. Arnold Hodgin, Rees's brother-in-law, was President Wiley's executive officer, discontent had already reached the boiling point. W. H. Tullis, the Idaho district superintendent, wired R. T. Williams that his people were not neutral. "We disapprove the action of Eckel and Walker," he stated. "We ask you in Jesus' name to reverse the action. Restitution alone now will satisfy us. Substitutes won't. We stand solid for Reese."[17]

Early in March, Dr. Reynolds telegraphed all who had served on the committee on *Manual* revision at the General Assembly of 1915 to explain to him why, in their view, the article giving superintendents power to disorganize churches was inserted in the law of the church, since no record existed of General Assembly action authorizing it. All but one of those who responded were positive that the committee had intended the power to be exercised only when a congregation proved too weak to survive or else stood in open violation of the church's doctrines.[18] Reynolds then called the general superintendents to meet in Kansas City on April 4, 1917. Dr. Walker, however, refused to come, and a committee of influential ministers in California wrote Reynolds they had advised him not to do so, on the grounds that "the right to review and revise the action of a General Superintendent having jurisdiction" in such matters was vested "solely in the General Assembly." The University Church, Walker wrote, was out of existence, and could be restored only by action of the next quadrennial gathering.

Reynolds, Goodwin, and Williams met without him. They examined the large file of telegrams, letters, and petitions which the superintendents had received. They then adopted and published in the *Herald of Holiness* an interpretation of the *Manual* which declared superintendents might disorganize churches only when they were too weak to continue their work or when they persisted in a "hopelessly unorthodox or immoral" course. The pronouncement specified, moreover, that any church so disorganized had the full rights of appeal, and continued without prejudice as an organization until its appeal was ruled upon. Although this courageous statement bore no legal authority, the moral force of the united opinion of the general superintendents, even when acting against one of their colleagues, was immense. Dr. Walker publicly withdrew his approval of Eckel's action.[19]

The University Church might have soon been welcomed back into the fold had Seth C. Rees been willing. But at some point during the controversy, whether before or after the disorganization of his congregation no evidence can show, Rees became convinced that he was to head a new movement. On May 26, at a meeting of his church board called to consider the terms of a settlement, Rees reported that documentary evidence had fallen into his hands proving that reinstatement in the Church of the Nazarene was impossible. "In order to save the credentials of the elders," he said, and to "carry on the work unhindered," he proposed that the group unite under a new covenant and adopt the name Pentecost-Pilgrim Church.

From June, 1917, onwards, then, the problem of the general superintendents was to prevent further secessions; reconciliation had clearly become impossible. By summer, they realized that keeping the Idaho churches in the denomination would be especially difficult. H. Orton Wiley, as we shall see in a moment, planned and executed almost singlehandedly the strategy which achieved this objective. But at the time few were able to see any blessedness in his peacemaking.[20]

H. Orton Wiley and Northwest Nazarene College

The broad desert valleys of the Far West were America's last frontier. Irrigation opened many of them to settlement in the twentieth century, giving to the sunset years of American pioneering a brilliant afterglow. One of the greatest of these is the Snake River valley, which winds four hundred miles through southern Idaho. Here an inexhaustible supply of water flows westward from the melting snows atop the continental divide toward the gorges of the Snake and the Columbia. Once the news spread that man-made canals were carrying some of this water to the sagebrush flatlands south and west of Boise, farmers from Kansas and the Dakotas, many of them "shouting Methodists," joined Mormons from Utah in the trek to Idaho. Friends, United Brethren, and Mennonite Brethren in Christ families were sprinkled among the first migrants, as well. From 1900 onward, holiness evangelists crisscrossed the valley, stretching their rag tents and alternately cheering the settlers' hearts with gospel music and chilling them with sermons on judgment day.

Eugene Emerson, a pioneer lumber dealer in this territory, spent the winter of 1912-13 in southern California. There, at the altar of Seth C. Rees's University Church, he professed the experience of sanctification. Emerson joined the Nazarenes and returned to the town of Nampa, dreaming of a holiness church and school in the community where his growing business provided material for pioneer homes. He attended the Idaho-Oregon District Assembly of 1913, where the leaders discussed founding an elementary school for their people. Emerson invited a chief promoter of the scheme, C. H. French, to begin in Nampa. They rented a little building recently vacated by a Mennonite group and enrolled thirteen pupils in the school, among them Emerson's children.

In the fall of 1914, Emerson persuaded Harry Hays, a Friends evangelist, to become pastor of the local Nazarene congregation and head of the school. The church's trustees secured a large tract of land at the southern edge of Nampa, under an agreement by which the town was to provide irrigation. At the end of the second year they turned the undertaking over to the district assembly. That body elected twelve trustees, subscribed $6,000 to erect a building, and named it the Idaho-Oregon Holiness School. Meanwhile another former Friends minister, Lewis I. Hadley, succeeded Hays as pastor in Nampa. Families came from all over the valley and bought homesites from the college plot. They hoped thus to help finance the venture as well as to assure their children of both a godly environment and an incentive to learning.[21]

By the spring of 1916 the sagebrush and tumbleweed on the new campus were giving way to flowers and trees, and a rambling frame building housed classes from the primary grades to "college." One hundred and thirty-three students were enrolled. The district voted that year to change the name to Northwest Holiness School and to send their superintendent to the neighboring assembly in the state of Washington to seek a broader base of sponsorship. Hearing of H. Orton Wiley's resignation at Pasadena, the trustees invited him to become president of the institution. Wiley went to Nampa in June, and laid before the group an ambitious program. He demanded, however, the same terms he had recently been refused at Pasadena, namely, a five-year contract, and full authority and responsibility in the conduct of the school. Explaining that he was unable to move to Nampa for the space of a year, he promised to recommend others to conduct the work in his absence. The board accepted these terms readily. Wiley thereupon named G. Arnold Hodgin to be dean, and Fred J. Shields, a Pasadena graduate, to be professor in charge of the college department.[22] Inevitably, therefore, when the crisis broke open at Pasadena the following winter, the seceding students and faculty members chose Nampa for their resting place.

For the next two years the affairs of the Northwest college were interwoven with the conflict over Rees. Wiley's policy, once he got on the ground in May, 1917, was to support Rees's constitutional and spiritual position, but to maintain unyielding loyalty to the Church of the Nazarene. He found on his arrival, however, that the senior class had requested the University Church pastor to be their commencement speaker. The trustees, led by Eugene Emerson, had not only sanctioned the move but had encouraged District Superintendent W. H. Tullis to invite Rees to stay over a few days and serve as the night speaker for the district assembly, scheduled to follow immediately. Tullis kept to himself the fact that he had received strenuous objections to the plan from the assembly's presiding officer, R. T. Williams. On his arrival in Nampa, therefore, the young general superintendent must have greeted with scant enthusiasm the news that a brass band and a crowd of five hundred people had met Seth Rees at the train. Before the assembly was over, however, N. B. Herrell, a staunch friend of both Wiley and the church, had replaced Tullis as district superintendent, and Wiley and Williams had come to an understanding, if not to full agreement, as to what the policy of the college president would be.[23]

Wiley's next task was to allay fears among members of the neighboring Northwest District that his loyalties were questionable. His visit to their assembly in July seems to have dispelled all doubts. The delegates made him chairman of their educational committee. The young president seized the opportunity to push through a recommendation that all the denomination's educational institutions be placed under the full control of the General Board of Education. He thus balanced the weight of the Washington Nazarenes, whose spiritual and financial support was necessary to the success of the Idaho school, against the Nampa leaders, whose sympathies lay largely with Rees. A private letter to C. Howard Davis, pastor in Spokane, made his position plain. Harry Hays and Bud Robinson, Wiley wrote, were as greatly admired in the Nampa community as was Brother Rees. Moreover, Nazarenes all over the Northwest resented the injustice of the disorganization of the University Church. The college, therefore, should reject schism and ecclesiasticism alike, but support earnest spirituality from whatever quarter. In late August, Dr. Williams wrote Wiley that one of the greatest joys that had come to him was the attitude the Nampa president was taking.[24]

By that time, however, Wiley had already embarked on a bid for general reconciliation which tested to the breaking point the faith of his friends who were loyal to the church and the good will of those who were not. He sanctioned the decision of the Nampa camp meeting board to invite Rees and John Matthews to be their evangelists for the session scheduled for September 21-30, but did not relay news of the plan to General Superintendent Reynolds, who had agreed to speak at the missionary convention held in connection with the camp. When Reynolds learned who the camp meeting evangelists were, he wrote Wiley to ask if he really intended to remain true to the church. Wiley responded frankly that he had approved the arrangement in the hope of achieving a general reconciliation, but that he was depending on the presence of Dr. Reynolds, Mrs. DeLance Wallace, and other "loyal workers" to balance matters out. Reynolds then agreed, reluctantly, to keep his engagement.

When Rees and Matthews arrived, Wiley informed them in a "plain talk" that the college leaders "were Nazarenes and intended to remain so." After some initial tension, a tide of spiritual victory seemed to prevail in both the camp meeting and the missionary convention. Dr. Reynolds himself raised the offering to send to India Myrtle Belle Walters, one of the students who had come up with the group from Pasadena the year before.[25]

Somewhat encouraged, Wiley now launched a campaign for an adjustment of the wrong done in the disorganization of the University Church. To a troubled pastor in Freewater, Montana, the young president wrote bluntly that "the Church cannot have the smile of God upon her and hold the respect of her people unless that action is repudiated." "If all eyes are upon Idaho," he wrote to E. G. Anderson on October 6, "the people of Idaho are watching to see whether the Nazarenes intend to stand for the right regardless of personalities." In an early issue of the *Nazarene Messenger*, official publication of the college, Wiley discussed fully his program of loyal reform. He first announced that the board of trustees had placed the institution under the supervision of the General Board of Education. He then explained that the name of the paper, borrowed from Bresee's old weekly, was chosen to dramatize the point that the founder's version of the Nazarene way, and not that of latter-day leaders, was the one the college would support. "We may be drifting from some of our great principles," his editorial warned; the ideal of a gospel for the common people, of a message of full salvation through "the indwelling of the Holy Ghost," must not be lost.

That fall, Wiley wrote letters "to brethren all over the country" urging revisions of the *Manual* which would make impossible the disorganization of flourishing churches, and which would require that the powers of the general superintendents be exercised by the whole group, acting as a board. He announced to all his determination to spend a considerable portion of time arousing such sentiment as he could in favor of these measures. "I can see no reason," he said, "why the people who prefer a distinctively Holiness Church should be compelled to submit to an autocratic government. . . ."[26] In the following months, his proposals gained wide support. They seemed to men in many sections a sound compromise which would preserve the balance Nazarenes had struck between congregationalism and episcopacy.

At first, however, extremists in both camps opposed all compromise. Dr. Walker, in a blunt article in the *Herald of Holiness*, advocated doing away with the general superintendency unless the office could be strengthened, supported, and honored. E. A. Girvin and H. D. Brown both pleaded for more, not less, supervision. Brown urged that the power to appoint and remove pastors, the crucial factor in the Pasadena situation, be vested Methodist-fashion in an assembly committee acting jointly with the district and general superintendents. Personal elements in the debate steadily diminished, however, especially after Dr. Walker's serious illness and death in 1918.[27]

By the time the delegates gathered at Kansas City for the Fourth General Assembly in October, 1919, the combustibles of conflict were thoroughly dampened. In the last issue of the *Herald of Holiness* published before the assembly, Wiley joined A. M. Hills in the view that "radical congregationalism" could never succeed. The general superintendents disarmed budding gladiators with rulings from the chair which were free of arbitrariness and, as a visiting layman put it, permeated with "a spirit of piety, fatherly affection, and perfect love." In the committee on *Manual* revision, a very large majority eventually voted to allow the disorganization of churches, but only "by the action and formal pronouncement of the Board of General Superintendents on the recommendation of the district superintendent." This was about what Wiley had proposed. The committee turned back efforts to curb the power of congregations to call pastors, but specified that the general superintendents, acting again as a board, must decide cases where local churches and district superintendents could not agree on a man.[28]

Wiley was equally successful on the embattled local scene at Nampa. True, he was unable to prevent the secession of a small but influential group of Pilgrim sympathizers in January, 1918. But an almost continuous revival enabled him to minimize its effect. During the following years his fervent spiritual leadership strengthened the loyalty of the Idaho Nazarenes to both the college and the church.[29] One proof of this fact was the remarkable growth of the school. Student enrollment leaped from 133 to 183 in his first year, 1916-17. Three years later it numbered 320, this in a period when declining wartime registrations forced struggling church colleges all over the country to close their doors. Wiley persuaded Olive M. Winchester to come from Eastern Nazarene College to fill the professorship of Biblical literature in 1917, thus balancing the loss soon after of Fred J. Shields, who became president of the eastern school. Idaho District Superintendent N. B. Herrell and C. Warren Jones, the latter pastor at Spokane, mounted a tremendous "victory campaign" in 1919, to raise $100,000 for new buildings. Although this and succeeding efforts failed to solve the financial problems besetting the institution throughout Wiley's ten-year administration, the president could never again complain that the churches had neglected their duty.[30]

The early flowering of foreign missionary zeal at Nampa was both a cause and a result of the growing sentiment of denominational loyalty. It was nurtured by a succession of revivals which in both emotional intensity and personal consecration seemed a sufficient answer to all who feared that the fires lit by the founders were burning out.

From the day Wiley arrived in Nampa he declared it his purpose to make the Northwest College a "missionary school." Esther Carson, previously a graduate of Pasadena College and later a heroine of Nazarene work in Peru, was one of three missionary candidates in the small graduating class of 1918. By 1922 the most important student organizations were the six mission bands, and thirteen Nampa alumni were already on foreign fields. Prescott and Bessie Beals, graduates of 1918, sailed for India in 1920. Soon after, Fairy Chism joined Louise Robinson in Africa, and Professor F. C. Sutherland shortly began a ten-year term in China. And Dr. Thomas E. Mangum presided over a flourishing "Missionary Sanitarium and Institute" at which every woman who was a candidate for overseas work received some nurse's training.[31]

A graduate of the University of Texas Medical School at Galveston, Dr. Mangum gave up medical practice at Ballinger, Texas, in 1916, to launch a small hospital and nursing school in connection with the Nazarene college at Hamlin. When it became evident that this institution could not survive, Reynolds and Wiley encouraged Mangum to move his work to Nampa. The college trustees purchased a house for his use at the edge of the campus; Dr. Wiley and N. B. Herrell donned overalls to install the heating plant. In 1920 the sanitarium received its own corporate charter, and thereafter regarded itself as the property of the entire denomination, though local people always footed most of the bills. The Mangums donated their own newly built home to help get the struggling venture on its feet. A. E. Sanner, who became district superintendent in 1923, raised $40,000 from the Idaho and Oregon churches. Dr. Mangum's fame as a physician spread steadily; he was elected to the American College of Surgeons in 1932.[32]

Attracted by the excellent free medical care, missionaries on furlough usually made Nampa their headquarters for a part of their stay in the homeland. Their presence added much to the preoccupation of the community with overseas work. The emphasis upon medical missions, moreover, assured a longer life here than elsewhere to the ideal of holiness social work inherited from the earliest Nazarenes. Thus Fairy Chism, taking note in 1922 of the modernist's tendency to divorce social responsibility from personal piety, declared that service and sacrifice would bear no fruit in the world unless bound up in love for Christ. She repeated Dr. Wiley's dictum that the symbol of Christianity was neither a cross nor a crown, but a towel. Dr. Mangum, as beloved a preacher as he was a doctor, echoed the same theme throughout his life, in sermons which warned that Nazarenes must not substitute orthodox professions and the building of beautiful churches for obedience to Christ's law of service to suffering men.[33]

Looking back upon this story, the measure of Dr. Wiley's achievement in this his second major assignment from the church seems large indeed. He kept his own heart strong and loving under severe pressure and inspired a band of devoted young preachers and prospective missionaries to stay by the denomination. He led the way in reforms aimed at maintaining within the communion the spirituality which Rees believed could exist only outside. The institution at Nampa became during his administration the strongest Nazarene college. Meanwhile, as we shall see later, this intrepid administrator prodded the General Board of Education into actions which raised standards of Nazarene schools everywhere. In 1926 the trustees at Pasadena invited Wiley to return to the presidency of the college which was his first love. It had suffered much from the controversies which he had deplored but had been powerless to prevent. True to his principles, however, Wiley accepted the post only after they had agreed to the same terms he had presented without success ten years before. And so began a new day in the life of this good man.[34]

Clearly, the crisis of leadership which beset the denomination for ten years after 1915 had already begun to produce in the Great Northwest a corps of young stalwarts whose dedication could not be doubted. President Wiley, Dr. Mangum, District Superintendents Herrell and Sanner, pastors like C. Warren Jones, and missionaries such as Louise Robinson (now Mrs. J. B. Chapman) could be counted upon to preserve and extend the church which Bresee and Reynolds had founded. They had been tested in the fire.

The Fear of Spiritual Decline in the Second Generation

The church which these and other new leaders preserved, however, was not quite the same as the one they had inherited. In the nature of the case, it could not have been. Change is the essence of history. The tumultuous events of the year 1917 signaled but the beginning of a reshaping of the denomination which was complete by 1933. Far more than personal rivalry, therefore, or a reform of the superintendency, was at stake in this time of troubles. The Rees controversy seems to have been a symptom of a deep anxiety which altered significantly the outlook of the church. The fear grew on all hands that the faith of the fathers might not outlive the second generation. To understand the source and the nature of this fear is to see more completely why, as suggested earlier in this volume, the Nazarenes sharpened in this period the lines of their separation from both the secular and the religious world around them.

The church's pioneer leaders had felt their mission to be to preserve a doctrine and a way of life once dominant in older communions from the corrupting effects of social and religious change. They thought the formation of a specifically holiness denomination in the 1890's was a temporary strategy, necessary only until such time as the larger Christian community was ready to receive the truth again. By the end of two decades, however, events had almost eclipsed these hopes. The spread of a frank liberalism in the older churches produced increasing disdain for the evangelical Wesleyan heritage. More alarmingly, many children reared in the new denomination itself seemed less spiritual, less intense in their loyalties than they should have been. A spiritual rivalry, at once noble and opportunistic, among young firebrands who sought in every section to win for themselves the prestigious role of "true" champions of the faith of the fathers, stretched taut the lines of anxiety. The loss between 1914 and 1917 of many of the first strong leaders, some by death and infirmity and others by the decline of their earlier influence, simply triggered the trapsticks of fear.[35]

Such a crisis of the spirit has often swept over American denominations in their second generation, particularly those whose principal purpose was to conserve something which they felt threatened in a changing world. Professor Perry Miller and his distinguished student, Professor Edmund Morgan, have brilliantly demonstrated how this fear of declension affected the Puritan settlers of New England after 1645. The recently published diary of Henry M. Muhlenberg, the works of Michael Schlatter, and a growing body of recent scholarship on colonial Anglicanism indicate that when congregations of so-called "state" churches challenged the wilderness, they too passed through the same experience, and reacted by a similar tightening of denominational bonds.

In the years since the War for Independence, most new movements in American religion have professed conservative rather than revolutionary aims. The story of their second quarter-century is the same. Even those which, like the Disciples of Christ, the Latter-day Saints, and the Seventh-day Adventists, claimed at their founding to be guided by apocalyptic vision soon found themselves enshrining the memory of an orthodox past. Then, with the passing of but one additional generation, they too were torn by anxiety and dissension over how to preserve it. The pattern of fear, and the consequent quickening of sectarian tendencies in the second generation of American denominations, is therefore a familiar one, though sociologists of religion usually overlook it.[36]

The Nazarene experience, however, like that of every other group, had unique aspects which deserve careful consideration here. The slow adjustment of the rank and file to the revolution in church government which had been necessary to consolidate the unions of 1907 and 1908 provided some of the ingredients of dissent. Wise leadership had frayed but could not break the cords which, in New England, in the Old Southwest, and in the city mission movement, had bound congregational independency to popular perfectionism. When wisdom gave way to a rash abuse of power, men in all sections took alarm. Their concern was not simply constitutional; it was spiritual. The holiness pioneers had learned the hard way that ecclesiastical machinery was a threat to vital piety.

Hence the effectiveness of the bitter pamphlet which John Matthews published in 1920, entitled *The Rise and Fall of the Church of the Nazarene*. "There are Boards sufficient to build a second Noah's Ark," Matthews quipped, and each gave birth to others so rapidly that their entire energies were absorbed in raising their own expenses. He complained more seriously, however, of other matters, appealing at every step to the contrary example of the founders. The multiplication of committees and officials fettered the freedom of the Holy Spirit. Fund-raising campaigns threatened to make money the predominant theme in church assemblies. "Bogus universities" made false claims about their academic standards and cultivated patrons by generous grants of doctor's degrees. Ministers accepted into fellowship at the time of the unions turned out to have been divorced and remarried, a point on which the law of some parent bodies had not been clear. Most dangerous of all, however, was the fact that zeal for the denomination was becoming an acceptable substitute for submission to the Holy Spirit.

This broadside, written after its author had resigned his pastorate in Kansas City to join Seth C. Rees in his Bible school at Pasadena, is no record of objective observation to be sure. Within months, Matthews himself suppressed it, and acknowledged publicly that the dangers of radicalism far outweighed the benefits of independence. But the booklet nonetheless focused attention on the kinds of issues which a large majority of Nazarenes thought were of vital importance. Ever since, the danger of a compromising ecclesiasticism has remained a major and vocal concern.[37]

Another factor contributing to the general anxiety was the mental struggle over children reared in the church. Fears that they might water down the faith of their fathers were matched by equally powerful but more vague feelings that the church somehow belonged to them. The latter stemmed from the familial ties which flourished naturally in young congregations.

Here, again, the Nazarene story illustrates a little noticed but persistent trend in American church life. From the earliest settlement of the Atlantic seaboard, pioneer religious congregations, whether on rural or urban frontiers, began as a kind of family community, a home for homes. The first colonists had suffered profound emotional shock at being uprooted from their European village communities. They left behind a host of kin and other relationships which had given their lives direction and security. In the New World, the church congregation became a substitute for all the bonds of solidarity they had known before. Only religious awe, perhaps, could have evoked the kind of sentiments necessary to fashion new associations as satisfying as the old. The configuration of emotions in these congregations, therefore, whether New England Puritan, Pennsylvania Mennonite or Lutheran, New Jersey Presbyterian, or Virginia Baptist, was not simply religious but social and familial. This was true also of the worshiping communities into which Methodist circuit riders and Baptist farmer-preachers gathered succeeding generations of Americans as they moved westward toward the Pacific. On each new frontier, the churches were the first organized units of society. Their role was not so much denominational as it was cultural and congregational. They sustained and nurtured the growth of order, morality, and humane feeling, under circumstances which dictated the repeated dissolution of more natural ties of kin and community.

When, toward the end of the nineteenth century, mass emigration from the countryside to the city created an equally unstable social frontier, new urban congregations filled a similar function for newcomers there. This was particularly so for the earliest congregations of the Church of the Nazarene, as we have seen. Not many years passed before men and women who as "strangers to one another but not to God" had united with Bresee's church in Los Angeles or McClurkan's in Nashville would testify that their Christian brothers were dearer to them than their closest relatives.

For such persons, making sure that their own children remained loyal to the faith became a familial compulsion as well as a spiritual responsibility. They determined to engraft their youngsters' lives into the life of the church. Children who on maturing found themselves at odds with the denomination, whether from what they believed was a greater or a lesser spirituality, simply could not be told to line up or get out—a point which Brother Rees, for example, never understood. Getting out would be a kind of cultural suicide. Already, in this second generation, being a Nazarene was a symbol of belonging which they felt it perilous to break. It was much easier, as in all family troubles, to endure strife at home than to go homeless. Before long the new leaders found a better answer, anyway. They set out to produce by means both human and divine revivals of sufficient power to overcome all the attractions which a worldly life held for young people. Then, between revivals, they could shelter them in church schools and youth programs from polluting contact with evil.

A third major factor underlying the great fear of declension was the loosening of standards of dress and personal behavior in American society generally in the 1920's. The speed of the change opened a wide gap between the countryside and the sophisticated city. These were the days when Rudolph Valentino made the moving picture screen a symbol of lust and infidelity, when the hip flask, the cigarette, and the "Charleston" seemed to old-fashioned mothers symbols of a corruption which threatened the very foundations of morality. As late as 1928, a distinguished group of New York city club women and socialites rebuked in public print short skirts, brief bathing attire, bright make-up, and a number of other practices which they felt young ladies of high ideals should renounce. Under these circumstances, evangelical Christians needed no new surge of rebellion to widen their separation from the world. If they stood still, or merely accommodated themselves slowly to the new ways of dress and amusement, the world would fly on by. Such a situation inevitably deepened the sense of isolation among Nazarenes and taught them to despair of ever making the cities of America a garden of the Lord.[38]

Finally, it is important to note that the era of anxiety in the young church coincided with the outbreak of the fundamentalist controversy in older communions. This cultural and religious conflict, which reached its peak in America during the period from 1915 to 1930, stemmed from widespread apprehension that the nation itself was forsaking its spiritual heritage, and that the Christian faith had been betrayed in the house of its friends.

The organized protest against modernism began in 1910, with the publication of a series of tracts entitled *The Fundamentals; a Testimony to the Truth.* These affirmed orthodox Christian doctrine to rest upon five beliefs: the verbal inspiration of the Scriptures, the virgin birth of Christ, the substitutionary atonement, the bodily resurrection of Jesus, and His premillennial second coming. Several of the statements were cast in terms which, as we have seen, many early Nazarene leaders would have found confining. By the end of World War I, however, emotional factors had become as important as doctrinal issues in the fundamentalist crusade. Essentially religious fears—of modernism in religion, of evolution in education, and of the decline of personal morality in society—catalyzed and combined with social anxieties created by the war and by the general uprooting of people who went to work then and afterwards in boom-town factories. In these altered circumstances, as we shall see in a following chapter, Bresee's successors could not and did not escape involvement with fundamentalism.

For the Nazarenes, then, the crisis of the second generation was compounded of many elements: the passing of early leaders, the lag between legal unity and traditions of congregational independence, the fear that children reared in the church would betray its ideals, the reaction to the sudden weakening of standards of personal morality in the "flapper" age, and the pessimism which the fundamentalist controversy nurtured.

Interpreting the reaction of the young denomination to this manifold crisis is not an easy task. Looking backward toward the Rees controversy and forward to the resurgence of evangelism in the 1920's, three areas of religious concern seem to have received enlarged emphasis in the effort to head off spiritual decline. None was very successful when tried alone. Only when these emphases were combined in such a way as to balance one another, and then submerged in a renewal of Bresee's old crusade to evangelize the cities of the nation, did they set a pattern which Nazarenes could unite upon.

Of the three, the one which produced most discussion was the increased stress upon outward standards of behavior and adornment. The assumption was natural that one who was more strict than the founding fathers could not be less religious. To make not simply modesty but nonconformity the standard of women's dress; to insist that lodge members must give up not only their fellowship but their insurance protection in order to belong to the church; to forbid the wearing of wedding bands on the ground that they too were jewelry; to discourage social activities for church youth groups, and indeed to forbid the use of any part of church buildings for fellowship or recreation; and to frown upon educational "frills," whether in athletics or the fine arts, which brought the colleges into association with institutions of the "world"—by these devices, some employed in one locality and some in another, Nazarenes sought to prove both to themselves and others that the fountain of grace had not failed.[39]

The drift of events became painfully evident in a long debate over mixed bathing at the General Assembly held in Columbus, Ohio, in 1928. Sentiment in favor of rewriting the church's constitution had prompted the appointment of a commission on *Manual* revision at the assembly held four years before. Former General Superintendent E. P. Ellyson was made chairman; other members were E. J. Fleming, general church secretary, H. Orton Wiley, E. A. Girvin, John Gould, and P. L. Pierce. A group less likely to make radical changes could scarcely have been chosen. Nevertheless, as the assembly approached, expectations rose that a major effort would be made to revise the General Rules. The report of the commission, however, recommended exactly the same statement as before, except for the addition of the phrase "including movies" in the passage forbidding attendance at the theater. To everyone's surprise, General Superintendent Williams was able to gavel the recommendation through the committee of the whole without discussion.

At this point, however, a young Illinois pastor arose to complain that the commission had left out something far more serious than movies, mixed public bathing. The response from the floor was too great for Dr. Williams to restrain; he agreed reluctantly to allow reconsideration of the question. The Columbus newspapers took keen delight in reporting the debate which followed. The general superintendents themselves finally intervened to denounce those who, as one newspaper reported the statement, would turn the church aside "from the essentials of preaching the Gospel to matters of mere reformation." A compromise resolution then carried, providing that no mention of public bathing should appear in the church *Manual*, but that the General Assembly should go on record as disapproving it. The argument did not end, however, until the general superintendents announced on their own authority that the resolution would appear in an appendix of the *Manual*. Later General Assemblies found that the inclusion of such resolutions in the appendix, requiring only a simple majority vote, afforded a ready means of amending the church's conscience without changing its constitution.[40]

Another way to certify piety in the face of charges of declension was to encourage the freer demonstration of emotions in camp meetings and revivals, particularly those carried on in college communities. From the time of the awakening at Pasadena in 1914, displays of great fervor, as at Nampa under Dr. Wiley, became a frequent and reassuring occurrence in the colleges of the church. They were always widely reported. An earlier fear of fanaticism thus took second place to the new fear of backsliding. Dr. Bresee's oft-quoted phrase, "Get the glory down," took on a new tinge of meaning as men became uncommonly anxious to keep the tempo up. In staid New England, District Superintendent Nathan H. Washburn had rejoiced in 1914 that the churches "were never more free" from the "objectionable methods and manners" which had sometimes created "unnecessary prejudice." In 1925, however, E. T. French answered for his congregation at Lynn, Massachusetts, the question, "What is the greatest need in the evangelistic work of the church?" by saying:

> To my mind it is good victorious public services, with rousing song services, red hot testimonies, and a victorious swing that would make us different from other churches. We absolutely must not be like other churches. We must keep on fire.[41]

Tightening rules and intensifying emotions were not necessarily alternatives, of course. Many believed that both were vital to the rejuvenation which the church required. They became alternatives only when radical men, thinking to preserve the piety of the communion by surgical operation, charged their brothers with compromise. Then other leaders, emotionally as well as spiritually incapable of rending the fabric of fellowship, prayed for revivals in which scenes of unparalleled fervor would prove the charges false.

A final way of dealing with the problem which the transition to a new generation produced was to magnify denominational loyalties. James B. Chapman, who became editor of the *Herald of Holiness* in 1923, seems to have realized that this solution might isolate the church from other holiness communions, as well as from the world, and bring to a halt the long quest of Wesleyan unity. In an early editorial he deplored the tendency of denominationalism to degenerate into sectarianism, and affirmed stoutly that "every man, woman and child in the whole wide world who has accepted Jesus Christ as his Savior is my brother or sister in the Lord." He acknowledged this, he said, "without any reservations as to race, color or education; without reference to creeds, denominations, or any other barrier." He urged the Nazarenes to press for an early union with the Pilgrim Holiness, the Wesleyan Methodist, and the Free Methodist churches, so as to afford evangelical Christians a sound alternative to independent and radical connections.⁴² That such pleas won little response is, perhaps, proof enough that the denominationalism which the founders thought inappropriate for men seeking a reformation of American Christianity became for their successors the hallmark of orthodoxy.

CHAPTER XIII

The Laymen's Holiness Association on the Northern Plains

The Laymen's Holiness Association was the fruit of a Methodist evangelistic crusade which sprang up in North Dakota during the first and second decades of the twentieth century. Under J. G. Morrison's leadership, hundreds of its members united with the Church of the Nazarene in 1922 and 1923. The story of the organization, however, is more important than the relatively small numbers involved would suggest. It illustrates in detail how a Wesleyan variety of fundamentalism spread through the small towns and rural communities of the Middle West, loosening the ties of faith and sentiment which bound countless men and women to Methodism, and causing many of them to turn to younger denominations. Thus energies which these plainsmen had once directed against economic exploitation found release after 1915 in what seemed a more important crusade against infidelity and compromise in Christendom. The shift of attention from worldly to otherworldly concerns was evident during this period on a broader scope in the strange career of William Jennings Bryan, whose youthful battle for social justice gave place in his last years to a defense of the old-time religion.

The Origin of the Laymen's Movement

The Dakota prairies were the last frontiers settled in the Mississippi Valley. The suppression of the Sioux Indians, which General Custer's brave stand at Little Big Horn helped make possible, enabled farmers to move rapidly into the eastern fringes of the territory after 1880, especially along the Missouri River bottomlands. Congress granted statehood to both the northern and southern divisions in 1889. During three following decades successive tiers of counties to the westward slowly filled up with homesteaders willing to brave the blizzards, the grasshoppers, and the unending toil necessary to establish a prairie farm. Among the earliest settlers were a Methodist preacher and schoolteacher named S. A. Danford, and James and Amanda Morrison, whose tenth child, Joseph G., was one day to be a general superintendent in the Church of the Nazarene.

Danford was only twenty years of age when, in 1886, he was elected superintendent of schools in Sergeant County. He held the office four years, preaching all the while, and managed to organize the first normal school in the territory, at Milnor. Thereafter he gave his full time to the Methodist ministry. In 1899, while serving the church at Jamestown, North Dakota, he sought and found the experience of holiness. Bishop Joyce appointed him presiding elder of the Fargo District, covering the entire state, in 1904. Danford and his associates made the North Dakota Methodist Camp Meeting Association a principal instrument of their work. This organization sponsored an annual gathering, first in 1905 at White Rock, South Dakota, and thereafter at Jamestown. Methodist evangelists like Beverly Carradine, C. J. Fowler, and J. L. Glascock appeared frequently on its platform, and also held numerous revivals in churches across the district.[1]

Danford's preachers soon showed how the consecration and spiritual passion prompted by the experience of sanctification could nurture Methodism's growth under the most forbidding circumstances. Each summer found a corps of student evangelists living in huts and tents along the westernmost fringe of settlement, laying the groundwork for the churches they hoped to establish the next year. Some of their converts were transients, there merely to stake out a claim for later sale. But many had come to make the land their own. In the towns, meanwhile, more experienced pastors built small congregations into flourishing institutions.

By 1909, the Fargo District was so large as to require division. Danford was assigned to the frontier section; Jamestown was just inside its eastern border. He determined to take this area for Methodism. Membership on his district increased each year by more than twice the number of additions in other parts of the conference. He made the Ladies Aid societies an arm of the holiness revival, and promoted the Epworth League, the Methodist youth organization, with all his might. He arranged for the annual convention of the latter to meet at Jamestown campgrounds, so as to get its leaders under the preaching of the evangelists there. He also established a conference paper, placing it under the editorship of J. G. Morrison, who was by then pastor at Jamestown and Danford's right-hand man.[2]

The issues of this periodical which have survived indicate that the mood of anxiety out of which Methodist fundamentalism grew flowered early in the Dakotas. "Every great Church drifts with the lapse of time," Morrison declared in his editorial for August, 1910, and Methodism was no exception. "The child of an ardent holiness revival now slumbers complacently," he warned, "while the new theology teachers . . . drain her of the last bit of vitality left." But he believed that a great revival, beginning right here on the northern plains, might reverse the trend. "Brethren of the ministry," he cried, "preach the fundamentals."[3]

From 1909 to the outbreak of World War I, however, the North Dakota preachers were entirely loyal to their bishops. Danford steadily refuted the notion that "holiness" men were "marked for slaughter" by the "powers that be." This had not been true in his case, he insisted in 1913; everyone in authority, high and low, had encouraged his work. "The Methodist Church is a 'holiness church,'" the presiding elder told his people, and no other organization was needed to promote that doctrine. To officials who nonetheless questioned their loyalty, he cited the fact that no Nazarene congregation had ever been organized on either district he had served![4]

As had happened earlier in other sections of Methodism, however, three institutions gradually linked this independent association with the national holiness movement, whose leaders had long since fallen from the good graces of the bishops. These were the camp meeting, the holiness college, and the holiness paper. Evangelists from all over America appeared at Jamestown campgrounds. They were joined there by school representatives who encouraged young converts to enroll at Asbury College, Wilmore, Kentucky; God's Bible School, Cincinnati; Taylor University, Upland, Indiana; and Central Holiness University, in Oskaloosa, Iowa, in preference to nearby colleges under denominational control. Meanwhile the *Christian Witness* and Henry Clay Morrison's *Pentecostal Herald* joined Morrison's *North*

Dakota Methodist on parlor tables all over the area. The fame of Danford and Morrison traveled far beyond the territory also. Visitors to the camp meeting rarely failed to report in some journal the unusual fact that at Jamestown the superintendent of a district as large as the state of Ohio stood at the head of the work, and that all of his fifty-six pastors were advocates of the "second blessing." This frontier of Methodism, therefore, was never isolated. Nor was it ever dependent upon official sources alone for its information about the course the denomination was taking.[5]

By 1915 such a situation had become an embarrassment to the Methodist leadership. Danford experienced increasing opposition from his neighboring district superintendents, and from the new presiding bishop as well. His strongest preachers found themselves transferred to obscure country circuits. In 1916 he bowed to the inevitable and accepted a transfer to the pastorate of the First Methodist Church in Eugene, Oregon. Morrison departed soon after for an appointment in Sebring, Florida. Both men, however, retained their positions at Jamestown camp, and continued to serve jointly as editors of the paper, now renamed the *Little Methodist*. They also encouraged the formation of the Inter-State Camp Meeting Association to sponsor local gatherings in various parts of North Dakota and Minnesota.

By July, 1917, when the time for the Jamestown gathering rolled around again, the laymen had determined to form an alliance of their own which would operate beyond the reach of episcopal control. They organized the Methodist Laymen's Holiness Association, pledged salary and expenses to support an executive field secretary, and asked Morrison to fill the post. The crusading editor accepted immediately. He announced in the columns of his paper a threefold campaign "to carry the fight for orthodoxy" in the church, to "promote the sweet truth and experience of holiness," and to secure the money and subscriptions necessary to continue publication of the *Little Methodist*. On the first point especially, Morrison spoke sharply. "Our Sunday school literature is poisoned," he declared; "our Preachers' Course of Study is filled with . . . destructive criticism, thus ruining our young ministers." The only hope was for earnest Wesleyans to turn the glare of publicity and the aggressive power of revival upon those who were selling Methodism out to modernism.[6]

A Methodist Association

The first project of the Laymen's Holiness Association was a bold attempt to pressure their bishop into removing Danford's successor from the presiding eldership and appointing Morrison to the post. In a general "call to prayer," published on the eve of the annual conference in October, the association's officers charged that the decline of spiritual power in Methodism was due in part to a conspiracy among university men "to shift our Church's teachings . . . to a Christianity obtained by Education, Culture, Improved Social Environment, and the general processes of modern civilization." They meanwhile circulated petitions in behalf of Morrison's appointment which, when presented to Bishop R. J. Cooke, bore upwards of 1,000 names.

The bishop met the challenge head on. He began the conference with a clear and indeed beautiful exposition of the doctrine of Christian perfection. He admitted frankly that the new "Conference Course of Study" for licensed ministers was in part unorthodox, but he choked off all public criticism of it. Then, warming to his task, Cooke denounced the holiness crowd as "a disgruntled, restless group of religious I. W. W.'s," and declared that he would not appoint a minister to serve in any organization not under the control of the church. Scorning the petition proposing Morrison as presiding elder, he named instead one of the neighboring district superintendents who had been an outspoken opponent of the "second blessing."[7]

Meanwhile the presiding bishop in Florida, Frederic D. Leete, refused to accept the minister who had volunteered to complete Morrison's year of responsibility there, and summoned the North Dakota leader to trial for deserting his charge. Morrison published his correspondence on the matter in an effort to force postponement of the proceedings. His defense was that he had accepted appointment from the Laymen's Association in order to prevent the growth among them of disloyalty to the church. Bishop Leete persisted, however. As Morrison had predicted, the action by which he was officially dropped from the Methodist ministry only confirmed the laymen of North Dakota in the determination to proceed with their crusade.[8]

They believed from the outset, then, that loyalty to the spirit of Methodism might require them to disregard the wishes of ecclesiastical officials. The executive committee approved in January, 1918, a plan to form local "auxiliary holiness associations" wherever a group of their people were not receiving "suitable care." The secretary declared in March that, although Morrison's revivals were bringing numerous converts into Methodist membership, the organization would not "bow the knee to Baal or Bishop." "If the church authorities don't want you in the Conference," he wrote Morrison, "you can know that the laymen will stand by you. . . ." Thereafter, the association operated within but not as a part of the denomination. Its lay character was not dictated by any real protest against the traditional prerogatives of clergymen. Rather, it served as a legal device to prevent interference by bishops and presiding elders in the work the organization had set out to do.[9]

Nor was the movement ever genuinely interdenominational, despite the fact that at the very first meeting a provision was added to the bylaws welcoming to membership all Christians who subscribed to the doctrines of the Wesleys, whether or not they were Methodists. The association published the *Methodist* without changing either its form or its title until 1919. The district Epworth League convention still met annually at Jamestown, and S. A. Danford journeyed all the way from Oregon each summer to take part in business meetings, even after he became a presiding elder in the far western state. The ministers who accepted positions as field agents were all Methodists. Some of them, like James M. Taylor, had recently served as official "conference evangelists."[10]

The "North Dakota idea," as it was called, spread rapidly across the Upper Mississippi Valley, though the numbers were never large. During the first year, two evangelists besides Morrison were employed full time. In 1918, five more were added to the list. North Dakota and several adjacent states were divided into districts, with one "field agent" assigned to each. H. O. Jacobson, a member of the Norwegian-Danish Conference of the Methodist Episcopal church and president of the Scandinavian Holiness Association, led his group into the organization in 1918. He prepared a column in Norwegian for the *Methodist* each month. The Yellowstone Holiness Association, serving the area around Billings, Montana, united with the group also, and underwrote the salary of W. G. Bennett, one of Danford's men. Morrison had earlier established important contacts in Michigan. By the summer of 1920 he had organized four "districts" there. E. O. Rice, an Asbury graduate, was field agent of the one centered in

Detroit, and George W. Marine, a former Nazarene who had recently held a Methodist pastorate in North Dakota, supervised another. Morrison visited the Oakland City, Indiana, camp meeting in October, 1919, and organized a laymen's association to carry on the work of three such annual gatherings in that state. The same year J. M. Taylor persuaded the Central Kansas Holiness Association that the adoption of the Dakota idea would cultivate throughout the year a constituency for their camp meeting. In August, 1920, the Kansas group voted themselves into the Laymen's Association and appointed T. J. Nixon, official evangelist of the Northwest Kansas Conference, as their field agent. In southeastern Missouri, the Dunklin County Holiness Camp Meeting Association took the same step.[11]

By the summer of 1919 most of the ministers serving as evangelists or field agents had given up or otherwise lost their standing in their conferences. The estrangement from Methodist fellowship and the attraction of a few non-Methodists to the ranks provoked a reorganization along interdenominational lines. Pastors from the Salvation Army and the Evangelical Association, and at least one Nazarene, W. H. Tullis, former superintendent in Idaho, joined the group. A "Bible conference" for young people replaced the annual Epworth League convention at Jamestown. The word "Methodist" was dropped from the title of the organization and the paper was renamed the *Holiness Layman*. Several co-operating groups now gave up their identity entirely to join the larger body. The treasury was combined with that of Jamestown camp, and the leaders announced their willingness to take over actual direction of all the holiness camp meetings in Minnesota and North Dakota. The lay members enthusiastically undertook a campaign to raise $15,000 a year to support the seven evangelists. Ira E. Hammer was elected financial field agent, to supervise collections.

Morrison insisted that these actions signified no departure from Wesleyan doctrines or standards, but were intended rather to free the program of evangelism from all obligation to the Methodist church. He noted that, although the association had recently felt compelled to accept the care of a few independent congregations which had been organized to shelter their people from a liberal ministry, the leaders planned no new denomination. Sectarianism, he said, had outlived its day. The members of the association should remain in the churches to which they belonged. What was needed was an interdenominational holiness crusade, whose fruit would be not new churches "but thousands of church members made new by the Baptism of the Holy Ghost and fire."[12]

During the next year the association sponsored a total of thirteen camp meetings besides the large one at Jamestown. Income, boosted by wartime prosperity, totaled $20,000. The salaries of all eight evangelists were paid in full. Two thousand persons professed experiences of grace at their altars. And F. J. Mills and W. G. Bennett opened up new work in Michigan and Wisconsin.

The annual meeting of 1920 assigned to district organizations primary responsibility for the salaries of all the evangelists save Morrison, but retained full control of policy. The delegates also authorized a foreign missionary department which, in co-operation with the National Holiness Association, sent a young woman to China. Appeals for support of overseas evangelism, like those for missions at home, stressed the fear of modernism. "Much of the work being done in many places in the foreign fields," one plea ran, "has been so honey-combed with higher criticism and 'social service,' that the really spiritual work that holiness people want their money to do is not being done."[13]

One measure of the success of the Laymen's movement was the reaction of the Methodist leadership. In the summer of 1919 the presiding bishop appointed an official evangelist for each of the districts in North Dakota. All were known to be clear preachers of the doctrine of sanctification; one was Guy Wilson, until recently a Nazarene. The conference also established its own "holiness" camp meeting, at Mandan, North Dakota. Reports circulated that the bishop had written the district superintendents to urge their men to preach Christian perfection earnestly. Whether this was true or not, Methodist pastors seem to have felt free to employ field agents of the association to conduct their revivals during this and succeeding years. But the result was simply to multiply the numbers who were discontented with the course of events elsewhere in the denomination.[14]

Wesleyan Fundamentalism

The literature of the Laymen's Holiness Association was permeated with the spirit of what we must call Wesleyan fundamentalism. A comparison of the sermons, reports, and exhortations of this group with those of the holiness associations which flourished in the 1890's turns up some striking differences. In the earlier period the twin passions seem to have been evangelism and social work. The North Dakota group, by contrast, combined the idea of sanctification with attacks upon modernism, science, and public education, and with the expectation of an imminent Second Coming. Christian social service was explicitly rejected. In many ways, indeed, the laymen's movement revealed a fear of spiritual decline in Methodism which resembled closely the mood which, as we have seen, gripped earnest souls in the young Church of the Nazarene during these years.

A long series of articles denouncing modernism accompanied the organization of the association in 1917. Methodist universities and seminaries, the Conference Course of Study for licensed ministers, and the denomination's Sunday school literature all came in for sharp attack. A laymen's letter published in the *Little Methodist* in April complimented the editor for "taking some bark off the barren fig trees of Methodism." What Wesley's successors needed to halt declining attendance at Sunday evening services, Morrison wrote, was not forums and book reviews but the old-time religion. The church, he declared, "must cease abusing those who stand for the doctrine and the experience it urged them to seek"; and the power of university men must be curbed before it was too late. "THE HIGHER CRITICS AND THEIR SYMPATHIZERS ARE NOT METHODISTS," he declared; "we propose to wage a tremendous warfare to drive the critics out of control of the church."[15]

This objective, as we have seen, dictated the organization's initial strategy of absolute loyalty to Methodism. Morrison announced that the Laymen's Association would hold sacred the doctrines of the church, and have nothing to do with come-outism. "We are urging all our converts to unite with Methodist churches," he said, "and all our supporters to stand by the churches they are in." Although deploring "the awful apostasy" into which Wesley's denomination had fallen, he insisted as late as September, 1918, that his group had "no sympathy whatever with the current teaching that she is 'Babylon,' and that God is calling His people out of her. This is, we believe, a bit of pessimistic fanaticism."[16]

Powerful forces were at work, however, eroding the sentiments which bound the laymen to their church, and increasing their attachment to fundamentalism. One was fear. Another was the farmer's feeling of alienation from urban culture. The third was the heightened sense of human tragedy which World War I and its aftermath produced. First at the emotional level, and then in rational argument, these influences played their part. Here, as elsewhere in Methodism, they aroused and enflamed the strains of puritanism and pessimism which in other days had yielded first place to the perfectionist idealism dominant in Wesleyan faith.

The fear was a product of both religious and social tensions. In leading articles published in the fall of 1917, Morrison spelled out fully the reasons for religious alarm. While the laymen were attending to farms, shops, banks, and businesses, he charged, "German infidelity" had "invaded Methodist schools in the subtle guise of evolution, scholarship and modern research." For a long time ordinary church members could not believe that the ministry would allow such an apostasy, but the fire bell of events had awakened them. "The good ship Methodism," he wrote, "has been seized by those who have no right to her, who do not believe and love her doctrines, and who eat dishonest bread every day they remain in the church...."

He predicted, however, that "a frank proclamation of what the liberal scholars who have seized the church do believe" would array ten thousand preachers and two million laymen against them. "Turn on the light, and they will have to run," he declared; "we propose to stay in, and turn on the light." What he meant was plain from an article in the September issue, entitled "Death in the Pot." It was the first of a series which described works of liberal scholarship recently added to the list of books in the Conference Course of Study, a list from which Wesley's sermons had been eliminated.[17]

When Morrison linked his attacks on modernism to anti-German prejudice, many readers protested. The editor denied that he was simply exploiting wartime hatred for the national enemy. German scholars had invented higher criticism, he said. "It is German poison, ... German fever hatched from German 'kultur' and dropped into the wells of English, French and American fountains of learning." He quoted approvingly an article from the *Christian Witness* which traced modern heresies to a Teutonic plot to "break down all moral and spiritual standards" as a preparation for the enslavement of the world. "Let the church pitch the pro-Germans from the pulpit," Morrison cried.[18]

But this passion cooled quickly. As early as 1920 he arranged for the conduct of a German department in Jamestown camp meeting. By then, however, another fear had come to hand. The great "Red Scare," prompted by the Bolshevist revolution in Russia, had replaced anti-German feeling in the public mind. "The whole world is in danger from the menace of socialism, Bolshevism, and revolution generally," Morrison declared in March of 1921; only a great revival, one which would make the nation truly Christian, could dispel the danger.[19]

Another component of Wesleyan fundamentalism was the farmer's feeling that the urban world had passed him by, playing all the while a demonic "Pied Piper's" tune which his children could not resist.

A note of rural protest against the apostasy which flourished in cities runs like a purple thread through all of the literature of the laymen's movement. It became more insistent as the postwar depression ground farmers to the wall. A church hierarchy, one wrote, not only suppresses piety; it "cultivates the rich and powerful, since it desires to be rich and powerful itself." By contrast, the Laymen's Association sought to evangelize the common man. "It is especially to the out-of-the-way places that we are called," Morrison wrote, "to the schoolhouse, to the deserted country church, to the cross-roads hall."

In 1920 the editor warned his readers with utter seriousness that farming communities were seething with a spirit of discontent which endangered the life of the nation. As long as revolutionary sentiments were confined to the lower classes in cities, he said, America could easily weather the gale. But now the country people were aroused. "They feel that they have not been fairly dealt with. Unhappiness is in the air. Revolution of various grades from the peaceful ballot to the red bomb and flaring torch is now freely talked in every country home." His solution? Take the rural communities for Jesus. Thus, if Christ delayed His coming, the Laymen's Association could help save the nation from destruction. If not, they would have helped to gather out the bride of the Lord.[20]

The mounting evidence of "godlessness" in education was an important ingredient of this sense of estrangement between country church and urban culture. The Dakotans noted with alarm a survey which claimed that over 50 per cent of American college professors did not believe in God. Billy Sunday also impressed them with his flat statement that "college professors, generally, Harvard and . . . University of Chicago professors particularly," were atheistic. The group's response was not to deny the importance of education, of course, but to shape it into an instrument they could use. That the Christian cause needed leadership, skill, and intelligence to match that in Satan's camp was to them an axiom; they simply had no faith that such leadership could come out of institutions where the old-time gospel was an object of scorn. Hence their well-developed plan for a holiness academy at Jamestown. It was cut short of fulfillment only by their union with the Nazarenes, who had schools aplenty.[21]

Compounding the fear and the feeling of estrangement was the tragic blight which World War I seemed to lay on Christian hopes for a better world. Evangelists who had once proclaimed the approaching conversion of all mankind now professed to see no prospects for the kingdom of God save through the second coming of Christ. "There is no use talking, it is harder to get people to yield to God than in all my experience," Evangelist J. M. Taylor wrote in February, 1918. "This war, or something. . . . The final battle is on. We have not been deceived. Jesus is coming soon and Satan is surely coming down in great wrath."[22]

Thereafter, premillennialists attacked even holiness people who shared the traditional Methodist view that Christians must prepare a Kingdom for their King. The editor's effort to mediate this controversy collapsed in 1920 and 1921, when leading articles declared flatly that postmillennialism had "no foundation in the Scriptures," that it was the theology of the "great so-called 'Forward Movements' " which had "abandoned the programme of the Holy Ghost." Taylor called the doctrine "the supreme heresy of modern times," and a key weapon in "Satan's . . . final effort to seize the kingdom of God." Its popularity among Methodist leaders seemed to him proof that "the whole . . . Hierarchy has opened a concerted and world-wide assault upon the Bible teaching of the Second Coming of Christ. . . ."[23]

Here, then, was a new form of agrarian revolt, calling the nation to otherworldly piety rather than, as in the 1890's, to social reform. Not the economic power of Wall Street but the godless influence of universities, not the sufferings imposed by an unjust money system but the spiritual bankruptcy of an unfaithful church alarmed these plainsmen. The mood of protest and withdrawal evident in all farming communities was to dominate evangelical religion in America for the next thirty years. Whenever praying families moved from the countryside to the city, they identified themselves with Bible-believing congregations, adding new thrust to the force of urban fundamentalism as well. Such Christians, whether of Wesleyan, Baptist, or Presbyterian persuasion, thought of life primarily in terms of the pilgrim's heavenly journey; and they expected even that to be cut short by the coming of the Lord.

Uniting with the Nazarenes

Beginning as early as 1908, when H. D. Brown appeared in North Dakota to organize a Church of the Nazarene at Sawyer, intermittent contacts kept Danford's men informed of the growth of Bresee's young denomination. Evangelists crossed one another's paths repeatedly, of course. Several Nazarene ministers were active in the Laymen's Holiness Association, as we have seen. One Dakotan, F. J. Drewry, served a Nazarene pastorate across the border in Canada, at the same time helping to spread the association's work there.[24] Thus when Morrison's followers began to wonder whether their growing alienation from Methodism might not require a new church after all, they turned quite naturally toward the Nazarenes.

If public statements may be taken at face value, however, the nondenominational idea died hard. Down to a very few months before they joined the Church of the Nazarene, Morrison and other leaders professed supreme confidence in the "association plan." They organized holiness prayer bands on an interchurch basis and denied any intent ever to form a new sect. In November, 1920, Morrison announced that the coming annual meeting would "settle the Interdenominational aspect of the movement" so completely that the churches would lay aside permanently their fear that the association was "generating another denomination." The evening preacher for this seven-day session, however, was the sweet-spirited John W. Goodwin, general superintendent in the Church of the Nazarene. Dr. Goodwin wisely avoided all mention of possible union, and in fact praised publicly Morrison's careful definition and defense of the nondenominational idea. But he won the hearts of the North

Dakotans; a year later they were to accept him as a trusted friend and counselor.²⁵

In the following months, however, Morrison crowded every issue of the *Holiness Layman* with arguments against organizing or joining a new church. "The whole spirit of the age is opposed to denominationalism," he said; the "Layman's Idea" alone would succeed in preserving the Wesleyan heritage. Nevertheless he could not halt the process by which local holiness bands evolved into nonsectarian missions and then, sometimes within months, organized as independent churches. Replacing a band by a mission was, he agreed, sometimes an unhappy necessity, but the next step was a mistake. New converts should join existing churches. If pastors proved unhelpful, members of the association must renew their faith in the priesthood of individual believers. Their mission was to "populate the land with holiness bands"; the field agents could provide the "general oversight" required.²⁶

But what was to be done when no local church would accept the converts from bands and missions? The alternatives of denominationalism or disorder were as distasteful to Morrison and his associates as they had once been to John Short, Phineas Bresee, and J. O. McClurkan. Between the two, the Dakota Methodist preachers, reared in a disciplined fellowship, unhesitatingly chose order.

A chief factor in hastening their decision was financial. In 1920 a sharp postwar depression hit the northern plains. This, combined with the growing tendency to settle pastors in independent missions and churches, deprived the laymen's organization of the income necessary to pay the salaries of its evangelists. Up until the annual meeting of January, 1921, each one of these had received $1,800 a year plus necessary expenses, except for Morrison, whose stipend as president was $600 more. That meeting, however, directed the districts to arrange to support their evangelists independently after July 1, 1921. Economic conditions worsened, however.

By the fall of 1921, appeals for funds overshadowed all other matters in the *Layman*. Morrison urged some well-to-do person to "take the support of the president on his tithing account," so as to relieve him to campaign for the other men. He also published a series of articles calling upon the people to refuse further support to "any pastor who is not a genuinely spiritual man," and instead to channel all their tithes to the association. The annual convention which met in January, 1922, found all finances "in desperate condition," though every evangelist had managed to finish the year in the field and to reach the meeting. The laymen who had given generously during the wartime boom were now powerless; shrinking income and mounting debts plagued both farm and village undertakings. The evangelists were caught between a rock and a hard place.[27]

At this critical moment one of the evangelists fell under the spell of Aimee Semple McPherson, raising among the group the specter of what many of them believed was fanaticism. James M. Taylor returned to his native California in 1921, aiming to establish an arm of the association there. Within a short time he was filling his column in the *Holiness Layman* with accounts of Mrs. McPherson's work. When Morrison sought to moderate his enthusiasm, Taylor became only more ecstatic. On March 9, 1922, the editor yielded to demands that he print in full Taylor's latest review, which described her as "the supreme miracle of this generation." Four weeks later, at the close of a revival he conducted for E. E. Wordsworth in Minneapolis, Minnesota, Evangelist Morrison and his wife and daughter united with the Church of the Nazarene. To him, order and superintendency in a holiness church were preferable in every way to the freedom which could lead to such alliances as Taylor proposed.[28]

Morrison did not at once announce his decision to the readers of the *Holiness Layman;* but from that moment on, he labored to bring as many of them as possible into the denomination he had chosen. He moved quickly. Bud Robinson was engaged to conduct the camp meeting at Jamestown that summer. Within a few weeks the famous editorial "Hatching Chickens for the Hawks" appeared. In it Morrison pointed out bluntly the folly of "thrusting converts into a church that opposes holiness." He advised the laymen either to find a spiritual church or to make one of their own. The following week he printed in full Joseph H. Smith's courteous but firm rejection of any claim Mrs. McPherson might have on the loyalties of Wesleyan Christians. The June 1 issue contained Evangelist W. G. Bennett's article, "Seven Reasons Why I Can Remain No Longer in the Methodist Episcopal Church and Ministry." Bennett's previously unquestioned loyalty and his careful denial of any mistreatment by the bishops made even more effective his denunciation of the spread of modernism through the church and of the diversion of consecrated money to what he believed were unworthy purposes. These things, he said, left him no choice but to join a group like the Nazarenes, though he knew full well that "many precious brethren, both among the ministry and laity," would remain in the older communion.[29]

Indeed, the holiness missions had already begun to constitute themselves Nazarene churches, without waiting for the annual meeting of the association at Jamestown. New Rockford, North Dakota, was the first to do so, late in March. In May the important group at Jamestown followed suit, followed soon after by those at Valley City and Ellendale, North Dakota, and Billings, Montana.[30]

At the time of the Jamestown camp meeting, the news had circulated that W. L. Brewer would not be a candidate for re-election as superintendent of the North Dakota-Minnesota District of the Church of the Nazarene. Its assembly was scheduled to meet at Velva, North Dakota, July 12. The new congregations organized from the Laymen's Association began at once to advocate the election of Dr. Morrison to the post. When the delegates reached Velva, however, they learned that Brewer had changed his mind. Dr. Reynolds thereupon persuaded the assembly to divide the district into a northern and southern portion, representing roughly the areas in which the older and newer congregations were located. He appointed Morrison superintendent of the Jamestown-Minneapolis District. It contained as yet only 7 churches, 2 in Minnesota and 5 in North Dakota, with a combined membership of 245. In a long resolution welcoming the members of the Laymen's Association to the denomination, E. E. Wordsworth expressed the hope that upwards of a thousand members and twenty ministers would eventually follow their leader into the Nazarene fold. Nevertheless, he explained, both the Jamestown camp meeting and the *Holiness Laymen* were to remain for the present non-denominational agencies. A month later the Nazarenes in South Dakota voted to unite with the new district, thus placing an additional 12 churches and 285 members under Morrison's supervision.[31]

Partly by circumstance and partly by design, therefore, Morrison found himself simultaneously holding the offices of

Nazarene district superintendent, president of the Laymen's Holiness Association and editor of its official journal, and head of the Jamestown Camp Meeting board. Moreover, his two closest associates in the unsectarian work, Ira Hammer and Mrs. Nellie Hoffman, had been the first to follow him into the Nazarene fellowship. He was thus able to use all of these positions to draw his followers into the church. By the end of August, Evangelists S. C. Taylor and R. A. Wilson, who had recently been elected by the South Dakota State Holiness Association to lead a nondenominational campaign in that state, had thrown in their lot with him. The same month the editor reiterated the complete reversal of his previous position on "organized holiness." In an article in the *Layman,* he wrote: "Just a prayer band, at first, then a holiness mission, then a holiness church. That's the divine plan...."[32]

Succeeding issues of the journal described Morrison's supervision of Nazarene churches, independent missions, and Laymen's Association affairs with fine disregard of distinctions between them. Even sermons printed by the paper contained frequent references to the history of the Church of the Nazarene. At the district meetings of the association in the fall, men already in the Nazarene fold were elected to serve as chairmen and evangelists. In November, the superintendent introduced the denomination's foreign missionary work to the readers of the *Layman,* with only a slight bow to their missionary already in the field.

The success of Morrison's strategy was obvious by the time of the association's annual meeting in January, 1923. Every speaker on the program was a Nazarene. The discussion which followed a paper entitled "Holiness, Organized or Unorganized, Which?" produced the unanimous conclusion that without a satisfactory church home three-fourths of their converts would be lost. Nevertheless, the delegates voted to continue the old organization, so as to nurture the bands and missions which were not yet ready to turn themselves into Nazarene congregations.[33]

At the end of his first year as district superintendent, Morrison reported 10 new churches, 6 in Minnesota and 4 in North Dakota, and an increase of 344 members. During the following year, 16 new congregations were admitted, and the district's membership reached a total of 1,121. Clearly, not all of the laymen had chosen to follow their leader. But the number who became Nazarenes was sufficient to give the denomination a foothold in the territory stretching from Michigan to the mountains of Montana. As far west as Oregon, H. O. Jacobson persuaded several units of the Scandinavian Holiness Association to reorganize as Nazarene churches. Elsewhere, in Missouri, Kansas, Indiana, and California, other small groups took the same step.[34]

Thus was the "church question" settled in the Dakota movement. As earlier and in other places, after a brief experiment with an independent association, former Methodist preachers led the way toward denominational affiliation. Their work in this instance was made easier by the fact that the Laymen's Association had never fostered congregational independency. It relied from the beginning upon the superintending oversight of evangelists and field agents. The chief prerogative which the laymen exercised was to participate with ministers in the joint councils which determined the policies of the organization, an arrangement which was fast becoming the custom in the Church of the Nazarene as well.

Ever a practical man, Morrison framed his philosophy of life into the title of a book, *Achieving Faith*. His optimism, his flair for superintendency, and his embodiment of the spirit of Wesleyan fundamentalism then sweeping across the denomination he had adopted marked him for greater usefulness. In the spring of 1926 he was elected to succeed H. Orton Wiley as president of Northwest Nazarene College. The following year the General Board chose him to be executive field secretary of foreign missions, a post which he held until 1936, when he became a general superintendent.[35]

The Nazarene Response to Fundamentalism

The several thousand Methodist preachers and laymen who transferred their membership to the young denomination as a result of the spiritual conflicts of the 1920's added new impetus to the rapid growth of the Church of the Nazarene in the Upper Mississippi Valley. Quite naturally, however, they brought with them both the ideas and the attitudes of what we have called Wesleyan fundamentalism, including especially a deeply ingrained fear of ecclesiastical compromise, and an abhorrence of personal worldliness and fashionable forms of worship. Their anxieties matched precisely those which the crisis of the transition to a second generation had already stirred in the Nazarene fold. The fact that all American Wesleyans shared during this period some of the same alarms heightened the temptation to subordinate the distinctive heritage of holiness to other issues involved in the fundamentalist-modernist controversy.

The accession of the Laymen's Association, therefore, made immediately pressing a careful definition of the relationship of the Church of the Nazarene to the non-Wesleyan fundamentalists on one hand, and to the tongues-speaking "Pentecostal" movement on the other. The outcome was the elaboration of a point of view which was more distinctively denominational than before. But the point of view was also clearly Wesleyan. That this development drew a circle of isolation around the young church which excluded even many evangelical Christians was perhaps not so much a proof of deliberate sectarianism as an indication that the gospel of holiness had fallen on an unreceptive age.

J. G. Morrison himself had no sooner joined the denomination than he undertook to show his followers the uniqueness of the Nazarene way, as compared with other conservative religious movements in America. To be sure, he never let up for a moment his attacks on modernism in the churches and evolution and infidelity in the schools.[36] But he repeatedly explained that Wesleyans stood for *both* an inspired Bible and salvation from all sin, whereas other fundamentalists, nurtured chiefly in Baptist and Presbyterian traditions, gave little or no place to the doctrine of entire sanctification. Morrison also explained carefully the differences between Nazarenes and other perfectionists. Though zealous for a radical, sin-cleansing experience, they rejected rasping, unkind preaching. "Lashing can never convict people," Morrison declared; "the office of convicting men belongs to the Holy Ghost." He also exhorted his followers to avoid "boisterous praying, great bodily exercise," and "vociferous and constant shouting," and to shun those who taught that sanctification was certified by visions, dreams, and impressions, or by speaking in "other tongues."[37]

On issues other than the doctrine of holiness, however, the fundamentalist outlook made steady progress among Nazarenes. The growing popularity of premillennialism among them is a case in point. The doctrine which Tennessee and Texas leaders had failed to get written into church law at the General Assemblies of 1908 and 1911 became so dominant in the 1920's as to make postmillennialists suspect.

The rapid growth of the church in the Midwest, where premillennialism and perfectionism had become allies, goes far to explain this development, of course. But another factor was the advancement of a remarkable group of Texans to important positions in the church: James B. Chapman to the editorship of the *Herald of Holiness*, and, in 1928, to the general superintendency; Henry B. Wallin to the pastorate of Los Angeles First Church; and E. P. Ellyson, C. A. McConnell, S. S. White, and Thomas E. Mangum to places of leadership in the educational institutions. The shock of war also played its part. In 1918, C. B. Jernigan, who was soon to leave the prairies of Oklahoma to be district superintendent in New York state, published a volume entitled *The World War in Prophecy,* which ran the gamut of fundamentalist fears. Three years later L. A. Reed set forth in the church paper what came to be a widely held opinion: getting ready for "the near coming of Jesus Christ," he declared, was "almost the greatest incentive" preachers could employ to persuade Christians to seek the second blessing. Nevertheless, no change at all was made in the church's doctrinal statement on the subject.[38]

Nazarenes also accepted readily the fundamentalist belief that the public schools threatened to become seedbeds of godlessness. Many of the congregations in southern California had established parochial elementary schools in their early years. At one time or another each of the colleges had maintained one. Eugene Emerson urged in 1915 that every district establish a Christian academy and every local church a primary school. The postwar controversy over evolution, therefore, served only to confirm a long-standing conviction. William Jennings Bryan delivered at Olivet College his famous address called "Tampering with the Main-Spring" three years before he acted as prosecuting attorney in the trial of John T. Scopes. By then, what had once been a reasonably broad Nazarene attitude toward science instruction was yielding to the prevailing mood of suspicion. Curiously enough, however, the prejudices were not translated into practice; parochial education for younger children made no headway at all in the denomination during the 1920's, and enrollment in the church's secondary schools declined steadily.[39]

The increasing antipathy toward labor unions in this working-class church is another indication of the pervasive influence of rural fundamentalism. Before America's entry into World War I, B. F. Haynes, editor of the *Herald of Holiness*, professed great sympathy for labor's aims. Christians could not be content, he said, with a situation which kept ten million citizens in poverty and forced seventeen hundred thousand children of school age "into the poisonous atmosphere of factory, shop, and mine," while millionaires indulged the "vulgar display of superfluous money." The persistence of such inequalities, he noted, had brought other civilizations to ruin. In 1919, however, Haynes reversed his position. The federal government, he charged, had so "pampered and spoiled" unions during the war that they were now "practically threatening revolution." At the General Assembly that year delegates from several districts renewed an old proposal that the *Manual* equate labor organizations with secret societies and outlaw Nazarene membership in them. Though the measure did not pass, anti-union pronouncements became more commonplace as years went by.[40] Happily, however, the church's clear stand against secret societies ruled out involvement with the Ku Klux Klan, a movement which gained much support among fundamentalists in the South.[41]

In such circumstances the historic Nazarene faith in social progress through a revival of personal holiness lost ground rapidly. As early as 1912, Editor Haynes, in an article denouncing "Material Millennialism," declared that Christians who hoped for a perfect society were doomed to disappointment. "This is the devil's world," he wrote, "so claimed by him and so declared repeatedly by the authority of God's word."[42] Consequently the social work which had inspired so much devotion in the early years suffered from steadily increasing neglect. Rescue homes and missions disappeared from district programs. Pronouncements on social issues, when made at all, were buried in the reports of committees on public morals whose real preoccupation was standards of personal behavior among church people. The order of deaconesses, once a great source of spiritual power in the denomination, declined in both numbers and influence. Even the ancient commitment to prohibitionism was restated in terms of personal rather than social regeneration. In 1918 young Hugh Benner told an audience at Olivet that the sale of liquor was a national social problem and required federal legislation. Fourteen years later D. Shelby Corlett, executive secretary of the Nazarene Young People's Society, summoned the Wichita General Assembly to what in retrospect seems a rear-guard action in the face of the imminent return of the saloon. His major appeal was for educational campaigns aimed at securing individual abstinence.[43]

An editorial which J. B. Chapman published in the *Herald of Holiness* in 1924, entitled "An Apology for the Church of the Nazarene," was the high-water mark in the effort to make common cause with embattled fundamentalists. Those who clung to orthodox Christianity must either triumph in the great denominations, Chapman said, or withdraw. Unity was impossible between men who believed "in baptismal regeneration and a program of social and educational services" and "those who insist upon spiritual regeneration and a world-wide program of Pentecostal evangelism." Liberals, he noted, might tolerate fundamentalists, but the latter could never "cater to the doctrines and efforts of the social reformer." Chapman expressed the hope that many conservative Christians would find a home with the Nazarenes. He pointed out that the founders of the church had been liberal on questions of church polity and ordinances, but orthodox on all historic doctrinal matters. There was not "a Modernist nor a Higher Critic" among them, and they stood foursquare for a world-wide program of evangelism.[44]

As time passed, however, the gulf between Wesleyan and other kinds of fundamentalists became more apparent. J. Gresham Machen and a few of his colleagues left Princeton in 1924 to found Westminster Seminary in Philadelphia. Thereafter, in books, articles, and sermons, they strove to identify conservative Christianity with orthodox Calvinism. At the opposite extreme intellectually were the Bible schools, the traveling evangelists, and the pastors of independent "tabernacle" churches. Most of them taught, under either Southern Baptist or Plymouth Brethren influences, the doctrine of the eternal security of baptized believers. Many of them made a hobby of detailed speculations about the Second Coming. Others preached a second work of grace according to the Keswick view, declaring it to consist in an empowering for service rather than an inward cleansing and perfect love.

Meanwhile, from another point on the popular religious compass, the "Pentecostal" churches made rapid gains in both rural and urban environments. Their preachers combined Wesleyan and Keswick views by teaching that the baptism of the Holy Spirit went beyond sanctification and was in fact a "third blessing" with "signs following afterwards."

The chief among these signs was the "gift of tongues." Its possessors thought this to be a heavenly language, but outsiders saw only an emotional release of unrelated syllables. The spread of this teaching finally prompted the Nazarene General Assembly of 1919 to drop the word "Pentecostal" from the denomination's name, in order to avoid identification with the new movement. Opponents of the change argued that to do so was to surrender both a word and the memory of a crucial Christian event to those who proclaimed a gift quite different from the well-known tongues in which men heard the disciples preach at Pentecost. Certainly Nazarenes everywhere agreed that the change of name represented no surrender of their claim, as the editor of the *Herald of Holiness* put it, "to be called and recognized and distinguished as pentecostal."[45]

By the time the Nazarenes met at Columbus for their Seventh General Assembly in 1928, the challenge of all these ideas to their own traditional Wesleyan position was clear. After extensive discussion, that body adopted a new statement on the doctrine of free will. The aim was to define more clearly than the older *Manuals* had done the denomination's rejection of Calvinism. At one stage, the delegates, acting as a committee of the whole, approved a wording which affirmed boldly that man retained a "godlike ability of freedom," despite the Fall. "No decree of God, no chain of causation behind his will, no combination of elements in his constitution, compels his moral choice," the proposed statement ran; "the gracious aid of the Holy Spirit is only suasive, not necessitative." The theologians present secured approval of a more moderate wording, however. It affirmed that, on account of the Fall, man "cannot now turn and prepare himself by his own natural strength and works to faith and calling upon God." Nevertheless, "the grace of God through Jesus Christ is freely bestowed upon all men, enabling them to turn from sin to righteousness, believe on Jesus Christ for pardon and cleansing from sin, and follow good works pleasing and acceptable in His sight."[45]

Of equal significance was the assembly's careful rephrasing of the doctrine of sanctification, so as to stress their belief that it "comprehends in one experience the cleansing of the heart from sin and the abiding, indwelling presence of the Holy Spirit." The delegates also directed that no Nazarene educational institution should thereafter "employ or retain permanently in its employment any faculty member who is not in full accord with the doctrine of, and in the experience of, entire sanctification."[46] Four years later another General Assembly completed the break with fundamentalism by approving an amendment to the creed which declared that a person "in the possession of the experience of regeneration and entire sanctification may fall from grace and apostasize and, unless he repent of his sin, be hopelessly and eternally lost."[47]

Thus did events of the 1920's dictate an increasing isolation of the Nazarene denomination, not only from the older churches but from younger evangelical groups as well. In retrospect, however, the consolidation of inward loyalties provided the young church, still a tender planting, with both the shelter and sustenance which it needed to survive the wintry blasts of depression, war, and theological storm which, all unseen, lay ahead in Christendom. But when the storm had passed, the great question would be whether the flower of Christian brotherhood, of ecumenical holiness, could bloom again.

CHAPTER XIV

The Renewal of Leadership and the Resurgence of Evangelism, 1921-33

Neither the inward tensions evident in the Church of the Nazarene in the decade following World War I nor the outward challenges presented by modernism and fundamentalism were able to becloud the young denomination's vision of its future. In every department of the church's work, steady-handed leaders took the helm whenever the passage became perilous. As a result, the rank and file learned to rely on the good counsel of men like H. Orton Wiley and J. B. Chapman in the field of education and church publication, Roy T. Williams and E. J. Fleming in church administration, M. Lunn in financial and business affairs, and J. W. Goodwin and J. G. Morrison when spiritual issues were at stake. On both foreign and home missionary fields, meanwhile, a score of youthful district superintendents began turning dreams of world-wide holiness evangelism into reality.

The frankly denominational viewpoint of these new leaders undoubtedly curtailed somewhat the church's earlier dedication to the task of "Christianizing Christianity." Indeed, the loyalty and enthusiasm they inspired helped as much as doctrinal conservativism to set the movement off from American religion generally, where a postwar mood of apathy prevailed. By 1928 it was clear that the Nazarenes had determined to sail on course, regardless of how other ships in the convoy reacted to the gathering storm.

The Enlarged Role of Education in Denominational Strategy

The younger leaders believed that education was the key to the success of their plans. Far from neglecting the colleges, they persuaded the Nazarenes to enlarge their support year after year. Meanwhile the publishing house encouraged increasing emphasis upon Christian nurture through literature, and editors of Sunday school materials adapted the child-centered methods of the new "progressive" school of religious education to the task of teaching the old-time religion to the young.

James B. Chapman pointed out on one occasion that colleges were the first permanent institutions which twentieth-century Wesleyan groups established, and that their original aims had scarcely been altered through the years. Those aims, he said, were to protect young men and women from the apostasy growing in the world around them, and to raise up a holiness ministry for the church. In 1917, while serving as president of the school at Peniel, Texas, Chapman restated these objectives in terms applicable to the new situation at that institution. Peniel would no longer call itself a university, he wrote, since it never had and never could come up to such a title. Rather, it would seek to become a first-rate college, a position which he believed only one or two holiness schools in America had attained. The statement foreshadowed what was to be a thirty-year struggle for accreditation of Nazarene colleges. But the struggle was begun as part of their closer identification with denominational goals. Peniel College, Chapman declared, would follow closely the policies of the General Board of Education, shunning the dangers of local, and hence divisive, control. He regretted that an average of only 20 per cent of its students in the previous six years had prepared for the mission field or the ministry, and hoped these figures would increase.[1]

The increased exercise of vigilance against campus "worldliness" illustrates the closeness of the bond being forged between college and church. The first printing of detailed rules concerning personal behavior for students at Bresee College, Hutchinson, Kansas, in 1916, not only forbade on pain of expulsion the use of tobacco and obscene language, but prohibited also slang, chewing gum, "light and trashy literature," and "worldly songs and ragtime music." In 1922 the General Board of Education, in response to the urging of the general superintendents, resolved to oppose "undue emphasis upon athletics and competitive games" in the colleges, and the sponsorship of "dramatics and other forms of literary entertainment out of harmony with the beliefs and practices of the Church of the Nazarene." Various actions of the General Assembly the following year fully backed up these resolutions.[2]

The other side of the story was that the churches now for the first time shouldered heavy financial burdens in support of their colleges. The "victory campaign" by which H. Orton Wiley and N. B. Herrell raised the money to place the institution at Nampa on a sound footing was only one of several highly successful drives for funds. Between 1917 and 1921 the general superintendents were closely associated with similar campaigns in behalf of Olivet, Pasadena, and Eastern Nazarene colleges. They conducted rallies, wrote publicity, and preached sermons at educational services in district assemblies and conventions which helped stamp upon the Nazarene mind the idea that the future of the church was bound up with its program of higher education.[3]

J. B. Chapman's address as president of the General Board of Education in 1920 summarized thoughtfully the task ahead. Only an educated ministry could conserve and spread the Wesleyan gospel, Chapman declared. Holiness theological seminaries were not enough, however, for they got men too late to mold them. Nor would a strong Bible school and ministerial training institute provide future pastors and foreign missionaries with the solid preparation in arts and letters necessary for Christian leadership. The Nazarenes must concentrate instead on building substantial liberal arts colleges, he said, and be willing to spend money on the gymnasiums and laboratories which some thought quite unnecessary for the training of ministers.[4]

The rapidly rising prestige of the General Board of Education in the years from 1918 to 1925 enabled Chapman and his friend H. Orton Wiley to move the church decisively in the direction this address pointed. At its organization in 1917 the board authorized Wiley, as secretary, to notify the presidents and principals of all the church's educational institutions to send to the next meeting a representative who, by previous conference with their trustees or directors, would be prepared to state definitely whether or not their schools would be "placed under the direct control of the General Board of Education for the purpose of enabling that body to properly correlate the educational work of our church." They were also to bring with them for inspection by the board "the charters, Articles of Incorporation, By-laws, deeds, mortgages, and other papers of a legal nature affecting the institution."[5]

It is scarcely surprising that few representatives appeared the next year with the authorization or the documents requested.

Nevertheless, General Superintendents Reynolds and Goodwin met with Wiley, Delance Wallace, Olive Winchester, and J. B. Chapman at Portland, Oregon. The group resolved to recognize schools and colleges as belonging to the denomination only when the members of their boards of trustees were required to be Nazarenes, elected under conditions which made them responsible to the church, and when they had placed their activities under the supervision of the General Board of Education. The board also divided the church into six "educational districts," corresponding roughly to the territories now assigned to the six Nazarene colleges in the United States. Yet at that time two colleges existed in the Southeastern area and four were struggling for survival in the Southern district, comprising the states of Arkansas, Louisiana, Oklahoma, Texas, and New Mexico.[6]

Clearly, the restriction of new institutions and the merging of existing ones was the first requirement if the plan to enhance the academic status of the schools was to succeed. Fortunately a combination of circumstances, including the wartime cut in enrollments, the lack of experienced teaching and administrative personnel, and the breakdown of regional isolation through the constant interchange of evangelists and pastors, made consolidation as desirable as it was necessary.

On the eve of the General Assembly of 1919, the board issued a six-page document which explained for the first time that the educational districts were designed to sustain only one college within their bounds. Nazarenes would be free, of course, to support with funds or students a college outside their zone if they wished; but an institution enjoying official denominational sponsorship would not make systematic campaigns either for funds or students in another's territory. The board further recommended the adoption of minimal academic standards for the classification of institutions and asked authorization to summon annually a conference of school executives "to harmonize, adjust and correlate" the work.[7]

The merging of the various schools in the South proceeded rapidly. As early as 1918, E. P. Ellyson persuaded the sponsors of the Shingler Holiness College at Donalsonville, Georgia, to follow the advice of the General Board of Education and unite with Trevecca, at Nashville. In 1919 the board classified Peniel as a college, and the institutions at Hamlin, Texas, Bethany,

Oklahoma, and Des Arc, Missouri, as junior colleges. The school at Vilonia, Arkansas, retained the status of an academy only. Early in 1920 the board considered recommending that all of these unite and locate in a large city such as Dallas. But within the year, financial and other problems overwhelmed Peniel, and its leaders agreed to merge with the school at Bethany. The board promptly designated Bethany-Peniel the official senior college for the Southern district. Thus Oklahoma City rather than Dallas was destined to become the urban hub of Nazarene work in the Southwest. The sponsors of the weaker institutions at Hamlin, Vilonia, and Des Arc soon gave up their efforts to carry on alone. Only Bresee College, at Hutchinson, stood apart from the union movement. In 1940, however, both logic and financial necessity brought its students and faculty to Bethany as well.[8]

A second major problem confronting the General Board of Education was the financial one. Little progress indeed had been made in the period of local or district control. In 1922 the total estimated value of school property was $780,815, but liabilities amounted to $414,599. At their meeting that year Wiley and Chapman proposed to deal with the problem through greater centralization of authority. The board called for an allotment of $60,000 annually from the General Budget, equal to $2.00 per member, to be administered at their discretion on the basis of the church membership within each educational district. Although the general superintendents in their address to the quadrennial assembly the next year did not go that far, they did propose that the Board of Education be given a voice in framing the operating budget and planning the expansion program of each institution. The schools must no longer be allowed "to involve themselves heavily in debt and consequently bring disrepute and dishonor upon the church at large," they declared. But the church for its part must support them better. The growing demand for standardization and accreditation only magnified this necessity. "We must get out of debt and we must stay out of debt," the superintendents concluded. "It is better for us to do what we can and do it with honor than to undertake the impossible and end in disgrace."[9]

These proposals came, however, at the moment when the denomination's national activities were being placed under a single General Board, to which the Board of Education was subsidiary. The result was to reverse the tendency toward centralizing financial and administrative direction of the colleges. Regional control and support, however, rather than local or district, became the rule. Boards of trustees elected by all the district assemblies in a given college zone became the focal points of the effort to sustain and relate to denominational objectives the church's program of higher education. In this effort the influence of the district superintendents, who were almost always elected to these boards, was paramount.

The Inner Life of the College Communities

Meanwhile, local circumstances within each college community worked steadily to fasten loyalties more closely to the denomination, and to diminish contacts with the world outside. Bethany and Olivet were thoroughly Nazarene villages from the beginning, of course. In them college, church, and "public" school shared common purposes with the homes of the community. The nearest theaters were miles away; the sale even of tobacco was forbidden, and dancing and drinking were known only as sins of great cities reported in the daily newspapers. Similarly Nampa, whose population was large enough to sustain sizable congregations of many denominations, was still small enough for the Nazarene group to feel that their part of town, at least, was their own. As moral and religious confusion grew in the world beyond, these communities became sheltered retreats, in which educators hoped to train a force strong enough to seize and hold some major outposts against a brighter day. Real estate promotions helped both to provide the colleges with funds and to attract families to live in the villages around them.[10]

At both Eastern Nazarene College and Pasadena, financial needs combined with basic religious commitments to forestall any tendency toward identification with the urban communities in which they were situated.

Repeated acts of personal sacrifice by ordinary New England laymen had made possible the purchase of a new campus for the eastern institution at Wollaston, on the south shore of Boston Bay, in 1919. The deed to the school's property was then for the first time assigned to trustees who officially represented the Church of the Nazarene. Similar financial support made possible its steady growth thereafter under Presidents **Fred J.**

Shields and Floyd Nease, both of whom had graduated from Pasadena during Wiley's first administration there. Not for many decades did the college receive any noteworthy contributions from the local community, and it never attracted large sums from wealthy donors.[11]

Pasadena's problems were more severe, due to the loss of confidence of so many during the troubles of 1916 and 1917. General Superintendent Walker himself accepted the presidency of the institution in the fall of the latter year, after a grandiose scheme based upon promised support of an interested millionaire fell through. Of a total debt of $260,000 at that time, $111,000 was unsecured. The bank holding the mortgage on the property had already begun foreclosure proceedings. The Southern California District launched a campaign in June, 1917, to raise $100,000. Subscribers to this fund engaged to form a corporation which would purchase the mortgage from the bank and liquidate the debt. The committee in charge was Walker, Howard Eckel, E. A. Girvin, C. E. Roberts, A. O. Hendricks, and F. L. Winn, treasurer and business manager of the school. Hendricks seems to have held title to the property personally for a time; indeed, he carried a crushing burden of responsibility for the next five years. But growing numbers of ordinary church members made substantial annual gifts.

In 1926, Wiley returned to take charge at Pasadena, but financial matters improved very little. His friend and admirer, Orval J. Nease, succeeded him in the presidency in 1928. Nease constructed the administration building through an incredible loan arrangement, but laymen of moderate means kept sacrificing year by year to bring the college through. When President Wiley returned from a tour of duty as editor of the *Herald of Holiness* in 1933, only six girls were living in the dormitory and the current debt amounted to $135,000. But the great depression merely crystallized a situation already in existence. Throughout the twenty years of struggle which followed the crisis of 1917, the hopes of Pasadena rested in a marriage both spiritual and financial to the mission of the church. The marriage was helped along, of course, by the fact that the Rees secession had drawn off many of a more independent turn of mind. But hard necessity lay back of the announcement in 1918 that the college would henceforth be even more fully dedicated "to the teaching of those distinctive religious principles set forth in the *Manual* of the Pentecostal Church of the Nazarene."[12]

Similar financial troubles plagued Olivet College, despite the fact that this institution was relatively unaffected by the controversies which afflicted the church at large during the period. Here, indeed, the problems seem to have been local. A procession of presidents changed office almost annually until 1926, when T. W. Willingham, youthful pastor of a flourishing church in nearby Danville, assumed the office which no one else seemed to want. In a manner reminiscent of Wiley's early work at Nampa, Dr. Willingham combined business acumen, personal integrity, and spiritual leadership to place the school on firmer ground.[13]

By contrast with all the others, Trevecca College sought throughout these years to maintain its former interdenominational sources of support in the city of Nashville. As in J. O. McClurkan's time, the principal sponsors considered Trevecca's work both a social and educational ministry to the poor, and solicited funds for it on that basis. The result proved almost disastrous.

McClurkan's school, like his paper, legally had been a private venture, operated in the name of the Pentecostal Mission by a small board of trustees who were members of the Nashville congregation. When the founder died in 1914, Trevecca was heavily in debt. Instead of turning the institution over to the Church of the Nazarene, the trustees continued to operate for several years under the old arrangement. President C. E. Hardy, a medical doctor and preacher, was the dominant figure for nearly two decades. For brief periods in 1919-20 and 1925-28, Stephen S. White and A. O. Hendricks assumed the presidency. Neither, however, proved able to unite fully the local with the denominational aims and control. Even when, under Hendricks, some financial progress was made, the generosity of Nashville patrons provided the margin of survival, enabling H. H. Wise, McClurkan's successor in the Nashville pastorate, and other local figures to keep a firm hand upon even the smallest details of the school's administration.[14]

The depression which began in 1929 dried up the flow of funds from both the Nashville churches and the local community. Bills for fuel and groceries went unpaid, and the college was faced with bankruptcy. Dr. Hardy proposed to reorganize under a new charter, and to purchase the campus of what had once been a Baptist college for Negroes, in South Nashville. A series of lawsuits, one by faculty members for unpaid salaries, delayed the move, but the new corporation, called the Southeastern Educational Board of the Church of the Nazarene, finally got the institution under way at the new location in 1932. When the students appeared, however, they found that the furniture had been retained by court order at the old site. They slept on the floor for a time, and studied and prayed until interested friends carted in beds and chairs enough to furnish the dormitory rooms. Since Nashville men remained as much in control of the new as of the old corporation, pastors and district superintendents elsewhere inevitably wondered whether the denomination's interests had really become paramount. In that first year on the new campus, however, there came to the faculty a tall, gaunt young man from the Kentucky hills, named A. B. Mackey. His patience and persistence through the years ahead enabled the churches of the southeast Atlantic states to make the school their own.[15]

By the time of the General Assembly of 1928, the Board of Education was able to report an increase of $340,845 in the value of property belonging to the colleges, and a decrease in indebtedness of $135,217. Although total enrollment in the several institutions had decreased, this was chiefly due to the reduction of elementary school and academy programs. The number in college departments had risen steadily, establishing a trend which was to continue even during the depression ahead. Moreover, practically all of the schools had operated without a deficit in current expenses throughout the preceding four years.

The report made a point of attributing the absence of doctrinal differences among the Nazarenes to their educational system. "That we are not rent and torn by discussions of modernism and fundamentalism," they said, "is due to the fact that the colleges are true to the fundamental tenets of our church." What gave such a statement weight, however, was the growing confidence of the rank and file in the wisdom and integrity of educators like Fred Shields, A. O. Hendricks, Bertha Munro, C. A. McConnell, Olive M. Winchester, H. Orton Wiley, and the brothers Floyd and Orval Nease. A new generation had proved its ability to carry out, with some change of perspective, to be sure, the educational vision of the church's founders.[16]

Christian Education in Local Congregations

The history of the church's educational program is only half told, however, until we point out the influence during this period of the Sunday schools, the young people's societies, and the periodicals which the people read.

Remarkably enough, the decade of the 1920's, which saw conservatives in older denominations battling furiously with modernists over the relative claims of religious education and evangelism, witnessed the Nazarenes laying the foundations of a thoughtful program of Sunday school work. Here, again, denominational loyalty dictated an enlarged role for education. The key figure was E. P. Ellyson, elected chief editor of Sunday school publications at the General Assembly of 1923. Ellyson's report to the Columbus Assembly in 1928 tells the story well. In the five years since 1922, he noted, enrollment had gained 12,865 a year, a rate of nearly 16 per cent annually. The publishing house had circulated during these years over 9,000,000 pieces of literature. The General Sunday School Committee had adopted graded lessons suited to the needs of young children, instituted a program of teacher training in local churches, published a booklet to guide in the establishment of vacation Bible schools, and laid out a complete program for general, district, and local church school board organization.

The denomination could not escape responsibility for the religious education of its children, Ellyson declared. "The rush of business and society" had so changed the character of home life that the church must fill a larger place in the lives of the young. Even in the most religious households family prayer and an orderly program of Bible study were proving difficult to maintain. Ellyson discussed with complete frankness the fears that Sunday school literature might become, as in some older communions, "the open door of modernism into the church." The preparation of Nazarene graded lessons was in fact necessary, he believed, because the International Council of Religious Education was about to release a new graded course "built on the theory that . . . ideal character can be formed without the supernatural work of divine grace in any crisis experiences." The editor thus urged the church to answer unsound teaching not with ignorance but by education which was both efficient and orthodox. The assembly, needless to say, gave this report and its various recommendations wholehearted approval, and directed that the Sunday School Committee continue to operate separately from the General Board so as to reach its fullest usefulness.[17]

The formation of the General Nazarene Young People's Society during these years provided similar centralized planning and promotion for local Sunday evening fellowships, regional rallies, and, later on, summer camps. With the strong encouragement of General Superintendent R. T. Williams, a committee of interested youth leaders drew up a proposed constitution for a national organization, and distributed it to district assemblies and local societies prior to the General Assembly of 1923. Although young people's work had long held an important place in the programs of the oldest congregations, sharp debate greeted the plan. The General Assembly finally voted to ask a committee headed by Donnell J. Smith to bring in a revised constitution. A week later, when the committee's report was read, a second round of searching discussion preceded its adoption. Active membership in local societies was limited to those who were full members of a local church, and hence subject to the discipline of the *Manual*. All activities were to be under the supervision of the pastor and the church board. The constitution specified devotional, evangelistic, missionary, and visiting committees, but pointedly left out all reference to the social functions which, everywhere, were inevitably a part of teen-age work. Assured thus of its close tie to the church, the assembly gave the new organization its approval. The first General N.Y.P.S. Convention, held the same week, elected D. Shelby Corlett executive secretary, an office which he filled for the next thirteen years. His close association with the denomination's leaders and his persistence in preaching on the theme of entire sanctification at youth gatherings all over the nation eliminated all but a fragment of the old doubts as to the wisdom of a national organization of young people's work.[18]

That the youth program had caught the imagination of the church at large, however, was a fact already evident from the statistics. In the five years preceding 1920, membership in young people's societies increased nearly 70 per cent, while church membership advanced only 11 per cent. In the succeeding eight years, while church membership doubled, that of the youth organization multiplied almost five times. At the end of 1927 the local societies contained more than a third as many members as the church itself, and by 1933 over 43 per cent as many. Clearly, the Nazarenes were building a youth-centered denomination.[19]

Family discipline, nevertheless, remained an important channel by which children were taught the way of holiness, particularly in the homes of ministers. In this decade, and even long after youth and children's camps had become commonplace, pastors generally took their youngsters to the district camp meeting with them. There, intensified family worship combined with children's hours, "ring meetings" for personal testimonies, and long altar services to stamp the fear of sin, death, and judgment deep on impressionable minds, and to give boys and girls images of saintliness beyond those they saw in their parents upon which to try to model their lives. In local congregations as well, families from village and countryside attended revival meetings together. They also went as a unit to missionary rallies, prayer meetings, and Sunday school. The organization of life according to age-groups had not yet greatly affected the plain people, even in large towns. Their children worked hard at "chores" and looked forward to a trip to "meeting" as a release from drudgery. Not only the music and informal atmosphere there, but the sermons as well, could usually be counted on to interest young people. They may have appealed by turns to fear or sentiment, but they were never dull. A preacher with two rows of children seated across the front of a church or camp meeting shed could not afford to get lost in logical abstractions. This is one reason why the denomination's evangelists became famous above everything else as tellers of "true life" stories with a spiritual point.[20]

Looking back across the development of Nazarene education during these years, one is struck anew by the inadequacy of the view current among sociologists that religious education is a "churchly" activity, while its absence is a mark of sectarianism. Zeal for learning may, indeed, in the church as well as the nation, reflect a determination to preserve an older heritage as well as to cultivate broader outlooks. The leaders of the Church of the Nazarene clearly thought education a device for building the inward strength necessary to resist pressures from without. Their success, in country Sunday schools no less than college classes, goes far to explain the recovery of momentum in the young denomination in the period between the two world wars. Nazarene education and evangelism were "true yoke-fellows," E. P.

Ellyson wrote in the *Bible School Journal* in 1936, hitched like faithful oxen to the same load, pulling together to redeem lost men.[21]

The Committee System of General Church Administration

Successful voluntary associations require a clear pattern of organization, and one which strikes a rough balance between the claims of democracy and efficiency. In religious movements, however, local congregations tend to lean heavily toward democracy, and pastors toward all which preserves their individual freedom of action. When a denomination grows from grass-roots origins, as did the Church of the Nazarene, this bent toward independent judgment may greatly retard the growth of the framework of law and custom necessary to efficient operation of general programs. The result is often confusion and estrangement between local churches and their denominational leaders. It is not surprising, therefore, that the administration of the national foreign missionary, publishing, and educational ventures during the church's first ten years was so imperfect. What is remarkable is that the Nazarenes were able to correct so many of the weaknesses during the stormy years from 1918 to 1925, when independency contended openly with the drive toward centralization. The event was proof that the heritage of discipline, of organization, from Wesley was as virile as that of holiness.

Until 1919 the General Boards of Publication, Education, and Foreign Missions carried on their work quite independently of one another, each being responsible only to the quadrennial General Assembly. Campaigns for funds or the scheduling of regional conventions frequently conflicted, giving an impression of competition among groups whose objectives were or ought to have been the same. In many cases the policies of these boards were neither approved by the general superintendents nor communicated adequately to district leaders. Yet the direct relationship of these men with local churches made their support of critical importance.[22]

The problems of the Board of Publication illustrate the extent of the confusion. Ten years after the establishment of the central publishing house the enterprise was still operating on faith, rather than capital. In 1918, in its customary frank statement of its affairs to the church, the board noted a staggering annual loss of $20,000, most of it stemming from the publication at less than cost of the *Herald of Holiness* and the missionary paper, the *Other Sheep*. Even when subscription lists were assigned an inflated value of $20,000 in the statement of assets, the institution had no net worth at all. Although the General Assembly of 1915 had authorized a campaign to raise $50,000 capital for the business, and a "world-wide, hallelujah march" offering on March 28, 1917, did bring in $35,000 of that amount, special fund-raising drives could not offset continued losses of these dimensions. A famous "Christmas love offering" in 1919, promoted heartily by the general superintendents, merely served to postpone the day of reckoning.[23]

By contrast, the problems of the General Board of Foreign Missions were not financial but administrative. The crux of the matter was the absence of a real executive officer empowered to carry forward throughout the year the policies laid down at annual meetings. Instead, the entire group endeavored each year to tend to the accumulated details of administration. They listened interminably to letters on minor matters and passed specific resolutions on individual purchases of small significance. Both E. G. Anderson, the general treasurer, and H. F. Reynolds, the general superintendent charged specially with overseeing foreign enterprises, made extensive separate reports and recommendations. Both insisted that the board must act on every item. Even when that group had acted, however, neither of these two could wield executive authority—Reynolds because he was reluctant to assume prerogatives which would set him above the other general superintendents, and Anderson because he had to work with Dr. Reynolds, rather than simply under the board.[24]

The reaction against a strong superintendency which the Rees affair provoked made it difficult for the General Assembly of 1919 to increase executive authority at any point, despite the plea of the presiding officers for more "system" in the church's work. Instead, the power of decision was spread out even more widely among boards and committees. The Board of Education, for example, was granted its every wish, while individual general superintendents were required henceforth to act in concert with their colleagues in many important matters. The assembly turned down the proposal of the Board of Foreign Missions that they be allowed to appoint and direct the activities of a general superintendent for overseas work. The board succeeded, however, in making E. G. Anderson both treasurer and executive secretary.

This reduced somewhat General Superintendent Reynolds' prerogative, but did little to create a responsible executive. Meanwhile the assembly gave final sanction to the national organization of the Woman's Foreign Missionary Society, a proposal which had won initial approval in 1915. This added another wheel to the machinery but no new gears.[25]

Far from simplifying the work of other national boards, the General Assembly added a General Orphanage Board and authorized it, under President Theodore Ludwig's direction, to raise $100,000 to establish a central institution for the care of homeless children. It also approved the plan of the General Board of Church Extension to employ a full-time secretary to raise gifts and loans to use in financing church building projects—this despite the fact that during several years of effort the group had accumulated only a little over $4,000.[26] The delegates also created a new Board of Home Missions and Evangelism, composed of L. Milton Williams, president, and several aggressive district superintendents, including N. B. Herrell, U. E. Harding, and C. B. Jernigan. Although the assembly refused to authorize a full-time general field secretary, one of the earliest actions of the new board was to divide up the country into six zones, somewhat as the General Board of Education had done, and appoint a field secretary for each. These officers were to be empowered to spend, under the direction of the national group, one-half of the home mission funds raised within their respective zones. The obvious confusion of authority with that of district superintendents prompted immediate protests, however, so the plan never really got off the ground.[27]

More promising was the assembly's action requiring all the general boards to meet annually in a joint session designed to correlate their activities. In obedience to this order, the first meeting of what inevitably came to be called the "corrugated boards" assembled in February, 1920. A committee on organization recommended that the approval of the whole body be required for any programs which might be "construed as affecting the entire church," and proposed that all financial plans be scrutinized by a general ways and means committee. These recommendations were politely referred to the separate boards for their consideration. The result was vigorous opposition, especially from those finding it easiest to raise money. A commission consisting of the general superintendents and one member

THE RENEWAL OF LEADERSHIP 337

from each board was granted power to approve all financial campaigns, but the adoption of a general budget was deferred. One thoughtful resolution urged all district superintendents to attend this annual gathering. The next year these officers were granted full membership. But their enthusiasm could scarcely have been great in the face of the continued insistence of the General Board of Home Missions that its plan to spend one-half of all the money which districts raised for that purpose would help the church keep its "connectional spirit" as well as strengthen "weaker and smaller districts."[28]

Soon, however, a harrowing series of financial crises gave the general superintendents an opportunity to assert the great but dormant powers of their position and to develop the systematic organization of the church's business which they had long believed necessary.

R. T. Williams and the Forming of the General Board

The day before the boards gathered for their meeting of 1922, the group responsible for publishing affairs asked the general superintendents to meet with them and pledge their help in a new drive for desperately needed funds. The facts proved so appalling, however, that the superintendents refused their aid unless the board would consent to allow them to appoint a committee of three men—John T. Benson, F. M. Messenger, and E. G. Anderson—to take charge of the business entirely. Not, in fact, until the Correlated Boards gave the superintendents "full authority to act . . . in all matters pertaining to the management and expenses of every department of the Publishing House" did they agree to mount one last campaign to pay off the debt of over $100,000. Led by R. T. Williams, the superintendents first persuaded a young accountant named M. Lunn, an employee since 1913, to accept the position of general manager. Soon afterward, when three permanent members of the Board of Publication resigned, the presiding officers promptly nominated Anderson, Messenger, and one of their own number, John W. Goodwin, to replace them.

Under these circumstances the "victory campaign" understandably got off to a slow start. Only $30,000.00 came in the first year; but all of this sum was paid on old bills. By February, 1923, the financial statement looked respectable enough, though the listed assets still included a good many uncollectable accounts and much outdated merchandise. The superintendents pressed ahead, however, ably assisted by Lunn, who operated the house at a profit and collected thousands of dollars due from churches. By the time the delegates met for the General Assembly of 1923, the total debt of $115,346.86 had been paid in full.[29]

The other general boards, however, proved as unwilling as ever to give up control over their affairs. Thus in 1922, when E. A. Girvin presented plans for an executive committee to direct the work of the Correlated Boards, the groups in charge of foreign missions, home missions, and education turned thumbs down. Save for his initial victory in the publishing house matter, therefore, Dr. Williams had to content himself that year with powerful speeches stressing the importance of economy in church administration.[30]

By September, 1923, when the General Assembly met in Kansas City, a new kind of financial crisis enabled the superintendents to persuade the delegates to meet the issues head on. The assembly demolished with one blow the Boards of Home Missions, Foreign Missions, Publication, and Church Extension, and took away all discretionary authority over financial matters from other boards as well. These powers were then placed in the hands of six ministers and six laymen, elected at large, to serve under the chairmanship of the Board of General Superintendents in what was first called a General Council, soon renamed the General Board. The new board met at once and drew up a departmental organization of its work under which all final decisions were to be made by the whole group. It ordered all the bodies which it was displacing to turn over their assets, records, deeds, and other documents, and made the office of General Church Secretary E. J. Fleming its clearinghouse. Fleming's fine touch for administration smoothed the way for the reorganization at every step; thereafter he made certain that communication was full and deliberation possible on every issue.[31]

Here, then, was formed for the first time a tightly knit system of carrying on the denominational program. The general superintendents now possessed a constitutional means of exerting the full weight of their influence. They had produced from their own ranks a fearless and resourceful leader, R. T. Williams. Moreover, they had taught the church to rely on the sound business sense of leading laymen in order to halt the recurrent plunges into insolvency.

But the occasion of this reform was a sad one for the church's leaders. For nearly a decade the investment of various trust and annuity funds belonging to the Boards of Foreign Missions and of Publication had been left in the hands of Secretary-Treasurer E. G. Anderson. Although a small committee was charged with advising him, the investments were not adequately supervised or reported. On the eve of the General Assembly of 1923, news leaked out of what came to be called the "North Dakota land deal," a speculation involving wheatlands allegedly worth $200,000 to $300,000. Church funds had been invested in this scheme, secured by both the land and the personal notes of L. Milton Williams, who at the time of the transaction had been chairman of the Board of Home Missions and Evangelism.

A succession of investigations and explanations made during 1924 and 1925 produced sympathy and understanding, but only partial vindication of those involved. From Bethany, Oklahoma, C. A. McConnell finally wrote his friend, R. T. Williams, what proved to be the sentiments of the church at large. "My dear boy," McConnell began,

> It seems to me that there is just the same need for our entire church as there was for the Publishing House when you had the supreme courage to take hold of that situation. I mean that you and you alone must pray through on a plan and then take hold of the situation and work it out as you did with the Publishing House. . . . I am confident that we shall make the most dismal failure in Church history if we do not put an end once and for all to these big deficits. . . . Suspend every benevolence that asks for a dollar, close half of the mission stations, base our budget not on paper memberships of women and children, but on paying members, and then go in to sell the Budget to the local churches.[32]

Dr. Williams responded to this challenge with the vigor which in succeeding years made his name synonymous with firm leadership. Not only was the administration of foreign missions totally reorganized, as we shall see in a moment, but at a meeting in September, 1925, M. Lunn was elected general church treasurer in Anderson's place. Characteristically, Lunn accepted only after the General Board had approved policies he proposed calling for full publicity regarding every phase of finances, strict control of the rate of expenditure of the funds allotted annually to the various departments, including especially that of foreign missions, and a clear definition of the treasurer's responsibility.³³ At the General Assembly of 1928, Dr. Williams laid the whole matter before the church once more, and amidst considerable enthusiasm raised pledges of $109,000 to eliminate the deficit in missionary trust funds.

An indirect outcome of the affair was the achievement of a more effective management of the foreign missionary program. At first, however, the irregularities involved in the "land deal" gave the advantage to those who wished to decentralize the administration of overseas work. The General Assembly of 1923 directed that the General Board elect three superintendents to reside on foreign soil, one for each of three "zones"—Africa and the Near East, the Orient, and Latin America. The board chose George Sharpe, of the British Isles, for the first of these, J. E. Bates for the second, and J. D. Scott for the third. In informal discussions the board agreed that these men should, in the words of J. W. Goodwin, "be clothed with all authority on the field, [and] be free to formulate field policies, which are to be reported to the Board of General Superintendents."

The problem of administration was not solved, however, by simply transferring the responsibilities of the old foreign missionary board to the Board of General Superintendents. What was needed was a single administrator in the homeland with ample authority to carry out agreed-upon policies. Whether he did this through three missionary superintendents or through a dozen men responsible for individual fields was an important but a secondary issue. Undoubtedly the Board of General Superintendents would have allowed E. G. Anderson such authority in practice had not the fateful disclosures of that year intervened.

The economy drive which followed on the heels of these events brought the experiment in missionary superintendency to an end almost before it began, however. At this point Joseph G. Morrison was called from Northwest Nazarene College to become general secretary of foreign missions. He served directly under the General Board, in consultation with the general superintendents. Abroad, district superintendents chosen from among the missionaries on each national field became second in command to the general secretary in Kansas City. Although Dr. Morrison was preoccupied with raising the funds needed to keep mission stations alive during a period of retrenchment and, after 1930, of financial disaster, when he left office in 1936 to become a general superintendent the principal elements necessary for an efficient administration of the church's overseas program had been developed.

The cost was great, however. And it weighed heaviest upon the missionaries themselves, to whom financial stringency became a way of life. Twenty-nine missionaries were recalled in the year 1926, and the operating budget cut by over one-third. Many of those who stayed on dipped into their scanty personal funds in order to keep alive mission posts and dispensary projects which the general church could no longer fully support.[34]

Thus it was that out of trying times there emerged a group of young men whose powers of leadership became an inspiration to the church for the next two decades. At the moment when the publishing house bordered on bankruptcy, James B. Chapman accepted the editorship of the *Herald of Holiness,* and M. Lunn became manager of the business itself. In succeeding years Brother Lunn added to his load the heavy burdens of the general treasurership, and Chapman founded the *Preacher's Magazine,* a journal which he was to edit with distinction until long after his election to the general superintendency in 1928.[35] Meanwhile, E. J. Fleming introduced the order and efficiency necessary for continuous communication between members of the General Board, the general and district superintendents, and the church at large. And J. G. Morrison labored amidst great handicaps to give the foreign missions the kind of supervision which H. F. Reynolds had aimed at during the first years following the union of 1908. All these men took office in a period when the denomination had declared war on bureaucracy and waste. All had a passion for efficiency. They believed that through hard work and sound operation small staffs could get major tasks done. Standing alongside a group of general superintendents who had at last found ways to assert their influence, they each made important contributions to the spiritual rejuvenation which was taking place throughout the denomination.

Evangelism at Home and Abroad

On both home and foreign missionary fields the years between 1921 and 1933 witnessed the emergence of a corps of able district leaders as well. These men thereafter bore the brunt of the denomination's campaign to plant holiness churches around the world.

In many ways the most fascinating story of superintendents of overseas districts was that of Harmon Schmelzenbach, who pioneered Nazarene work in Swaziland, a British protectorate near the southeastern coast of Africa. Like two others whom we shall discuss—Roger Winans in Peru, and Richard B. Anderson in Guatemala—Schmelzenbach began his career as a "faith" missionary, without regular denominational support. He sailed from New York early in May, 1907, and spent his first year in South Africa with the independent White Holiness Mission at Port Elizabeth. At the end of the year he married a young woman who had come over with another party of missionaries on the same boat.

Not until February, 1909, did Schmelzenbach receive word that his home church at Peniel, Texas, had joined the Nazarene denomination. Another eighteen months passed before he received approval from the Nazarene foreign missionary board to move into Swaziland, an appointment which, however, carried no assurance of financial support. The young couple had already mastered the language of the Zulu tribesmen when, late in the year 1910 (which in South Africa, of course, is springtime), they ventured into the rugged mountain country which was to be their home for the rest of their lives. After an agonizing delay in getting permission to work in the country, they settled at a station which they named Peniel.[36]

Schmelzenbach then set out in earnest to break the hold of the witch doctors over the minds of the tribesmen. He mastered a medical book which a missionary friend had given him for a wedding present, and fixed up a small kit containing castor oil, Epsom salts, quinine, calomel, homemade ointments for sores and burns, and forceps for extracting teeth. At the beginning, he had only the patients whom the tribal practitioners had given up to die. But as the knowledge of the missionary's "Jesus medicine" spread, more and more natives accepted care, and a few, by 1914, accepted Christ as well. Meanwhile Schmelzenbach established a reputation for great courage, a virtue highly regarded in this primitive society. He trained one of his first native converts for the ministry, and placed him in charge of an outstation. When the man was unfairly persecuted, Schmelzenbach appeared at the native "trial" before the elders of the village, outwaited and outwitted the chief, and then appealed dramatically to the queen herself for protection for his men.

As years went by, the Swazi mission grew, more from feverish labor than from large financial investment. In 1925 a new day dawned. The British government, anxious to bring doctors to the Zulu tribes, offered the Nazarenes thirty-five acres of land near Bremersdorp for a hospital. In May of the same year, David Hynd, a recent graduate of the medical school at Glasgow University, came to invest his life in medical missions in South Africa. Hynd had married Agnes Kanema Sharpe, daughter of the founder of the Church of the Nazarene in Scotland, who was serving at the time as superintendent of overseas work in Africa and the Near East. Three days after these two courageous young people arrived on the bare hilltop where they were to establish a center of healing, Hynd himself lay seemingly at death's door with a raging fever, diagnosed as paratyphoid. He recovered soon, however, and within a few months had begun the erection of the Raleigh Fitkin Memorial Hospital. Two of Schmelzenbach's first converts gave the young doctor invaluable aid, Peter Dlamini as his interpreter and James Malambe as pastor of the native congregation at Bremersdorp. By 1930, Hynd had already graduated a class of nurses and was promoting the acceptance of native South Africans into medical schools without discrimination on account of their race. His hospital and outstation dispensaries were then treating over 30,000 patients a year.[37]

By 1928, Schmelzenbach's churches contained 800 Swazi members in full standing. A like number were candidates on probation, undergoing the long period of testing imposed upon native Christians. In 1933 these figures had practically doubled. Twenty-six missionaries were then serving under Nazarene appointment in Swaziland, including young men like C. S. Jenkins and W. C. Esselstyn, both of whom were to serve in turn as district superintendents and leaders in Bible school work.[38]

Meanwhile, in the equally forbidding mountains of northern Guatemala, in Central America, a determined group of missionaries was making similar progress. First on the field was Richard S. Anderson, a representative of McClurkan's Pentecostal Mission. Anderson spent the year 1907 at Coban, in the center of the coffee-growing district of Verapaz. Here he began to study the art of printing, and issued that year the first numbers of *El Christiano*, a periodical which for nearly forty years was the organ of Nazarene evangelism in Spanish-speaking lands. He struggled almost alone until 1915, however, hampered by uncertainties about the future of the Pentecostal Mission. By 1920 reinforcements had come from the United States and the success of the mission was assured. Typical of the new helpers was Eugenia Phillips, a graduate of Pasadena College, who arrived in 1917. In 1921, Miss Phillips established the Nazarene Bible Training School, chiefly to educate native ministers. She served as its director during three long periods, the last one ending in 1944.[39]

In Mexico, where foreign missionaries were forbidden to preach after the revolution of 1912, Dr. V. G. Santin, a citizen of the country and a medical doctor, drew together a flourishing congregation in Mexico City. In 1919, Santin became the first national minister to be appointed superintendent of a Nazarene mission field. He set out promptly, with the encouragement and advice of J. D. Scott and General Superintendent John W. Goodwin, to reopen the missions southward in Chiapas province which had been closed seven years before. By the end of 1927, 11 national pastors reported that their 12 congregations contained 745 members—almost as many as the mission field in Africa could count, despite the fact that only Dr. Santin was under regular appointment by the General Board.[40]

The missionary story which in later years caught the imagination of the denomination, however, was that of Roger and Esther Carson Winans, who first took Christianity to the headhunting Aguaruna Indians of northwestern Peru. Winans and his first wife had early sought appointment as Nazarene missionaries, but were unsuccessful. In 1912, heeding Dr. H. F. Reynolds' admonition that if God had called them they must go anyway, they ventured first by faith into Mexico. Soon excluded from that country, they made their way in 1914 to the seacoast town of Pacasmayo, Peru. Here Winans supported himself by teaching English and selling Bibles, part of the time as an agent of the British and Foreign Bible Society. Meanwhile he set his heart upon opening a mission to the Aguarunas.

In February, 1917, Winans was at last appointed as the first Nazarene missionary to Peru. He began work at once in Pacasmayo, and received from the start a favorable response from both other missionaries and the people of the country. The next year two young women, Esther Carson and Mable Park, were sent out to assist him, and other denominations turned over several stations to him, notably one at Monsefu, where the Bible school was begun. Mrs. Winans, however, passed away in 1918, leaving two small boys. Misses Carson and Park now had to care for the boys as well as get the school under way, while the superintendent traveled the field and made plans for the advancement of the work. In December, 1919, Esther Carson became the second Mrs. Winans, and a year later her own baby was born, adding both care and joy to her missionary adventure.[41]

Esther Carson had been one of the most beloved students at Pasadena College during Wiley's first presidency there. She had proceeded to the University of California to study languages before joining Wiley as a teacher and student at Northwest Nazarene College, in Nampa. Lithe of body and spirit, and blessed with an abundant sense of humor, she brought to her missionary task the same enthusiasm for work and study which her friends had observed in college days. She early caught Winans' vision of taking the gospel to the Aguarunas. After several years of planning, therefore, she and her husband gave up the superintendency of the Spanish missions in Peru and departed for the headwaters of the Amazon, across the Andes Mountains to the east.

The young mother lived barely two and one-half years among the Aguaruna tribe, and these were split by a year of furlough to America. She died in November, 1928, two days after the birth of her second child. In this period, however, she prepared an elementary grammar of their language and wrote out a group of Bible stories, in a paraphrase of the Gospel of Luke which she intended to be the basis for a later translation of the New Testament. It remained for her husband, staggered now the second time by the loss of a companion and helper, to finish the work of translation and win the Aguarunas to the Christian faith.[42]

Meanwhile, in the Orient, two other superintendents distinguished themselves, L. S. Tracy in western India, and W. A. Eckel, in Japan. Both gave first attention to the development of a national church and ministry. Eckel built the Japanese mission on the shoulders of three Japanese preachers who had been converted in America and educated at the college in Pasadena. Mr. and Mrs. J. I. Nagamatsu arrived in Fukuchiyama in 1913 with Miss Cora Snider. The Nagamatsus stayed on after Miss Snider's return the next year to make their ten Sunday schools and their weekday kindergarten beloved to hundreds of Japanese children. Hiroshi Kitagawa went to Japan late in 1914 with Mr and Mrs. M. B. Staples. He founded at once and taught for many years the Bible school at Kumamoto, from which several able native pastors graduated. Kitagawa eventually became the first national superintendent of the Japanese churches. The third member of the trio was N. Isayama, who had been Eckel's interpreter for two years at the Japanese mission in Los Angeles before accompanying him to the Orient in 1915. First at Kure, then at Kyoto and elsewhere, Isayama was right-hand man to both Eckel and Kitagawa. Although by 1932 Eckel was the only foreign missionary under regular appointment in Japan, and he spent part of his time teaching in the public schools, General Superintendents Williams and Goodwin found the twenty-five organized churches there thriving under native leadership. They recommended strongly that building an indigenous national church on every field should be the cornerstone of Nazarene missionary policy.

In China a larger missionary force was able to establish a foothold in an area stretching 125 miles through western Shantung and Hopei provinces. Bresee Memorial Hospital, completed in 1932 under the direction of C. J. Kinne, son-in-law of Dr. Bresee, provided a strong basis for further progress. By the time the Chinese mission could resolve a group of frustrating inner problems, however, the Japanese invasion threatened, and the stability of the native church was in doubt.[43]

On most of their mission fields the Nazarenes, like the Methodists before them, found the camp meeting an institution easily adapted to evangelism in agrarian societies, whether primitive or civilized. In Swaziland, in Guatemala, in China, and in India the annual gathering in an open grove attracted large crowds of new Christians. Doubtless the informality of the atmosphere hastened the development of native spiritual leaders as well, both lay and ministerial. Susan B. Fitkin told of visiting a "great people's meeting, out under the shining moon" on the island of Barbados in 1928. Four hundred persons stood in an oval ring, singing and clapping, swaying to the rhythm of the music. The testimonies, the weeping, and the joy, she said, particularly when the group turned to singing songs about heaven, made her feel at home. "It was a real American Camp Meeting off the little narrow Barbados street," she wrote; "at the close, three young men knelt and gave their hearts to God, adding the crowning touch of glory to that wonderful service."[44]

Medical missions, by contrast, were a new venture, prompted by the needs which missionaries faced on the fields themselves. In 1932 the General Assembly heard a detailed report by J. G. Morrison, E. J. Fleming, and Mervel Lunn summarizing their study of the church's overseas hospitals, dispensaries, and clinics, and the related work of the Missionary Sanitarium and Institute at Nampa, Idaho. The report undertook to answer the questions raised by those who wondered whether medical missions might supplant evangelism, and social ministries take the place of spiritual. These trusted leaders recommended, nonetheless, that as soon as the weight of the depression was past, the church should declare itself firmly in favor of medical missions, but at the same time look for safeguards "to prevent professional healing from displacing salvation usefulness in the conduct and equipment of these institutions."[45]

The foundation of the growing program of missions abroad, however, was laid in the work of a new generation of district superintendents who began bringing to fruition Bresee's vision of establishing a holiness church in every town and city of the United States. In the Midwest, E. O. Chalfant, of the Chicago Central District, and C. A. Gibson, of the Ohio District, were outstanding among a number of superintendents who by 1933 could claim credit for the organization of a hundred congregations or more. All over the nation, however, with the sole exception of the seaboard states of the southeast Atlantic, where the denomination's home missionary expansion lagged until the 1940's, the story was the same. Where Methodism had flourished in the nineteenth century, the Nazarenes found a receptive audience for their appeals in the twentieth.[46]

Nor was personal heroism any less evident among the missionaries at home than abroad. Although district superintendents might plan new outposts, men and women must be found willing to go with their children for periods short and long into a strange town and announce that their purpose was to gather a congregation of Nazarenes. They held nightly meetings under cloth tents or in open-air tabernacles. Sometimes they managed to lease or buy a church building made vacant by the merger of congregations of older denominations, or their removal to the suburbs.

In another decade the church world at large was to notice this mushrooming growth and mistakenly attribute it to the unsettling impact of the depression. Actually the expansion had begun long before the crash of 1929. A chart of membership gains during four-year periods after 1911 showed over 56 per cent increase between 1911 and 1915, only 5½ per cent the next quadrennium, then additions of 45 per cent, 35 per cent, 35 per cent, and 40 per cent in the four-year periods following, until 1935. The denomination's remarkable growth continued through the years of World War II, when working-class people were more prosperous than at any time in our country's history.[47]

The needs to which the Nazarene and other holiness denominations ministered were broader and deeper than merely economic privation. The America of the late nineteenth century was a fundamentally religious land. The twentieth century, with its succession of wars, depressions, and cityward migration, heightened the hunger for religious solace at the very moment when intellectual and cultural leaders of the nation were either rejecting traditional Christianity or modifying its message so much that common people felt themselves spiritually orphaned. The latter turned quite naturally to leaders from their own ranks who spoke clearly the ancient language of sin and judgment, of forgiveness and redemption, of faith and everlasting life. In the Nazarenes they found another quality also—enthusiasm to counteract the dead weight of personal and social despair. "Time and again," wrote a young sociologist who surveyed religion in the prairie cities of Illinois in the mid-thirties,

> one would hear that the Nazarenes were the only live group in town. In several places their ministers were said to be receiving the largest salaries of any ministers in the community and their church services well attended. Generally speaking, "life" and "real enthusiasm" were attributed to this group. . . . Many of the old line denominational groups were pretty "dead."[48]

A FORWARD GLANCE

Such books as this often close with a look backwards. But the story of the Nazarenes is only begun here. It is not finished, and the writer and editors believe that we ought not to attempt to finish it now.

In the thirty years since the General Assembly of 1932, the denomination has shown a net gain of 2,812 churches in cities large and small around the world. The Nazarene people have multiplied their membership by 80 per cent, expanded and improved their Sunday school and youth work, and increased the beauty and utility of their church buildings so much as to make the total property worth an estimated fifty-six million dollars. Missionaries now serve on 42 overseas fields, guiding the development of national churches whose 57,000 members are moving steadily toward self-support. In the United States, all but one of the six schools established in the early days are fully accredited by their regional associations as four-year liberal arts colleges, and two more have been added outside the country, in Canada and the British Isles. The enrollment at all these institutions in 1961-62 reached 5,680. A graduate theological seminary, founded at Kansas City in 1945, interestingly enough at the behest of James B. Chapman, has already granted degrees to 656 ministers. A weekly radio program meanwhile carries the Nazarene message to every continent, through 450 stations. The Nazarene Publishing House in Kansas City has branches in Toronto, Canada, and Pasadena, California, and depositories in Britain, Australia, and South Africa. Its sales in 1961 exceeded $3,000,000.

Yet as far as close observers can tell, the devotion of the denomination to its distinctive belief in the doctrine and experience of entire sanctification and the commitment of its people to the firm discipline of the General Rules are as great as ever. If the notion has any validity that church organizations inevitably pass through a cycle from youthful intensity and orthodoxy to mature accommodation with the world and, then, spiritual decay, one can find little evidence to support it thus far in the story of the Nazarenes. On the contrary, the people of the church are still marked by their total abstinence from tobacco and alcohol, still notable for their renunciation of movies and excessive adornment, still nurtured by revivals and camp meetings in which the experience of perfect love is the keynote of preaching and the constant quest of seekers at the mourners' bench.

If we compare the daily life of today's Nazarenes with that of the church world around them, we must conclude that their separation is as great as that which set their grandparents off from the Methodists and Presbyterians of fifty years ago. Indeed, the generation of leaders who were youths in the 1920's grew up with an intense awareness of the apparent grip of the cycle of development and decay upon some of the older denominations. They determined at all costs to prevent its operation in theirs, without turning to either legalism or emotionalism as a substitute for the spiritual commitment they knew was required.

The story of the last thirty years would for these reasons alone be a tempting one for us to try to tell. But the time is not yet ripe for it. To appraise accurately the significance of the deeds of men still living and to evaluate the programs and the controversies in which they have taken part would be far more difficult than writing the narrative of earlier decades, and much less appropriate in a volume being published by the denomination itself. Perhaps the perspective of time, and the grace of a kindly Providence in raising up scholars to undertake the task, will make possible such a volume a decade or two hence. Until then, the present generation of Nazarenes will likely be content to make history, rather than write it.

In closing, two comments seem necessary. The first is addressed to scholars generally who may read this book. The second is for the people of the church.

We have tried to tell here the story of what happened, as best we could find out about it from the records available. The author and the editors, of course, all acknowledge deep kinship and affection for the persons whose lives we have chronicled and for the church they loved. We believe that a reasonably objective estimate of the facts is no less possible for historians who write from a viewpoint sympathetic to their subject than for those who approach it from the outside. Neither kind of student can understand fully the life of the persons or groups he describes without a thorough grasp of what they believed their lives to mean.

A creature from Mars, with no worldly preconceptions whatsoever, would see both this story and all of human history differently, to be sure; but until he saw events in terms which the actors on earth's stage thought vital, he would not be seeing them at all. On the other hand, those who write the story of their own family, church, or nation must chasten both mind and emotion at every turn in the road, lest their history become mere propaganda—a tale spun out to influence the present by distorting the past. For this reason, history written by "insiders" ought especially to be subjected to rigorous analysis. To enable interested scholars to make the fullest possible check upon the accuracy and appropriateness of statements made here, we have provided more than the usual number of references to the sources of information.

And now to the people of the church. The writer of this volume and those who have assisted him believe, in common with Christians generally, that God is at work in the affairs of men, and particularly in the life of His Church. Each of us has at times been awed and at other times properly disappointed by events in which he felt he saw a providential hand at work, or the foolish and erring hands of men frustrating His design. But we have made no attempt here to trace out by human scholarship the deeds of the Holy Spirit. As Jesus said to Nicodemus, He is like the wind, whose sound we hear but whose path we cannot see.

The reader, therefore, must evaluate for himself the significance of the men and events which compose the history of the Nazarenes. We shall be content if in telling the story we have provided new and important information upon which thoughtful persons may ponder the meaning of American Christianity, the part played by the small denominational families into which so much of it has recently been divided, and the relevance of Wesleyan perfectionism to a generation awed by its rediscovery of the deep sinfulness of man.

NOTES

The materials upon which this book is based are virtually all available to qualified scholars, in either their original form or on microfilm, at the Nazarene archives, in Kansas City, Missouri. Interested persons should inquire of the General Secretary, Church of the Nazarene Headquarters, 6401 The Paseo, Kansas City, Missouri.

CHAPTER I

THE HOLINESS REVIVAL, 1858-88

1. See Timothy L. Smith, *Revivalism and Social Reform in Mid-Nineteenth-Century America* (N.Y., 1957), chaps. 7-9; and John L. Peters, *Christian Perfection in American Methodism* (N.Y., 1956), for detailed discussions of Wesley's doctrine and its cultivation in America.

2. *Proceedings of Holiness Conferences, Held at Cincinnati . . . and at New York . . .* (Philadelphia, 1878), pp. 139-40; *Guide to Holiness*, L (October, 1866), 123-25.

3. *Guide to Holiness*, L (August-November, 1866), 58-59, 88-91, 122-23, 152-54, 188, and LI (May, 1867), 155; S. Olin Garrison, *Forty Witnesses, Covering the Whole Range of Christian Experience* (N.Y., 1888), p. 95.

4. A. McLean and Joel W. Eaton, eds., *Penuel, or Face to Face with God* (N.Y., 1869), contains, pp. 6-15, Inskip's account of the association's origin. Cf. George Hughes, *Days of Power in the Forest Temple . . .* (Boston, 1874), pp. 39-60, the "official" history of the first fourteen national camps; Henry B. Ridgaway, *The Life of the Rev. Alfred Cookman . . .* (N.Y., 1874), pp. 314-28; and William McDonald and John E. Searles, *The Life of Rev. John S. Inskip . . .* (Boston, 1887).

5. Ridgaway, *op. cit.*, pp. 349-50; Hughes, *op. cit.*, p. 65; McLean and Eaton, eds., *op. cit.*, pp. 158-59, 254-68. See also Raymond W. Albright, *A History of the Evangelical Church* (Harrisburg, Pa., 1942), pp. 268-78.

6. Simpson's sermon is quoted from McLean and Eaton, eds., *op. cit.*, p. 468; cf. pp. 381-85. See also Ridgaway, *op. cit.*, pp. 359-61; and Hughes, *op. cit.*, p. 69.

7. Ridgaway, *op. cit.*, pp. 369-70, 414-18, 420-23; *New York Christian Advocate and Journal*, July 13, 1871, p. 220; *Proceedings of Holiness Conferences*, pp. 127-28.

8. Hughes, *op. cit.*, pp. 51-87; Ridgaway, *op. cit.*, pp. 378, 422-23; *The Double Cure, or Echoes from the National Camp-Meetings* (2nd ed., c. 1895), pp. 7-8.

9. Matthew Simpson, *A Cyclopedia of Methodism . . .* (Philadelphia, 1878), pp. 288-89, 638; *Proceedings of Holiness Conferences*, pp. 133-34; Ridgaway, *Cookman*, p. 318; McLean and Eaton, eds., *op. cit.*, pp. 462-66,

473; and George Hughes, *The Beloved Physician: Walter C. Palmer* . . . (N.Y., 1884), p. 227.

10. E. Harrison Stokes, *Ocean Grove, Its Origin and Progress* . . . (Philadelphia, 1874), pp. 10, 60, and the same author's *Beatitudes by the Sea* . . . (Philadelphia, 1886), pp. 50, 65, 69-70, are more complete on the holiness emphasis than Morris S. Daniels, *The Story of Ocean Grove* . . . (N.Y., 1919), pp. 1-15, 26-27, 69; cf. Hughes, *Beloved Physician*, pp. 264-66 ff. Ridgaway, *op. cit.*, pp. 359-65, 402, 405, 426 ff., covers Cookman's last year and death.

11. McDonald and Searles, *op. cit.*, pp. 213, 216-17, 221-23, 308-9, 313-14, 344; Simpson, *op. cit.*, pp. 546, 830; *Proceedings of Holiness Conferences*, p. 111. Paul F. Douglass, *The Story of German Methodism* (N.Y., 1939), pp. 1-70, charts Nast's career, but ignores holiness. The sketch of Daniel Steele in the *Dictionary of American Biography* does the same.

Lewis R. Dunn wrote "Entire Sanctification," *Methodist Quarterly Review*, XLIX (1867), 555-72; "Christian Purity," the same, LV (1873), 206-29; *The Mission of the Spirit* . . . (N.Y., 1871); and *Sermons on the Higher Life* (N.Y., 1882), containing an introduction by Bishop Simpson.

12. Phoebe Palmer, ed., *Pioneer Experiences* . . . (N.Y., 1867), pp. i-ix; *Journal of the General Conference of the Methodist Episcopal Church* . . . *1872* (N.Y., 1872), 236, 300, 305-7; Hughes, *Days of Power*, pp. i-v; McLean and Eaton, eds., *op. cit.*, pp. 466-67. Cf. Smith, *op. cit.*, pp. 119-20.

13. *Journal of the General Conference of the Methodist Episcopal Church, South,* . . . *1870* (Nashville, 1870), p. 164; cf., the same, *1866* (Nashville, 1866), and *1878* (Nashville, 1878), p. 33.

14. *Proceedings of the Ecumenical Methodist Conference* . . . *1881* (Cincinnati, 1882), pp. 63, 84, 122-24, 145, 151, 154-55; Simpson, *op. cit.*, pp. 288-89, 638. William Warren Sweet, *Indiana Asbury—DePauw University, 1837-1937* . . . (N.Y., 1937), pp. 139-51, omits reference to DePauw's participation in the holiness revival.

15. George Hughes, *Fragrant Memories of the Tuesday Meeting and Guide to Holiness* . . . (N.Y., 1886), pp. 71-76; see also pp. 64, 77, 93, 129-30, 142-43.

16. Hughes, *Beloved Physician*, pp. 244-47; McLean and Eaton, eds., *op. cit.*, pp. 469-70; Hughes, *Days of Power*, pp. 422, 425.

17. Phoebe Palmer, ed., *op. cit.*, pp. 65-70, 109-19, 172-75, 196-202, 361 ff., contains testimonies of Presbyterian ministers; Garrison, *op. cit.*, preserves those of Moody, Cullis, and many others. Cf. John Q. Adams, ed., *Experiences of the Higher Christian Life in the Baptist Denomination* . . . (N.Y., 1870); Absalom B. Earle, *Bringing in Sheaves* (Boston, 1869), pp. 54 ff., 239 ff., 280-94 ff.; A. P. Graves, *From Earth to Heaven* (14th ed., Chicago, 1882), pp. 193-200; William E. Boardman, *Faith Work Under Dr. Cullis in Boston* (Boston, 1876); and Asa T. Mahan, *Out of Darkness into Light* . . . (Boston, 1876), pp. 190-92.

18. Dougan Clark and Joseph H. Smith, *David B. Updegraff and His Work* (Cincinnati, 1895); David B. Updegraff, *Old Corn* (Boston, 1892), pp. xiii, 373, and "press notices" on the back flyleaves; *Christian Witness and Advocate of Bible Holiness*, October 29, 1896, p. 2. Dougan Clark's two most significant works are *The Offices of the Holy Spirit* (Philadelphia, 1879) and *The Theology of Holiness* (Chicago, 1893).

Arthur O. Roberts, "The Concepts of Perfection in the History of the Quaker Movement" (B.D. thesis, Nazarene Theological Seminary, 1951), pp. 111-15, and elsewhere, summarizes these developments.

19. Lewis R. Dunn, "Christian Purity," *Methodist Quarterly Review*, LV (1873), 229; Hughes, *Days of Power*, 440 ff., and McLean and Eaton, eds., *op. cit.*, pp. 11-13, make plain the position of the National Association. Cf. Richard Wheatley, *The Life and Letters of Mrs. Phoebe Palmer* (N.Y., 1876), pp. 436, 442, 447-48; Edward Davies, *Illustrated History of Douglas Campmeeting* (Boston, 1890), p. 33; and John Peters, *Christian Perfection*, p. 136.

20. Hughes, *Tuesday Meeting*, p. 186; Benjamin B. Warfield, *Perfectionism* (2 vols., N.Y., 1931), II, 458-59; Phoebe Palmer, *Four Years in the Old World* (N.Y., c. 1864), pp. 113-20 and elsewhere; *Guide to Holiness*, LI, 4 (April, 1867), 154-55; McDonald and Searles, *op. cit.*, pp. 310-25.

21. Arthur T. Pierson, *The Keswick Movement in Precept and Practice* ... (N.Y., 1903), pp. 18-38; and Warfield, *op. cit.*, I, 313-30, II, 469-83, are standard accounts, the latter severely critical. See also Clark, *Offices of the Holy Spirit*, IV, 120.

22. Pierson, *op. cit.*, pp. 46-64; Warfield, *op. cit.*, II, 470-71. Cf. R. A. Torrey, *The Baptism with the Holy Spirit* (N.Y., 1895), p. 5; the sketch of Torrey in *The National Cyclopedia of American Biography*, XXI, 428; and Aaron Merritt Hills, *Scriptural Holiness and Keswick Teaching Compared* (Manchester, England, c. 1900).

23. G. S. Railton, *The Authoritative Life of General William Booth* (N.Y., 1912), pp. 48-71, 95-96; Catherine Booth, *Aggressive Christianity* (Boston, 1883), introduction by Daniel Steele; Clarence W. Hall, *Samuel Logan Brengle, Portrait of a Prophet* (N.Y., 1933).

24. See, for examples, John Charles Ryle (Lord Bishop of Liverpool), *Holiness. Its Nature, Hindrances, Difficulties and Roots* ... (London, 1883), pp. v-x; and Henry Drummond, *The Ideal Life; Addresses Hitherto Unpublished* (N.Y., 1898), pp. 172-77, 296-97. Cf. William Booth, *In Darkest England and the Way Out* (N.Y., 1890), pp. i-viii and elsewhere, on the relationship of holiness to social hope, a subject treated at great length in Smith, *op. cit.*

CHAPTER II

THE CHURCH QUESTION, 1880-1900

1. F. G. Smith, *Brief Sketch of the Origin, Growth and Distinctive Doctrine of the Church of God Reformation Movement* (pamphlet, Anderson, Indiana, 1926), pp. 1-20; *Michigan Holiness Record*, II, No. 4 (July, 1884), 27, quoting Mrs. Warner's letter.

2. *Proceedings of Holiness Conferences ... 1877* (Philadelphia, c. 1878), pp. 85, 90, 99; Clarence E. Cowen, *A History of the Church of God (Holiness)* (Overland Park, Kansas, 1949), pp. 43-47, 147-49; John P. Brooks, *The Divine Church* (Columbus, Mo., 1891). M. L. Haney, *The Story of My Life* (Chicago, 1906), pp. 248, 311, is the best account of the early holiness movement in Illinois.

3. Cowen, *op. cit.*, pp. 20-33, 41-55; J. A. Kring, *The Conquest of Canaan* (Kansas City, Mo., 1930), pp. 3-4; *Christian Advocate and Journal*, January 12, 1888, p. 20.

4. Quoted from B. F. Gassaway in Macum Phelan, *A History of the Expansion of Methodism in Texas, 1867-1902* . . . (Dallas, Texas, 1937), pp. 118-19. See also Haney, op. cit., pp. 293-97; and C. B. Jernigan, *Pioneer Days of the Holiness Movement in the Southwest* (Kansas City, Mo., c. 1920), pp. 18-19.

5. Jernigan, op. cit., pp. 19-22; Phelan, op. cit., pp. 119-20; articles by Cyrus T. Hogan and John Paul in *Texas Holiness Advocate*, July 12 and 26, 1906; and the general account in George McCulloch, *History of the Holiness Movement in Texas, and the Fanaticism which Followed* (Aquilla, Texas, 1886).

6. Mrs. Josephine M. Washburn, *History and Reminiscences of the Holiness Church Work in Southern California and Arizona* (Pasadena, c. 1911), pp. 7-8, 23-24, 53-54, 58-61, 98-103, 123, 145-46, 213-14, 156, 163, 228-29. Dennis Rogers, *Holiness Pioneering in the Southland* (Hemet, California, 1944), pp. 11-26, is very inaccurate on dates.

7. *Michigan Holiness Record*, II (April, June, August, and October, 1884), 5-6, 21, 39, 2-3; the same, III (February, 1886), and V (July, 1887), 20; S. B. Shaw, *Touching Incidents and Remarkable Answers to Prayer* . . . (Grand Rapids, Mich., 1895), 204-5; and Brooks, op. cit., pp. 281-82.

8. See especially Shaw's editorial, "A New Church—Not Quite," *Michigan Holiness Record*, VII (August and September, 1889), 13-14, 18-19. On the Chicago Assembly see the same, II (September and November, 1884, and April, 1885), 47, 56, 86; III (June and July, 1885), 9-12 and passim; V (October, 1887), 46-47; and VII (February, 1890), 9.

9. On the National Association, see Isaiah Reid's column in *Christian Witness*, January 10 and December 12, 1895, and July 9, 1896; Haney, op. cit., pp. 341-62, 371, 374-76; S. B. Shaw, *Echoes of the General Holiness Assembly . . . 1901* (Chicago, 1901), pp. 3-11 and passim; Joseph Smith, "Open Letter to the National Holiness Association," reported in *Nazarene Messenger*, July 16, 1903, p. 7. Cf. *Yearbook of the Holiness Union . . . 1904* (Memphis, Tenn., 1904); A. E. Thompson, *The Life of A. B. Simpson* (N.Y., 1920); and Maury E. Redford, "History of the Church of the Nazarene in the South" (M.A. thesis, Vanderbilt University, 1935), pp. 122-36.

10. Jernigan, op. cit., pp. 33-37, 109-25; *History of the Organization of the Reformed Baptist Denomination* . . . (1938), p. 1; J. A. Huffman, *History of the Mennonite Brethren in Christ Church* (New Carlisle, Ohio, 1920), pp. 59-73, 159-63; *Christian Witness*, October 10, 1895, p. 8.

11. John S. McGeary, *The Free Methodist Church* . . . (Chicago, 1917), pp. 124 ff., is superseded by Wilson T. Hogue, *History of the Free Methodist Church of North America* (2 vols., Chicago, 1915), Vol. II; Raymond W. Albright, *A History of the Evangelical Church* (Harrisburg, Pa., 1942), pp. 268-78, 306; H. J. Bowman, *Voices on Holiness from the Evangelical Association* (Cleveland, Ohio, 1882); *Michigan Holiness Record*, VI (February, 1889), 68. On all these groups see John L. Peters, *Christian Perfection in American Methodism*, p. 124 and passim.

12. George Watson, *White Robes* . . . (Cincinnati, Ohio, 1883), pp. 151 ff., the chapter on "Useless Adornment"; "The Evils of Worldly Conformity in Dress," *Michigan Holiness Record*, II (June and July, 1884); Beverly Carradine, *Fifteen Objections to Church Entertainments* (New Orleans, c. 1892); L. L. Pickett, *The Book and Its Theme* (Nashville, 1893), pp. 253 ff. Even

E. E. Shelhamer, *Popular and Radical Holiness Contrasted* (Atlanta, Georgia, 1906), reveals a surprisingly intelligent grasp of the issues.

On Methodism's attitude toward popular amusements see, generally, William W. Sweet, *Methodism in American History* (N.Y., 1933), pp. 336-45; Hunter Dickinson Farish, *The Circuit Rider Dismounts: A Social History of Southern Methodism, 1865-1900* (Richmond, Va., 1938), pp. 342-51; *Journal of the General Conference of the Methodist Episcopal Church . . . 1872* (N.Y., 1872), pp. 238, 379; *ibid., 1880* (N.Y., 1880), pp. 432-33; *ibid., 1896* (N.Y., 1896), pp. 51-52; and *Proceedings, Sermons, Essays, and Addresses at the Centennial Methodist Conference . . . 1884* (N.Y., 1885), p. 72.

13. *Central Christian Advocate*, January 18, 1882, p. 2, printed both letters. For evidence that the holiness leaders were already on the defensive at this point see *Proceedings of Holiness Conferences . . . 1877*, pp. 103 ff., 111-12; and Thomas K. Doty, *Lessons in Holiness* (Cleveland, Ohio, 1881), pp. 195-224.

14. J. E. Searles, *History of the Present Holiness Revival, A Sermon* . . . (Boston, 1887), pp. 29-32.

15. *Michigan Holiness Record*, II (April, 1884), 2, and III (October, 1885), 47, lists these periodicals, as does *The Holiness Year Book* (N.Y., 1888). See also *Proceedings of Holiness Conferences . . . 1877*, pp. 111-12; and William McDonald and J. E. Searles, *The Life of Rev. John S. Inskip* (Boston, 1885).

16. William Taylor, *Story of My Life* (N.Y., 1896), pp. 687-95; *Journal of the General Conference . . . 1884* (N.Y., 1884), pp. 209, 211, 654-57; *Central Christian Advocate*, March 15, 1882.

17. Taylor, *op. cit.*, pp. 695 ff.; Edward Davies, *History of Silver Lake Camp Meeting* . . . (Reading, Massachusetts, 1899), pp. 9-11, 23-24; Edward Davies, *Illustrated History of Douglas Campmeeting* (Boston, 1890), pp. 38-41; *Pacific Christian Advocate*, October 9, 1895; T. L. Jones, *From the Gold Mine to the Pulpit* (Cincinnati, 1904), pp. 90-92, 118-25, indicating Taylor's role in Oregon; *The Double Cure or Echoes from National Camp Meetings* (Boston, c. 1894), 254-66.

18. *Journal of the General Conference . . . 1888*, pp. 47-48, 59-60, and, generally, pp. 392-96, 440, 482-85, 645, 653.

19. *Journal of the General Conference . . . M.E. Church (South) . . . , 1894* (Nashville, 1894), p. 25; John A. Porter, W. B. Godbey, and others, *Christian Perfection, an Address by the Southern Holiness Associations* (pamphlet, Nashville, c. 1890); Leonidas Rosser, "Sanctification," *Quarterly Review of the M.E. Church (South)* (November, 1887), p. 237.

20. Phelan, *op. cit.*, pp. 391-94. John L. Peters, *Christian Perfection in American Methodism* (N.Y., 1956), pp. 145-48, is brief but excellent on the controversy over measures; cf. Robert Lee Harris, *Why We Left the Methodist Episcopal Church, South* (pamphlet, Milan, Tenn., 1894); "Come-Out-Ism and Put-Out-Ism," in Beverly Carradine, *The Sanctified Life* (Cincinnati, 1897), pp. 200-220; and James B. Chapman, *History of the Church of the Nazarene* (Kansas City, Mo., 1926), p. 129.

21. See Timothy L. Smith, *Revivalism and Social Reform in Mid-Nineteenth-Century America* (N.Y., 1957); Jesse T. Crane, *Holiness the Birthright of All God's Children* (N.Y., 1874), reviewed in *Methodist Review*, LVI (1874), pp. 490-93; J. T. Crane, "Christian Perfection and the

Higher Life," the same, LX (1878), pp. 696-97; and Stephen M. Merrill, *The Aspects of Christian Experience* (N.Y., 1882), preface, pp. 188 ff., 217-34, irenic in tone.

L. L. Pickett, *Entire Sanctification from 1799 to 1901* (Louisville, 1901), illustrates the success of the holiness party in the debate.

22. J. M. Boland, *The Problem of Methodism* . . . (Nashville, 1888), was reviewed in *Quarterly Review of the M.E. Church, South*, favorably by John E. Edward, n.s., X (1888-89), 41 f. and Joseph B. Cottrell, XI (1889-90), 106, and unfavorably by Josephus Anderson, X (1888-89), 373. Benjamin F. Orr's review of George H. Hayes, *The Problem Solved*, ibid., XIII (1891-92), 91-106, defended the second-blessing view, as did S. H. Wainwright, "Dr. Boland and the Ninth Article," ibid., XIV (1894), and H. R. Withers, ibid. Related articles, all opposing Boland and Hayes, are R. H. Mahon, "The Nature of Sin and Holiness," XI (1889-90), 28; John J. Tigert, "Colossians 3:1-16," XIV (1894), 274-77; and O. E. Brown, "A Comparative Study of Methodist Theology," XV (1895), 201 ff. See also Leonidas Rosser, *A Reply to the Problem of Methodism* (Nashville, 1889).

All this material is discussed at length in Claude H. Thompson, "The Witness of American Methodism to the Historical Doctrine of Christian Perfection" (Ph.D. dissertation, Drew University, 1949).

23. See J. M. Boland, "A Psychological View of Sin and Holiness," *Quarterly Review of the M.E. Church, South*, n.s., XII (1892), 339-54, and especially his "The Problem and Its Critics," ibid., XIII (1893), 349-50. Cf. "The Bishops on Christian Perfection," ibid., XIV (1894), 692-93; Bishop E. R. Hendrix, "The Perfecting of the Saints," ibid., XV (1895), 55-64, an article which was reprinted alongside Bishop J. C. Granberry's "Entire Sanctification" in a pamphlet which Tigert issued in 1896; and Bishop Joseph S. Key's introduction to Pickett, *The Book and Its Theme*.

24. B. F. Haynes, *Tempest-Tossed on Methodist Seas* (Kansas City, Mo., 1914), pp. 98-258, passim; *Christian Witness*, October 29, 1896, p. 13.

25. See the long and favorable review of James Mudge, *Growth in Holiness Toward Perfection* . . . (N.Y., 1895) in *Methodist Review*, LXXVII (1895), 663-65; Daniel Steele, *A Defense of Christian Perfection* . . . (N.Y., 1896), pp. 18, 29-31; Lewis R. Dunn, *A Manual of Holiness and Review of Dr. James B. Mudge* (Cincinnati, 1895), pp. 58, 87-88, 109; Asbury Lowery, "Dr. Mudge and His Book," *Methodist Review*, LXXVII (1895), 954-59; and Bishop J. C. Granberry, "Dr. Mudge on Growth in Holiness," *Quarterly Review of the M.E. Church, South*, n.s., XVI (1896), 198-210.

26. See D. W. C. Huntington, *Sin and Holiness* . . . (Cincinnati, 1898); George W. Wilson, *Methodist Theology versus Methodist Theologians* (Boston, 1904), introduction, pp. 329 ff., and passim; William McDonald to Phineas Bresee, quoted in *Peniel Herald*, I, No. 3 (December, 1894), 3, and No. 5 (February, 1895), 3; *Christian Witness*, January 10, 1895, pp. 4-5, and September 12, 1895, p. 4.

27. The quotation is from *Peniel Herald*, I, No. 7 (April, 1895), 5; for comments on General Booth see ibid., Nos. 1 and 4 (October, 1894, and January, 1895), pp. 3, 1.

See also Washburn, *The Holiness Church*, pp. 26-52; Jernigan, op. cit., p. 92; Haney, op. cit., pp. 360-61; P. P. Faris' sketch of A. B. Simpson in

The *Dictionary of American Biography;* files of *Vanguard* for 1894-98, in the St. Louis Public Library; and *Holiness Evangel* (Pilot Point, Texas) for 1903-5, in the Nazarene archives. Cf., on H. D. Brown, C. R. Starck, Jr., "Fifty Years with Children," *Seattle Spokesman Review,* December 8, 1946; and Frank J. Bruno, *Trends in Social Work, 1874-1956* . . . (2nd ed., N.Y., 1957), pp. 60-61.

28. See the bishops' address in *Journal of the General Conference . . . 1888,* pp. 58-59; Haney, *op. cit.,* pp. 360-61, 375-76; *Christian Witness,* September 5, 1895, p. 4, November 28, 1895, p. 4, November 12, 1896, p. 13, June 3 and 24, 1897, p. 13; Church of the Nazarene, Spokane, Washington, "Minutes of the Official Board" (in church office), p. 9, entry for November 10, 1902.

29. *Los Angeles Times,* October 22, 1894, p. 4; *Peniel Herald,* I, No. 1 (October, 1894), 1-2, No. 2 (November, 1894), 1; M.E. Church, Southern California Conference, *Journal . . . 1894* (Los Angeles, 1894), pp. 3-7, 15, 18-19. *Infra,* 106-9.

30. See Amanda Smith's letter in *Christian Witness,* November 11, 1897, p. 13; *Peniel Herald,* I, No. 3 (December, 1894), 1-2; comments on Rees and Mrs. M. W. Knapp in *Burning Bush,* September 10, 1903, pp. 6-7, and November 26, 1903, p. 6; Jernigan, *op. cit.,* p. 109; and Maury E. Redford, *Church of the Nazarene in the South,* pp. 136-46. *Infra,* 278 ff.

31. *Peniel Herald,* I, No. 4 (January, 1895), 1, 3, No. 8 (May, 1895), 1, No. 9 (June, 1895), 1; William McDonald to P. F. Bresee, *ibid.,* I, No. 2 (November, 1894), 2, No. 3 (December, 1894), 3, No. 5 (February, 1895), 3, and No. 7 (April, 1895), 4.

32. *Christian Witness,* September 5, 1895, p. 13, and August 19, 1897, pp. 2-3, indicates events in Nebraska, where Bresee and H. D. Brown played key roles. *Ibid.,* October 22, 1896, p. 5, January 21, 1897, pp. 4-5, and M. L. Haney, *op. cit.,* pp. 336-86, *passim,* illustrate the progress of the revival in Iowa.

CHAPTER III

NAZARENE BEGINNINGS IN THE EAST

1. *History of the Revival of Holiness at St. Paul's M.E. Church, Providence, R.I.* (Providence, 1887), p. 57. The preceding paragraphs are based on the earlier portions of this pamphlet.

2. *Ibid.,* pp. 58-87.

3. Reports in *Beulah Items,* September-December, 1888, and January-February, 1889. The issue for July, 1890, contains, p. 3, W. C. Ryder's account of the origins of the work at Rock.

4. *Ibid.,* April, 1889, pp. 1, 3.

5. *Ibid.,* July, 1890, pp. 3-4, and October, 1890, p. 3; Church of the Nazarene, New England District, *Second District Assembly Journal . . . 1909,* pp. 36-37.

6. *Report of the Central Evangelical Holiness Association . . . March 25 and 26, 1891* (Lynn, Mass., 1891), pp. 5, 7; *Beulah Items,* March, 1890, p. 3, November, 1890, p. 1. See also *ibid.,* February, 1889, p. 2, and June, 1889, p. 3.

7. *Christian Witness* for 1892: April 21, p. 4, April 28, p. 2, May 26,

p. 4, October 13, pp. 1-2, 5. Cf. also *ibid.*, May 5, 1892, p. 4, for J. N. Short's account of his work at Central Church, Lowell.

8. H. F. Reynolds, "Autobiography" (Ms in Nazarene archives), pp. 178, 181, 185-87, 192-94 ff., and *passim;* Edith Carey, Johnson, Vt., June 9, 1956, to T. L. Smith (Nazarene archives). O. J. Copeland, "Scrapbook" (in possession of Rev. Chester A. Smith), contains a clipping, "Gone to Be with Christ," by J. C. Bearse, and a letter of H. F. Reynolds, Wollaston, Mass. (about 1932), to O. J. Copeland. All these and the conversation of Edith Carey with the writer, February 20, 1956, find corroboration in the files of *Christian Witness,* May 5, 1892, p. 5, May 12, 1892, p. 5, August 18, 1892, p. 5, November 3, 1892, p. 4, April 6, 1893, p. 5, January 3, 1895, p. 13, and August 1, 1895, p. 13.

9. The columns of *Christian Witness* from 1892-97 provide the best contemporary account of the emergence of the N.E. Conference of the Evangelical Association. See especially the news columns for October 6, 1892; February 14, March 7, June 27, November 7, and November 14, 1895; April 2, May 28, June 11, and July 2, 1896; January 21, May 6, May 20, and June 10, 1897; and April 14 and 21, 1898. Cf. Everett, Mass., Church of the Nazarene, "Church Record" (in the church office), p. 1.

10. *Christian Witness,* January 24, September 26, October 10 and 17, 1895; January 7 and April 22, 1897; and May 12, 1898. See also Lynn, Mass., Church of the Nazarene, "Proceedings of the Church Board, 1894-1904" (in the church office), pp. 61-62; and Mary Webber, "Diary" (in the possession of her descendants in Cliftondale), p. 28, entry for June 14, 1897.

11. Edward Davies, *Illustrated History of Douglas Campmeeting* (Boston, 1890), pp. 11, 19, 46 ff., and *passim;* Association of Pentecostal Churches, Missionary Committee, "Minutes, April 13, 1901, to April 13, 1907" (Ms in the Nazarene archives), pp. 37-59; *Christian Witness,* August 1, 1895.

12. See *Christian Witness,* June 25, October 8, and November 26, 1896, and April 14 and August 18, 1898; *Beulah Items,* September, 1890, pp. 2-3.

13. Reynolds, *op. cit.,* pp. 222 ff.; *Christian Witness,* January 3 and February 21, 1895; and J. C. Bearse's fine account, *Nazarene Messenger,* July 4, 1907, p. 3.

14. *Christian Witness,* February 21 and 28, October 3, and November 21, 1895.

15. Copeland, "Scrapbook," clipping "Gone to Be with Christ"; Reynolds, *op. cit.,* pp. 198-202.

16. See the quotations in *Christian Witness,* April 23, 1896, p. 9, and July 9, 1896, p. 13; Reynolds, *op. cit.,* pp. 198-202 ff.

17. Lynn, Mass., Church of the Nazarene, "Proceedings," *loc. cit.,* p. 49; Association of Pentecostal Churches of America, *Minutes . . . 1897.*

18. Edna Skinner, "A Brief History of John Wesley Church," in *John Wesley Nazarene Messenger,* February, 1926; Basil Miller, *Susan N. Fitkin: For God and Missions* (Kansas City, Mo., n.d.), pp. 44-53; the *Herald of Holiness,* August 20, 1938; Cliftondale, Mass., Church of the Nazarene, "Church Record," pp. 1-14; Mary L. Webber, "Diary," *loc. cit.,* pp. 1-22; *Christian Witness,* December 10, 1896, and January 14, 1897.

NOTES TO PAGES 71-83   361

19. *Ibid.*, May 20 and 27, 1897, and April 28, 1898; Association of Pentecostal Churches, *Minutes* . . . *1898.*
20. Association of Pentecostal Churches of America, *Articles of Faith*, pp. 9-10.
21. *Ibid.*, p. 10; Lowell, Mass., Church of the Nazarene, "Minutes of the Church Board, 1903-1905" (in the church office), p. 49; Lynn, Mass., Church of the Nazarene, "Proceedings," *loc. cit.*, p. 82.

CHAPTER IV

THE ASSOCIATION OF PENTECOSTAL CHURCHES, 1897-1907

1. *Christian Witness*, June 17 and November 11, 1897, and May 19, 1898; Lowell, Mass., Church of the Nazarene, "Minutes of the Church Board, 1903-1905" (in the church office), pp. 4, 46, 81-83, 103-4.
2. C. W. Griffin, conversation with the writer, July 24, 1955; *Christian Witness*, June 3 and November 4, 1897; Edward Davies, *A History of Silver Lake Camp Meeting* (Reading, Mass., n.d.), pp. 23, 26; Association of Pentecostal Churches of America, *Minutes* . . . *1898*, pp. 41-44; Edith Carey, conversation with the writer, February 20, 1956, and June 21, 1956.
3. U.S. Census, *Compendium of the Eleventh Census, 1890* (Washington, 1890), pp. 600 ff.; New England District, Church of the Nazarene, *Journal* . . . *1925*, p. 33; conversation with Henry Hadley, Everett, Mass., 1951; Assoc. of Pent. Ch. of Am., *Minutes* . . . *1903*, p. 36.
4. *Pentecostal Era*, February 3, 1910; conversation of the writer with J. H. Shrader, October, 1956.
5. Assoc. of Pent. Ch. of Am., Missionary Committee, "Minutes, April 15, 1897, to April 10, 1901" (Ms in Nazarene archives), pp. 81, 112; *Christian Witness*, August 26, 1897, p. 12; *Nazarene Messenger*, November 19, 1908, pp. 6-7, 9-10.
6. Assoc. of Pent. Ch. of Am., Missionary Committee, "Minutes, 1897-1901," *loc. cit.*, pp. 6-9, 14; *ibid.*, Executive Committee of the Missionary Committee, "Minutes" (Ms, Nazarene archives), pp. 7-11.
7. *Ibid.*, pp. 37, 114. See also H. F. Reynolds, Westport Factory, Mass., May 23, 1900, to Charles BeVier; H. F. Reynolds, Westport Factory, Mass., February 16 and March 25, 1901, to J. H. Norris; H. F. Reynolds, Westport Factory, Mass., May 6, 1901, to C. Howard Davis (all in Reynolds papers, Nazarene archives).
8. Assoc. of Pent. Ch. of Am., *Minutes* . . . *1904*; *ibid.*, Missionary Committee, "Minutes, 1901-1907," pp. 16, 20, 24, 33-35.
9. John Short, *Divine Healing* (Providence, R.I., n.d.); conversation with Dr. J. Glenn Gould, October 17, 1955.
10. *Christian Witness*, May 5, 1898, p. 12; Records of the Grace Pentecostal Church, Saratoga Springs, N.Y., p. 39; *Beulah Christian*, August-November, 1900, *passim;* Pentecostal Collegiate Institute, *First Annual Catalogue, 1900-1901*, pp. 6, 26-27, and *passim;* Assoc. of Pent. Ch. of Am., *Minutes* . . . *1902*, p. 38; L. S. Tracy, correspondence, copies from originals at the Eastern Nazarene College library (in Nazarene archives).
11. H. N. Brown, Brooklyn, N.Y., May 22, 1902, to H. F. Reynolds (Reynolds correspondence, Nazarene archives).
12. H. N. Brown, Brooklyn, N.Y., May 26 and June 7, 1902, to H. F. Reynolds (Reynolds correspondence, Nazarene archives); Records of

Grace Pentecostal Church, Saratoga Springs, N.Y., pp. 82, 84, 95-96, 100-102, 144-46; *Pentecostal Witness*, June 7, 1902; O. J. Copeland, "Scrapbook," clippings on "The People's Church."

When Pettit resigned the Brooklyn church to become a Presbyterian minister, his congregation elected to join the Disciples of Christ, becoming the first unit of that denomination in the New York area.

13. Assoc. of Pent. Ch. of Am., Missionary Committee, "Minutes, 1901-1907," pp. 48, 61-63, 78-79, 83.

14. *Ibid.*, 1897-1901, pp. 9-12, 17, 20, 55, 63, 76-78, 128, 138; H. F. Reynolds, Westport Factory, Mass., December 28, 1899, May 16, 1900, September 6, 1900, and April 23, 1901, to M. D. Wood; Assoc. of Pent. Ch. of Am., *Minutes . . . 1903*, p. 28.

15. Olive G. Tracy, *Tracy Sahib of India* (Kansas City, Mo., 1954), pp. 24, 44.

16. Assoc. of Pent. Ch. of Am., *Minutes . . . 1906*, pp. 28, 29, 32; *ibid.*, Missionary Committee, "Minutes, 1901-1907," pp. 82, 85, 110-12.

17. Assoc. of Pent. Ch. of Am., *Minutes . . . 1906*, p. 16; *ibid.*, Missionary Committee, "Minutes, 1901-1907," pp. 78, 99-105.

18. See Lynn, Mass., Church of the Nazarene, "Proceedings of the Church Board, 1894-1904" (in the church office), pp. 24, 28-29, 31, 53; and Basil Miller, *For God and Missions: Susan N. Fitkin* (Kansas City, Mo., n.d.), pp. 57-58, 62-64.

19. See, for the foregoing quotations, *Christian Witness*, April 28, 1898, p. 9; Pentecostal Collegiate Institute, *Fourth Annual Catalogue*, p. 7; Assoc. of Pent. Ch. of Am., *Articles of Faith*, p. 3.

20. Lowell, Mass., Church of the Nazarene, "Minutes, 1903-1905," pp. 41-44.

21. F. A. Hillery, comp., *Songs of Beulah* (Providence, R.I., n.d.), No. 7.

CHAPTER V

PHINEAS BRESEE AND THE CHURCH OF THE NAZARENE

1. For the foregoing see E. A. Girvin, *P. F. Bresee, A Prince in Israel* (Kansas City, Mo., 1916), pp. 23-37, 39-40, and, for the quotation, pp. 42-43; M.E. Church, Iowa Conference, *Minutes . . . Fourteenth Session . . . 1857*, p. 26; *Fifteenth Session . . . 1858*, p. 13; *Sixteenth Session . . . 1859*, p. 8; *Seventeenth Session . . . 1860*, pp. 4, 26; and *Eighteenth Session . . . 1861*, pp. 8, 16.

2. Girvin, *op. cit.*, pp. 45-70, *passim;* M.E. Church, Des Moines Conference, *Register . . . Tenth Session . . . 1873*, pp. 10-11, 55; and *ibid., Iowa Conference, Official Record . . . Thirty-third Session . . . 1882*, pp. 2, 18. The quotation is from W. L. Kershaw, *History of Page County, Iowa . . .* (2 vols., Chicago, 1909), I, 179. See also P. F. Bresee, "The Pastoral Office," in *Proceedings of the Second Iowa Methodist State Convention . . . 1881* (Burlington, Iowa, 1881).

3. Girvin, *op. cit.*, p. 50.

4. *Ibid.*, pp. 51-52.

5. *Ibid.*, p. 81. Cf. also pp. 50-52, 54, 56, 65, 84-85; *Nazarene Messenger*, October 26, 1905, p. 5.

6. M.E. Church, Des Moines Conference, *Official Record* . . . *Twenty-fourth Session* . . . *1883*, pp. 7, 30. See also Girvin, *op. cit.*, pp. 72-80; sketch of Knotts in anon., *Biographical History of Pottawattamie County, Iowa* . . . (Lewis Pub. Co., 1891), pp. 493-95; record of author's conversation with Mrs. Bertha Parker, Phineas Bresee's daughter, August 26, 1955, on file in the Nazarene archives.

7. Girvin, *op. cit.*, pp. 81-85. See also Leslie Gay's account in *Southern California Methodist Quarterly*, II, No. 1 (March, 1885), 1; and Fred Shields, "Biography of Dr. P. F. Bresee," in *La Sierra* (yearbook of Pasadena College), June, 1915, which antedates Girvin's account. For the memories of old-timers, see the record of the conversation of the following persons with the writer, in the Nazarene archives: Mrs. Bertha Parker, August 26, 1955; C. W. Griffin, July 24, 1955; H. Orton Wiley, August 2, 1955.

8. Girvin, *op. cit.*, pp. 82-83. Cf. also *Nazarene Messenger*, January 7, 1909, p. 1, for J. W. Goodwin's poem about Bresee's experience.

9. Girvin, *op. cit.*, pp. 84-85.

10. *Southern California Methodist Quarterly*, I, No. 2 (April, 1884), 13, and No. 3 (July, 1884), 38-55.

11. *Ibid.*, "Wesley on Christian Perfection," I, No. 2 (April, 1884), 12-13, and 6, 17-18; *ibid.*, II, No. 1 (March, 1885), *passim*, No. 2 (June, 1885), 97-98, 103, No. 3 (September, 1885), 113-19, 121, and No. 4 (November, 1885), 123.

12. *Ibid.*, II, No. 3 (September, 1885), report of "Children's Day" at Long Beach, and No. 3 (November, 1885), 127-31, 136-38. For Bresee's relation to the University of Southern California in the 1880's, see: *ibid.*, I, No. 2 (April, 1884), 6, No. 3 (July, 1884), 38, 52, and III, No. 2 (June, 1885), 97-98; and M.E. Church, Southern California Conference, *Minutes* . . . *Eleventh Session* . . . *1886*, pp. 4-6, 50, 53.

13. Girvin, *op. cit.*, pp. 86-88; M.E. Church, Southern California Conference, *Minutes* . . . *Twelfth Session* . . . *1887*, pp. 46, 85-86, *Thirteenth Session* . . . *1888*, pp. 45, 89, 86, *Fourteenth Session* . . . *1889*, pp. 30, 64, 68, and *Fifteenth Session* . . . *1890*, p. 3. See also "A Visit to Pasadena," *Southern California Christian Advocate*, December 30, 1887, and references in issues for February 4 and 18 and April 14, 1888, and January 3, April 25, and September 12, 1889.

14. M.E. Church, Southern California Conference, *Minutes* . . . *Twelfth Session* . . . *1887*, pp. 5-7, 83, *Thirteenth Session* . . . *1888*, pp. 3-4, and, on the holiness movement in the conference, *ibid.*, *Fourteenth Session* . . . *1889*, p. 31. See also, in *Southern California Christian Advocate*: "Holiness Meetings," February 11, 1888; "The Work of Cleansing," December 30, 1888; references in issues for February 18 and April 28, 1888, January 24 and February 28, 1889; reports of the preachers' meetings, March 28, April 18, and May 2, 1889; and of the camp meetings, July 25, August 1, and October 10, 1889. Cf. J. E. Searles, *History of the Present Holiness Revival* (Boston, 1887), p. 36.

15. M.E. Church, Southern California Conference, *Minutes* . . . *Fourteenth Session* . . . *1889*, p. 51, and *Fifteenth Session* . . . *1890*, pp. 28-29; *Southern California Methodist Quarterly*, I, No. 7 (July, 1885), 18; *Southern*

California Christian Advocate, January 10 and July 11, 1889; Hiram A. Reid, *History of Pasadena* . . . (Pasadena, California, 1895), pp. 246, 273-74. Cf. Gilman M. Ostrander, *The Prohibition Movement in California, 1848-1933* (Berkeley, Calif., University of California, Publications in History, No. 57, 1959).

16. William McDonald, "Holiness and the Church," *California Christian Advocate,* January 1, 1890, and replies in the issues for February 19 and March 26, 1890; and S. F. Sterrett, "Revivals," *ibid.,* December 16, 1891. Cf. J. C. Simmons, *History of Southern Methodism on the Pacific Coast* (Nashville, Tenn., 1886), p. 432.

17. The best running account of Bresee's revival crusade is found in William McDonald's reports to the *Christian Witness,* which appeared in each week's issue from January 28 to May 5, 1892. See also M.E. Church, Southern California Conference, *Minutes . . . Sixteenth Session . . . 1891,* pp. 11, 36, 58; *Daily Christian Advocate* (for the General Conference), quoted in *California Christian Advocate,* May 11, 1892; and, on Simpson Church, *Southern California Christian Advocate,* July 18, 1889.

18. M.E. Church, Southern California Conference, *Minutes . . . Seventeenth Session . . . 1892,* pp. 24-27, 62; Girvin, *op. cit.,* pp. 95-96.

19. Girvin, *op. cit.,* pp. 97-98; M.E. Church, Southern California Conference, *Minutes,* as follows: *1891,* pp. 48-49; *1892,* pp. 38-40; *1893,* pp. 3-4, 11, 30-32; and *1894,* p. 42.

20. See University of Southern California, Board of Directors, "Minutes" (in the university archives), entries for October 2, 1884, September 1, 1885, for the year 1890 generally, and for January 11, 1892, p. 210; and E. T. W., "Joseph Pomeroy Widney, A.M., M.D., D.D., LL.D.," reprinted from *California and Western Medicine,* XLIV (April, May, June, 1936), 3-6.

21. See the University of Southern California, College of Liberal Arts, Board of Directors, "Minutes" (in the university archives), pp. 16-17, for the quotation, and, for other matters, *passim;* and Leslie Gay, Jr., "History of the University of Southern California" (M.A. thesis, the University of Southern California, 1910), pp. 84, 171, 213-30.

22. On Widney, see *An Illustrated History of Los Angeles County, California* . . . (Chicago, Ill., 1889), pp. 200-201, 804; *Southern California Christian Advocate,* February 14, May 30, June 13, 20, and 27, and October 10, 1889; and *California Christian Advocate,* November 21, 1894. A sculptured bust of Widney stands in the foyer of the Los Angeles County Medical Association Building.

23. *Supra,* 49 ff.; M.E. Church, Southern California Conference, *Minutes . . . Nineteenth Session . . . 1894,* pp. 9, 15, 18-19, 33; *Los Angeles Times,* September 29 and 30 and October 1, 1894, and (for a brief history of Peniel Mission) October 7, 1895; *California Christian Advocate,* October 9 and 31, 1894; Mamie P. Ferguson, *T. P. Ferguson, The Love Slave,* summarized in M. E. Gaddis, "Christian Perfectionism in America" (Ph.D. dissertation, the University of Chicago, 1929), pp. 499-502; *Peniel Herald,* October, 1894, pp. 1, 3, November, 1894, pp. 2, 4, and March, 1895, p. 1. I. G. Martin and Frank J. Stevens, pastor of St. James M.E. Church, Pasadena, in conversations with the writer, August 3, 1955, and January 20, 1956, agree that Bresee's motive in joining Peniel Mission was not primarily doctrinal but evangelistic.

24. *California Christian Advocate*, Dec. 26, 1894, and April 17, May 12, June 5, 26, 1895; *Peniel Herald*, Nov., 1894, pp. 1, 3, and Feb., 1895, p. 3.
25. *California Christian Advocate*, May 29 and July 17, 1895; *Peniel Herald*, July, 1895, p. 4, August, 1895, pp. 2, 4, and September, 1895, p. 12.
26. *Los Angeles Times*, October 7 and 21, 1895; *Peniel Herald*, October, 1895; Girvin, *Bresee*, pp. 112-16, 144-51; Fred J. Shields, "Historical Sketch of the Name, Nazarene," *La Sierra* (yearbook of Pasadena College), I, No. 1 (February, 1914), 10; *Nazarene Messenger*, May 17, 1900.
27. One copy of the flyer may be found inserted in the copy of the Church of the Nazarene, *Manual . . . 1898*, in the rare-book collection of Pasadena College library. Cf. "The Nazarenes," "California Tracts," No. 5 (Los Angeles, 1895), photostat in the Nazarene archives.
28. *California Christian Advocate*, October 9, 16, 23, and 30, 1895.
29. Girvin, *op. cit.*, pp. 117-25; *Nazarene Manual . . . 1898*, pp. 15-18; record of the writer's conversation with H. Orton Wiley, July 18, 1955, and with I. G. Martin, July 17, 1955.
30. *Nazarene Messenger*, July 3, 1899; *Nazarene Manual . . . 1898*, p. 2; Bresee's sermon, "The Poor Have the Gospel Preached to Them," in Ms volume in possession of the book editor, Nazarene Publishing House, pp. 80-82. Cf. the *Nazarene Manual . . . 1908*, p. 2.
31. *Nazarene Messenger*, 1898.
32. Girvin, *op. cit.*, pp. 106-9.
33. *Nazarene Manual . . . 1898*, pp. 28-30. Cf. *Discipline of the Methodist Episcopal Church 1896*, pp. 30-31. Item 4 in the second section must have been intended to be part of the first section, but if so, it was not corrected until 1905.
34. *Nazarene Messenger*, Dec. 6, 1900; and compare issues for Sept. 14 and Nov. 30, 1899, Apr. 18, 1901, and July 2, 1903. See also the *Nazarene Manual . . . 1908*, p. 20; Church of the Nazarene, Northwest District, *Fiftieth Anniversary Book . . .* (E. E. Zachary, ed., Spokane, Wash., 1954), pp. 16-17; and, in the Nazarene archives, records of the following conversations with the writer: H. Orton Wiley, July 19 and Aug. 2, 1955; John E. Moore, July 22, 1955; and Mallalieu Wilson, Aug. 15, 1955.
35. *Nazarene Messenger*, December 29, 1904, p. 7.
36. *Nazarene Manual . . . 1898*, pp. 13-14.
37. See W. E. Shepard's articles in *Nazarene Messenger*, August, 1899, and March 22, 1900; and my notes on conversations with Mallalieu Wilson, August 15, 1955, and with H. Orton Wiley, August 2, 1955.
38. Girvin, *op. cit.*, pp. 110-11, 124, 133-34; *Nazarene Messenger*, July 25, 1901, and August 6 and 20, 1903.
39. Girvin, *op. cit.*, pp. 120-42, 375-76; *Nazarene Messenger*, May 3, 1900, May 28 and June 18, 1903, and *passim;* and, in the Nazarene archives, my notes on conversations with H. Orton Wiley, July 19, 1955, I. G. Martin, July 20, 1955, and Mallalieu Wilson, August 15, 1955.
40. Girvin, *op. cit.*, p. 153; *Pacific Christian Advocate*, October 25, 1899; Leslie F. Gay, Jr., *loc. cit.*, pp. 188-89; and my notes on conversations with H. Orton Wiley, August 2, 1955, I. G. Martin, August 3, 1955, and Mrs. Samuel Widney, August 2, 1955. Cf. J. P. Widney, *The Faith That Has Come to Me* (Los Angeles, 1932), pp. 8-9, 22-23, 52-55, 148-49, 202 ff.
41. Girvin, *op. cit.*, pp. 120, 152-53.

Chapter VI
The Nazarenes Become a National Church

1. *Nazarene Messenger*, August 31, 1905, p. 10; Church of the Nazarene, Tenth General Assembly, *Proceedings . . . 1905*, p. 51.

2. *Nazarene Messenger*, March 26, 1903; Phineas Bresee, *Certainties of Faith; Ten Sermons by the Founder of the Church of the Nazarene* (Kansas City, Mo., 1958), introduction by Timothy L. Smith. I have relied much on a conversation with H. Orton Wiley, July 18, 1955. Cf. *Christian Witness*, June 3 and 17 and October 24, 1895, June 11 and October 15, 1896, and May 27, 1897.

3. *Nazarene Messenger*, July 20 and August 31, 1899.

4. *Ibid.*, May 17, 1900, quotes L. B. Kent's article from *Christian Witness;* see also editorials for July 26 and August 2, 1900.

5. *Ibid.*, March 15, April 5, and June 28, 1900. Cf. the issues for July 20 and December 14, 1899, and January 4 and May 24, 1900.

6. *Ibid.*, for these years, especially, April 19, September 13, and October 18, 1900 (from which the quotation of Bowers is taken), and March 14, 1901.

7. *Ibid.*, July 20, 1899, and August 12 and June 7, 1900; a special prohibition issue appeared April 26, 1900. For the general background, see Gilman M. Ostrander, *The Prohibition Movement in California, 1848-1933* (Berkeley, Calif., University of California, *Publications in History*, No. 57, 1957), pp. 63 ff., 88-89, 90, 95 f. Cf. *San Francisco Call*, December 11, 1895, p. 6, for a letter of E. A. Girvin opposing a Prohibition party.

8. See, in *California Christian Advocate*, articles by J. A. Wood, February 21, June 6, and October 10, 1901; material on the Beulah Park Camp, issues of April 18 and May 9, 1901; and A. C. Bane's article, "Sanctification: A Statement of 'the Great Distinguishing Doctrine' of Wesleyan Methodism," June 20, 1901.

9. *Nazarene Messenger*, February 13, 1902; see also issues for March and April, May 15, and May 26, 1902, and May 14, 1903. Cf. I. G. Martin, "What is the Church of John Wesley Doing?" *ibid.*, July 31, 1902.

10. S. B. Shaw, ed., *Echoes of the General Holiness Assembly Held in Chicago, May 3-13, 1901* (Chicago, 1901), pp. 33-34, 37, and *passim*. The *Nazarene Messenger*, May 23, 1901, contains Shepard's final view of the assembly, more favorable than that which appears in his earlier reports in the issues of May 9 and 16.

11. See Shaw, *op. cit.*, pp. 30-31, 275-76, 325-26; and W. E. Shepard's reaction to this question in *Nazarene Messenger*, May 9 and 23, 1901.

12. The Library of Congress has a complete file of the *Burning Bush;* material for the foregoing paragraph may be found in issues for January, February, and March, 1903. See also issues for August 13, 1903, and July 20, 1905, on labor unions; April 21, 1904, on W. E. Shepard's reappearance in Los Angeles; nearly all those for 1904, on the divorce question; and November 16, 1905, on Alma White's defection. The issue for June 9, 1904, contains a bitter attack on Bresee and J. P. Widney, complete with a scornful cartoon.

13. See *Nazarene Messenger*, October 31, 1901, January 30, March 20, and August 7, 1902, and March 26, 1903; a weekly summary of a sermon by Ruth appears in each issue after February 7, 1902. Cf., for Ruth's

NOTES TO PAGES 130-39   367

early life, *Short Sketches from the Life of Rev. and Mrs. C. W. Ruth* (Louisville, Ky., n.d.), pp. 1-11; and occasional notes in *Christian Witness,* September 12 and October 10, 1895, and *passim.*

14. *Nazarene Messenger,* May 21, June 23, August 13, and September 3, 1903, and *passim.*

15. *Ibid.,* April 9 and 23, July 9 and 16, and August 6, 1903.

16. *Ibid.,* November 12, 1903.

17. *Ibid.,* December, 1900, to February, 1901, *passim;* October 31 and November 28, 1901, March 20, 1902, March 23 and October 1, 1903, November 3, 1904, and October 12 and November 2, 1905. Cf. "History of the First Church of the Nazarene, Pasadena, California," Ms in the church office, pp. 1-4.

18. *Nazarene Messenger,* April 19, 1900, and May 7, 1903; *Peniel Herald,* I, No. 8 (May, 1895), 1; *San Francisco Call,* June 3, 1896, and November 26, 1903; and Girvin, *op. cit.,* p. 123.

19. See Tenth Assembly, *Proceedings* . . . *1905,* p. 18; *Nazarene Messenger,* May 7, July 27, and November 2, 1905; E. A. Girvin, San Francisco, California, June 4, 1909, to P. F. Bresee (letter in possession of Mr. Horace Bresee, Los Angeles, California).

20. *Nazarene Messenger,* July 25, 1901; clippings in the Countess Hurd "Scrapbook," Nashville, Tennessee, I, 87-88, II, 121. Cf. Girvin, *Bresee,* pp. 133-34.

21. Church of the Nazarene *Manual* . . . *1898,* pp. 37-46; *1903,* pp. 49-63. *Nazarene Messenger,* January 8, April 17, May 8, June 12, July 10, and August 7, 1902, and issues for May and June, 1903, describe the sacramental services.

22. *Nazarene Messenger,* February 21, 1901, July 31, 1902, March 26, 1903, and August 18, 1904.

23. Ninth Assembly, *Proceedings* . . . *1904,* p. 34; Tenth Assembly, *Proceedings* . . . *1905,* pp. 17, 45; Church *Manual* . . . *1905,* p. 36; Countess Hurd "Scrapbook," I, 86; Church of the Nazarene, Northwest District, Ms, "Minutes" (district office), pp. 11, 26; H. Orton Wiley, conversation with the writer, July 17, 1955.

24. Girvin, *op. cit.,* pp. 181-82; *Nazarene Messenger,* August 23, 1900, May 1, June 19, and August 7, 1902; Ninth Assembly, *Proceedings* . . . *1904,* pp. 8-9, 26; Church of the Nazarene, Los Angeles District, Home and Foreign Missionary Board, Minutes (Ms in the district office), entry for July 21, 1912; Ida S. Edgar, Los Angeles, January 3, 1907, to W. P. Trumbower, appended to First Church of the Nazarene, Los Angeles, Ms, "Minutes of the Official Board," January 28, 1907; and *ibid.,* April 22, 1906.

25. *Nazarene Messenger,* August 17, 1899, September 12, 1901, June 12, 1902, and November 30, 1905, pp. 4-5; *Christian Witness,* June 17, 1897. For comparable Methodist views, see *California Christian Advocate,* April 10, 1895, and January 31, April 18, June 13, and September 12, 1901.

26. *Nazarene Messenger,* July 3, 1899, January 18, 1900, July 4, 1901, July 3, 1902, and *passim;* Ninth Assembly, *Proceedings* . . . *1904,* p. 32.

27. The early history of the school can be found only in the columns of the *Nazarene Messenger:* see Leora Maris, "A Short History of Pacific Bible College," July 27, 1905; and other references and announcements in the issues for July 31 and August 14, 1902, June 4 and 11, 1903, and

October 26 and November 22, 1905. See also Girvin, *op. cit.*, pp. 178-79, and the founder's statement, quoted above, in Ninth Assembly, *Proceedings . . . 1904*, pp. 11, 29-30.

28. *Supra*, 99; Bresee's sermon, reported in *Christian Witness*, August 22, 1895, pp. 1-8; Countess Hurd, "Scrapbook," II, clipping, 120; Tenth Assembly, *Proceedings . . . 1905*, report of the educational committee, pp. 37-38.

29. See Girvin, *op. cit.*, pp. 178-79. Cf. *Nazarene Messenger*, May 17, 1906, pp. 6, 10; May 31, 1906, pp. 7, 10; July 5, 1906, pp. 21-22; June 6, 1907, p. 8; September 12, 1907; and notes on the author's conversations with H. Orton Wiley, August 2, 1955, and with Horace Bresee, July 24, 1955.

30. T. L. Jones, *From the Gold Mine to the Pulpit* (Cincinnati, 1904), pp. 85-95, 118-25; Walton Skipworth, Portland, Oregon, December 1, 1943, and December 9, 1943, to William W. Youngson (in Skipworth papers, Willamette University); *Pacific Christian Advocate*, October 22 and September 17, 1885, February 7, 1894, and January 2, February 27, and October 9, 1895.

31. See Albert Atwood, *Glimpses of Pioneer Life on Puget Sound* (Seattle, 1903), pp. 400, 457-59; Methodist Episcopal Church, Puget Sound Conference, *Journal . . . 1887*, p. 3, *Journal . . . 1888*, pp. 43-44, *Journal . . . 1889*, p. 36, and appointment lists in the *Journals* for 1896 to 1901; *Christian Witness*, August 29, September 5, and October 24, 1895; and W. N. Coffee, Rosette Douglas, and others, "A Brief Outline History of the Oregon Conference of the Free Methodist Church" (Ms in the Willamette University Library), pp. 1-9.

32. I. G. Martin, conversations with the author, August 3 and 17, 1955; photostat of clipping dated "Great Falls, Montana, March, 1901," from I. G. Martin's notebook (in the Nazarene archives); First Church of the Nazarene, Spokane, Washington, "Minutes" (Ms in church office), pp. 1-2; *Northwest Nazarene*, XXIV, No. 2 (June, 1953), 1; *Nazarene Messenger*, January 16 and 23, 1902, and July 27, 1905.

33. *Nazarene Messenger*, August 15 and September 26, 1901; M.E. Church, Puget Sound Conference, *Journal . . . 1902*, pp. 16, 24, *Journal . . . 1903*, pp. 20, 79, *Journal . . . 1904*, p. 61. *Supra*, 48.

34. See the accounts of Bresee's journey in *Nazarene Messenger*, June 26, July 10 and 17, and (for his description of the church in Spokane) July 24, 1902. Cf. M. L. Haney, *Pentecostal Possibilities, or Story of My Life* (Chicago, 1906), pp. 386-87.

35. See *Nazarene Messenger*, December 22 and 29, 1904. *Northwest Nazarene*, XXXIV, No. 3 (July, 1953), 1, contains Mrs. H. D. Brown's account of her husband's decision to join the denomination.

36. *Nazarene Messenger*, July 6, 13, and 20, 1905, October 18, 1906, and March 14, 1907, p. 4; Church of the Nazarene, Northwest District, "Minutes" (Ms in the district superintendent's office), p. 9.

37. The First Church, Spokane, "Minutes," tell this story on pp. 9, 13, 38, 60-66, 77, 82, 88-89, 93, 97, 104. Cf. H. D. Brown's report, *Nazarene Messenger*, September 14, 1905.

38. See *Nazarene Messenger*, March 8, 1900, on Kent's meetings; and March 7, April 25, and Sptember 19, 1901, for representative reports from the Buffums.

NOTES TO PAGES 146-56 369

39. See reports in *ibid.*, June to September, 1900, especially August 23, 1900, where the quotation concerning Scottsville camp appears; and *ibid.*, issues for September 5, October 3 and 24, and December 19, 1901.

40. *Ibid.*, June 14, 1900, November 28, 1901, and March 13, May 15, May 22, and June 19, 1902. See notes on similar ventures in Colorado Springs, Colorado, and St. Joseph, Missouri, in the issues for January 10 and September 19, 1901, and January 15, 1902.

41. *Ibid.*, January 23, March 13, and November 5, 1903, for J. A. Smith's work; and July 16, August 13 and 20, and December 24, 1903.

42. See *Nazarene Joy Bells*, I, 2 (April, 1906); First Church of the Nazarene, Chicago, Illinois, *Twenty-fifth Anniversary*, an account apparently written by Mrs. Jack Berry; First Church of the Nazarene, Chicago, Illinois, "Record Book" (Ms in church office), pp. 1-51; Illinois State Holiness Association, *Yearbook* . . . *1906*, pp. 7-8; *Nazarene Messenger*, July 13, 1905.

43. Chicago First Church, *Twenty-fifth Anniversary*.

44. *Nazarene Joy Bells*, I-II, Nos. 1, 2, 3, 4, 8-10 (March-June, October-December, 1906); Chicago First Church, *op. cit.*; Chicago First Church, "Record Book," pp. 90, 91, 97, 102, 111; Church of the Nazarene, Eleventh Annual Assembly, *Proceedings* . . . *1906*, p. 39; Illinois State Holiness Association, *Yearbook* . . . *1906*.

45. *Nazarene Messenger*, August 9, 1906, pp. 4, 9; August 16, 1906, p. 6; and August 23, 1906, pp. 4, 6. *Cf. Nazarene Joy Bells*, II, No. 7 (September, 1906), 1, No. 8 (October, 1906), and III, No. 9 (September, 1907), 8; and Mark R. Moore, *Fifty Years . . . and Beyond; A History of the Chicago Central District, Church of the Nazarene* (Kankakee, Illinois, 1954), pp. 13-14.

CHAPTER VII
FROM THE CUMBERLAND TO THE RIO GRANDE:
THE HERITAGE OF HOLINESS IN THE OLD SOUTHWEST

1. George McCulloch, *History of the Holiness Movement in Texas and the Fanaticism Which Followed* (Aquilla, Texas, 1866), pp. 7-9, 13-17; *Cumberland Presbyterian*, LVI, No. 10 (September 9, 1897), 2; and *ibid.*, No. 11 (September 16, 1897), article by J. B. Mitchell, "The Discussion on Sanctification."

2. McCulloch, *op. cit.*, pp. 53-55; Mrs. R. B. Mitchum, "Personal Diary" (Ms in the possession of Mrs. Countess Hurd, Nashville, Tenn.), clipping, p. 183, apparently from *Way of Life*, August 9, 1893; *Memphis Advocate*, December 7, 1893, p. 7; R. L. Harris, *In America and Africa* (Chicago, 1887), chaps. 5-7, *passim*; R. L. Harris, *Why We Left the Methodist Episcopal Church* (Memphis, Tenn., 1893), pp. 9-11; Maury E. Redford, "History of the Church of the Nazarene in the South" (Master's thesis, Vanderbilt University, 1936), pp. 36-40; *Michigan Holiness Record*, IV, No. 6 (October, 1886), 43, No. 7 (November, 1886), 53, No. 9 (January, 1887), 67, and V, No. 1 (May, 1887), 3.

3. Redford, *op. cit.*, pp. 40-47; Mitchum, *op. cit.*, pp. 16-22; *Government and Doctrines of the New Testament Church* (pamphlet, Milan, Tennessee, 1894), *passim*.

4. Mitchum, *op. cit.*, pp. 54-103; Redford, *op. cit.*, pp. 50, 59; The Church of Christ, Milan, Tennessee, "Record Book" (Ms in the Nazarene archives,

Kansas City, Mo.), p. 3, entry for October 18, 1898 (on Murphree's accession); William E. Fisher, conversation with the writer, August 12, 1955; C. B. Jernigan, *Pioneer Days of the Holiness Movement in the Southwest* (Kansas City, Mo., 1919), pp. 116-19; Mary Lee Cagle, *Life and Work* . . . (Kansas City, c. 1928), pp. 21-22, 40-83, *passim*.

5. W. B. Godbey, *Women Preachers* (Nashville, Tenn., n.d.), pp. 11-12; Fannie McDowell Hunter, *Women Preachers* (Dallas, 1905), pp. 53-55, 70-74, 79-83, 85-87, 90-93. For material in the preceding paragraph, see Mitchum, *op. cit.*, p. 177, and personal letters in the possession of Mrs. Countess Hurd, Nashville.

6. Mrs. E. H. Sheeks prepared some years later the early pages of the New Testament Church of Christ "Journal" (Ms in the Nazarene archives, Kansas City, Missouri), pp. 2-6, apparently with the help of the original Church of Christ "Record Book"; see the latter, pp. 7-14.

7. Church of Christ, "Record Book," pp. 15-19.

8. Redford, *op. cit.*, pp. 62-67; New Testament Church of Christ, "Journal," pp. 9-10, 16-20.

9. Redford, *op. cit.*, pp. 58-60; Jernigan, *op. cit.*, pp. 120-31; New Testament Church of Christ, *Council and Guide Book* . . . (Dallas, Texas, 1905), pp. 30-33; *New Testament Church of Christ, Texas Annual Council* . . . *Second Session* . . . *1903*, p. 9; Cagle, *op. cit.*, pp. 89 ff.

10. The chapter in Jernigan, *op. cit.*, pp. 17-23, is reliable, having been based upon George McCulloch, *op. cit.*, pp. 1-17, 51. See also John Paul, "Scottsville Camp Meeting, a Historic Sketch," *Texas Holiness Advocate*, July 26, 1906, p. 1, and W. E. Shepard's "Report of the Waco Camp," *Peniel Herald*, I, No. 12 (September, 1895), 4. Cf. *supra*, 30-31.

11. J. T. Smith, *Entire Sanctification (Heart Purity) and Regeneration, as Defined by Mr. Wesley, One and the Same* . . . (pamphlet, Marshall, Texas, 1895), pp. 3-4; Macum Phelan, *A History of the Expansion of Methodism in Texas, 1867-1902* (Dallas, Texas, 1937), p. 383; and John H. McLean, *Reminiscences* . . . (Dallas, Texas, 1918), pp. 261-62. Cf. James W. Hill, ed., *The North Texas Conference* . . . *Pulpit* (Nashville, Tennessee, 1880), pp. 60-64, 66; and R. Crawford, *Sanctification Calmly Considered, or Thoughts and Conclusions on Justification, Regeneration, Sanctification, and Christian Perfection* (Georgetown, Texas, 1883), pp. 14-21. See also James B. Chapman, *Bud Robinson, A Brother Beloved* (Kansas City, Mo., 1943), pp. 39-43.

12. Jernigan, *op. cit.*, pp. 68-69; anon., *Christian Perfection. An Address by the Southern Holiness Associations* (pamphlet, Nashville, n.d.); W. B. Godbey, *Christian Perfection* (Atlanta, Georgia, 1886), p. 12; Phelan, *op. cit.*, pp. 118-20.

13. Homer S. Thrall, *Methodism in Texas* (Houston, 1872), pp. 290-91; *Zion's Outlook*, February 14, 1901, p. 4; Methodist Episcopal Church, Gulf Mission Conference, *Journal* . . . *Annual Session* . . . *1897*, pp. 12, 18; *ibid.*, 1898, pp. 30, 32-33; *ibid.*, *Official Journal* . . . *Annual Conference* . . . *1904*, title page, pp. 94, 99, 109; and *ibid.*, 1905, pp. 28-29, 33-36. Cf. R. L. Selle's report as presiding elder in San Antonio in *Christian Witness*, June 17, 1897, p. 13, and reports of his work in Denton in *Zion's Outlook*, June 27, 1901, pp. 1, 8. By 1904, the Gulf Mission Conference *Journal* was being printed at the *Pentecostal Herald* press, in Louisville.

14. *Holiness Evangel*, June 1, 1907, p. 1; and Jernigan, *op. cit.*, p. 86.
15. *Texas Holiness Advocate*, July 5, 1906, p. 1.
16. Jernigan, *op. cit.*, pp. 97-100.
17. The only contemporary account, in *Texas Holiness Banner*, I, No. 3 (December, 1899), 7, agrees with Jernigan, *op cit.*, pp. 100-102. See also *Nazarene Messenger*, November 19, 1908, p. 29; Viva C. DeJernett, conversation with the writer, fall, 1959; and Texas Holiness University, *First Catalogue . . . 1900*, pp. 8-9.
18. Jernigan, *op. cit.*, pp. 102-4, quotes C. A. McConnell's editorial in *Texas Holiness Banner*, written between the two meetings of November and December, which makes matters clear. See also the reconstruction from much later memory in Dennis Rogers, *Holiness Pioneering in the Southland* (Hemet, California, 1944), pp. 28-30, and compare Jernigan, *op. cit.*, pp. 90-93.
19. Jernigan, *op. cit.*, pp. 94-96, prints what he asserts were the complete minutes of the association, but several important items, including the statement of doctrine and the plan to ordain ministers, are left out; see *Minutes of the Northwest Texas Holiness Association, held at the Holiness Camp Ground, Sunset, Texas, August 9, 1899; also Form and Plan of Local Organization, Adopted by the Association* (the only copy I have seen is in the possession of M. L. Locke, of Bridgeport, Texas).
20. Jernigan, *op. cit.*, pp. 104-7; *Texas Holiness Banner*, I, No. 8 (May, 1900), 5.
21. See Huckabee's editorial, "Signs of the Future," *Pentecostal Advocate*, June 28, 1906, p. 45; and Texas Holiness University, *Catalogue*, for the years 1902-7 (at the Bethany Nazarene College library), especially that for 1905-6, in which Professor L. B. Williams described at length his "commercial department." *Living Water*, April 6, 1905, p. 8, notes the change in ownership of the *Advocate*.
22. See, for the quotation, Texas Holiness University, *Third Catalogue . . . 1902-3*, p. 9, and *1905-6*, pp. 49-55. Cf. W. G. Airhart, "Why You Should Move to Peniel," *Texas Holiness Advocate*, July 12, 1906, p. 4; the article by L. B. Williams, *ibid.*, June 28, 1906; and Chapman, *op. cit.*, p. 46.
23. See in *Pentecostal Advocate*: "History of the Holiness Work on the Plains," January 3, 1907; "Central Plains College," November 7, 1907; and J. B. McBride, "History of Missouri Holiness School, July 25, 1907.
24. *Ibid.*, November 21, 1907, p. 8. On the mood of optimism and brotherliness, see "Organized Bands," April 4, 1907, pp. 8-9, and "Holiness Association of Texas," October 24, 1907, p. 2; on camp meetings, see the issue for June 21, 1906, pp. 6, 13.
25. Jernigan, *op. cit.*, pp. 110-14; D. Shelby Corlett, *Spirit-filled; the Life of the Rev. James Blaine Chapman, D.D.* (Kansas City, n.d.), pp. 61-66.
26. Jernigan, *op. cit.*, pp. 114-15. Neither the files of the *Texas Holiness Advocate* for these years nor the records of the councils of the Independent Holiness church have survived.
27. *Ibid.*, pp. 56-58.
28. *Ibid.*, pp. 61-65; Mrs. Annie Scott, "Mission Work in Arkansas," *Highways and Hedges*, October 1, 1906, p. 7.
29. New Testament Church of Christ, "Journal," pp. 30, 32-38; cf. *ibid.*, pp. 35-36, and Jernigan, *op. cit.*, pp. 122-23.

30. See Mitchum's report to the annual meeting of 1902, describing his work as a drummer, in New Testament Church of Christ "Journal," p. 15; miscellaneous flyers describing the churnless butter process, in the Nazarene archives; Redford, *op. cit.*, pp. 71-75; and notes on the writer's conversation with Mrs. Countess Hurd, Mitchum's daughter, November 12, 1955.

31. B. F. Neely, conversation with the writer, July 10, 1955; New Testament Church of Christ, *Government and Doctrines* (1903), pp. 15-18; Holiness Church of Christ, *Yearbook and Minutes . . . 1905* (in possession of M. E. Redford), *passim*. On the laity, see Jernigan's comments in *Highways and Hedges*, October 15, 1906, p. 1, and *ibid.*, December 1, 1906.

32. New Testament Church of Christ, "Journal," p. 64.

33. See Cagle, *op. cit.*, pp. 100-111; *Holiness Evangel*, February 1 and 15, 1907; Arkansas Holiness Literary School, "Minutes of the Board" (Ms in possession of Dr. Roy Cantrell, Bethany, Oklahoma), entries for December 28, 1905, February, March 24, April 26, May 8, and May 15, 1906, and March 10 and 11, 1913; J. D. Scott's report in *Holiness Evangel*, February 1, 1907; New Testament Church of Christ, "Journal," p. 99.

34. New Testament Church of Christ, "Journal," pp. 64-65, 70; Holiness Church of Christ, *Yearbook and Minutes . . . 1905*, pp. 26-28; *Highways and Hedges*, September 15, 1906, p. 8, and November 15, 1906, p. 7; *Holiness Evangel*, April 1, 1907, p. 4, and April 15, 1907, p. 7; and R. M. Guy, "Freedom," *Zion's Outlook*, May 2, 1901, p. 2. William E. Fisher shared his memories of R. M. Guy and C. B. Jernigan in a conversation with the writer, August 12, 1955.

35. *Highways and Hedges*, September 15, 1906, p. 4.

36. *Ibid.*, December 1, 1906, p. 4; New Testament Church of Christ, "Journal," pp. 84-85, 93; and Mrs. Cagle's letter in *Holiness Evangel*, February 15, 1907, p. 6.

37. The quotation is from "Minutes of the Ninth Annual Council, Holiness Church of Christ, Little Rock, November 12, 1907," in *Holiness Evangel*, January 15, 1908, p. 12. For material in the preceding paragraphs, see *Highways and Hedges*, September 15, 1906, p. 6, and December 1, 1906, p. 3; Mrs. Johnny Jernigan, "A Tragic Night in the Slums," *Holiness Evangel*, April 15, 1907; and "Report of Home Mission Commission," *ibid.*, December 15, 1906, p. 5.

38. *Highways and Hedges*, October 1, 1906, pp. 4-5, and December 1, 1906, p. 6. Cf. editorial, "The Holiness Church of Christ and Missions," *Holiness Evangel*, May 1, 1907; and, *ibid.*, July 15, 1907, p. 7, for advertisement of the second annual missionary camp meeting.

39. New Testament Church of Christ, "Journal," p. 80; *Holiness Evangel*, August 1 and 15, 1907; Holiness Church of Christ, *Manual . . . 1907*, p. 39; and Rest Cottage Association, *The White Slaves of America* (Pilot Point, 1907), pp. 35-38, 30-34, and *passim*.

40. Holiness Church of Christ, *Yearbook and Minutes . . . 1905*, pp. 49-55, lists the congregations. Cf. Jernigan, *op. cit.*, p. 124, and *Highways and Hedges*, September 15, 1906, p. 5, on the Buffalo Gap congregation.

41. J. B. Chapman's account in *Highways and Hedges*, October 15, 1906, pp. 2, 8, and C. B. Jernigan, *ibid.*, November 15, 1906, p. 4; cf. *Living Water*, June 1, 1905, p. 12.

42. The quotation is from New Testament Church of Christ, "Journal," p. 98; see also pp. 102, 106-7. Cf. Holiness Church of Christ, *Yearbook and Minutes* . . . *1905*, pp. 13-14; J. D. Scott, "The Church of Christ," *Highways and Hedges*, October 1, 1906, p. 1, setting forth a spiritual basis for the idea of apostolic succession; and *Highways and Hedges*, September 15, 1906, p. 4.

43. *Holiness Evangel*, January 15, 1907, p. 1, and July 15, 1907, p. 2.

44. Quotations in the paragraph may be found in the New Testament Church of Christ, "Journal," pp. 103, 124-25, and *Highways and Hedges*, November 1, 1906, p. 2. See, for numbers of ordained elders, *Holiness Evangel*, December 15, 1906, pp. 7-8, and January 15, 1907, p. 7. For other views, see J. B. Chapman, "The Church and Revivals," *Highways and Hedges*, December 1, 1906, p. 2, and "Pastors Needed," *ibid.*, October 1, 1906, p. 2; and Joseph N. Speakes, "Pastor and People," *Holiness Evangel*, March 1, 1907, p. 2.

45. The quotations are from R. M. Guy, "Interdenominationalism," *Holiness Evangel*, February 15, 1907, p. 2; Jernigan's editorials in *Highways and Hedges*, October 15, 1906, p. 4, and *Holiness Evangel*, June 15, 1907, p. 4, and July 15, 1907, p. 4; and J. B. Chapman, "Church Union," *ibid.*, September 15, 1907, p. 2.

46. Editorial, *Texas Holiness Advocate*, June 28, 1906, p. 8; W. E. Fisher, "Our Meetings," *ibid.*, July 5, 1906; and representative notices of holiness associations, Southern and Northern Methodist churches, Free Methodists, etc., in *ibid.*, June 21, 1906, p. 13, and July 12, 1906, p. 6.

47. *Texas Holiness Advocate*, for 1906: July 5, p. 7, and July 12, p. 9; and incidental notices of Jernigan, Fisher, Rogers, and the rescue home at Pilot Point in the issues for June 13, June 21, June 28, and July 5, 1907. Cf. Holiness Church of Christ, *Yearbook and Minutes* . . . *1905*, pp. 12, 18; and *Highways and Hedges*, December 1, 1906, p. 8.

48. Editorials in *Holiness Evangel*, for 1908: issues of February 1, p. 4; March 1, p. 2; March 15, p. 2; April 15, p. 7; August 20, p. 4; and September 16, p. 2.

CHAPTER VIII

THE PENTECOSTAL MISSION IN TENNESSEE, 1898-1915

1. *Zion's Outlook*, September 22, 1898, p. 2, November 1, 1900, p. 1, February 21, 1901, p. 1, July 18, 1901, p. 1, and October 17, 1901, p. 12; B. F. Haynes, *Tempest-Tossed on Methodist Seas* (Kansas City, 1914), pp. 98 ff; Maury E. Redford, "History of the Church of the Nazarene in Tennessee" (B.D. thesis, Vanderbilt University, 1934), pp. 30 ff.; *supra*, 44.

2. The quotation is from the *Cumberland Presbyterian*, February 23, 1899, p. 232. See references to McClurkan's life in *Zion's Outlook*, April 11, 1901, p. 1, and October 20, 1904; Trevecca College, *Darda, Volume IV, 1928, Historical and Pictorial Edition* (Claude Galloway, ed., Nashville, 1928), "Historical Sketch"; and Merle McClurkan Heath, *A Man Sent from God; the Life of J. O. McClurkan* (Kansas City, 1947), pp. 21-24, 27-28, 30-36, 40-41, 51-52. On "Keswick" influences, see J. Wilbur Chapman, "God's Plan for Us," *Zion's Outlook*, November 14, 1901; *ibid.*, October 25, 1900, p. 1; excerpts from Charles G. Finney's writings, *ibid.*, March and April, 1901; and *ibid.*, October 10, 1901, p. 2.

3. M. E. Redford, "History of the Church of the Nazarene in the South"

(M.A. thesis, Vanderbilt University, 1936), pp. 123-25, 132-33; Heath, *op cit.*, pp. 53-57.

4. *Zion's Outlook*, February 7, 1901, p. 8. For other references to the foregoing, see *ibid.*, October 25, 1900, p. 5, November 1, 1900, p. 6, May 2, 1901, p. 8, October 10, 1901, p. 12, and January 28, 1904, p. 1. Cf. *ibid.*, October 4, 1906, p. 8, for McClurkan's denunciation of race prejudice and mob action in Atlanta. See also Redford, "Church of the Nazarene in Tennessee," pp. 34-52, and Redford, "Church of the Nazarene in the South," pp. 125-30.

5. The quotations are from *Zion's Outlook*, April 25, 1901, p. 3, and May 30, 1901, p. 4. Cf. the weekly columns written by Mrs. May Anderson Hawkins throughout these years. See also J. O. McClurkan, *Wholly Sanctified* (Nashville, n.d.), pp. 109-12, for decisive statements on the idea of eradication; contrast A. B. Simpson, *The Fullness of Jesus; or, Christian Life in the New Testament* (N.Y., n.d.), pp. 8-10, 110-18, 220.

6. The doctrinal statement is quoted from *Zion's Outlook*, April 19, 1900, in Redford, "Church of the Nazarene in Tennessee," p. 45.

7. The quotations are from *Zion's Outlook*, editorial for February 28, 1901, p. 8; see also the article, "Behold, He Cometh," April 18, 1901, p. 6, and "A Temperate View of Dowie," November 4, 1901, p. 5. Cf. *ibid.*, March 7, 1901, p. 13, April 11, 1901, pp. 1, 8; and the editorial "When Faith Healers Disagree, Who Shall Decide?" *Cumberland Presbyterian*, December 9, 1897, p. 716.

8. Redford, "Church of the Nazarene in the South," pp. 136-37, 139-40.

9. *Zion's Outlook*, February 28, 1901, pp. 1, 8; and April 14, 1901, p. 4. Cf. *ibid.*, August 15, 1901, p. 8, August 29, 1901, p. 8, and November 28, 1901, p. 12.

10. *Ibid.*, editorial, "The Church Question," May 30, 1901, and editorial, "Judging," September 12, 1901, p. 8. Practically every issue during this year pointed up the same theme.

11. M. E. Redford had access to the minutes of the Pentecostal Alliance for November 4, 1901, which he quotes in "Church of the Nazarene in the South," pp. 137-39; I have seen substantially the same information in *Zion's Outlook*, November 7, 1901, p. 9.

12. *Zion's Outlook*, November 7, 1901, pp. 8-9, November 28, 1901, p. 8, and the page 1 story on Peniel Missions, August 29, 1901. The issue for April 21, 1901, p. 6, first listed missionaries specifically sponsored by the Pentecostal Alliance, an indication that the separation from the Christian and Missionary Alliance was already patent by that time. Cf., however, the issue for December 12, 1901, pp. 4-5, for a sermon by A. B. Simpson; there was evidently no break in fellowship.

13. *Living Water*, October 22, 1903; see also issues for June 5, 1902, p. 8, and July 16, 1903, p. 3; and Redford, "Church of the Nazarene in the South," pp. 146-47.

14. The quotation is from *Living Water*, August 16, 1903, p. 15; see also issues for December 8, 1904, p. 12, February 18, 1904, p. 1, and September 19, 1907, p. 16.

15. See accounts of the institutions at Meridian in *Zion's Outlook*, March 7, 1901, p. 5, May 9, 1901, p. 3, September 26, 1901, October 24, 1901, p. 12, July 16, 1903; *Yearbook of the Holiness Union . . . 1904* (Memphis,

Tennessee, 1904), pp. 14-17; Miss Pallen I. Mayberry, conversation with the writer, August 25, 1955. In 1904 Professor R. E. Smith led a secession of students from the Meridian Male College to establish Ruskin Cave College, Tennessee, thirty miles south of Nashville; C. E. Hardy, who attended school at Ruskin Cave, supplied information on this institution in a conversation with the writer, November 12, 1955.

16. Quoted in Heath, *op. cit.*, p. 65. Cf. *ibid.*, pp. 66-72; *Zion's Outlook,* March 7, 1901, p. 8, May 30, 1901, p. 8, November 21, 1901, p. 12, September 14, 1905, p. 1, and October 11, 1906, p. 16; Trevecca College, *op. cit.*, "Historical Sketch"; and Redford, "Church of the Nazarene in Tennessee," pp. 64-66.

17. *Yearbook of the Holiness Union . . . 1904*, pp. 51-52; *Zion's Outlook,* June 5, 1902, p. 8; *Living Water,* March 30, 1905, p. 12, and November 1, 1906, p. 12.

18. F. L. Chappell, *The Eleventh Hour Laborers* (South Nyack, N.Y., 1898), was reviewed in *Zion's Outlook,* March 7, 1901. Cf. *Living Water,* November 3, 1904, pp. 1, 8.

19. *Ibid.,* August 17, 1905, p. 8, September 14, 1905, p. 1, and October 11, 1906, pp. 8, 17. On establishment of Trevecca College, see *ibid.*, June 24, 1909, pp. 1-2, quoted in Redford, "Church of the Nazarene in Tennessee," p. 90.

20. The editorials quoted in the preceding paragraphs appeared May 12, 1904, and January 22, 1905; cf. *ibid.,* August 1, 1907, p. 8.

21. *Zion's Outlook,* February 21, 1901, p. 4, March 21, 1901, p. 4, April 25, 1901, June 6, 1901, p. 3, August 22, 1901, p. 8, and November 20, 1902, p. 6; and *Living Water,* October 22, 1903, p. 6. On contacts with the New Testament Church of Christ, see *Zion's Outlook,* June 5, 1902, p. 12, and November 20, 1902, p. 9; *Living Water,* November 1, 1906, p. 12; New Testament Church of Christ, "Journal" (Ms in the Nazarene archives, Kansas City), pp. 62, 70, 86; record of conversation of Mrs. Countess Hurd with the writer, November 5, 1955. Cf. Huckabee's editorial in *Texas Holiness Advocate,* July 12, 1906.

22. J. O. McClurkan, *How to Keep Sanctified* (pamphlet, Nashville, 1899), p. 29, and *passim; Zion's Outlook,* March 28, 1901, p. 3; T. C. Young, conversation with the writer, November 8, 1955.

23. *Living Water,* August 17, 1905, p. 8. See also, on the mystic tradition, *ibid.,* October 22, 1903, p. 5, January 28, 1904, p. 2, and March 9, 1905, p. 1; and *Zion's Outlook,* January 31, 1901, pp. 1, 8.

24. *Living Water,* November 3, 1904, p. 9; cf. *ibid.,* April 13, 1905, pp. 1-2, and June 8, 1905, p. 5.

25. McClurkan, *Wholly Sanctified,* pp. 109, 112; *Living Water,* March 14, 1907, p. 8; Stephen S. White, conversation with the author, January 8, 1956; Joseph H. Smith, "Anger," *Living Water,* November 3, 1904, p. 9. See also P. R. Nugent, *Scriptural Sanctification* (pamphlet, Nashville, n.d.), pp. 9-11, stressing cleansing without use of the term eradication; and C. E. Cornell in *Nazarene Joy Bells,* III, No. 5 (May, 1908), 2 (file at First Church of the Nazarene, Chicago, Illinois).

26. J. O. McClurkan, Nashville, Tennessee, January 1, 1907, to P. F. Bresee (carbon copy in possession of M. E. Redford, microfilm in Nazarene archives); P. F. Bresee, Los Angeles, California, August 1, 1907, to J. O.

McClurkan (original in possession of M. E. Redford, microfilm in Nazarene archives).

27. J. O. McClurkan, Nashville, Tennessee, to C. E. Cornell (the carbon copy, with date mutilated, in possession of M. E. Redford, and on microfilm in Nazarene archives) seems to be the same letter to which Redford refers in his "Church of the Nazarene in the South," p. 148; it was published in *Nazarene Messenger*, September 19, 1907.

28. Redford, "Church of the Nazarene in the South," pp. 149-53, is complete on these points, and is based upon the minutes of the Pentecostal Mission. On women preachers, see *Nazarene Messenger*, October 31, 1907, p. 9, November 14, 1907, p. 2, December 12, 1907, p. 7, March 12, 1908, p. 4, and August 6, 1908, p. 7; Church of the Nazarene, First General Assembly, *Proceedings* . . . *1907*, pp. 33-34; Heath, *op. cit.*, pp. 82-83; and the *Holiness Evangel*, April 15, 1908, p. 3.

29. Redford, "Church of the Nazarene in the South," quotes from the Pentecostal Mission, "Minutes, 1907-1914," pp. 44-48, *passim*. See also J. O. McClurkan, Nashville, Tennessee, March 5, 1907, to B. W. Huckabee (carbon copy on microfilm in the Nazarene archives; original in possession of M. E. Redford), for an indication that H. C. Morrison's public attacks upon McClurkan in 1907 may have helped to alienate McClurkan, especially in view of the fact that Morrison was in that year urging the Texas groups to unite with the Church of the Nazarene; and Bresee's letter to McClurkan, cited above.

On the fact that women preachers were welcome in the Pentecostal Mission, so long as they did not insist upon ordination, see Mrs. George C. Needham, "Woman's Ministry," *Living Water*, November 1, 1906, p. 7; incidental references to their work, *ibid.*, June 2, 1904; *Zion's Outlook*, January 10, 1901, p. 1, January 24, 1901, p. 4; notes on T. C. Young's conversation with the author, November 8, 1955 (in the Nazarene archives), a conversation which also indicates the growth of Freemasonry among some of McClurkan's most loyal followers.

30. See copy of McClurkan's letter in that of E. P. Ellyson, Peniel, Texas, November 28, 1910, to H. F. Reynolds (in Reynolds papers, Nazarene archives).

31. Pentecostal Church of the Nazarene, *Official Minutes, Third General Assembly* . . . *1911*, pp. 26, 34, 54; *ibid.*, General Foreign Missionary Board, "Minutes, 1908-1913" (in the Nazarene archives), pp. 57-58, 60, 66. The general superintendents' correspondence, in the Reynolds papers, gives indispensable background: see H. F. Reynolds' letters to E. P. Ellyson from Chicago, January 31, March 15, April 28, and May 8, and one from Nashville, February 22, 1911; and Ellyson to Reynolds, Peniel, Texas, March 7 and May 1, 1911.

32. *Second General Assembly* . . . *1908*, p. 3; H. F. Reynolds, Chicago, February 1, 1910, to E. P. Ellyson (in Reynolds papers, Nazarene archives); Church of the Nazarene, Clarksville District, Second Annual Assembly, *Minutes* . . . *1912*, "Statistical Report," inside back cover, and pp. 3-4, 12; Church of the Nazarene, Tennessee District, Third Annual Assembly, *Minutes* . . . *1915*, p. 19.

33. H. F. Reynolds, October 25, 1910, to E. P. Ellyson (in Reynolds papers). See history of the early Georgia work in *Christian Witness*,

June 11, 1896; and *Zion's Outlook,* June 13, 1901, p. 17, July 4, 1901, p. 4, and July 25, 1901. Cf. *The Discipline of the Holiness Church, Headquarters, Donalsonville, Georgia* (Louisville, n.d.); and Florence Shingler, "History of the Donalsonville Church of the Nazarene" (Ms in Bethany Nazarene College library).

34. Redford, "Church of the Nazarene in Tennessee," pp. 94, 97-102; C. E. Hardy, Tim H. Moore, Edward W. Thompson, and John T. Benson, Nashville, Tennessee, October 21, 1914, to the General Foreign Missionary Board, Pentecostal Church of the Nazarene (in Nazarene archives, correspondence of the General Foreign Missionary Board); Mrs. Countess Hurd, conversation with the writer, November 5, 1955. Cf. the packet of records for the year 1915, marked, "Trevecca College Receipts, etc.," in the archives of the college.

35. Redford, "Church of the Nazarene in Tennessee," pp. 102-6; "Articles of Agreement between the Pentecostal Church of the Nazarene and the Pentecostal Mission" (in Nazarene archives, attached to letter to Foreign Missionary Board cited in the preceding footnote); C. E. Hardy, conversation with the writer, November 13, 1955.

36. See especially Richard D. Hofstadter, *The Age of Reform: Bryan to F. D. R.* (New York, 1955); George E. Mowry, "The California Progressive and His Rationale: A Study in Middle Class Politics," *Mississippi Valley Historical Review,* XXXVI (September, 1949), 239-50.

37. Charles Howard Hopkins, *The Rise of the Social Gospel in American Protestantism, 1865-1918* (New Haven, 1940); Lawrence A. Cremin, "The Progressive Movement in American Education," *Harvard Educational Review,* XVII (fall, 1957), 251-70; Gilman N. Ostrander, *The Prohibition Movement in California, 1848-1933* (Berkeley, Calif., University of California, *Publications in History,* No. 57, 1957), Chap. VI, p. 57.

38. Pentecostal Church of the Nazarene, First General Assembly, *Proceedings . . . 1907,* p. 57; J. D. Scott, "God's Standard," *Holiness Evangel,* January 15, 1907, p. 1; "Internationalism, Interdenominationalism," *Pentecostal Advocate,* December 5, 1907.

39. Church of the Nazarene, Ninth Assembly, *Proceedings . . . 1904,* p. 37; Pentecostal Church of the Nazarene, First General Assembly, *Proceedings . . . 1907,* p. 43.

40. See Liston Pope, *Millhands and Preachers: A Study of Gastonia* (New Haven, 1942); Walter G. Muelder, "From Sect to Church," *Christendom,* Vol. X (autumn, 1945); and H. Richard Niebuhr, *The Social Sources of Denominationalism* (N.Y., 1929). For later views, see Charles S. Braden, "The Sects," and Liston Pope, "Religion and the Class Structure," in Roy H. Abrams, ed., *Organized Religion in the United States* (*The Annuals of the American Academy of Political and Social Science,* March, 1948).

CHAPTER IX

UNION AND LIBERTY—ONE AND INSEPARABLE

1. For quotations, see J. B. Chapman, "A Builder with Ample Plans," *Herald of Holiness,* December 17, 1938 (Bresee Centennial Number), p. 7; *Pentecostal Advocate,* January 10, 1907, p. 9. Cf. *ibid.*: February 21, 1907, p. 2; C. A. McConnell's editorial, "A Broader Love," October 17, 1907, p. 8;

and the unsigned article "Interdenominationalism, Internationalism," December 5, 1907.

2. The quotation is from J. W. Goodwin, "The Church of the Nazarene as I Have Seen It," *Nazarene Messenger*, December 14, 1905, p. 4. Cf. A. E. Sanner, *John W. Goodwin, A Biography* (Kansas City, 1945), pp. 75-76, 81-82, 84-85. See also, on Deacon Morse, *Nazarene Messenger*, March 26, 1903, p. 3; and, on other matters, C. W. Griffin, conversation with the writer, July 16, 1955; Association of Pentecostal Churches of America, Missionary Committee, "Minutes, April 13, 1901, to April 13, 1907" (Ms, in Nazarene archives), pp. 89, 92.

3. *Nazarene Messenger*, August 9, 1906, pp. 6-7; Association of Pentecostal Churches of America, Missionary Committee, "Minutes, 1901-1907," p. 104; John Bricker, "A Life of E. E. Angell" (seminar paper, Eastern Nazarene College History Department, 1950); references to C. W. Ruth's role, in *Nazarene Messenger*, November 19, 1908, pp. 15, 19; and Ruth's address in the Church of the Nazarene, Eleventh Assembly, *Proceedings . . . 1906*, pp. 9-10, 22-23.

4. *Nazarene Joy Bells*, II, No. 7 (September, 1906), 4; *Nazarene Messenger*, September 27, 1906, pp. 6-7; E. A. Girvin, *Phineas F. Bresee, A Prince in Israel* (Kansas City, 1916), p. 316; H. Orton Wiley, conversation with the writer, August 18, 1955; Countess Hurd, "Scrapbook" (in possession of Mrs. Hurd, Nashville, Tennessee), I, 88, clipping, from an unknown California newspaper.

5. On the public receptions, see Church of the Nazarene, Eleventh General Assembly, *Proceedings . . . 1906*, pp. 7, 9, 21-24; and J. N. Short's report to *Beulah Christian*, reprinted in *Nazarene Messenger*, December 6, 1906, p. 3.

6. Church of the Nazarene, *Manual*, 1898, pp. 15, 17.

7. *Ibid.*, 1903, pp. 37-38; cf. *ibid.*, 1905, pp. 53-54.

8. Church of the Nazarene, Northwest District, "Minutes . . . 1905" (Ms, in the district office), pp. 31-34; and *Nazarene Messenger*, October 26, 1905, p. 9.

9. *Nazarene Messenger*, October 26, 1905, pp. 1, 4-5; and J. B. Creighton's statement in Northwest District, "Minutes . . . , 1907," pp. 73-74. Cf. *supra*, 77-81.

10. *Nazarene Messenger*, October 11, 1906, p. 6, indicating that the plan of union had been in fact "formulated by Dr. Bresee"; and Short's statement, *ibid.*, December 6, 1906, p. 3.

11. The emphasis upon holiness evangelism, especially in great cities, as the chief purpose of the union appears in nearly every editorial and comment on the subject. See Church of the Nazarene, Eleventh General Assembly, *Proceedings . . . 1906*, p. 9; *Nazarene Messenger*, August 9, 1906, p. 7, December 6, 1906, pp. 3, 6, February 14, 1907, p. 6; and J. G. Pingree, "What Shall be Done with Our Cities?" *ibid.*, August 8, 1907, p. 2.

12. See Bresee's editorial, "Church Union," *Nazarene Messenger*, February 14, 1907, p. 6. H. F. Reynolds, "Why I Voted for the Union" (Ms, Reynolds papers, Nazarene archives), presented on the occasion of the twenty-fifth anniversary of the Chicago Central District, is summarized in more refined tones in H. F. Reynolds, "Autobiography" (Ms in Nazarene archives), I, 230.

A sample of the problems which easterners had faced is found in "People's Pentecostal Church of West Brooklyn, to the Missionary Committee of the Association of Pentecostal Churches of America" (Ms, June, 1905, Reynolds papers, Nazarene archives); a lawsuit was necessary to settle the ownership of the church property after this secession.

13. "Church Unity Again," *Nazarene Messenger,* March 7, 1907, p. 6.

Bresee's reference to "fanaticism" was not a casual one. The outbreak of the "tongues" movement, calling itself Pentecostal, had created wide concern among the holiness people in the South and West. See Bresee's editorial, *Nazarene Messenger,* December 13, 1906, p. 6, and references to the movement in other holiness papers as follows: *Nazarene Joy Bells,* II, No. 9 (November, 1906), 5; *Texas Holiness Advocate,* July 26, 1906, p. 4; *Pentecostal Advocate,* January 10, 1907, pp. 2, 13, and February 21, 1907, pp. 8-9; *Holiness Evangel,* January 1, 1907, p. 1, February 15, 1907, p. 5, March 15, 1907, p. 5, and September 16, 1908, p. 2; *Living Water,* May 30, 1907, p. 8. C. W. Sherman's defection and return are noted in *Pentecostal Advocate,* September 5, 1907, p. 9.

14. See Association of Pentecostal Churches of America, *Minutes . . . Twelfth Annual Meeting . . . 1907,* pp. 12-13; P. F. Bresee, Los Angeles, California, August 1, 1907, to J. O. McClurkan (in possession of M. E. Redford, microfilm in Nazarene archives).

Interestingly enough, the Lincoln Place congregation in Pittsburgh had been at the point of withdrawing from the Pentecostal Association because of the lack of proper supervision; the pastor advised the annual meeting that if the union was consummated "and the united body was more connectional," they might be induced to remain. See Association of Pentecostal Churches of America, *Minutes . . . 1907,* p. 16; and cf. letter from T. L. Wieand, Allentown, Pennsylvania, to *Nazarene Messenger,* July 18, 1907, p. 4.

15. See again Girvin's article in *Nazarene Messenger,* April 25, 1907, p. 7; his article in *Nazarene Joy Bells,* II, No. 4 (April, 1907), 2; D. Rand Pierce's account, describing Hoople's speech, in *Beulah Christian,* April 20, 1907, p. 5; and Association of Pentecostal Churches of America, *Minutes . . . 1907,* p. 30.

16. *Ibid.,* p. 19.

17. The *Christian Witness* article is quoted in *Nazarene Messenger,* May 2, 1907, p. 4; cf. Association of Pentecostal Churches, *Minutes . . . 1907,* pp. 15, 21. See, on Morrison, *Nazarene Messenger,* March 21, 1907, pp. 6-7, and March 19, 1908, pp. 6-7; and P. F. Bresee, Los Angeles, California, August 1, 1907, to J. O. McClurkan (microfilm, Nazarene archives).

18. Pentecostal Church of the Nazarene, First General Assembly, *Official Minutes . . . 1907,* pp. 43-59; *Nazarene Messenger,* October 31, 1907, p. 1.

19. See Dr. Bresee's report, in Pentecostal Church of the Nazarene, First General Assembly, *Official Minutes . . . 1907,* pp. 22-23; and, *ibid.,* references to Reynolds' election, p. 32. The *Nazarene Messenger,* September 12, 1907, pp. 1-2, describes the first organization of the Los Angeles District, with C. V. LaFontaine as district superintendent. The Church of the Nazarene *Manual, 1905,* pp. 46-51, compares closely with the Pentecostal Church of the Nazarene *Manual, 1907,* pp. 41-47, 56. See also Cornell's note on the

Committee on Superintendency in *Nazarene Joy Bells*, II, No. 10 (October, 1907), 1, and in *Nazarene Messenger*, November 14, 1907.

20. *Nazarene Messenger*, May 2, 1907, p. 6, and October 31, 1907, p. 7. *Supra*, 94-95.

21. *Infra*, 245-46.

22. Jernigan's note in *Highways and Hedges*, November 15, 1906, p. 8; and Association of Pentecostal Churches of America, Missionary Committee, "Minutes, 1901-1907," pp. 108-9.

23. *Holiness Evangel*, January 15, 1907, pp. 1, 4. Cf. *ibid.*, June 15, 1907, p. 4.

For evidence of the depth of this strong tradition on tobacco, dress, and secret societies, see Mrs. R. B. Mitchum, "Personal Diary" (in possession of Countess Hurd, Nashville, Tennessee), pp. 60-62, 68, 79; Mary Lee Cagle, *Life and Work ... An Autobiography* (Kansas City, c. 1928), pp. 19, 32; New Testament Church of Christ, "Journal" (Ms in Nazarene archives), pp. 3, 20-21, 65; *Government and Doctrines of New Testament Churches* (Waco, Texas, 1900), p. 2; and New Testament Church of Christ, *Government and Doctrines . . . 1903*, p. 7. In 1905, however, it was agreed that "the taking out of a part of a man's wage without his consent" by a labor union which maintained itself as an oath-bound secret order would not be considered as making him a member or supporter of the order; see Holiness Church of Christ, *Yearbook and Minutes . . . 1905*, pp. 18-19.

24. Pentecostal Church of the Nazarene, First General Assembly, *Official Minutes . . . 1907*, pp. 15, 39-42; *Holiness Evangel*, November 1, 1907, p. 6. Cf. Church of the Nazarene, *Manual . . . 1905, With Changes Adopted at the Assembly of 1906*, p. 33.

25. *Holiness Evangel*, November 15, 1907, p. 1. See also Pentecostal Church of the Nazarene, First General Assembly, *Official Minutes . . . 1907*, pp. 28, 35.

26. See report in *Holiness Evangel*, December 1, 1907, p. 4; and "Minutes of the Ninth Annual Meeting, Eastern Council, Holiness Church of Christ," *ibid.*, January 15, 1908, p. 11. The Holiness Church of Christ, "Journal," comes to an abrupt end with the reading of the manuals, p. 128. Cf. *Nazarene Messenger*, February 13, 1908, p. 5, for Speakes's report of his progress in placing the churches under Nazarene discipline.

27. "Minutes of the Annual Meeting of the Western Council, November 5-10, 1907," in *Holiness Evangel*, November 15, 1907, p. 7. On H. D. Brown's role, cf. *ibid.*, December 1, 1907, p. 4; *Pentecostal Advocate*, November 23, 1907; reports of Jernigan and Brown to *Nazarene Messenger*, November 14, 1907, p. 4, and December 26, 1907, p. 5; and notes on conversations of the author with William E. Fisher, July 12, 1955, and B. F. Neely, July 10, 1955.

28. C. E. Cornell's article in *Nazarene Messenger*, November 14, 1907, p. 2, and Pierce's, *ibid.*, October 31, 1907, p. 1; Church of the Nazarene, Northwest District, *Fiftieth Anniversary Book* (E. E. Zachary, ed., 1954), for pictures of Northwest Nazarene women, which show no fear at all of flowers and ruffles.

29. E. D. Hinchman, "Legalism Overdone," *Nazarene Messenger*, March 19, 1908, p. 2; Mrs. Cagle's report, *ibid.*, July 30, 1908, p. 10; a com-

plaint from an Arizona pastor, *ibid.*, pp. 4-5; and Mary Lee Cagle, *op. cit.*, pp. 129-30.

30. Cf. Short's article, *Nazarene Messenger*, October 1, 1908, p. 1, with B. F. Neely, conversation with the writer, July 10, 1955.

31. Lyle E. Akers, "The Life and Works of E. P. and M. Emily Ellyson" (B.D. thesis, Nazarene Theological Seminary, 1953), pp. 25-26, 29, 31. Cf. *Highways and Hedges*, December 1, 1906, pp. 4, 8; E. P. Ellyson, "The Church Natural and Necessary," *Nazarene Messenger*, November 19, 1908, pp. 5-6; and *ibid.*, December 19, 1901, p. 4, for Ellyson's first contact with a Nazarene evangelist in Iowa.

32. The quotations are from *Pentecostal Advocate*, October 17, 1907, p. 8, and January 23, 1908, p. 10. Cf. *ibid.*, November 4, 1908, p. 8; and C. A. McConnell, *The Potter's Vessel, My Life Story* . . . (Kansas City, 1946), pp. 6-10, 19, 26-31. See, on other matters, *Nazarene Messenger*, February 6, 1908; and Mrs. C. A. McConnell, conversation with the writer, July 8, 1955. Cf. First General Assembly, *Official Minutes* . . . *1907*, pp. 35, 58, indicating Ruth's earlier interest in the union with the South.

33. *Nazarene Messenger*, March 5, 1908, p. 7, March 12, 1908, pp. 5, 7, and April 2, 1908, p. 1.

34. See especially Dr. Bresee's own account in the first of a notable series of editorial letters in *ibid.*, April 16, 1908, p. 6; Professor Whitehurst's report, *ibid.*, April 23, 1908, pp. 4-5; *Holiness Evangel*, April 15, 1908, p. 3; Bresee's further reference to Bud Robinson's role in *Nazarene Messenger*, June 18, 1908, p. 1; and First Church of the Nazarene, Los Angeles, "Founders Day Bulletin," October 20, 1940, pp. 2-3. Cf. notes of my conversations with John E. Moore, July 22, 1955, B. F. Neely, July 10, 1955, and Mrs. C. A. McConnell, July 7, 1955, all of whom confused Robinson's earlier identification with Methodism with his alleged reluctance to join the Nazarenes.

35. *Nazarene Messenger*, April 23, 1908, p. 6, and June 4, 1908, p. 6; *Holiness Evangel*, May 15, 1908, p. 1.

36. See the long and detailed accounts of this journey in Bresee's editorial correspondence to *Nazarene Messenger*, April 30 to August 6, 1908; this is by far the best source of information on the churches during this critical period.

37. The quotation is from McConnell, *op. cit.*, p. 54. See also the same author's "The Fourth Wise Man" (undated Ms, Bethany College Library, photostatic copy in the Nazarene archives), pp. 3-4, noting that both the superintendents' wives wore wedding rings; Pentecostal Church of the Nazarene, Second General Assembly, *Official Minutes* . . . *1908*, pp. 47, 49; *ibid., Manual* . . . *1908*, p. 72; B. F. Neely, conversation with the writer, July 10, 1955; *Nazarene Messenger*, October 15, 1908, p. 5, and October 22, 1908, pp. 1-2.

38. On the "interdenominational" evangelists, see *Pentecostal Advocate*, July 18, 1907, p. 1; notes on the writer's conversation with Lee Hamric, July 12, 1955; and *Holiness Evangel*, May 15, 1907, p. 7. Cf. for those who turned temporarily to Northern Methodism, Methodist Episcopal church, Gulf Mission Conference, *Journal . . . Annual Session . . . 1905*, pp. 21, 27; *ibid., 1906*, p. 22; and *ibid., 1907*, pp. 26, 29. Cf. the "pentecostal" meetings at the same conference in 1908, *Journal*, pp. 45-46.

39. *Nazarene Messenger,* October 29, 1908; Second General Assembly, *Official Minutes . . . 1908,* p. 3.

40. Tenth General Assembly, *Proceedings . . . 1905,* p. 33; *Nazarene Messenger,* June 7, 1906, p. 6; *supra,* 114-15.

41. Joseph Speakes's account in *Pilot Point Post-Signal,* October 13, 1958. Cf. Girvin, *op. cit.,* pp. 412-14, and I. G. Martin, conversation with the writer, July 17, 1955; *Nazarene Joy Bells,* III, No. 10 (October, 1908), 1. For the hymn by L. Milton Williams and I. G. Martin, see *Nazarene Messenger,* November 19, 1908; the first stanza began:

> *The holiness bands from over these lands*
> *Are fast coming in and all joining hands,*
>   *Praise God! Praise God! Praise God for Jesus!*
> *With the Blood and the fire of the Holy Ghost*
> *We'll rout the foe and his black-winged host.*
> *March on, march on, march on with Jesus.*

Chapter X
Some Unheralded Accessions, 1908-15

1. See report of the union in *Christian Advocate* (New York), August 8, 1907, p. 37; *Nazarene Messenger,* May 23, 1907, p. 5; Association of Pentecostal Churches of America, Missionary Committee, "Minutes, 1901-1907" (Ms, Nazarene archives), pp. 124, 127.

2. *Nazarene Messenger,* May 23, 1907, p. 5; Pentecostal Church of the Nazarene, First General Assembly, *Official Minutes . . . 1907,* p. 21; *Holiness Evangel,* November 1, 1907, p. 5; and E. P. Ellyson, North Scituate, Rhode Island, July 29, 1909, to H. F. Reynolds (in Reynolds correspondence, Nazarene archives).

3. *Nazarene Messenger,* May 9, 1907, March 5, 1908, p. 9, and November 19, 1908, p. 21.

4. *Ibid.,* November 5, 1908, p. 6; *Christian Witness,* September 1, 1892, p. 2, and January 10, 1895, p. 2; and M. L. Haney, *Pentecostal Possibilities, or Story of My Life* (Chicago, 1906), pp. 347, 378-79. Walker's articles in issues of the *Nazarene Messenger* for the fall of 1908 may be compared with his earlier writings in the *Christian Witness;* see, for examples in the latter, issues for February 7, 1895, p. 2, September 26, 1895, p. 2, and November 26, 1896, p. 2.

5. First General Assembly, *Official Minutes . . . 1907,* pp. 19-20, 56; *Nazarene Messenger,* November 28, 1907, p. 9, April 30, 1908, p. 6, July 9, 1908, p. 6; Mark R. Moore, *Fifty Years . . . and Beyond: A History of the Chicago Central District Church of the Nazarene* (Kankakee, Illinois, 1954), p. 14.

6. H. F. Reynolds, Chicago, November 25, 1908, to P. F. Bresee (Reynolds papers, Nazarene archives); and *Nazarene Messenger,* November 12, 1908, pp. 8-9, and December 3, 1908, p. 3.

7. Mrs. Mattie Hoke, "Origin of the Work," in the Apostolic Holiness Bible School, *First Catalogue . . . 1906,* pp. 10-13; *ibid., Catalogue . . . 1907,* pp. 7-8; and *ibid., Catalogue . . . 1908,* p. 9.

8. C. B. Jernigan, *From the Prairie Schooner to a City Flat* (New York, 1926), pp. 58-59. E. Wayne Sears, "A History of the Origin and Growth of the Church of the Nazarene in Kansas" (M.S. thesis, Kansas State Teachers

College, 1949), pp. 37-39, quotes church records and correspondence unavailable elsewhere.

9. Sears, op. cit., pp. 38-41, 53-54, and, generally, pp. 56-81; and Third General Assembly, *Official Minutes* . . . *1911*, p. 25. Cf. *Nazarene Messenger*, August 30, 1906, p. 4, and October 4, 1906, describing Bresee's earlier appearance at Topeka in the role of a home mission evangelist. *Ibid.*, July 11, 1907, pp. 3-4, 6, refers to a previous "Nazarene mission" in Wichita.

10. See Holiness Association of Oklahoma, *Yearbook* . . . *1906-1907*, pp. 3-4, 13-15, 21; and reports of the school in *Pentecostal Advocate*, February 21, 1907, "Territory Page"; and *Nazarene Joy Bells*, II, No. 9 (September, 1907), 11. Cf. accounts of earlier holiness evangelism in Oklahoma, much of it under the auspices of the Methodist Episcopal Church, North, in *Christian Witness*, October 10, 1895; Haney, op. cit., pp. 368-70, 372; and C. B. Jernigan, *Pioneer Days of the Holiness Movement in the Southwest* (Kansas City, 1919), pp. 60-61 ff., 91 ff., 111.

11. See the fugitive paper Jernigan published announcing the founding of Bethany, *Highways and Hedges*, I, No. 1 (September, 1909), 1; C. B. Jernigan, *Prairie Schooner*, pp. 75-77; Jernigan, *The Nazarene Home* (pamphlet, Bethany, 1912), *passim;* Leona B. McConnell, "A History of the Town and College of Bethany, Oklahoma" (M.A. thesis, the University of Oklahoma, 1935), p. 2; and Ernest K. Farmer, "Attitudes of the Community Newspapers toward the Church of the Nazarene in Bethany, Oklahoma" (senior thesis, Bethany Nazarene College, 1956), pp. 5, 8.

12. Third General Assembly, *Official Minutes* . . . *1911*, pp. 18, 61; Jernigan, op cit., p. 59.

13. *Ibid.*, pp. 79-80. Cf. Dr. Bresee's visits to the Ponca reservation, reported in *Nazarene Messenger*, November 5, 1908, p. 6.

14. *Nazarene Messenger*, October 3, 1907, p. 4, October 10, 1907, p. 4; October 17, 1907, p. 4, January 16, 1908, pp. 4-5, February 20, 1908, and June 25, 1908, p. 2, for the work in the Northwest. Cf. for other districts, *ibid.*, September 19, 1907, p. 6, and September 26, 1907, p. 8. See also Church of the Nazarene, Northwest District, Sixth Annual Assembly, *Journal* . . . *1910*, p. 14. and *Journal* . . . *1914*, pp. 35-36; and E. E. Zachary, ed., *Northwest District, Church of the Nazarene, Fiftieth Anniversary Book* (Spokane, 1954), pp. 43, 45, 47.

15. J. Fred Parker, "The Historical Background of the Church of the Nazarene in Western Canada" (B.D. thesis, Nazarene Theological Seminary, 1950), pp. 10-44, 64-70, summarizes these developments.

16. Cf. statistical chart in Second General Assembly, *Proceedings* . . . *1908*, p. 54, with that in Third General Assembly, *Proceedings* . . . *1911*, p. 60.

17. E. A. Girvin, *P. F. Bresee, A Prince in Israel* (Kansas City, Mo., 1916), pp. 413-14.

18. In the absence of manuscript records, the best written account of these events is found in the *Nazarene Messenger* for 1908, as follows: January 2, p. 9, March 26, p. 6, May 14, p. 6, September 3, p. 7, October 1, p. 4, and November 19, pp. 6-7, 9, the last containing Trumbauer's account of the history of the denomination and H. F. Reynolds' estimate of its significance. See also C. W. Ruth's early report in *Christian Witness*, August 26, 1897, p. 12; and Milton H. Taylor, ed., *Pictorial Review of Washington and Philadelphia District* (pamphlet, c. 1950), pp. 5, 32.

19. Haney, *op. cit.*, pp. 349, 351, 384-85, 388; *Burning Bush*, March 12, 1903, pp. 2-3, and March 26, 1903, pp. 2-5. Cf. *supra*, 128-29.

20. *Nazarene Messenger*, March 7, 1907, p. 9, March 26, 1908, p. 4, June 11, 1908, p. 6, April 23, 1908, p. 10; and Deets Pacific Bible College, *Sixth Annual Catalogue, 1907-1908*, p. 17. Cf. *Holiness Evangel*, November 15, 1907, p. 1; and *Pentecostal Advocate*, March 21, 1907, p. 6, for B. W. Huckabee's description of the state of affairs in Colorado.

21. *Nazarene Messenger*, August 20, 1908, p. 5, August 27, 1908, pp. 5, 7, and October 8, 1908, p. 6.

22. See, in the Nazarene archives, photostat of "Historic Statement of the Origin of the Lee Holiness Mission," dated January 17, 1916, signed by Lee, taken from I. G. Martin's notebooks by the writer; and *Nazarene Messenger*, June 7, 1906, p. 4.

23. *Nazarene Messenger*, December 13, 1906, p. 7, November 14, 1907, p. 9, and January 21, 1909, p. 5.

24. See, on the union, the following letters (in the Reynolds correspondence at the Nazarene archives): P. F. Bresee, Los Angeles, December 21, 1910, to H. F. Reynolds; H. F. Reynolds, Des Arc, Missouri, January 17, 1911, to E. P. Ellyson; H. F. Reynolds, Chicago, February 18, 1911, January 31, 1911, and April 24, 1911, to E. P. Ellyson; E. P. Ellyson, Peniel, Texas, February 22, 1911, and March 7, 1911, to H. F. Reynolds. For the withdrawal, see William H. Lee, Colorado Springs, April 13, 1911, and January 6, 1912, to P. F. Bresee.

25. See Girvin's article, quoted in his *Bresee*, pp. 429-30.

26. See E. P. Ellyson, Peniel, Texas, November 14, 1910, to H. F. Reynolds (Reynolds papers, Nazarene archives), describing the Methodist Protestant proposal and the commission appointed to deal with it; Girvin, *op. cit.*, p. 430; Third General Assembly, *Proceedings . . . , 1911*, pp. 14-15, 27-28, 34-35, 54; and the writer's notes on a conversation with J. Glenn Gould, October 17, 1955. I have not had access to records or publications of the Methodist Protestant church during this period.

27. Church of the Nazarene, *Proceedings of the Various Districts . . . 1920* (Kansas City, Mo., 1920), p. 2.

28. Cf. *supra*; and see J. M. Wines, *Hoosier Happenings* (Kansas City, Missouri, 1926), pp. 69-72; and S. A. Danford, *Spreading Scriptural Holiness, or the North Dakota Movement* (Chicago, 1913), pp. 3, 29, 51, and *passim*.

29. *Nazarene Messenger*, January 11, 1906, p. 4, and December 6, 1906, p. 4; and Moore, *op. cit.*, pp. 14, 18-19. I. G. Martin, *My Scrapbook* (pamphlet, Mansfield, Illinois, 1936), p. 2, shows that he was appointed district superintendent first, but he did not serve.

30. *Nazarene Messenger*, February 7, 1907, p. 7, March 28, 1907, p. 9, September 26, 1907, p. 7, December 26, 1907, p. 6, February 20, 1908, p. 7, and February 27, 1908, p. 9. Cf. Moore, *op. cit.*, p. 20, and notes on the writer's conversation with S. T. Ludwig, January 5, 1957.

31. *Nazarene Messenger*, February 27, 1908, p. 5, and June 18, 1908, p. 1, the latter containing Bresee's account; Wines, *op. cit.*, p. 69; and Chicago Central District, Fifth Annual Assembly, *Journal . . . 1909*, p. 7. *Ibid., Journal*, in any year from 1908 to 1915, lists five or more Methodist ministers presenting their names for recognition of elder's orders.

32. *Nazarene Messenger,* June 18, 1908, p. 4, and August 13, 1908, p. 4; Wines, *op. cit.,* pp. 72-73.
33. *Nazarene Messenger,* November 28, 1907, p. 4, February 6, 1908, p. 4, April 2, 1908, p. 4, April 9, 1908, p. 4 (containing Imhoff's report on New Palestine), June 4, 1908, p. 3, and November 26, 1908, p. 5.
34. *Ibid.,* June 10, 1909, pp. 3-4; Third General Assembly, *Official Minutes . . . 1911,* p. 61; J. Glenn Gould, conversation with the writer, October 17, 1955; and Carleton D. Jones, *Church Directory of the Church of the Nazarene . . . Uhrichsville, Ohio* (pamphlet, Uhrichsville, Ohio, n.d.), p. 5.
35. George Sharpe, *This Is My Story* (Glasgow, c. 1948), pp. 7-8, 16-18, 21, 43.
36. *Ibid.,* pp. 43-52, 55-56.
37. *Ibid.,* pp. 62, 66-67, 71-73, 78; George Sharpe, *A Short Historical Sketch of the Church of the Nazarene in the British Isles* (pamphlet, n.d.), pp. 23-24, 27-29, 32-33; *Herald of Holiness,* April 22, 1914, p. 9.
38. *Nazarene Messenger,* June 17, 1909, pp. 3-4.
39. The quotation from Peavey's letter appeared in *ibid.,* December 26, 2907, p. 15. See also *ibid.,* September 17, 1908, p. 4, for Olive Winchester's first report; December 31, 1908, p. 7, announcing the opening of Sharpe's Bible school; and *ibid.,* April 1, 1909, p. 7, reprinting a letter from A. M. Hills to the *Pentecostal Herald.* Cf. *Pentecostal Advocate,* September 26, 1907, p. 3, and October 10, 1907.
40. Third General Assembly, *Official Minutes . . . 1911,* p. 24; Olive M. Winchester, Glasgow, Scotland, March 27, 1913, to H. F. Reynolds (copy in General Foreign Missionary Board, "Reports, etc., 1913," Nazarene archives).
41. *Ibid.*
42. See Walker's articles in *Herald of Holiness,* April 15, 29, and May 20, 1914; and H. F. Reynolds, Calcutta, India, May 7, 1914, to the General Foreign Missionary Board (in General Board, "Reports, etc., 1911-16," Nazarene archives).
43. Pentecostal Church of Scotland, "Minutes of the Meeting of the Provisional Committee held in Parkhead Pentecostal Church, October 2 and 6, 1914" (Ms carbon copy in General Board, "Reports . . . 1911-1916," Nazarene archives); and a thirteen-page document headed only, "Scotland" (in the Reynolds papers, Nazarene archives), which seems to be the extended report Dr. Reynolds provided for the General Foreign Missionary Board on his return, pp. 1-3, 6-7, 10-11.
44. *Herald of Holiness,* October 6, 1915, p. 5; Pentecostal Church of the Nazarene, General Board of Foreign Missions "Minutes, 1908-1914" (Ms, Nazarene archives), entries for October 26, 1914, and October 13, 1915; Fourth General Assembly, *Proceedings . . . 1915,* pp. 25-26; Sharpe, *Historical Sketch,* p. 58; and George Frame, *Blood Brother of the Swazis: The Life Story of David Hynd . . .* (Kansas City, Missouri, 1952), pp. 40-47, 56.

CHAPTER XI

ACHIEVING THE INNER REALITY OF UNION

1. First General Assembly, *Proceedings . . . 1907,* pp. 56-57; H. F. Reynolds, Monterrey, Mexico, March 31, 1910, to P. F. Bresee (in Reyn-

olds correspondence, Nazarene archives); *Pentecostal Era*, February 3, 1910 (which I have seen in M. F. Copeland, "Scrapbook," in possession of C. A. Smith); letter of H. B. Hosley, Washington, D.C., July 29, 1921, to a Reverend Mr. Keith (in Nazarene archives); and E. F. Walker, Eaton Rapids, Michigan, August 1, 1912, and Olivet, Illinois, March 10, 1913, to H. F. Reynolds.

2. *Nazarene Messenger*, June 10, 1909, pp. 3-4; H. F. Reynolds, Chicago, Illinois, November 25, 1908, to P. F. Bresee; and, on the capture of all of the Nazarene churches in Florida by the "tongues movement," *ibid.*, April 8, 1909, p. 9.

3. See the frank and loving account in A. E. Sanner, *John W. Goodwin, A Biography* (Kansas City, 1945), pp. 102, 104; and E. A. Girvin, *Phineas F. Bresee: A Prince in Israel* (Kansas City, Missouri, 1916), pp. 179, 416, 432. Cf., for sketchy but supporting evidence from contemporary sources, the sudden end of references to C. V. LaFontaine in *Nazarene Messenger*, December 2, 1907; their resumption in the issue for March 12, 1908, p. 9; *ibid.*, succeeding issues, describing his organization of a new church on Grand Avenue, Los Angeles; and *ibid.*, August 6, 1908, p. 2. On Whitcomb, see *ibid.*, February 6, 1908, p. 7, September 17, 1908, p. 7, June 17, 1909, pp. 8-9, and June 24, 1909, pp. 1-2.

4. See the printed "Prospective Schedule, General Missionary Secretary and Superintendent of Foreign Missions" for 1909 (in Reynolds papers, Nazarene archives); and reports in *Nazarene Messenger*, November 26 and December 3, 1908, and weekly after January 14, 1909.

5. See P. F. Bresee, Los Angeles, California, March 8, 1909, and June 12, 1909, to H. F. Reynolds; and E. P. Ellyson, Hollow Rock Camp, Toronto, Ohio, August 17, 1909, to Reynolds (both in Reynolds correspondence, Nazarene archives).

6. Girvin, *op. cit.*, pp. 417-18, 420-22; E. P. Ellyson, Malden, Missouri, October 8, 1909, and Peniel, Texas, March 15, 1910, to H. F. Reynolds; P. F. Bresee, Los Angeles, California, December 4, 1909, to H. F. Reynolds; and H. F. Reynolds, Mexico City, April 4, 1910, and Cordovo, Mexico, April 28, 1910, to E. P. Ellyson (all in the Reynolds correspondence, Nazarene archives).

7. See H. F. Reynolds, Chicago, Illinois, April 28, 1911, to E. P. Ellyson (in Reynolds correspondence, Nazarene archives).

8. Third General Assembly, *Official Minutes* . . . *1911*, pp. 12-13, 26.

9. *Ibid.*, pp. 32, 39, 50.

10. J. B. Chapman, "Dr. Reynolds, the Perfect Brother and Christian Gentleman," *Herald of Holiness*, August 20, 1938, p. 5; and I. G. Martin's article, *ibid.*, September 8, 1915, p. 6.

11. Fourth General Assembly, *Proceedings* . . . *1915*, p. 48, and *passim*.

12. *Ibid.*, p. 54.

13. R. T. Williams, Bethany, Oklahoma, January 20, 1916, to C. A. McConnell (in possession of R. T. Williams, Jr.; photostat in Nazarene archives); Gideon B. Williamson, *Roy T. Williams, Servant of God* (Kansas City, Missouri, 1947), pp. 12-19.

14. *Nazarene Messenger*, July 4, 1907, p. 9; Association of Pentecostal Churches of America, *Minutes* . . . *1907*, pp. 43, 52-53.

15. On the China Mission, see *Nazarene Messenger*, August 7, 1902,

p. 3, August 14, 1902, p. 2, and August 21, 1902, p. 3. See also Church of the Nazarene, Tenth Annual Assembly *Proceedings* . . . *1905*, pp. 10, 34-36; and cf. Fourth General Assembly, *Proceedings* . . . *1915*, p. 50.

16. See, for the foregoing, Church of the Nazarene, Home and Foreign Missionary Board, Ms, "Minutes," entries for April 30, May 19, September 5, and October 31, 1906; anon., *The Story of Mrs. Sukhoda Banargee and Hope School, Calcutta, India* (pamphlet, Los Angeles, 1906), pp. 17-18, 25-26, 27; Mrs. E. G. Eaton, comp., *Our Work in India: Hallelujah Village, Hope School, Calcutta* (pamphlet, Portland, Oregon, 1913), pp. 19-20; and *Nazarene Messenger*, May 10, 1906, p. 1, and October 11, 1906, pp. 2-3.

17. *Nazarene Messenger*, July 4, 1907, pp. 7-8. Cf. *ibid.*, June 6, 1907, p. 3, and a note on Bresee's address to the Association of Pentecostal Churches of America, *Minutes* . . . *1907*, p. 17.

18. See, for a convenient summary, *Nazarene Messenger*, November 19, 1908, pp. 12-14. Cf. *ibid.*, January 30, 1908, p. 4; First General Assembly, *Official Minutes* . . . *1907*, p. 39; *ibid.*, 1908, p. 35; and General Board of Foreign Missions, *History of the Foreign Missionary Work of the Church of the Nazarene* (pamphlet, Kansas City, Missouri, 1921), pp. 19, 37, 44.

19. First General Assembly, *Official Minutes* . . . *1907*, pp. 46-51; Mendell Taylor, *Fifty Years of Nazarene Missions*, Volume I, "Administration and Promotion" (Kansas City, 1952), pp. 15-19.

20. Pentecostal Church of the Nazarene, General Board of Foreign Missions, "Minutes, 1908-1914" (Nazarene archives), entries: for October 14, 1908; for the "Third Annual Meeting," October, 1909, pp. 37, 40, 43, 44-47; and for October 5, 1910.

21. Pentecostal Church of the Nazarene, Third General Assembly, *Official Minutes* . . . *1911*, pp. 39-40; *ibid.*, General Board of Foreign Missions, "Minutes, 1908-1914," entry for annual meeting of 1911; and the "field reports" in Church of the Nazarene, General Board, "Reports, etc., 1911-1916" (in Nazarene archives).

22. E. P. Ellyson, Peniel, Texas, January 19, 1910 (with copies of a proposed "contract" attached), and January 28, 1910, to H. F. Reynolds. Cf. General Board, *Foreign Missionary Work*, p. 45, for J. D. Scott's own account.

23. H. F. Reynolds, Chicago, Illinois, January 25, 1910, to E. P. Ellyson.

24. The quotation is from J. D. Scott, Pilot Point, Texas, February 17, 1910, to E. P. Ellyson. See also (in the Reynolds correspondence, Nazarene archives) E. P. Ellyson, Peniel, Texas, February 4, 1910, Lawrence, Kansas, June 15, 1910, to H. F. Reynolds; H. F. Reynolds, Chicago, Illinois, February 9 and December 28, 1910, to E. P. Ellyson; E. P. Ellyson, C. B. Jernigan, and W. T. McConnell, Peniel, Texas, May 11, 1910, to J. D. Scott and Dennis Rogers; C. B. Jernigan, Oklahoma City, April 7, 1910, to H. F. Reynolds; General Board of Foreign Missions, "Minutes, 1909-1914," entries for Thursday, October 6, 1910, p. 7, and for October 7 and 16, 1911; and General Board, *Foreign Missionary Work*, p. 45.

25. See H. F. Reynolds, en route from Calcutta to Buldana, India, April 17, 1914, to the General Missionary Board; a subsequent letter, Calcutta, India, May 7, 1914; and L. S. Tracy, Calcutta, India, June 20, 1914, to H. F. Reynolds (all in the Nazarene archives, General Board, "Reports,

etc., 1911-1916"). See also General Board of Foreign Missions, "Minutes, 1908-1914," entries for October 10, 1913, and April 10, 1914.

26. *Ibid.*, October 23, 1914, and October 13, 1915; Olive G. Tracy, *Tracy Sahib of India* (Kansas City, Missouri, 1954), pp. 82-83, 109; and General Board, *Foreign Missionary Work*, p. 34.

27. First General Assembly, *Official Minutes* . . . 1907, p. 53. Cf. *ibid.*, pp. 28-29; and Second General Assembly, *Official Minutes* . . . 1908, pp. 42-43. See also Roy F. Cantrell, "A History of Bethany Nazarene College" (D.R.E. thesis, Southwestern Baptist Theological Seminary, 1955), p. 68.

28. Arkansas Holiness Literary School, "Minutes of the Board" (Ms at Bethany College Library; pertinent photostats at the Nazarene archives), entries for February 18 and August 15, 1908, and January 1, 1909, the last containing the quotation above; and *ibid.*, entries for February 7, April 5, and November 29, 1910. The matter was never settled satisfactorily; see the "Minutes" for September 2 and 19, 1912, and notes on the conversation of Lee Hamric with the writer, July 12, 1955. Cantrell, *op. cit.*, pp. 68-70, and *passim*, summarizes the history of the institutions of the Southwest.

29. See H. F. Reynolds, en route to Blossom, Texas, October 25, 1910, to E. P. Ellyson (Ms carbon copy in Reynolds correspondence, Nazarene archives).

30. E. P. Ellyson, Peniel, Texas, February 11, 1911, to H. F. Reynolds; Reynolds, February 17, 1911, to E. P. Ellyson (in Reynolds correspondence, Nazarene archives). Cf. Ellyson's article in *Pentecostal Advocate*, August 8, 1907, p. 5.

31. Third General Assembly, *Official Minutes* . . . 1911, pp. 20, 40, 42-43.

32. *Herald of Holiness*, June 19, 1912; Mark Moore, *Fifty Years . . . and Beyond: A History of the Chicago Central District Church of the Nazarene* (Kankakee, Illinois, 1954), pp. 116-17; and Illinois Holiness University, Board of Trustees, "Minutes" (in the office of the president), entries for June 20, 1908, May 1, 1909, June 11, 1910, March 6 and 27 and November 20, 1911, January 26, February 8, June 13, July 23, and November 1, 1912, and October 6, 1913.

33. *Herald of Holiness*, April 14, 1915, p. 13, and April 25, 1917, p. 9.

34. Girvin, *op. cit.*, pp. 418-20; Sanner, *op. cit.*, pp. 107-9; *supra*, 140. Sue Bresee, "Personal Diary," entry for December 15, 1909, and I. G. Martin, conversation with the writer, August 3, 1955, confirm Bresee's active role in the move.

35. The general reader can find much of this story in Girvin, *op. cit.*, pp. 425-26, Sanner, *op. cit.*, pp. 110-15, and *Nazarene Messenger*, November 2, 1911, p. 21. In addition, see Bresee's series of manuscript reports to the Board of Trustees during 1911 and 1912, some of them undated, in the archives of Pasadena College (photostats are in the Nazarene archives). Cf. also, on Sanders, *College Clarion* (Pasadena, California), March-April, 1928; and, on the land operations, Nazarene University Park Company, "Minutes of the Board of Directors" (in the archives of the president), pp. 1-13, entries for July and August, 1911.

36. The quotation is from *Herald of Holiness*, April 17, 1912, p. 11.

See also *ibid.*, May 1, 1912, p. 13; Nazarene University *Bulletin* . . . *1912-1913*, pp. 10, 15, 28; and *ibid.*, *1913-1914*, pp. 12-14.

37. Pentecostal Collegiate Institute, *Bulletin* . . . *1910-1911*, p. 10; *Heart, Head, and Hand, P.C.I. Monthly Devoted to Industrial Education*, I, No. 3 (November, 1912), 1-2; *ibid.*, III, No. 10 (June, 1915), 4-6, article by R. Leon Roy, "The Value of a Commercial Education"; and *ibid.*, V, No. 3 (November, 1916), 1-2, "Education for Efficiency."

38. *Heart, Head, and Hand*, III, No. 1 (September, 1914), 1; *ibid.*, No. 2 (October, 1914), 6; *ibid.*, No. 3 (November, 1914), 3-4, containing the quotation; and *ibid.*, No. 10 (June, 1915), 1.

39. Bertha Munro, "Our Eastern College," *Heart, Head, and Hand*, V, No. 11-12 (July-August, 1917), 1-2, 4-6; *ibid.*, VI, No. 9 (May, 1918), 1; *ibid.*, VII, No. 1 (September, 1918), 1, 5; *ibid.*, No. 4 (December, 1918), 1-2; and *Eastern Nazarene College Monthly*, I, No. 2 (October, 1919), 2, and II, No. 2 (October, 1920), 1.

40. Fourth General Assembly, *Proceedings* . . . *1915*, p. 51; H. Orton Wiley's comments in the *Herald of Holiness*, December 17, 1938, p. 10; and E. A. Girvin's account of Bresee's last sermon at the college based on stenographic notes, *op. cit.*, pp. 440-41.

41. See H. F. Reynolds, Chicago, Illinois, February 16, 1910, to E. P. Ellyson; and E. P. Ellyson, Peniel, Texas, February 19, 1910, and April 5, 1911, to H. F. Reynolds (in Reynolds correspondence, Nazarene archives). Cf. advertisements of the "Clubbing List," offering joint subscriptions, in *Nazarene Messenger* for April and May, 1908.

42. Third General Assembly, *Official Minutes* . . . *1911*, pp. 22, 35, 53; and Girvin, *op. cit.*, p. 430.

43. Pentecostal Church of the Nazarene, General Board of Publication, "Minutes, 1911-1918" (Ms, Nazarene archives), entries for October 12 and 13, November 21 and 24, 1911, and April 15, 1912.

44. *Ibid.*, entry for February 5, 1913, to which are attached copies of the pertinent correspondence in a document filed as "Exhibit H"; and F. A. Hillery, Providence, Rhode Island, April 10, 1917, to the New England District Assembly of the Pentecostal Church of the Nazarene (carbon copy, with Hillery's signature, Nazarene archives).

45. The quotation is from the *Herald of Holiness*, August 25, 1915, p. 1. See also Fourth General Assembly, *Proceedings* . . . *1915*, pp. 59-60; Pentecostal Church of the Nazarene, General Board of Foreign Missions, "Minutes, 1908-1914," entry for October 9, 1913; Church of the Nazarene, Tennessee District, Third Annual Assembly, *Minutes* . . . *September 1-5, 1915*, pp, 18, 21.

46. Girvin, *op. cit.*, pp. 373-75; and cf., for an example, *Nazarene Messenger*, November 30, 1905, pp. 4-5.

47. Church of the Nazarene, *Manual, 1911*, pp. 87-89; Third General Assembly, *Official Minutes* . . . *1911*, p. 49; and, generally, the "commencement number" of the *Herald of Holiness*, June 26, 1929. Note also, on the effort to develop a pastoral tradition, the sharp words about evangelists in the *Herald of Holiness* symposium on "The Need of Pastors," May 8 and 15, 1912.

48. *Nazarene Messenger*, November 7, 1907, pp. 5-6; *Holiness Evangel*, November 15, 1907, p. 7, and January 15, 1908, p. 11; Association of Pente-

costal Churches of America, *Minutes* . . . *1907*, pp. 21-22; First General Assembly, *Official Minutes* . . . *1907*, pp. 53-61; Third General Assembly, *Official Minutes* . . . *1911*, pp. 47-48; and Church of the Nazarene, *Proceedings of the Various Districts* . . . *1920* (Kansas City, Missouri, 1920), p. 2.

49. Third General Assembly, *Official Minutes* . . . *1911*, pp. 43, 61; and Fourth General Assembly, *Proceedings* . . . *1915*, pp. 65-66, 73. Cf. First General Assembly, *Proceedings* . . . *1907*, p. 54, recommending against the organization of a national body; and Church of the Nazarene, Correlated Boards, "Minutes, 1921," entry for February 19, 1921.

50. The quotations are from *Nazarene Messenger*, September 19, 1907, November 21, 1907, p. 2, and Fourth General Assembly, *Proceedings* . . . *1915*, p. 60. See also First General Assembly, *Proceedings* . . . *1907*, p. 50; and Pentecostal Church of the Nazarene, General Board of Foreign Missions, "Minutes, 1915-1919," entry for Wednesday, October 18, 1916.

51. *Nazarene Messenger*, September 5, 1907, pp. 6-7; Third General Assembly, *Official Minutes* . . . *1911*, p. 30; Fourth General Assembly, *Proceedings* . . . *1915*, pp. 66-67.

52. See, for the quotation, pictures and Bresee's comments, *Nazarene Messenger*, July 5, 1906, pp. 2, 11. Cf. pictures in Moore, *op. cit.*, pp. 21 ff.; R. E. Bower, comp., *Bird's-eye View of the Washington Philadelphia District* . . . (Philadelphia, 1917), *passim;* M. H. Taylor, *A Pictorial Survey of the Washington and Philadelphia District* (pamphlet, c. 1945), *passim;* and E. E. Zachary, ed., *Church of the Nazarene, Northwest District, Fiftieth Anniversary Book* (Spokane, 1954), *passim.*

53. See Second General Assembly, *Official Minutes* . . . *1908*, pp. 43-45; Third General Assembly, *Official Minutes* . . . *1911*, p. 48; and Fourth General Assembly, *Proceedings* . . . *1915*, p. 67. Cf. *Nazarene Messenger*, August 15, 1907, p. 8 (on the Lynn, Mass., home), and June 17, 1909, p. 6, indicating H. D. Brown's intention to establish a home at Seattle.

54. Church of the Nazarene, Northwest District, Tenth Annual Assembly, *Journal* . . . *1914*, p. 40. Mrs. Countess Hurd, "Scrapbook," II, 124-25, contains clippings from two Los Angeles newspapers which recount the debate over the abandonment of Mrs. Seth Rees's "Hillcrest Home for Fallen Women."

55. *College Clarion* (Pasadena), Vol. II, Nos. 3 and 4 (March-April, 1928), contains a fine sketch of his life.

56. See, for quotations, *Herald of Holiness*, August 25, 1915, p. 1; Fourth General Assembly, *Proceedings* . . . *1915*, pp. 51, 60, 65-66; and Girvin, *op. cit.*, p. 440.

57. See Girvin, *Nazarene Messenger*, January 16, 1908, p. 6; Girvin, *op. cit.*, p. 440; and Board of General Superintendents, *Quadrennial Address, 15th General Assembly* (pamphlet, Kansas City, Missouri, 1960), pp. 8-9. Cf. "antisectarian" statements by Dr. Bresee in Church of the Nazarene, Chicago Central District, Sixth Annual Assembly, *Journal* . . . *1910*, p. 8; and by C. E. Cornell, in "The Greatest Religious Movement of the Century," *Nazarene Joy Bells*, V, No. 8 (August-September, 1910), 7.

CHAPTER XII

THE TRANSITION TO A NEW GENERATION

1. E. F. Walker, Olivet, Illinois, December 15, 1915, and February 1, 1916, to H. F. Reynolds (in Reynolds correspondence, Nazarene archives).

NOTES TO PAGES 272-77   391

2. See telegrams from Leslie F. Gay, C. E. Jones, Howard Eckel, and H. Orton Wiley, to H. F. Reynolds (in the Reynolds correspondence for 1916, accompanying the record of the ballots of the election of Williams and Goodwin); E. F. Walker, Olivet, Illinois, February 15, 1916, to H. F. Reynolds; and H. F. Reynolds, Santiago, Cuba, March 14, 1916, to E. F. Walker (in the same place).

3. A. Everett Sanner, *John W. Goodwin, a Biography* (Kansas City, Missouri, 1945), pp. 119-20, 122-25; J. W. Goodwin, San Diego, California, April 22 and April 28 and May 13, 1916, to H. F. Reynolds.

4. Paul Rees, *Seth C. Rees: The Warrior Saint* (Indianapolis, 1934), pp. 54-55; International Holiness Church, *Manual* (c. 1920), pp. 7-8; M. L. Haney, *Pentecostal Possibilities: The Story of My Life* (Chicago, 1906), p. 377; *Nazarene Messenger*, November 5, 1908, p. 8, and November 26, 1908, p. 7; and Mallalieu Wilson, conversation with the writer, August 15, 1955.

5. See my notes on conversations with H. Orton Wiley, July 19, 1955, with Weaver W. Hess, January 18, 1956, and with Mrs. Countess Hurd and Mr. Robbie Mitchum, November 12, 1955, covering these points. Cf. newspaper clippings summarizing Rees's sermons during these years in Mrs. Countess Hurd, "Scrapbook" (in possession of Mrs. Hurd, Nashville, Tennessee), II, 129-32.

6. See the sketch of Wiley's life in Northwest Nazarene College, *Twenty-five Years*, pp. 15-31; and notes on his conversation with the writer, July 18, 1955.

7. See contemporary accounts in Hurd, "Scrapbook," II, 150; "The Story of the Revival," in the Pasadena College yearbook, *La Sierra, 1915*, pp. 18-28, written principally by Floyd and Orval Nease; and notes on the writer's conversation with H. Orton Wiley, July 19, 1955.

8. See the notes on the author's conversations with Weaver W. Hess, January 18, 1956, and H. Orton Wiley, July 19 and August 2, 1955; and A. O. Hendricks, Pasadena, California, May 10, 1917, to an unknown correspondent in the Northwest (typed copy in the Wiley correspondence, Northwest Nazarene College library).

9. See Sue Bresee, "Personal Diary," entries for April 1, 2, 3, and 14, May 24, June 22, and August 30, 1915; Fred C. Epperson, Los Angeles, California, June 22, 1915, to P. F. Bresee; and F. R. Matthew, Pasadena, California, June 26, 1915, to P. F. Bresee (these items are all in the possession of Horace Bresee).

10. Sue Bresee, "Diary," entries for June 24, 26, July 4, and September 22, 1915; newspaper clippings in Mrs. Hurd's "Scrapbook," II, 122-25; Mallalieu Wilson, conversation with the writer, August 15, 1955; Church of the Nazarene, Fourth General Assembly, *Proceedings . . . 1915*, pp. 55-56.

11. See the author's notes on a conversation with H. Orton Wiley, July 19, 1955; Hurd, "Scrapbook," II, 126; and *infra*, 281-88.

12. See clippings concerning the trial in Hurd, "Scrapbook," II, 115 ff.; notes on conversations of the writer with C. W. Griffin (one of the jurymen at the trial), July 24, 1955, and with I. G. Martin, August 3, 1955; A. O. Hendricks, Pasadena, California, May 10, 1917 (the letter cited above); and J. W. Goodwin's letters to H. F. Reynolds, from San Diego

and Pasadena, April 22, May 13, June 3, and September 5, 1916 (in Reynolds correspondence, Nazarene archives).

13. See, on the Pasadena student body, notes on the writer's conversation with Mallalieu Wilson, August 15, 1955; and, on Publishing House matters, H. F. Reynolds, Kansas City, Missouri, January 16, 1917, to R. T. Williams; E. F. Walker, Glendora, California, February 19, 1917, to Reynolds; R. T. Williams, Nashville, Tennessee, February 20, 1917, to Reynolds; and minutes and documents pertaining to the meeting of the general superintendents, February 23 and 24, 1917 (all in Reynolds correspondence).

14. The basic printed documents may all be seen in the Nazarene archives, namely, Seth C. Rees, "An Open Letter," dated Pasadena, February 26, 1917; Howard Eckel, *A Plain Statement of Why the University Pentecostal Church of the Nazarene Was Disorganized* (Pasadena, March 8, 1917); and *Pilgrim*, Vol. I, Nos. 1-4 (undated, 1917). See also notes on the author's conversations with H. Orton Wiley, July 19, 1955, I. G. Martin, August 3, 1955, and Weaver W. Hess, July 18, 1956.

15. See J. W. Short, East Liverpool, Ohio, April 3, 1917, William Howard Hoople, New York, April 4, 1917, and Bud Robinson, Pasadena, California, March 26, 1917, to H. F. Reynolds (in the Reynolds correspondence); and E. P. Ellyson, Donalsonville, Georgia, August 7, 1917, and Charles A. McConnell, Donalsonville, September 17, 1917, to H. Orton Wiley (both in the Wiley correspondence, Nampa). Cf. C. A. McConnell, *The Potter's Vessel* (Kansas City, 1946), p. 60.

16. See Seth Rees, Pasadena, California, March 14, 1917, to J. W. Goodwin; H. Orton Wiley, Berkeley, California, April 2, 1917, to H. F. Reynolds; and other letters from various Californians (in the Reynolds correspondence).

17. See (in Reynolds correspondence) G. Arnold Hodgin, Nampa, Idaho, March 12, 1917, to Reynolds and others, and W. H. Tullis, Nampa, Idaho, April 2, 1917, telegram to R. T. Williams; record of writer's conversation with S. T. Ludwig, June, 1955; and R. E. Dunham, Hutchinson, Kansas, December 7, 1917, to H. Orton Wiley (in Wiley correspondence).

18. See (in the Reynolds correspondence) the series of notes and letters for March, 1917, numbered 45-62.

19. See Howard Eckel, C. E. Cornell, and others, Los Angeles, April 1, 1917, to H. F. Reynolds; E. F. Walker, Glendora, California, April 2, 1917, to Reynolds; "Minutes of General Superintendents' meeting, Kansas City, Missouri, April 4, 1917" (in Reynolds correspondence); and a document apparently by John W. Goodwin in the same place entitled "My Interpretation of Section I, Page 46, in the Manual."

20. See *Preacher: A Herald of Christian Liberty* (I. G. Martin, editor, Pasadena, California), No. 5; General Foreign Missionary Board, Church of the Nazarene, Ms documents dated April 23, 1917; J. W. Goodwin, Ellington, Missouri, May 24 and 25, 1917, to H. F. Reynolds; and University Church, Pasadena, California, "Minutes of the Board" (in the church office), May 26, 1917. Practically no news of any of these events appeared in the *Herald of Holiness;* see the explanation by William E. Fisher, May 16, 1917, p. 11.

21. See Northwest Nazarene College (abbreviated hereafter as NNC),

Oasis, 1918, pp. 14-20; NNC, *Twenty-five Years of Progress* (a volume prepared by Miss Bertha Dooley, Nampa, Idaho, 1938), pp. 5-7, 10-12; Northwest District, *Tenth Annual Assembly Journal* . . . *1914,* p. 43; articles by C. H. French and Eugene Emerson in *Nazarene Messenger* (Nampa, Idaho), V, No. 3 (March, 1922), 4, and No. 4 (April, 1922), 6; record of the author's conversation with W. D. Parsons, Nampa, Idaho, August 18, 1955; and, on L. I. Hadley's work at George Fox and Cascade colleges, notes on my conversation with President John E. Riley, August 19, 1955.

22. NNC, *Oasis,* 1917, pp. 7, 11, 13; NNC, *Twenty-five Years,* pp. 13-14; NNC, Board of Trustees, "Minutes (1916-1920)," pp. 16, 21, 28-32; H. Orton Wiley, Pasadena, California, May 1, 1916, to E. F. Walker, and Berkeley, California, June 17, 1916, to G. Arnold Hodgin (then in Greensboro, North Carolina); and H. Orton Wiley, conversation with the writer, July 19, 1955. Items of Wiley's correspondence cited here and in succeedings pages are located in the NNC library.

23. See notes on the writer's conversations with H. Orton Wiley, July 19, 1955, and with Russell DeLong, January 7, 1955; and "The Idaho-Oregon Episode," *Pilgrim,* I, No. 1 (no date [June, 1917?]), 3; and NNC, Board of Trustees, "Minutes, 1916-1920," p. 93.

24. H. Orton Wiley, Nampa, Idaho, September 1, 1917, to C. Howard Davis; notes on Wiley's conversation with the writer, July 19, 1955; R. T. Williams, Nashville, Tennessee, August 22, 1917, to H. Orton Wiley; Edward F. Walker, Gaines, Michigan, August 23, 1917, to Wiley; and E. E. Zachary, ed., *Northwest District, Fiftieth Anniversary Book* . . . (Spokane, 1954), p. 58.

25. H. F. Reynolds, Colfax, Washington, September 18, 1917, to H. Orton Wiley; H. Orton Wiley, Nampa, Idaho, September 20, 1917, to H. F. Reynolds; Wiley, October 1, 1917, to John T. Little; and *Nazarene Messenger* (Nampa, Idaho), October, 1917, pp. 4, 6.

For another facet of the story, however, cf. Seth C. Rees, Colorado Springs, August 15, 1917, to H. Orton Wiley; Wiley, Nampa, Idaho, August 21, 1917, to Rees; and Arnold Hodgin, Pasadena, August 20, 1917, to Wiley.

26. *Nazarene Messenger* (Nampa, Idaho), October, 1917, pp. 1, 4, and December, 1917, p. 6; NNC Board of Trustees, "Minutes, 1916-1920," p. 115; H. Orton Wiley, Nampa, Idaho, October 6, 1917, to E. G. Anderson; Wiley, November 1, 1917, to H. G. Cowan, and others (in the Wiley correspondence, Nampa).

27. E. F. Walker, "What Ought to Be Done with the General Superintendency?" *Herald of Holiness,* July 4, 1917, p. 8; H. G. Cowan, "The Revision of the Manual," *ibid.,* January 23, 1918, p. 11; E. A. Girvin, "Disorganization of Churches," *ibid.,* January 30, 1918, p. 8.

28. A. M. Hills, "A Matter of Profound Importance," *Herald of Holiness,* September 24, 1919, p. 9; H. Orton Wiley, "Brother Brown's Memorial," *ibid.,* p. 21; anon., "Impressions of the General Assembly," *ibid.,* October 22, 1919, p. 11; and Fifth General Assembly, "Minutes of the Manual Revision Committee" (Ms, Nazarene archives), pp. 5, 9, 12, 21.

29. NNC Board of Trustees, "Minutes, 1916-1920," p. 124; and H. Orton Wiley, Nampa, Idaho, to Mrs. Ada Bresee, March, 1918.

30. *Nazarene Messenger* (Nampa, Idaho), summer, 1921, p. 3, gives enrollment figures for five years. See also *ibid.,* February-March, 1919,

pp. 1, 5; *ibid.*, January, 1922, p. 8; NNC, Board of Trustees, "Minutes, 1920-1928," pp. 19, 134a, 148-49; and NNC, *Twenty-five Years*, pp. 24-26.

31. Statements by Wiley and Mrs. E. G. Eaton in the NNC *Oasis, 1917*, pp. 35, 40; *ibid., 1918*, pp. 4, 18-19, 33; *ibid., 1922*, pp. 82-85; *ibid., 1923*, p. 77; *Nazarene Messenger*, February, 1922, entire issue; *ibid.*, March, 1922, p. 5, April, 1922, pp. 2-4; Carol Gish, *Touched by the Divine: The Story of Fairy Chism* (Kansas City, 1952), pp. 28-35, 56; Olive G. Tracy, *Tracy Sahib of India* (Kansas City, 1954), pp. 126-29, and preface by Wiley. On college revivals, see, again, NNC, *Twenty-five Years*, pp. 28-30.

32. NNC Board of Trustees, "Minutes 1916-1920," p. 133, entry for April 9, 1918; H. Orton Wiley, Nampa, April 12, 1918, to T. E. Mangum; NNC *Oasis, 1922*, p. 58; Alline Swann, *Song in the Night: The Story of Dr. and Mrs. Thomas E. Mangum* (Kansas City, 1957), pp. 22-23, 30, 52-53, 57, 62, 68 ff.; the larger Ms for the same book (in Mrs. Swann's possession), pp. 98-99, 102, 105-6, 146; C. T. Corbett, *Our Pioneer Nazarenes* (Kansas City, 1958), p. 105.

33. See Fairy Chism's article, NNC *Oasis, 1922*, pp. 76-77. Cf. *ibid.*, p. 81; and Mangum's sermon (a recording of which is in the NNC library) quoted in Swann, Ms, pp. 112-14. The Olivet College *Aurora, 1921*, p. 97, describes an embryonic "medical department" there as well.

34. H. Orton Wiley, conversation with the writer, July 19, 1955; and *By-Laws of Pasadena College* (a pamphlet in the archives of the president), Article 2, Section 1.

35. Those who remember the uneasiness of the late 1940's when General Superintendents R. T. Williams, James B. Chapman, and H. V. Miller passed away, within a brief period also marked by war, social disruption, and religious anxiety, will understand better what happened thirty years before.

36. Perry Miller, *The New England Mind: From Colony to Province* (Cambridge, Massachusetts, 1954); and Edmund S. Morgan, *The Puritan Family: Essays on Religion and Domestic Relations in Seventeenth-Century New England* (Boston, 1944), especially chapter six, "Puritan Tribalism," pp. 90-106; Henry M. Muhlenberg, *Journals* (T. G. Tappert and John W. Doberstein, trans.; 3 vols.; Philadelphia, 1942-58); Michael Schlatter, *A True History of the Real Condition of the Destitute Congregations in Pennsylvania*, in Henry Harbaugh, *The Life of Rev. Michael Schlatter . . .* (Philadelphia, 1857), pp. 87-234; and H. P. Thompson, *Thomas Bray* (London, 1954).

37. John Matthews, *Rise and Fall of the Church of the Nazarene* (n.p., n.d.), pp. 18-19, 11, 30, 31, 12-13, 22-23; John Matthews, Pasadena, California, November 30, 1920, "Open Letter . . . to His Nazarene Brethren," (Ms in General Board "Reports, etc., 1915-1920," Nazarene archives); and "General Superintendents' Address," Sixth General Assembly, *Journal . . . 1923*, p. 183.

38. Preston W. Slosson, *The Great Crusade and After, 1914-1928* (A. M. Schlesinger and Dixon R. Fox, eds., *A History of American Life*, XI, N.Y., 1930), 149-57.

39. "A Many Sided Evil" (on church entertainments), *Herald of Holiness*, June 6, 1917, p. 16; editorial, *ibid.*, September 10, 1919, p. 1;

N. B. Herrell, "Our Stand on the Dress Question," *ibid.*, February 25, 1920, p. 12; Allie Irick, "Food for Thought," *ibid.*, August 15, 1923, p. 8.

40. Seventh General Assembly, *Journal* . . . *1928*, pp. 74, 113, 165-67, 202; newspaper clippings in Mrs. Countess Hurd, "Scrapbook," III, 93; and the very important notes on the writer's conversation with Mallalieu Wilson, August 15, 1955.

41. See Washburn's report in New England District, Seventh Annual Assembly, *Journal* . . . *1914*, pp. 22-23; E. T. French, "Pastor's Report for 1925-1926" (Ms in Church of the Nazarene, Lynn, Mass., "Records, 1924-1940"). Cf. John W. Goodwin, *Living Signs and Wonders* (Kansas City, 1920), pp. 126-27; and Seventh General Assembly, *Journal* . . . *1928*, p. 69.

42. See editorials in *Herald of Holiness*, June 25, 1924, p. 1, and November 5, 1924, p. 1.

CHAPTER XIII

THE LAYMEN'S HOLINESS ASSOCIATION ON THE NORTHERN PLAINS

1. C. T. Corbett, *Soldier of the Cross: the Life Story of J. G. Morrison, 1871-1939* (Kansas City, 1956), pp. 11-20, 30-40, a careful study based on thorough research; S. A. Danford, *Spreading Scriptural Holiness, or the North Dakota Movement* (Chicago, 1913), pp. 95-98; J. G. Morrison, *Other Days: Boyhood Reminiscences of Frontier Hardships* (Kansas City, n.d.), pp. 6-10, 12-13; Ira Hammer, "The North Dakota Holiness Movement" (Ms, Nazarene archives), pp. 10-12; and Mrs. Nellie Hoffman, "The North Dakota Holiness Movement" (Ms, Nazarene archives), pp. 1-2. The last two are based upon personal memories as well as contemporary documents.

2. Danford, *op. cit.*, consists principally of his annual reports for the Fargo District; see pp. 10, 26, 32, 36-37, 46, 51, 54, 63-65, 67, 72, 83. See also Hammer, *op. cit.*, pp. 15, 19-25; and *North Dakota Methodist*, II, No. 14 (August 1, 1910), 2-3.

3. Danford, *op. cit.*, p. 117; and *North Dakota Methodist*, August 1, 1910, pp. 1-2. Cf. other issues in the Nazarene archives.

4. Danford, *op. cit.*, p. 3; S. A. Danford, *Report of Sixth Year for Bismarck District of North Dakota Conference, M.E. Church* (pamphlet, Bismarck, North Dakota, 1915), p. 3; and Hammer, *op. cit.*, pp. 26-27.

5. Danford, *Spreading Scriptural Holiness*, pp. 7-9, reprints an article by G. A. McLaughlin from *Christian Witness*, July 4, 1912. Cf. Hammer, *op. cit.*, p. 36; and, on the role of holiness schools, *Holiness Layman*, July, 1919, p. 3.

6. *Little Methodist*, April 1917, p. 3; *Methodist*, 1917, p. 2, and August, 1917, p. 3; and Hammer, *op. cit.*, pp. 42-43.

7. *Methodist*, October, 1917, p. 1, and November, 1917, p. 4. Cf. Hammer, *op. cit.*, pp. 43-44.

8. This story is told in great detail in *Methodist*, January, 1918, p. 2, February 1918, p. 2, and March 1918, p. 3.

9. *Methodist*, February, 1918, p. 1, and March, 1918, p. 3.

10. See, on these matters, Methodist Laymen's Holiness Association, "Minutes, 1917-1919" (Ms, Nazarene archives), bylaws, p. 1, and entry for June 28, 1919; *Methodist*, February 1918, p. 1, July, 1918, p. 1, August, 1918, pp. 1-2; *Holiness Layman*, October, 1919, p. 4, January, 1920,

p. 1, and July, 1920, p. 1; and Laymen's Holiness Association, "Minutes, 1919-1922" (Ms, Nazarene archives), entries for June 27, 1919, and June 30, 1921.

11. Aside from the general account in Hammer, *op. cit.*, pp. 53-54, information about these new units must be gleaned from the *Methodist* and its successor, the *Holiness Layman*. See, in the former, September, 1917, p. 3, October, 1918, p. 1, November, 1918, p. 1, and January, 1918, p. 1; and, in the latter, September, 1919, pp. 1, 3, October, 1919, pp. 1, 4, March, 1920, p. 3, October, 1920, pp. 1, 3, and September, 1920, pp. 1-2.

12. The quotation is from Morrison's editorial in *Holiness Layman*, July, 1919, an issue which contains a complete summary of these events. See also *ibid.*, August 1919, p. 3, September, 1919, p. 1, November, 1919, p. 1; and Hammer, *op. cit.*, pp. 54-58. Morrison's valuable "historical statement" appears in Laymen's Holiness Association of America, *Journal . . . First Annual Meeting . . . 1920*, pp. 5-14.

13. Laymen's Holiness Association of America, *Journal . . . 1920*, p. 22, and *passim; Constitution of the Laymen's Holiness Association of America* (pamphlet, 1920), pp. 3-4, 14-16; and *Holiness Layman*, March, 1920, pp. 1-3, and July, 1920, pp. 1-2.

14. See "An Association By-Product," *Holiness Layman*, January, 1920, pp. 1-2; and "An Open Letter," *ibid.*, May, 1920, p. 1. Cf. *ibid.*, April 14, 1921, pp. 2-3.

15. *Little Methodist,* April, 1917, pp. 2, 4; and *Methodist*, July, 1917, pp. 2-3.

16. *Ibid.;* "Loyalty to True Methodism Affirmed," *Methodist*, April, 1918; *ibid.*, July, 1918, p. 2; "Comments on 'Babylon,'" *ibid.*, September, 1918, p. 1; and *ibid.*, November, 1918. Cf. Hammer, *op. cit.*, p. 28.

17. See editorials, *Methodist*, August, 1917, p. 1, and September 1917, p. 2; "There's Death in the Pot," *ibid.*, p. 1; and "Methodism in Danger, or Tainted Books," *ibid.*, October, 1917, p. 2.

18. *Methodist,* November, 1917, p. 1; "Pitch the Pro-Germans Out of the Pulpits," reprinted from *Christian Witness, ibid.,* August, 1918, p. 1; and "Purge Out Germanism," *ibid.*, p. 4.

19. *Holiness Layman,* April, 1920, p. 1, March 17, 1921, p. 1, and September 29, 1921, p. 1.

20. See editorials in *Methodist*, October, 1918, p. 4; *Holiness Layman*, July, 1920, p. 3; and Morrison's annual report in Laymen's Holiness Association of America, *Journal . . . 1920,* p. 8.

21. See, for early views, *Methodist*, September, 1917, p. 1. On the agitation for a college, see *ibid.*, July, 1917, p. 3, January 1918, p. 2, and succeeding issues, especially July, 1918, p. 3, and July, 1920, p. 1. Cf. "Education and Salvation," *ibid.*, April 14, 1921, p. 1.

22. See Taylor's statement in *Methodist*, February, 1918, p. 1. Cf. articles as follows: "The Great Apostasy," January, 1918, p. 3; "The Present World Crisis," April, 1918, p. 2; a gloomy view of the proposed League of Nations by C. Harris, July, 1918, pp. 3-4; and "Prophecy and the Second Coming," October, 1918, p. 3.

23. See "An Impending Controversy," *Holiness Layman*, August, 1919, p. 4; *ibid.,* March, 1920, p. 4; J. M. Taylor, "Why Are They Going?" *ibid.*, January 6, 1921, p. 4; and *ibid.*, June 15, 1922, pp. 1-2.

24. *Nazarene Messenger,* November, 1908, pp. 11, 17; Pasadena, College, *La Sierra, 1915,* section on chapel speakers, pp. 4-5; *Methodist,* October, 1917, p. 3, February, 1918, p. 4, and July, 1919, p. 2; *Holiness Layman,* September, 1920, February 24, 1921, p. 1, November 10, 1921, p. 4; and Laymen's Holiness Association, *Journal . . . 1921,* p. 44.

25. *Holiness Layman,* November, 1920, p. 2, and December, 1920, pp. 1-2; and Laymen's Holiness Association of America, *Journal . . . 1921,* pp. 6, 7, 12, 16-40.

26. *Holiness Layman,* September 22, 1921, p. 1, and October 13, 1921, p. 1; "An Unfounded Assertion," *ibid.,* November 3, 1921, p. 1; and "The Care of Holiness Bands," *ibid.,* November 24, 1921, p. 4.

27. See Laymen's Holiness Association, *Journal . . . 1920,* p. 21; *ibid., Journal . . . 1921,* p. 49; *Holiness Layman,* August 11, 1921, p. 2, September 1, 1921, p. 2, and September 15, 1921, p. 4; "Money and Bread," *ibid.,* October 20, 1921, p. 3; "Let the Laymen Awake," *ibid.,* November 3, 1921, p. 1; and *ibid.,* January 5, 1922, p. 1.

28. See "California Breezes," in *Holiness Layman,* November 10, 1921, pp. 3-4, January 5, 1922, pp. 3-4, and March 9, 1922, pp. 1-4; Morrison's "Editorial Correspondence," *ibid.,* February 9, 1922, p. 2, and April 6, 1922, p. 4; Taylor's autobiographical article, *ibid.,* June 30, 1923, p. 4; and Corbett, *op. cit.,* p. 49.

29. See in *Holiness Layman,* "Hatching Chickens for the Hawks," April 20, 1922, p. 2; Smith's answer, April 27, 1922, p. 2; and Bennett's article, June 1, 1922, pp. 1-4. Cf. W. G. Bennett, *The Supreme Command of Jesus* (publisher and date unknown), pp. 2, 5, 18-19.

30. *Holiness Layman,* April 6, 1922, p. 3, and June 8, 1922, pp. 3-4.

31. See the excellent account in Corbett, *op. cit.,* pp. 51-55; Hammer, *op. cit.,* pp. 66-72; Church of the Nazarene, Minneapolis-Jamestown District, *First Assembly Journal . . . 1922,* pp. 36, 45, 49; and Morrison's editorial announcement of his acceptance of the new position in *Holiness Layman,* July 20, 1922, p. 2.

32. "Organized Holiness," *Holiness Layman,* August 31, 1922, p. 2. Cf. *ibid.,* July 13, 1922, pp. 2, 4, and September 7, 1920, p. 2.

33. *Holiness Layman,* October 14, 1922, pp. 1, 3, October 21, 1922, p. 3, October 28, 1922, p. 3, December 7, 1922, p. 1, January 3, 1923, p. 1, and January 13, 1923, p. 1; and Corbett, *op. cit.,* p. 38.

34. Corbett, *op. cit.,* pp. 57, 60; and *Holiness Layman,* July 7, 1923, p. 4, January 26, 1924, p. 2, July 12, 1924, p. 1, and news columns in succeeding issues. On the Wisconsin and Oregon groups, see *ibid.,* January 26, 1922, p. 3, July 20, 1922, and August 4, 1923, p. 4.

35. J. G. Morrison, *Achieving Faith* (Kansas City, 1926), pp. 69-82; and Corbett, *op. cit.,* pp. 68-73, 106-7.

36. See, for examples, "Two Thousand 'New Theology' Missionaries in China," *Holiness Layman,* July 7, 1923; and "The Menace of the Public Schools," *ibid.,* December 23, 1922, p. 1. Cf. *ibid.,* July 21, 1923, p. 1; Jamestown Holiness Academy, "Opening Announcement" (broadside, in Laymen's Holiness Association papers, Nazarene archives); and Laymen's Holiness Association, *Journal . . . 1921,* pp. 23-25.

37. See, in *Holiness Layman,* "Radical Holiness," September 22, 1923, p. 1; the address of the General Holiness Convention, Fort Wayne, Indiana, October 13, 1923, pp. 1-3; the editorial for January 26, 1924, p. 2; and "Beware of Extremism," April 5, 1924, p. 1.

38. Illinois Holiness University, Board of Trustees, "Minutes" (Ms, president's office, Olivet College), entry for June 11, 1909; C. B. Jernigan, *The World War in Prophecy* (Ponca City, Oklahoma, n.d.), pp. 23, 25, 74, 77; L. A. Reed, "Today? Perhaps!" *Herald of Holiness,* September 14, 1921, p. 5; and Church of the Nazarene, Seventh General Assembly, *Journal . . . 1928,* p. 120. Cf. Jacob H. Rosenberg's anti-Semitic volume, *Startling Fulfillment of the Prophecies Concerning the Jews in the Last Days* (Nashville, 1917), *passim;* and the attack upon the postmillennialists in Henry Bell, "The Impending Church Split," *Herald of Holiness,* September 19, 1923, p. 5.

39. Northwest Nazarene College, *Twenty-five Years,* p. 7; H. O. Wiley, "The Grammar School," *Nazarene Messenger,* July-August, 1919, p. 1; and Olivet College, *Aurora, 1921,* p. 28. Contrast George Hare, "Science Cannot Account for Origination of Living Organisms," *Herald of Holiness,* August 18, 1915, p. 6.

40. Cf. Haynes's editorials in *Herald of Holiness* for September, 1915, p. 2, and June 6, 1917, p. 2, with that of August 27, 1919, p. 2. *Supra,* 234. Cf. notes on J. Glenn Gould's conversation with the writer, June, 1956; and H. Orton Wiley's scornful statement in *Nazarene Messenger,* January, 1922, p. 2.

41. See the "People's Forum" column, in *Herald of Holiness,* June 6 and 20, July 25, and August 15, 1923; and R. T. Williams, February 14, 1925, to C. J. Frost, of Jasper, Alabama (unsigned carbon copy, Williams papers, Nazarene archives).

42. *Herald of Holiness,* May 15, 1912, p. 1.

43. Cf. Hugh C. Benner, "A Democracy Safe for the World," in Olivet College, *Aurora, 1918,* pp. 84-86, and Fifth General Assembly, *Journal . . . 1919,* "Report of the Committee on the State of the Church and the Country," p. 116, with D. Shelby Corlett, *Prohibition at the Crossroads* (pamphlet, Kansas City, 1932), pp. 14-15, and *passim.*

44. *Herald of Holiness,* November 5, 1924, p. 1. Cf. again, Bell, "The Impending Church Split," *ibid.,* September 19, 1923, p. 5; and the general superintendents' address in the Church of the Nazarene, Sixth General Assembly, *Journal . . . 1923,* p. 183.

45. John Norberry, "Changing Our Church Name," *Herald of Holiness,* September 24, 1919, p. 11; editorial, *ibid.,* October 8, 1919, p. 1; Fifth General Assembly, *Journal . . . 1919,* p. 33.

46. Cf. Church of the Nazarene, *Manual, 1908,* p. 27, *1915,* p. 18, and *1919,* p. 19, with Church of the Nazarene, Seventh General Assembly, *Journal . . . 1928,* p. 118.

47. *Ibid.,* pp. 72, 119, 239.

48. See a folder entitled "Church of the Nazarene, Amendment to the Church Constitution, January 26, 1935" (in the Nazarene archives), for correspondence with district secretaries on the ratification of this amendment; it seems to have encountered strange opposition.

CHAPTER XIV
THE RENEWAL OF LEADERSHIP AND THE RESURGENCE OF EVANGELISM, 1921-33

1. See J. B. Chapman, History of the Church of the Nazarene (Kansas City, 1926), p. 80, and his "Peniel's Proposed Plan," Herald of Holiness, July 18, 1917, p. 11; and Church of the Nazarene, Sixth General Assembly, Journal . . . 1923, p. 237.

2. Bresee College, Catalog . . . 1916, pp. 26-27; General Board of Education, "Minutes, 1917-1923" (Ms, Nazarene archives), entries for February 16 and 17, 1922; ibid., entries for September, 1923; Nazarene Messenger, V, No. 3 (March, 1922), 9; and Sixth General Assembly, Journal . . . 1923, pp. 157-59.

3. J. W. Goodwin, Chicago, December 11, 1917, and Lynn, Massachusetts, November 20, 1917, to H. F. Reynolds (Reynolds correspondence, Nazarene archives); and Olivet University Trustees, "Minutes" (Ms, in president's office), November 9, 1921.

4. See General Board of Education, "Minutes, 1917-1923," for this significant address, appearing at the end of the record for February 18, 1920.

5. Ibid., entry for June 18, 1917.

6. Ibid., entries for January 10, 1918.

7. "Report of the General Board of Education," Fifth General Assembly, Journal . . . 1919, pp. 81-83.

8. See, on the founding of the Georgia school and its merger with Trevecca, Herald of Holiness, April 19, 1916, p. 12, and April 18, 1917, p. 11; Pentecostal Church of the Nazarene, Southeastern District, Proceedings, Seventh Annual Assembly . . . 1915, pp. 11, 16-17; and ibid., Georgia District, Proceedings, Fourth Annual Assembly . . . 1918, pp. 9, 14-15. See also General Board of Education, "Minutes 1917-1923," October 6, 1919, February, 1920, February 16-19, 1921, and February 15-19, 1922.

On the Bethany-Peniel merger, cf. C. A. McConnell, Potter's Vessel (Kansas City, 1946), pp. 63-64; notes on the writer's conversation with B. F. Neely, July 10, 1955; and Roy H. Cantrell, "A History of Bethany Nazarene College" (D.R.E. thesis, Southwestern Baptist Theological Seminary, 1955), passim. C. E. Cowen, History of the Church of God (Holiness), pp. 65-67, describes events at Clarence, Missouri, in terms sharply critical of the Nazarene leadership; J. C. Davis, Kansas City, Missouri, August 24, 1925, to W. I. DeBoard and H. F. Reynolds (Ms, Reynolds papers, Nazarene archives), covers the same story.

9. See General Board of Education "Minutes, 1917-1923," "Statistical Report," recorded February 15, 1922, and entry for evening session, February 16, 1922; and Sixth General Assembly, Journal . . . 1923, pp. 184-85.

10. Northwest Nazarene College, Oasis, 1917, p. 63; miscellaneous financial records in the archives of Trevecca Nazarene College pertaining to the sale of lots at the old site in East Nashville; and Ernest K. Farmer, "Attitudes of the Community Newspapers Toward the Church of the Nazarene in Bethany, Oklahoma" (senior seminar paper, Bethany Nazarene College, 1956), pp. 23-26, quoting articles from Daily Oklahoman, May 15, 1921, p. 8, and Oklahoma City Times, July 11, 1929, p. 7.

11. See Eastern Nazarene College, Catalog, 1921-1922, "Historical Statement," p. 8.

12. See the writer's notes on a conversation with H. Orton Wiley, July 19 and August 2, 1955; and *Nazarene University Messenger,* I (August, 1917), 1-4 (at the Pasadena College library), for financial details. Cf. Pasadena College, Board of Trustees, "Report at Meetings of . . . June 5, 1923" (unsigned Ms, archives of the president); and, for the quotation, Pasadena University, *Bulletin, 1918-1919,* p. 1, "Reason for Changing Name."

13. Olivet University, Board of Trustees, "Minutes" (Ms in the office of the president), entry for July 11, 1917; the Olivet *Aurora,* annual issues, 1918 to 1928.

14. Merle McClurkan Heath, *A Man Sent from God; The Life of J. O. McClurkan* (Kansas City, 1942), p. 89; notes on the author's conversations with A. B. Mackey, November 12, 1955; copy of a lease conveyed to C. E. Hardy, from the trustees of Trevecca College, May 15, 1916, in the Trevecca archives; *Herald of Holiness,* October 22, 1919, p. 7; and Trevecca College, Board of Trustees, "Minutes" (in the archives of the college), January 19, 1928, with attached letters, and entries for April 7, July 10, and August 20, 1928.

15. Most of the story is spread out in the pages of the *Trevecca Messenger;* see issues for September, 1931, pp. 1, 4, September, 1932, pp. 1, 3, November, 1932, p. 2, February, 1933, pp. 1, 3, and June, 1933, pp. 1, 3. See also trustees of Trevecca College, "Minutes, 1929-1933" (in the archives of the college), especially letters inside the front cover to and from faculty members, officers, and trustees.

16. Sixth General Assembly, *Journal . . . 1923,* p. 237; Seventh General Assembly, *Journal . . . 1928,* pp. 431-33; and H. Orton Wiley, "On Educational Standards," *Herald of Holiness,* October 25, 1933, p. 26, which reprints Bresee's address of 1915.

17. Seventh General Assembly, *Journal . . . 1928,* pp. 172, 415-20. Cf. Lyle E. Akers, "The Life and Works of E. P. and M. Emily Ellyson" (B.D. thesis, Nazarene Theological Seminary, 1953), pp. 79-81.

18. Church of the Nazarene, Correlated Boards, "Minutes . . . 1921," entry for February 19, 1921; and Sixth General Assembly, *Journal . . 1923,* pp. 54, 142, 145-47.

19. Sixth General Assembly, *Journal . . . 1923,* statistical chart, p. 295; Seventh General Assembly, *Journal . . . 1928,* p. 474; and Ninth General Assembly, *Journal . . . 1936,* p. 230.

20. Hannah Brown Smith, *For Heaven's Sake* (Boston, 1949), pp. 74, 87-98, 198-206, is a semifictional autobiographical account.

21. E. P. Ellyson, "True Yoke-Fellows," *Bible School Journal,* XXVI (January 5, 1936), 1.

22. Church of the Nazarene, General Board of Foreign Missions, "Minutes, 1915-1919," entry for Tuesday, October 17, 1916, morning session; H. D. Brown, "The General Assembly," *Herald of Holiness,* August 27, 1919, p. 9; and N. B. Herrell, "Dr. Wiley's Article," *ibid.,* September 10, 1919, p. 9.

23. General Board of Publication, "Minutes, 1911-1918" (Ms, Nazarene archives), entry for February 22, 1916; *Herald of Holiness,* April 12, 1916, pp. 8-9, May 9, 1917, and November 5, 1919, pp. 8-9.

24. General Board of Foreign Missions, "Minutes, 1908-1914," record of the annual meeting of October 22 to October 27, 1914; and, *ibid.,* "Minutes, 1915-1919" (Nazarene archives), afternoon session, October 18, 1916,

morning session, October 17, 1917, and afternoon session, October 18, 1917. Cf. *ibid.*, afternoon session, October 17, 1918, report of the Committee on Administration.

25. *Ibid.*, entries for 1919: morning session, September 23, morning session, September 24, evening session, September 30, and evening session, October 7; Fifth General Assembly, *Journal* . . . *1919*, p. 106; Susan N. Fitkin, *A Brief History of the Woman's Missionary Society, Church of the Nazarene* (pamphlet, Kansas City, n.d.), p. 406; and Church of the Nazarene, Woman's General Foreign Missionary Council, "Minutes of the Executive Committee . . . January 4, 1930—January 10, 1930" (Ms, Nazarene archives).

26. See, on the Orphanage Board, *Herald of Holiness*, October 29, 1919, p. 7, and November 19, 1919, p. 6; General Board of Church Extension, "Minutes" (Nazarene archives), entry for October, 1916, September 25, 1919, and October 6, 1919; and Fifth General Assembly, *Journal* . . . *1919*, pp. 102 ff., 106, 113.

27. *Ibid.*, pp. 86-88, 111; L. Milton Williams, Oskaloosa, Iowa, April 24, 1920, to H. F. Reynolds, in General Board, "Reports, etc., 1915-1920" (Nazarene archives).

28. Church of the Nazarene, Correlated Boards, "Minutes, 1920," *passim* (there are no page numbers); and *ibid.*, "Minutes, 1921."

29. General Board of Publication, "Minutes, 1919-1922," entries for the meetings of February 13-17, 1922; an untitled Ms in the Reynolds papers, dated March 1, 1922, pertaining to publishing house problems; Nazarene Publishing House, "Special Report, February 15, 1923" (Ms, Nazarene archives), with penciled notes on the back, apparently by R. T. Williams; and Sixth General Assembly, *Journal* . . . *1923*, pp. 181, 186, 239-41.

30. Correlated Boards, "Minutes, 1922," *passim;* and Mendell Taylor, *Fifty Years of Nazarene Missions*, Volume I, "Administration and Finance" (Kansas City, 1955), pp. 21-22.

31. Sixth General Assembly, *Journal* . . . *1923*, pp. 81-83, 104, 107, 128-29.

32. General Board, "Minutes . . . Executive Committee . . . June 23-25, 1924" (Nazarene archives), pp. 16-17, 20, 24; E. G. Anderson, Kansas City, Missouri, November 18 and December 24, 1924, to H. F. Reynolds (Reynolds correspondence); C. A. McConnell, Bethany, Oklahoma, August 21, 1925, to R. T. Williams, and R. T. Williams, August 31, 1925, to McConnell (Williams papers, Nazarene archives).

33. General Board, Church of the Nazarene, "Minutes of the Special Meeting . . . September 21, 1925," pp. 40, 43-44, 50, 54, 57, 67, 88-89; and *Herald of Holiness*, July 4, 1928, p. 24.

34. Church of the Nazarene, General Board, "Minutes, 1923" (Ms, Nazarene archives), pp. 15, 17; C. T. Corbett, *Soldier of the Cross: The Life Story of J. G. Morrison, 1871-1939* (Kansas City, 1956), pp. 72-88, containing numerous excerpts from Dr. Morrison's diaries; Sixth General Assembly, *Journal* . . . *1923*, pp. 202-8, for E. G. Anderson's report, deploring proposals for retrenchment; and Seventh General Assembly, *Journal* . . . *1928*, pp. 309-14, for a review of the successive reorganizations.

35. General Board of Publication, "Minutes, 1919-1922," entry for February 19, 1921, and February 13, 1922; General Board, "Minutes of the Meeting of the Executive Committee . . . June 23-25, 1924," p. 11; E. J. Fleming, Kansas City, Missouri, July 3, 1925, to members of the Department

of Publication (Ms, Nazarene archives), containing attached letters from M. Lunn and J. B. Chapman on the plan for *Preacher's Magazine;* and Sixth General Assembly, *Journal* . . . *1923,* pp. 59-65.

36. Lula Schmelzenbach, *The Missionary Prospector: A Life Story of Harmon Schmelzenbach* . . . (Kansas City, n.d.), pp. 7-17, 24; and General Board of Foreign Missions, *History of the Foreign Missionary Work of the Church of the Nazarene* (pamphlet, Kansas City, 1921), containing, pp. 9-14, Schmelzenbach's own sketch.

37. Schmelzenbach, *op. cit.,* pp. 83-89, 181, 183-87; and George Frame, *Blood Brother of the Swazis: The Life Story of David Hynd* (Kansas City, 1952), pp. 18-19, 28, 40, 46-47, 51, 81.

38. *Report of the General Board of the Church of the Nazarene . . . to the Seventh General Assembly* . . . *1928,* last three pages; and Ninth General Assembly, *Journal* . . . *1936,* p. 290.

39. Russell and Margaret Birchard, *Richard Simpson Anderson, Pioneer Missionary to Central America* (Kansas City, 1951), pp. 10-19, 43-60; notes on author's conversation with Eugenia P. Coats, January 18, 1956, and letter from Eugenia P. Coats to the author, January, 1956 (both in the Nazarene archives).

40. General Board of Foreign Missions, *History,* pp. 44-47; *Report of the General Board* . . . *1928,* last three pages; and A. E. Sanner, *John W. Goodwin: A Biography* (Kansas City, 1945), pp. 140 f.

41. To this point, Roger Winans' two articles in General Board of Foreign Missions, *History,* pp. 48-59, are indispensable to getting the facts straight. See also the author's notes on a conversation with Roger and Mable Park Winans, January 18, 1956; and Carol Gish, *Letters of Esther Carson Winans* (Kansas City, 1951), p. 36.

42. *Ibid.,* pp. 14-15, 30-31, 47-48, 57, 103, 122-24; and notes on the author's conversation with Roger Winans, January 18, 1956.

43. *Report of the General Board* . . . *1928,* last three pages; General Board of Foreign Missions, *History,* pp. 23-43; Church of the Nazarene, General Board, *Proceedings* . . . *1931,* p. 105; and Ninth General Assembly, *Journal* . . . *1936,* p. 290.

44. Susan N. Fitkin, *Grace Abounding,* pp. 94-96; compare pp. 67-69.

45. General Board, *Proceedings* . . . *1931,* pp. 108-9; "Report of the Special Hospital Committee of the General Board, Church of the Nazarene, in regular session January 12-18, 1932" (Ms, in Reynolds papers, Nazarene archives); notes on a conversation of F. C. Sutherland with the author, August 15, 1955; and, for the effects of the depression on the Bremersdorp Hospital, George Frame, *op. cit.,* pp. 53-56.

46. See report of the home mission service at the General Assembly of 1928 in *Herald of Holiness,* July 4, 1928, p. 27; E. O. Chalfant, *Forty Years on the Firing Line* (Kansas City, 1951), pp. 51-71; and sketches of District Superintendents R. J. Plumb, J. W. Short, D. E. Higgs, A. E. Sanner, C. A. Gibson, and R. V. Starr in C. T. Corbett, *Our Pioneer Nazarenes* (Kansas City, 1958), pp. 61-79, 91-96, 103-14.

47. See graph in Ninth General Assembly, *Journal* . . . *1936,* p. 240. Samuel C. Kincheloe, *Research Memorandum on Religion in the Depression* (N.Y., 1937), pp. 7-9, 93-94, comments penetratingly on this theme.

48. Kincheloe, *op. cit.,* p. 136.

INDEX

Abbott, Lyman	200	Barbados	346
Abolitionism	92	Barnhart, A. C.	91
Achieving Faith	315	Bates, J. E.	340
Address by the Southern Holiness Associations	160	Bathing, promiscuous	295
Advocate of Holiness	18	Bearse, J. C.	69, 261-62
Africa	343	Beeson, J. W.	187
African Methodist Episcopal church	126	Beeson, M. A.	187
Aggressive Christianity	25	Belden, Henry	22
Agnew, T. H.	150, 236-37	Bell, A. J.	100
Aguaruna Indians	344-45	Bell, Thomas	229
Airhart, W. G.	162	Benner, Hugh C.	9, 318
Akers, J. W.	148	Bennett, W. G.	303, 305, 312
Albrecht, W. E.	82-83	Benson, John T.	182, 186, 197-98, 337
Alfred University	20	Benson, Mrs. John T.	268
Allen, John	18	Berachah Rescue Home	158
Allentown camp meeting	63, 76	Berry, Jack	148
Allison, William	146-47	Bethany-Peniel College	227, 326-27
American Board of Commissioners for Foreign Missions	22	Bethany Mission	57
		Beulah Christian	70, 82, 86, 263, 265
American Outlook	44	Beulah Heights Academy and Bible School	226-27
Ames, Bishop Edward R.	18	*Beulah Items*	57
Anderson, E. G.	199, 256, 285, 335, 337, 339-40	BeVier, Charles	67, 69, 71, 78, 81
Anderson, Richard S.	187, 343	Bible Institute at Pilot Point	172
Andrews, Bishop Edward G.	20, 61	*Bible School Journal*	334
Angell, E. E.	66, 68, 70, 83, 206, 257, 261	"Board Tabernacle"	114
		Boardman, William E.	11, 21-26
Apostolic Holiness church	36, 167, 225	Boland, J. M.	42, 45
Apostolic Holiness Union	200	Bolton, Robert	239
Arkansas Holiness Association	169	Booth, Catherine	25
Arkansas Holiness College	172, 257-58	Booth, William	25, 47
		Boston Holiness League	64
Armour, Mrs. A. T.	138	Boston University	19, 54, 81, 126
Asbury Church	102	Bothwell, Mrs. Lilly	138
Asbury College	35, 45-46, 162, 300	Bounds, E. M.	44
Asbury, Francis	21	Bovard, M. M.	99
Asbury Grove	16	Bowers, Dr. Stephen	124
Ashcroft, Frank and Harry	141	Bowes, Alpin	231
Association of Pentecostal Churches of America	36, 64-65, 69-71, 74-90, 130, 145, 177, 206 ff. 250, 268	Bowman, Bishop Thomas	18, 62
		Bowne, Borden Parker	46
		Boxer Rebellion	251
		Boyd, Miss Lizzie	55
Averill, R. L.	160, 163	Brand, Walter C.	224
		Bremersdorp	343
Baldwin, Mrs. A. P.	110	Brengle, Samuel Logan	25
Ballantine, G. N.	55	Bresee, Mrs. Ada F.	268
Bane, A. C.	52	Bresee College	226, 326
Banner of Holiness	29, 34	Bresee, Maria Hibbard	92
		Bresee Memorial Hospital	346

Bresee, Dr. Paul 136
Bresee, Phineas F. 12, 36, 46, 48, 49-52, 77, 89, 91-121, 122, 179, 190, 192, 194-95, 198, 206 ff., 229, 231-32, 240, 245-49, 261-62, 271, 272, 275, 277, 311
  early years 91-96
  interest in prohibition 101 ff.
  personal peculiarities 120
  sanctification of 93-94, 97
  in southern California 96-121
Bresee, Sue 276
Bresee, Susan Brown 91
Brewer, W. L. 313
British and Foreign Bible Society 344
Bromley, C. A. 197, 236
Brooks, John P. 28-30, 34
Brotherhood of St. Stephen 134-36
Brown, H. D. 48, 141-44, 208, 210, 216, 220, 228, 229, 285, 310
Brown, H. N. 55, 60-61, 65-66, 68, 71-72, 76, 79, 81, 83, 88, 206, 207, 209
Brown, J. T. 183
Brown, O. E. 43
Brown, Tom M. 75
Browning, Francis J. 160
Bryan, William Jennings 298, 317
Buell, George N. 62
Buffum, Herbert and Lillie 137, 146
Burger, L. E. 231, 233
Burke, Dr. Edwin 148
Burning Bush 128
Bushnell, Horace 266

Cagle, H. C. 155, 158
Cagle, Mrs. Mary Lee; see Mary Lee Harris
Calgary, Alberta 229
California Christian Advocate 17, 101, 107-8, 112, 126
Campbell, S. W. 102
Canada 229
Cape Verde Islands 78, 84-87, 250
Carey, Edith 75
Carradine, Beverly 46, 52, 69, 71, 181, 299
Carson, Esther (Winans) 287
Cascade College 35
Caughey, James 23, 25
Central Evangelical Holiness Association 35, 58-59, 62, 64-65, 68-69
Central Holiness University 46, 236, 255, 258, 300
Central Idea of Christianity, The 19

Central Kansas Holiness Association 304
Chalfant, E. O. 347
Chafee, S. S. 132
Chapell, F. L. 189
Chapman, J. B. 32, 167, 169, 172, 175-78, 205, 216, 219, 248, 258, 296, 317, 319, 322-26, 341, 349
Chapman, J. Wilbur 25, 182
Chapman, Mrs. Louise Robinson 287-88
Chicago Evangelistic Institute 46
Chicago Holiness Assembly, 1885 33
Chicago Holiness Assembly, 1901 35
Chief White Eagle 227
China 251, 346
China Band 138
Chism, Fairy 287-88
Christian Advocate 20
Christian Alliance Bible School 47
Christian and Missionary Alliance 25, 35, 109, 146, 182, 186, 188, 200
Christian Purity 15
Christian Standard 19, 39, 52
Christian Standard and Home Journal 17
Christian Witness 39, 46, 51, 54, 60, 62, 64-65, 67-68, 123, 127, 136, 149, 211, 300, 307
Christian Worker 22
Christian's Secret of a Happy Life, The 24
Christmas Love Feast 118
Church History Commission 9-10
Church of Christ of Milan 152
Church of God (Anderson) 28, 235
Church of God (Holiness) 29, 30, 46, 122, 143, 235
Church of the Nazarene becomes a national church 122-50
  Los Angeles 91-121
  origin of name 110
City Evangelization Union 108
Clark, Dougan 22-23
Claypoole, Fannie 188
Cleveland Bible Institute (Malone College) 22, 46
Cochran, A. S. 226, 264
Codding, Roy G. 256
Colt, W. B. 30
Colorado Holiness Association 231
"Come-outism" 28-33, 57, 160
Communism 308
Company E 113, 134-35

Congregational Methodist
 Church   82
Congregational sovereignty 36, 72
Congregationalism, 54-58, 78, 170
Cooke, Bishop R. J.   302
Cookman, Alfred   15-18, 81
Copeland, O. J.   60, 68
Cordell, B. A.   162
Corlett, D. Shelby   172, 319, 332
Corlett, Lewis T.   172
Cornell, C. E.   122, 149, 195, 207,
                   217, 236, 243, 276
Correlated Boards   337-38
Creal, W. M.   264
Creighton, J. B.   30, 122, 143
Crist, Rose Potter   194
Crittenton, Charles N.   48
Crittenton Home   174
Cuba   187
Cullis, Charles C.   21, 25
Cumberland Presbyterians 152,
             159, 163, 178, 181-82
Curry, Daniel   40

Daily Christian Advocate   103
Danford, S. A.   299-303, 310
Danner, W. W.   245
Davidson, Rev. and Mrs. J. M.   85
Davis, C. Howard   57-59, 64, 66,
          69-71, 76-80, 89, 130, 243, 284
Deaconess order   318
Deets, Mr. and Mrs. Jackson 139,
                              260-61
Deets Pacific Bible College 202,
              217, 231, 245, 257
DeJernett, E. C.   160-62
DePauw, Washington C.   18, 20
Des Plaines camp meeting   190
Dewey, John   267
Dlamini, Peter   343
Dilley, Clyde T.   228
Disciples of Christ   290
Divine Church, The   29
Dodge   69
Dooley, Mr. and Mrs. J. A.   147
Door of Hope   49
Door of Hope Mission   185, 200
Douglas Camp Meeting 23, 40, 58,
                    64, 89, 206, 224
Drew Theological Seminary 15, 18
Drewry, F. J.   310
Duncan, Colonel   110
Dunklin County Holiness
  Camp Meeting Association   304
Dunn, Lewis R.   15, 19, 22, 45

Earle, A. B.   11, 21
Earlham College   22

East Mississippi Female
  College   187
Eastern Illinois Holiness
  Association   130, 147, 259
Eastern Nazarene College 65, 74,
     81-88, 202, 239, 257, 261-62, 286,
                              324, 327
Eaton, Mrs. E. G.   251, 256
Eckel, Howard   276-79, 328
Eckel, W. A.   197, 345-46
Education
  enlarged interest in   322 ff.
  organization of   257 ff.
El Christiana   343
Eleventh Hour Movement, The 189
Elhanan Training and
  Industrial Institute   188
Ellyson, Edgar P. 21, 146, 166, 195-
     98, 217-18, 221, 225, 228, 232, 246,
     249, 255, 257-58, 260-61, 271, 274,
              279, 295, 317, 331, 334
Emmanuel Church   79
Emerson, Eugene   283, 317
England, holiness revival in   23 ff
Epperson, Fred C.   260
Epworth League   19, 299
Ernest, Mrs. J. W.   111
Ernest, Mr. L. L.   136
Esselstyn, W. C.   343
Essentials in American History 267
Eternal security   319
Evangelical Association 37, 61-66,
                     72, 74, 76, 304
Evangelical church   16
Evangelist   156
Everett, T. J.   55

Family life   333
Farnsworth, R. W. C.   96, 98
Farson, Duke   128
Ferguson, Rev. and Mrs. T. P. 49-51,
                              109, 141
Fifth Street Mission   270
Finney, Charles G. 11, 22-23, 26,
                                   47
First Pentecostal Mission
  Church   147
Fisher, William E. 155, 158-59, 169,
                         172, 178, 221
Fitkin, Abram E.   70
Fitkin Memorial Hospital 242, 343
Fitkin, Susan N. 68, 70, 88, 268,
                                  346
Fitzgerald, Bishop John N.   106
Fleming, E. J.   295, 322, 338, 341,
                                  347
Fletcher, John   21

405

Florence Crittenton Home	135
Foote, J. B.	65
Foreign Missions, organization	250-57
Form and Plan of Local Organization	164
Foss, Cyrus D.	109
Foster, Randolph S.	15, 18-19
Fowler, Charles J.	27, 54, 60-65, 69, 71, 74, 123, 126, 130, 211, 244, 299
Franklin, George J.	257
Free Methodist	12
Free Methodist church	33, 37, 126, 141, 145, 159, 161-62, 172, 178, 235, 258, 296
French, C. H.	282
French, E. T.	296
Friends Expositor	22
Fundamentalism	14, 235, 271, 294, 298 ff.
Wesleyan	305 ff.
Galloway, Bishop	44
Garrett Biblical Institute	15
Gassaway, B. F.	31
Gay, Leslie F.	96, 98-100, 107, 251-53
Gay, Mrs. Leslie F.	110, 232
General Board, The	327, 334, 337-41
General Board of Church Extension	336
General Board of Education	284, 285-88, 323-27, 330, 334
General Board of Foreign Missions	334, 338
General Board of Home Missions and Evangelism	336, 338-39
General Board of Publication	334, 338
General Board of Rescue Work	269
General Educational Board	257
General Foreign Missionary Board	197, 240, 242, 247, 252-55, 257
General Holiness Assembly, 1901	126
General Holiness League	59-60
General Orphanage Board	269, 336
General Sunday School Committee	331
General Superintendents, Board of	9
George Fox College	35
Georgia Holiness Association	198
Gerrish, Dr. M. F.	225
Gibson, C. A.	347
Gibson, Julia R.	85
Gill, Joshua	54, 59-64
Gilmore, R. E.	226
Girvin, E. A.	132, 210, 233, 285, 295, 328, 338
Gladden, Washington	266
Gladney, L. L.	169
Glascock, J. L.	299
Glasgow University	240-41
Godbey, W. B.	156, 160
Godliness	25
God's Bible School	35, 46, 52, 237, 300
Good Way, The	29
Goodwin, John W.	21, 132, 140, 206, 245, 249, 260-61, 270, 272-73, 276-77, 310, 322, 325, 337, 340, 344, 346
Gordon, Adoniram J.	25
Gordon College	25
Gould, John	237, 295
Government and Doctrines of the New Testament Church	154
Graded lessons	331
Grandview Park Camp Meeting	206
Graves, A. P.	21, 224
Griffin, C. W.	206
Growth in Holiness Toward Perfection	45
Guatemala	342-43, 346
Guide to Holiness	12, 18-20, 34, 39, 54
Guthrie, M. J.	169
Guy, R. M.	169, 172, 174-77, 190, 221
Hadley, Lewis I.	224, 282
Hall, E. D.	55
Hall, J. N.	153
Hall, Phoebe and Sara	76
Hammer, Ira E.	304, 314
Hammond, G. M.	157-58, 169, 176
Haney, M. L.	30, 142, 148
Hanscome, Mrs. S. A.	58
Hanson, Isaac	76
Hardin, Wallace	28-31, 34
Harding, U. E.	336
Hardy, C. E.	198, 329
Harford-Battersby, Canon	24
Hargrove, Bishop	44
Harris, A. T.	150
Harris, Mary Lee	154, 158-59, 169, 171-73, 176, 216-17
Harris, Robert Lee	42, 153-59
Harris, W. L.	20
Hart, Albert Bushnell	267

Hartt, Aaron   58, 60, 62-63, 66, 76
Harvey, E. L.   128
"Hatching Chickens for the Hawks"   312
Hatfield, J. T.   128, 132
Haven, Bishop Gilbert   19, 93
Hawkins, C. L.   172
Hayes, George H.   43
Haynes, B. F.   44, 180, 182, 264-65, 318
Hays, Harry   280-82, 284
Hendricks, A. O.   132, 275, 328-30
Herald of Holiness   44, 265, 280, 286, 296, 317, 319-20, 328, 335, 341
Herrell, N. B.   283, 286, 288, 324, 336
Hertenstein, Ralph   275
Hess, Weaver W.   275
Higher Christian Life, The   11
Highways and Hedges   173
Hill, Mary A.   138, 250
Hillcrest Home   276
Hillery, Fred A.   55, 58, 60, 63-65, 69, 71, 78, 81, 83, 86, 89, 265
Hills, Aaron Merritt   21, 127, 162, 165-67, 190-91, 217, 236, 240, 241, 259, 278, 286
Hodgin, G. Arnold   279, 280, 283
Hoffman, Mrs. Nellie   314
Hofstadter, Richard   199
Hoke, Mrs. Mattie   225
Holiness Association of Texas   35, 161-66, 167, 169
Holiness Baptist church   36, 171
Holiness Christian Church Association   77, 161, 230
Holiness Christian church   129, 219, 230, 274
Holiness Christian Conference of Indiana   235
Holiness church   28, 32
Holiness Church of California   224
Holiness Church of Christ   171-79, 190, 198, 214-16, 221, 223, 244, 251-53, 267
Holiness Evangel   173-74, 178, 201, 214, 255, 264
Holiness Evangelist   34
Holiness Layman   304, 311-13
Holiness movement   9
Holiness Revival, 1855-88   11-26
Holiness revival in England   23 ff.
Holiness Union   35, 197, 222
Holmes, N. J.   188
Hoople, William Howard   21, 63-64, 66-73, 76, 78, 80-81, 83-84, 87-88, 130, 230, 240, 279

Hope School   251, 256
Hosley, H. B.   69, 72, 76, 78-79 83-85, 87, 219, 221, 230, 244, 265
Howland, Gardner   110
Huckabee, B. W.   165, 178, 190, 205, 217
Hudson Band   168
Huff, Will   123, 130, 244
Hughes, George   15, 19, 23, 34, 39
Hugus Ranch   260
Hunter, Mrs. Fannie McDowell   155
Huntingdon, Lady   189
Huntington, D. W. C.   45
Hynd, Dr. David   242, 343

Idaho-Oregon Holiness School   282
Illinois State Holiness Association   29, 143, 149, 235
Illinois Holiness University   259
Imhoff, C. A.   237
In His Steps   136
Independent Holiness church   32, 36, 159, 167-69, 171
India   78, 82, 84-87, 187, 199, 245-46, 205, 252, 256, 284
Ingler, Arthur   128
Inland Christian Advocate   93
"Inner Light"   22
Inskip, John S.   15-18, 23, 39
International Apostolic Holiness church   274
International Council of Religious Education   331
International Holiness Mission   241
International Holiness Union and Prayer League   274
Inter-State Camp Meeting Association   301
Iowa Holiness Association   224
Irick, Allie   169, 221
Isayama, N.   346

Jacobson, H. O.   303, 314
Jacques, J. R.   20
Jamestown Camp Meeting   314
Jamison, Joseph   137-38
Janes, Edmund S.   19
Japan   252, 345-46
Jefferies, A. G.   167
Jenkins, C. S.   343
Jernigan, C. B.   32, 161-64, 167-69, 173-78, 190, 214-15, 225-28, 258, 317, 336
John Wesley Church   70, 83, 206, 210
Johnson, Mrs. Herbert   137-38
Jones, C. Warren   286
Jones, Rufus   22

407

Jones, Sam P. 181
Jones, T. L. 140
Joyce, Bishop 299
Keen, Samuel A. 53, 107
Keith, C. M. 163-64
Kellogg, Mrs. E. J. 138
Kent, L. B. 122, 124, 127, 143, 145, 235
Keswick movement 21, 23-26, 124, 182-83
Keswick theology 319
Key, Bishop Joseph S. 44
King, J. W. 231
Kinne, C. J. 264, 270
Kitagawa, Hiroshi 345
Kletzing, H. F. 244
Knapp, Martin Wells 59-60, 274
Knapp, Mrs. Martin Wells 36, 52
Knott, Mrs. Lucy P. 135, 232
Knott, Mrs. W. S. 110-11, 113
Knotts, Joseph 94 ff., 213
Kring, J. A. 30
Kroft, Mrs. M. E. 111
Ku Klux Klan 318
Labor 136
Labor unions 234, 318
Ladies Aid societies 299
Ladies' Foreign Missionary Auxiliary 88
LaFontaine, C. V. 122
Lanpher, Lois E. 82
Latter-day Saints 290
Laymen's Holiness Association 234, 298-315
Lee Holiness Mission 231
Lee, Jason 141, 232
Lee, William 141, 231-32
Leete, Bishop Frederic D. 302
"Legalism Overdone" 216
Levy, E. M. 23, 55, 60, 64, 68
Liberalism 232
Linaweaver, P. G. 133
Little Methodist 301, 306
Lively, J. W. 160, 163
Living Water 44, 188-89, 198, 266
Lord Macaulay 5
Los Angeles County Medical Association 104
Los Angeles Times 107, 109-10
Lowell Holiness Mission 74
Lowery, Asbury 17, 19, 38, 45
Ludwig, Theodore 336
Lunn, M. 322, 337-39, 341, 347
Luscomb, Benjamin 58
Lynn Mission Church 57
McBride, J. B. 221, 279

McClean, John H. 160
McClintock, John C. 15, 18
McClurkan, J. O. 21, 27, 35, 44, 52, 175, 180-99, 210, 271, 311, 329
McConnell, C. A. 163-64, 166, 178, 201-2, 217, 249, 255, 265, 271, 279, 317, 339
McConnell, Will T. 264
McCulloch, C. O. 108
McDonald, William 18, 23, 27, 46, 52, 54, 59-60, 91, 97-102
McInturff, D. N. 49
McKee, Mrs. Leoti 138
McLaughlin, G. A. 149
McLean, Alexander 67
McPherson, Aimee Semple 312
McPherson, Miss Ethel 136
McReynolds, Mrs. A. F. 136
McReynolds, Mrs. Mary 251
Machen, J. Gresham 319
Macaulay, Lord 5
Mackey, A. B. 330
Mahan, Asa 11, 22-24
Malambe, James 343
Malden Mission Church 58
Mallalieu, Bishop Willard F. 20, 27, 46, 54, 102, 109, 161
Mallory, Mattie 226
Malone College 35
Mangum, Dr. Thomas E. 287-88
Manitoba, Saskatchewan 229
Mann, G. W. 157-58
Mann, Una P. 82
Marine, George W. 304
Maris, Miss Leora 137-38
Martha's Vineyard 18
Martin, I. G. 119, 130, 141, 148, 227-28, 232, 248-49, 279
Mateo Street Church 113
Matson, Henrietta 188
Matthews, John 278, 284, 290-91
Maybury, John Thomas 230
Medical missions 347
Mennonite Brethren in Christ 36, 235
Meridian College 46
Meridian Female College 187
Meridian Male College 187
Merrill, Bishop Stephen M. 18-19
Merrit, Timothy 54
Messenger, F. M. 128, 337
Methodism, The Methodist Church 9, 12, 15, 19-21, 26, 29-33, 35, 37-38, 39-46, 48-50, 52-57, 59-67, 71-72, 74-75, 91-109, 112, 115, 125-26, 140, 145, 151-52, 159-62,

408

164, 218, 222, 234-35, 238, 298-310, 347
Methodism, English 23
Methodist Episcopal church, Southern 32, 41, 52-53, 161, 180-82, 222
Methodist Laymen's Holiness Association 301
Methodist Protestant church 37, 159, 161, 168, 234
Methodist Quarterly Review 22, 40, 43
Methodist, The 17
Methodist Theology vs. Methodist Theologians 46
Metropolitan Church Association 36, 128, 231
Mexico 252, 254-55, 344
Michigan Holiness Record 34
Michigan State Association 33
Miley, John 38, 267
Miller, H. H. 227, 243
Miller, Perry 290
Mills, F. J. 305
Missionary Evangel 172
Missionary Sanitarium and Institute 287, 347
Missionary Training Institute 202
Missions, city rescue 48-53
Missouri Holiness College 258
Mitchum, R. B. 156-57, 169-70, 173, 176, 191, 199
Mitchum, Mrs. R. B. 48, 153, 155
Modernism 235
Moke, Henrietta 82
Monday Holiness Meeting 64
Moody Bible Institute 25
Moody, Dwight L. 22, 25
Moore, J. E., Sr. 172, 262
Moore, Timothy H. 186, 197-98
Morgan, Edmund 290
Morris, Thomas A. 17
Morrison, Henry Clay 27, 35, 42, 45, 69, 161, 167, 169, 177, 192, 211, 222
Morrison, J. G. 298-315, 316, 322, 340-41, 347
Morrison, James and Amanda 299
Morse, Deacon George 60, 64, 71, 206, 224
Mowry, George E. 200
Mudge, James 45-46
Muhlenberg, Henry M. 290
Munro, Bertha 262
Murphree, J. A. 155-56, 158
Nagamatsu, Mr. and Mrs. J. I. 345
Nashville Advocate 44

Nashville Holiness Tabernacle 185, 197, 199
Nast, William 19, 24
National Camp Meeting Association for the Promotion of Holiness 16, 33-34
National Association for the Promotion of Holiness: *see* National Holiness Association
National Holiness Association 23, 29, 35, 39, 54, 60, 65, 74, 81, 96, 100-101, 123, 127, 184, 221-22, 224, 236, 240, 305
Nazarene, The 118, 121
Nazarene Bible Training School 334
Nazarene Messenger 122-23, 125, 134, 136-37, 216, 240, 246, 252, 263-64, 285
Nazarene Publishing Company 136
Nazarene Publishing House 263 ff., 264, 270, 278, 322-23, 331, 334, 337, 349
Nazarene University: *see* Pasadena College
Nazarene Young People's Society 319, 332
Nease, Floyd 275, 328, 330
Nease, Orval 275, 328, 330
Nebraska State Holiness Camp Meeting 141
Nebraska Wesleyan University 45
Neeley, B. F. 159, 171, 176, 216
New Brunswick Baptist Association 36
New England Union Holiness Convention 57
Newman, John P. 20
"New Orthodoxy" 14
New Testament Church of Christ 36, 48, 153-59, 168-71, 190
New York State Holiness Association 67-68
New York Yearly Meeting of Friends 70
Nixon, T. J. 304
Norberry, John 64, 67, 74, 78, 128
Norris, John 72, 77, 80, 82, 237
"North Dakota idea" 303
"North Dakota land deal" 339
North Dakota Methodist 300-301
North Dakota Methodist Camp Meeting Association 299
Northwest Holiness School 282
Northwest Nazarene College 270, 277, 281 ff., 324

409

Northwest, Nazarenes in the 140-44
Northwest Texas Holiness Association 31, 42, 159, 163-64
Oakland City camp meeting 304
Oberlin College 11, 22
Oberlin movement 21
Oberlin theology 182
Ocean Grove (New Jersey) camp 18
Ohio Yearly Meeting of Friends 36, 145, 235
Oklahoma Holiness Association 227
Oklahoma Holiness College 227
Old Orchard Beach 17
Olivet Nazarene College 130, 259-60, 272, 317, 324, 327, 329
"One New Testament Church" 29
Osborn, William B. 15, 18
Other Sheep 265, 335
Oxford Union Meeting for the Promotion of Scriptural Holiness 24

Pacific Bible College 133, 137-38
Park, Mable (Mrs. Roger Winans) 344
Parkhead Congregational Church 239
Park Street Church 21
Palmer, Phoebe 12, 19-21, 23, 26, 40, 47, 200
Palmer, Dr. and Mrs. 15, 18, 21, 23
Pasadena College 137, 139-40, 196, 260, 270, 272, 288, 328, 344
Peavey, L. D. 240, 264
Peck, Jesse T. 19-20
Peniel 161-66, 260
Peniel College 323, 325
Peniel Hall 49-51, 106, 134
Peniel Herald 50
Peniel Mission 49-51, 106, 141
Pennsylvania Methodist 126
Pentecost-Pilgrim Church 281
Pentecostal Advocate 165-66, 217-18, 240, 247, 255, 265
Pentecostal Alliance 35, 182
Pentecostal Church of Scotland 234, 238-42
Pentecostal Church of the Nazarene 170, 178, 201, 211, 219, 320
"Pentecostal" churches (unknown tongues) 319-20
Pentecostal Collegiate Institute: see Eastern Nazarene College
Pentecostal Era 244, 265

Pentecostal Herald 177, 300
Pentecostal League 84, 87
Pentecostal Mission 36, 44, 52, 169, 175, 179, 180-99, 200, 251, 239
Pentecostal Mission Hall 74
Pentecostal Movement 316
Pentecostal Preachers' Association 81, 88
Pentecostal Trade Schools 262
Pentecostal Union 169
People's Evangelical churches 54-58
People's Mission 129
People's Mission Church 232
People's Mission, Spokane 232
People's United Church 49
Perfect Love 50
Perry, Mrs. Ella 85
Perry, Ernest 82, 83
Perry, George E. 55
Perry, Gertrude 82, 85
Personalism 54
Peru 287, 342
Pettit, Lyman C. 82
Phillips, Eugenia (Mrs. Coats) 344
Pickett, L. L. 69
Pierce, Robert 133, 142, 214, 216
Pierce, R. L. 295
Pike, J. M. 186
Pilgrim 279
Pilgrim Holiness church 36, 274, 281, 296
Pillar of Fire church, 128, 231
Pilot Point 9, 12, 28, 47, 152, 167-68, 170, 194, 219, 220-23
Plain Account of Christian Perfection 31
Plumb, R. J. 30
Plummer, F. W. 58
Plymouth Brethren 319
Preacher's Magazine, The 341
Premillennialism 25, 118, 184, 194, 214, 309
Primitive Holiness Mission 34
Primitive Methodist church 23
Pritchard, Augustus B. 120
Pritchard, Calvin W. 22
Problem of Methodism, The 42
Problem Solved, The 43
Progressive movement 199-204
Prohibition 101 ff., 124, 201, 318

Raleigh Fitkin Memorial Hospital: see Fitkin Memorial
Ramsay, A. J. 274, 275-77
Ransom, A. S. 186, 197
Rauschenbusch, Walter 200
Red Deer, Alberta 229

Reed, L. A. 317
Rees, Byron J. 79
Rees, Paul S. 273
Rees, Seth C. 21, 36, 52, 64, 70, 128, 140, 165, 167-68, 261, 273-78 ff., 280-81, 284, 291-92
Reformed Baptist church 36, 76
Reid, Isaiah 30, 46, 48, 122, 127, 224
Rest Cottage 168, 173, 175
Reynolds, E. E. 60, 74
Reynolds, Hiram F. 12, 60-61, 63-66, 68-72, 74, 76, 77-81, 83-86, 88, 130, 194-96, 198-99, 212-14, 219, 225, 230-32, 240-41, 244-45, 247-49, 252-53, 256, 258, 265, 272-73, 279, 284, 313, 325, 335, 336, 341, 344
Reynolds, Mrs. Hiram F. 88
Rice, E. O. 303
Rice, S. 148
Riggs, A. B. 60, 64, 66, 68, 71, 74, 76, 78, 81, 88, 206-7, 209, 232
Rise and Fall of the Church of the Nazarene, The 290
Rising Star Union of 1904 168-71
Roberts, C. E. 174, 328
Roberts, John 169, 174
Roberts, J. P. 168, 214, 220
Robinson, Bud 42, 123, 130, 160-61, 165-67, 217-18, 221, 240, 264, 279, 284, 312
Robinson, T. E. 98-99
Rogers, Dennis 32, 163-64, 169, 178, 255
Rogers, J. G. 228
Rose, O. W. 158
Rosser, Leonidas 41, 43
Round Lake 16, 22
Rural tradition 28
Russell, I. A. 157-58
Ruth, C. W. 49, 122, 129-30, 135, 142, 147, 206-7, 217, 219, 230, 236
Ryder, W. C. 58, 64, 69
Rye, J. J. 196-97
Rye, Martha 181

Sails, T. L. 140
St. Louis Advocate 44
Salvation Army 25, 47, 49, 124, 200, 202, 304
San Antonio Holiness Association 147
Sanders, J. F. 261, 270
Sanner, A. E. 30, 288
Santin, Dr. V. G. 344

Scandinavian Holiness Association 303, 315
Schlatter, Michael 290
Schmelzenbach, Harmon 242, 342
Scopes, John T. 317
Scott, J. D. 168, 172, 175-76, 178, 201, 214-15, 221, 255, 340, 344
Scott, Colonel William T. 159
Scottsville Camp Meeting 31, 159
Searles, J. E. 39
Seattle Pacific College 141
Second generation 289-97
Secret orders 128, 215
Sect and church 266-71
Seiss, J. A. 184
Selle, R. L. 161
Seventh-day Adventists 290
Seymour, Dr. A. L. 138
Seymour, Mrs. A. L. 137-38
Sharpe, Agnes Kanema (Mrs. David Hynd) 242, 343
Sharpe, George 21, 238, 242, 340
Shaw, S. B. 28, 33, 35, 153
Sheeks, E. H. 170, 172, 254
Sheeks, Mr. and Mrs. E. H. 153, 155, 157, 174, 176, 214-15
Sheldon, Charles M. 136
Shepard, W. E. 137, 146
Sherman, C. W. 48, 153, 169
Shields, Fred J. 263, 275, 283, 286, 328, 330
Shingler Holiness College 325
Shingler, T. J. 198, 214, 258
Short, James W. 279
Short, J. N. 60, 61, 63-64, 74, 80-81, 206-7, 209, 217, 311
Shroyers, Nina E. 85
Silver Lake Camp Meeting 61, 64, 75
Simpson, A. B. 25, 36, 47, 109, 182, 184
Simpson Church 103-4
Simpson, Bishop Matthew 15-16, 18, 20
Sin and Holiness 45
Sloat, F. W. 69
Smith, Mrs. Amanda 41, 51
Smith, Donnell J. 332
Smith, Hannah Whitall 24
Smith, J. A. 147
Smith, Joseph H. 50, 52, 59, 312
Smith, J. T. 160
Smith, Robert Pearsall 23-24
Smith, Timothy L. 9
Snider, Miss Cora 345
Social concern 135
  Bresee and 101 ff., 108 ff., 114 f.

Social gospel 200
Social work 269-70, 318
  holiness 47-53
South Dakota State Holiness
  Association 314
South Providence Holiness
  Association 55
Southeastern Educational Board
  of the Church of the Nazarene
    330
Southern Baptist church 319
Southern California and Arizona
  Holiness Association 31-32
*Southern California Christian
Advocate* 100-102
*Southern California Methodist
Quarterly* 98-99
Southern Methodist Episcopal
  church 32, 41, 52-53, 161,
    180-82, 222
Southwestern Arkansas Holiness
  Association 169
Southwestern Holiness
  Association 29
Speakes, Joseph 158, 172, 214
Spear, G. H. 55
Sprague, F. L. 57, 60-61, 64, 69,
    71, 78
Sprague, Lillian M. 84-85
Stafford, S. M. 174, 214, 252
Stanfield, John 163
Staples, Mr. and Mrs. M. B. 346
Staten Island camp meeting 69, 71
Steele, Daniel 19, 25, 27, 38, 45-
    46, 54, 59, 64
Stive, Miss Emma 111
Studd, G. B. 49, 51
Suddarth, Mrs. Fannie E. 172
Sunday, Billy 309
Sunday school 134
Sunday school literature 267
Sunday school work 331 ff.
Sunset Camp Meeting 168
Superintendency 36, 77-81
Superintendency, General 245 ff.
Superintendents, Board of
  General 285 ff.
Surrendered Life, The 182
Sutherland, F. C. 287
Swaziland 342, 346
Syracuse University 19

Tait, W. B. 229
Tanner, Fillmore 49
Taylor, Carrie E. 84
Taylor, James M. 303-4, 309, 312
Taylor, S. C. 314

Taylor University 35, 46, 300
Taylor, William 18, 40, 41, 140
Teel, George M. 32
Tennessee Methodist 44, 180
Terry, Milton S. 38
Texas Holiness Advocate 163-64,
    178
Texas Holiness Association 31, 159
Texas Holiness University 46, 160,
  162, 165, 168, 178, 217-18, 246,
    257-58, 259
Thomas, David 241
Thompson, C. A. 229
Thompson, Charles E. 229
Tigert, John J. 43-44
Tillett, Wilbur 45
Torrey, R. A. 25
Tracy, L. S. 76, 82, 256, 345
Trevecca Nazarene College 188,
  189, 197-98, 258, 325, 329
Troy Conference Grounds 16
Truax, A. B. 61
Trumbauer, Horace G. 77, 230
Trumpet 153
"Tuesday Meeting for the
  Promotion of Holiness" 12, 20
Tullis, W. H. 280, 283, 304

Union Gospel Mission 49
Union Holiness Mission 142
Union Mission Association 169
Union Mission of San Antonio 147
United Brethren church 33, 126
University of Southern
  California 50, 99, 104-6, 139
Upchurch, J. T. 158, 216
Updegraff, David B. 22
Upham, T. C. 23, 191
Urban tradition 28
Utica Avenue Tabernacle 67

Vacation Bible schools 331
Vanderbilt University 45
Vanderpool, D. I. 30
Vanguard Mission 48, 153
Vennard College 35
Vermont Holiness Association
    60-61
Vermont Methodist Seminary 60
Victoria, B. C. 229
Vincent, Bishop John H. 103, 124
Vineland (New Jersey) camp
    15, 26
Volunteers of America 49, 185,
    200, 202

Waco Camp Meeting 31, 42, 190
Wainwright, S. H. 43
Walden, Bishop John M. 140, 160

Walker, Edward F.   21, 127, 130, 186, 196-97, 224, 226, 238, 241, 245, 247, 249, 272, 277-78, 285, 328
Wallace, DeLance   141, 143, 264, 325
Wallace, Mrs. DeLance   207, 284
Wallace, Hardin   159
Wallin, Henry B.   218, 317
Walters, Myrtle Belle   284
Walthall, W. J.   171
Warner, Daniel S.   28, 34
Warren, W. F.   108
Warrior Saint, The   273
Washburn, James F.   32, 34
Washburn, Mrs. James F.   32
Washburn, Nathan   66, 71, 75, 296
Washington State Children's Home Society   58, 142
Washington State Holiness Association   141
Watson, George D.   91, 97-98
Webber, Mrs. Mary   70
Weiand, T. L.   76
Wesley, John   9, 21, 42
Wesley Pentecostal Church   74
Western Holiness Association   29
Western Union Holiness Convention   23
Wesleyan Methodist church   33, 37, 145, 235, 296
Wheat, T. J.   30
Whitcomb, A. L.   139, 244
White, Mrs. Alma   128
White Holiness Mission   342
White, Mrs. Kent   231
White Slaves of America, The   175
White, Stephen S.   262, 317, 329
Whitehurst, Z. B.   218
Wholly Sanctified   192
Widmeyer, C. B.   226
Widney, Arabella E.   98, 111
Widney, Dr. J. P.   50, 99, 104-5, 109, 111-12, 118, 121, 139

Wiley, Fred P   84
Wiley, H. Orton   140, 207, 261, 273-74, 277, 279, 280, 281 ff., 288, 295, 315, 322, 325-27, 330, 345
Willard, Frances   15
Willard, Mary J.   110
Williams, L. Milton   224-25, 229, 236, 238, 259, 336, 339
Williams, R. T.   218, 234, 243, 249 267, 272, 273, 283, 295, 322, 332, 337-41, 346
Williamson, G. B.   30
Willingham, T. W.   329
Wilson, George W.   46
Wilson, Guy   305
Wilson, R. A.   314
Wilson, W. C.   42, 122, 132, 207, 249, 272, 276, 277
Winans, Esther Carson   344-45
Winans, Roger   342, 344
Winchester, Olive M.   240, 262 286, 325, 330
Wines, John M.   236, 237
Winn, F. L.   328
Wise, H. H.   329
"Wise Men from the East"   207
Woman's Foreign Missionary Society   268, 326
Women Preachers   156
Wood, John Allen   15, 50, 52, 100-102
Wood, Rev. and Mrs. M. D.   84-85
Wordsworth, E. E.   312-13
World War in Prophecy, The   317
Yellowstone Holiness Association   303
Young Men's Holiness League   236
Zion's Herald   19, 54
Zion's Outlook   181-85, 187-91

www.ingramcontent.com/pod-product-compliance
Lightning Source LLC
Chambersburg PA
CBHW070436100426
42812CB00031B/3309/J